JACK LONDON

A Study of the Short Fiction

Also available in Twayne's Studies in Short Fiction Series

Sherwood Anderson: A Study of the Short Fiction by Robert Papinchak

Samuel Beckett: A Study of the Short Fiction by Robert Cochran

Jorge Luis Borges: A Study of the Short Fiction by Naomi Lindstrom

Paul Bowles: A Study of the Short Fiction by Allen Hibbard

Raymond Carver: A Study of the Short Fiction by Ewing Campbell

Anton Chekhov: A Study of the Short Fiction by Ronald L. Johnson

Charles W. Chesnutt: A Study of the Short Fiction by Henry B. Wonham

Kate Chopin: A Study of the Short Fiction by Bernard Koloski

Robert Coover: A Study of the Short Fiction by Thomas E. Kennedy

Julio Cortázar: A Study of the Short Fiction by Ilan Stavans

Mary Wilkins Freeman: A Study of the Short Fiction by Mary Reichardt

John Gardner: A Study of the Short Fiction by Jeff Henderson

Charlotte Perkins Gilman: A Study of the Short Fiction by Denise D. Knight

Graham Greene: A Study of the Short Fiction by Richard Kelly

Shirley Jackson: A Study of the Short Fiction by Joan Wylie Hall

Franz Kafka: A Study of the Short Fiction by Allen Thiher

Gabriel García Márquez: A Study of the Short Fiction
    by Harley D. Oberhelman

Bobbie Ann Mason: A Study of the Short Fiction by Albert Wilhelm

Flannery O'Connor: A Study of the Short Fiction
    by Suzanne Morrow Paulson

John O'Hara: A Study of the Short Fiction by Steven Goldleaf

Edgar Allan Poe: A Study of the Short Fiction by Charles E. May

Jean Rhys: A Study of the Short Fiction by Cheryl Alexander Malcolm
    and David Malcolm

Leslie Marmon Silko: A Study of the Short Fiction by Helen Jaskoski

Wallace Stegner: A Study of the Short Fiction by Jackson L. Benson

Mark Twain: A Study of the Short Fiction by Tom Quirk

Eudora Welty: A Study of the Short Fiction by Carol Ann Johnston

John Edgar Wideman: A Study of the Short Fiction by Keith E. Byerman

Twayne publishes studies of all major short-story writers worldwide. For a complete list, contact the Publisher directly.

Twayne's Studies in Short Fiction

Gary Scharnhorst and
Eric Haralson, Editors

JACK LONDON.
Arnold Genthe. © California State Parks, Jack London Collection.

JACK LONDON
A Study of the Short Fiction

Jeanne Campbell Reesman
University of Texas at San Antonio

TWAYNE PUBLISHERS
New York

Twayne's Studies in Short Fiction, No. 75

Twayne Publishers
1635 Broadway
New York, New York 10019

Library of Congress Cataloging-in-Publication Data

Reesman, Jeanne Campbell.
    Jack London : a study of the short fiction / Jeanne Campbell
Reesman.
        p.   cm. — (Twayne's studies in short fiction ; no. 75)
    Includes bibliographical references and index.
    ISBN 0-8057-1678-5 (alk. paper)
    1. London, Jack, 1876–1916—Criticism and interpretation.
2. American fiction—Themes, motives.   3. Short story.   I. Title.
II. Series.
PS3523.O46Z8665   1999
813'.52—dc21   98-55670
                                                                 CIP

This paper meets the requirements of ANSI/NISO Z3948-1992 (Permanence of Paper).

10 9 8 7 6 5 4 3

Printed in the United States of America

For Earle Labor,
with profound gratitude
from a
"Young Wise One"

Contents

Preface   *xi*
Acknowledgments   *xix*

PART 1. THE SHORT FICTION

1. The Klondike   3
2. Stories of Social Realism   67
3. Fictional Experimentation   94
4. The Pacific   126

PART 2. THE WRITER

Introduction   197
From *John Barleycorn* (1913)   199
From *Martin Eden* (1907)   203
From "The Terrible and Tragic in Fiction" (1903)   206
Selected Letters   211

PART 3. THE CRITICS

Introduction   223
Edgar Lucien Larkin   225
Charles A. Sandburg   227
Earle Labor and King Hendricks   232
Lawrence I. Berkove   237
James Slagel   245

Chronology   *253*
Selected Bibliography   *260*
Index   *265*

Preface

"And work," admonishes Jack London, concluding a 1903 litany of advice to young writers published in *The Editor*:

> Spell it out in capital letters, WORK. WORK all the time. Find out about this earth, this universe; this force and matter, and the spirit that glimmers up through force and matter from the magnet to Godhead. And by all this I mean WORK for a philosophy of life. . . . The three great things are: GOOD HEALTH; WORK; and a PHILOSOPHY OF LIFE. I may add, nay, must add, a fourth—SINCERITY. Without this, the other three are without avail; and with it you may cleave to greatness and sit among the giants.[1]

London's own philosophy of life, the work he performed to express it, and his artistic sincerity find their greatest fulfillment in his short stories. Notwithstanding the merits of his nonfiction and his novels, such as the world classic *The Call of the Wild* (1903), which made him America's leading international author; his compelling socialist works such as *The Iron Heel* (1907) and *The People of the Abyss* (1903); his autobiographical novel, *Martin Eden* (1909), inspiration for many young authors; and the haunting visionary work *The Star Rover*, a response to California labor and class injustices, it is London's nearly two hundred short stories written from 1893 to his death in 1916 that contain his greatest treasures as a writer.

London was one of the inventors of the modern short story, perhaps second in importance only to Poe, and his oeuvre presents an astonishing range of narrative experimentation, diverse characters, and international settings that prepared America's reading public for the advent of literary modernism. Through the icy existentialism faced by the hero of "To Build a Fire," the ragged aesthetic that consumes the heart of the child laborer in "The Apostate," and the religious and racial alterity of the old Hawaiian fisherman in "The Water Baby," London imagined the outlooks and voices of hundreds of characters, from the Indians of the Klondike as they confront the gold-seeking "Sunlanders" to the native peoples of the Pacific Rim, who encounter the tortured psyches of their colonizers. London's call for the writer to encompass the world was a fitting one for the writer who perhaps, surprisingly for some, best embodies Emerson's description of the American Scholar: one who would learn from nature, learn from books, be a man of action, and, finally, act as a consummate observer. London's famed eclecticism and seemingly inexhaustible energy found their discipline as well as their release in the carefully crafted form of the short story.

Too often in the past, critics have allowed London's adventurous life to obscure the central activity within that life, which was writing. Living in the great age of the magazine in America, and faithfully writing his 1,000 words per day, Jack London spent a majority of his time and thought crafting his short stories and novels. His was an unusual apprenticeship, combining as it did the rigor of library and typewriter with another kind of rigor as he struggled to come to terms with certain sensational aspects of his youth. His early life as a child laborer, his oyster pirating, living as a hobo, and gold prospecting made way for his true calling after he found his metier in "An Odyssey of the North," published in the *Atlantic Monthly* in 1900.

His was a representative voice of his time, describing economic uncertainties at home, imperialistic excursions abroad, and emergent movements such as socialism, Darwinism, and feminism. Fin de siècle America had grown impatient with the bland romanticism proffered in the nation's periodicals. In *John Barleycorn* (1913), London says of his entry into the successful magazine market that "[s]ome are born to fortune, and some have fortune thrust upon them. But in my case I was clubbed into fortune, and bitter necessity was the club."[2] This is a key statement about his own personal sense of realism and how that realism was mirrored by the new desires of his audience. London made no secret of his writing for cash; this was part of the new American realism—literary naturalism—he helped invent. But he never lost sight of his own self-described cardinal virtue, his sincerity, and neither did his audience.

Alongside William Dean Howells, Edith Wharton, Mark Twain, Stephen Crane, Frank Norris, Theodore Dreiser, and others, London developed literary naturalism into new and diverse forms. In his late South Seas fiction in particular, however, while not relinquishing his realism and his commitment to socialism, he joined his determinism with an inner sense of a world beyond the material. Since the publication of the two three-volume sets *The Letters of Jack London* and *The Complete Sto-*

ries by Stanford University Press in 1988 and 1993, respectively, London's range and depth are available to scholars as never before. Despite frequent characterization as merely a "red-blooded" naturalist writer for men and boys, in his 197 stories London reveals that his abiding interest was not in a clichéd notion of "man vs. nature" but in *human* nature, like Faulkner's notion of the "human heart in conflict with itself." And like Faulkner, London writes of this conflict within class, race, and gender questions, and also places it within spiritual constructions. Throughout his career London attempts to enter community after community and to show them from the inside; the need to belong that drove him as a youth was at last transmuted into a dynamic new art for a new century. The burgeoning numbers of critical books and articles on London as well as new editions of his works are bringing more and more scholarly attention to his canon; his popular audience has never left him, but students and scholars alike are beginning to encounter him more and more in the classroom and at academic conferences such as the Modern Language Association, American Literature Association, and Popular Culture Association, as well as the biennial Symposia conducted by the Jack London Society, founded in 1990 to promote the study of London's life and works. The present volume is only the second book ever published devoted exclusively to London's short fiction—the first being James McClintock's influential *White Logic: Jack London's Short Stories* (1975).

Part 1 of this study combines some biographical material with examination of sources and contexts in order to support its central focus: analysis of specific stories. It touches upon dozens of tales, but focuses extended treatment upon a dozen or so important or problematic texts. Although the major elements of London's work span his entire career, his stories are best framed by the *topoi* of the Klondike and the Pacific, with special attention to his social criticism and his literary experimentation.

Chapter 1, "The Klondike," examines London's apprenticeship and early career and his mastery of the short story, with most of the chapter devoted to close analysis of his Northland tales. These stories, drawn from the year he spent prospecting for gold in the Klondike, are written throughout his entire career and comprise the largest segment of his short fiction. In them London dwells upon the theme of men and women in nature. On the stark stage of the vast White Silence, London portrays with epic intensity, in part drawn from Greek mythology, the terrible choices his characters must make as to how to live and what values to live by. Although the Northland tales depict men and women struggling to survive in the harsh lands of the Yukon, the stories' premise is that those who survive are those who subscribe to the Northland Code of fair play, integrity, and honesty with the self. But as powerful as the code is, in certain stories London reveals its weakness in the face of racial differences. When the whites confront the Indians, and vice versa, a different code can take over, one of sheer survival based on strength and cunning. London's idealistic vision of human justice is sometimes tainted with a racial determinism that undermines a universalized ethics. Community is the central value, but it can be delimited in his works by racial barriers.

Similarly, as presented in chapter 2, "Stories of Social Realism," there are contradictions within London's treatment of the theme of social justice. Here, men and women confront each other within society, largely within the setting of the city, and the theme of justice developed in the Klondike takes on a stronger socialistic cast. Instead of the White Silence, there is the silence of the capitalists toward the poverty of laborers. London's socialism, derived both from his reading of Marx, Engels, and others and his own burning awareness of being born into the "work beast" class, preached so passionately in his lectures and essays, is an important factor in much of his fiction, but is especially so in a handful of stories with explicit socialist themes. Class always lies close to the essential impulse behind London's stories, and within that he addresses some of our most pressing contemporary problems: race and gender inequality, poverty, unemployment, exploitation, homelessness, addiction, gangs. When socialism per se is compromised in these tales, as it is in novels such as *Martin Eden* and *The Iron Heel*, it is comingled with the strong strain of individualism London developed from his reading of Nietzsche and other philosophers. London was never a "doctrinaire" socialist writer, if there is such a thing, and he tends to complicate any question of social justice. But if reading these stories reveals weaknesses in his theories, it also makes clear that his characters are his focus, after all: the agonies of the fighters in stories like "A Piece of Steak" or "The Mexican" speak as loud if not louder than any of London's nonfiction polemics.

Chapter 3 is concerned with some particularly intriguing examples of London's fictional experimentation. Although he is clearly a writer who discovered that plots drawn from any and every source available would work for his fiction if he adhered to particular formulae for constructing stories, paradoxically he never ceased to experiment with new ideas, even when they meant unsalable stories. One might speculate that London's continued success at selling his work had the effect of merely leading him into hack work to maintain his rising level of income and keep pace with his expenses, mounting from projects such as the *Snark* and Wolf House. It is certainly true that London wrote his share of pot-boilers and that he bought some plots—and that he had pressing expenses. But it also seems that his success allowed him to experiment quite radically with his fiction in ways that clearly resist labeling. London's entire life was a sort of experiment, and he could not resist the challenge of seeing life from as many vantage points as possible, from within ethnic communities scattered across the Pacific Ocean, from feminine as well as masculine points of view, from the minds of both the sane and the insane, and from the perspectives of both the ruling class and the ghetto. While he benefited from finding an easy publishing niche with such collections as *Tales of the Fish Patrol* (1905), *Smoke Bellew* (1912), and the David Grief stories (1912), London continued to experiment with subject, structure, language, and point of view throughout his career, including such innovations as experiments with his tried-and-true frame structure, multiple narrators, dialogic structures, and narrative ambiguity. Such unusual stories as "The Night-Born," "Samuel," and "Told in the Drooling Ward" illustrate the surprising range of his fictional portraits.

The oceanic setting of the Pacific, the subject of chapter 4, makes up the next-largest group of his stories after the Klondike. Two major groups of stories take place in the Pacific: those set in the South Seas and those set in Hawaii. To the voyagers aboard London's ketch the *Snark*, which sailed the Pacific in 1907 and 1908, the South Seas, despite the many attractions, too often seemed a tropical hell where the nihilism of the White Silence was replaced by the screams of head-hunters and the curses of dissipated white colonizers. London could not believe his eyes when he visited Nuka Hiva—could this be the Typee that Melville lovingly described, its natural beauties wasted by the predations of colonizers and its inhabitants practicing unspeakable savagery? In contrast, Hawaii was Paradise Regained. London turned to the Hawaiian theme after a four-year hiatus in short story writing that lasted from 1912 to the spring of 1916. It was a place for a weary mind and body to find peace. Its greenness was also fertile ground for the imagination, with its rich mythology and traditions. The cultural and psychic transformations London encountered there beginning in 1907 bore fruit in his fiction until his very last story, "The Water Baby," and caused reorientations in his views of race, gender, his craft itself, and his spiritual life. The *Snark* voyage was truly the turning point in his view of the world. Notwithstanding the perspective he stated that he had gained in the Klondike, the Pacific was a stage larger and vastly more complex than anything else imaginable. It is a tragic irony, given London's artistic and personal breakthrough with the Hawaiian tales—his questioning of his long-held racist views, his renewed respect for women, and his newfound interest in the unconscious and even spiritual dimensions of reality—that his career was abruptly cut short by his early death at age 40.

Surprisingly, there is no chapter here on California, London's home, site of his beloved Beauty Ranch in the Valley of the Moon. Although the few California stories he wrote will be analyzed, for the most part London chose to make California a setting for novels rather than short stories—as in his three novels, *Burning Daylight* (1910), *The Valley of the Moon* (1913), and *The Little Lady of the Big House* (1916). In the short fiction, the twin poles of the Klondike and the Pacific Ocean inspire tale after tale; together with the California novels his work suggests that London should be viewed as one of America's first Pacific Rim writers.

Part 2 of the volume consists of excerpts from London's writings on writing and the creative process, demonstrating an interesting shift from London the bookish literary aspirant to the worn but game mentor for hordes of young writers who contacted him. In hundreds of lines of letters London was willing to share advice based on his own exceptional self-awareness and understanding of writers, the craft of fiction, audience, and market. These selections include London's essay "The Terrible and Tragic in Fiction"; letters from his voluminous correspondence to fellow writers, editors, and friends; and selections from his semi-autobiographical works *Martin Eden* and *John Barleycorn*. Part 3 includes several important biographical and critical essays on the writer and on individual stories that further elaborate key issues raised in part 1 and offer the reader new directions in which to pursue study of the short stories of Jack London.

Discussions of the stories follow near-chronological order within each of the chapters. I have chosen to follow the editors of the Stanford edition of *The Complete Short Stories of Jack London* in dating the stories according to London's magazine sales records; thus, dates given for short stories are dates of first submission, unless otherwise noted, and the stories are treated individually for the most part, not as parts of the collections London published. This approach allows me to examine with much greater accuracy developments in subject matter and narrative structure from story to story. Dates given for any novels mentioned are dates of book publication.

Notes

1. Jack London, "Getting into Print" (1903; reprinted in *No Mentor but Myself: A Collection of Articles, Essays, Reviews, and Letters, by Jack London, on Writing and Writers*, ed. Dale L. Walker, Port Washington, N.Y.: Kennikat Press, 1979), 57–58.

2. Jack London, *John Barleycorn: Alcoholic Memoirs* (New York: Century, 1913), 237–38.

Acknowledgments

One of the rewards of writing this book has been the opportunity for conversations on the short stories with other London scholars. These have taken place at conferences, including those of the American Literature Association and the Jack London Society, and in my office and classrooms at the University of Texas at San Antonio. I am most deeply indebted to Earle Labor for his friendship over the years and for his careful reading of an earlier version of this project. I am also grateful to Gail Jones for the many hours of discussion of London's stories we have enjoyed. She contributed significant insights especially in the readings of London's early Klondike stories. For help with London's sources, I wish to thank Chaddie Kruger, Paul Alessi, Mark Allen, and Kevin Harty.

To Milo Shepard I extend my heartfelt thanks for his generosity in making the first editions of the stories available to me. I was also fortunate to have the assistance of Sara S. Hodson, Curator of Literary Manuscripts at the Henry E. Huntington Library; William Sturm, Librarian, Oakland History Room, Oakland Public Library; and Glenn Burch, California State Parks and Recreation Department, Sonoma, California, in locating unpublished materials. Susan Streeter and Jeff Turpin served ably and enthusiastically as research assistants.

My thanks also to Gary Scharnhorst and Eric Haralson, Twayne Studies in Short Fiction series editors; Anne Davidson, Twayne Publishers project editor; and Mary Jo Heck and Mary Boss at Impressions Book and Journal Services.

I gratefully acknowledge the following for permission to reproduce materials: The Trust of Irving Shepard and the Henry E. Huntington Library for permission to quote from Charmian London's diaries (Huntington Library JL 218); the Trust of Irving Shepard and the California Department of Parks and Recreation for permission to reproduce the Arnold Genthe portrait of Jack London, © California State Parks, Jack London Collection; the Henry E. Huntington Library for permission to quote excerpts from the letters of Joseph Conrad (JL 5130) and Mary Austin (JL 1993); and Stanford University Press for permission to reprint letters from *The Letters of Jack London*, three volumes, edited by

Acknowledgments

Earle Labor, Robert C. Leitz, III, and I. Milo Shepard © 1988 by the Board of Trustees of the Leland Stanford Junior University.

Lawrence I. Berkove's "A Parallax Correction in London's 'The Unparalleled Invasion' " first appeared in *American Literary Realism* Vol. 24:2 © 1992 and is reprinted by permission of McFarland & Company, Inc., Publishers, Jefferson, NC 28640. James Slagel's "Political Leprosy: Jack London the '*Kama'āina*' and Koolau the Hawaiian" is excerpted from *Rereading Jack London*, edited by Jeanne Campbell Reesman and Leonard Cassuto with an Afterword by Earle Labor. Used with permission of the publishers, Stanford University Press © 1996 by the Board of Trustees of the Leland Stanford Junior University. "Jack London's Twice-Told Tale" by Earle Labor and King Hendricks first appeared in *Studies in Short Fiction* Vol. 4 © 1967 and is reprinted by permission of the publisher.

Material on "To Build a Fire" in chapter 1 appeared in different form in " 'Never Travel Alone': Naturalism, Jack London, and the White Silence," *American Literary Realism* Vol. 29:2 © 1997 and is reprinted by permission of McFarland & Company, Inc., Publishers, Jefferson, NC 28640. Some of the discussion of "The Red One" in chapter 4 appeared in different form in " 'Falling Stars': Myth in 'The Red One,' " *Jack London Newsletter,* Vol.11 (1978). Material on "The Water Baby" appeared in different form in "The Problem of Knowledge in 'The Water Baby,' " *Western American Literature* Vol. 23 (1988) and appears here by permission of the publisher.

At the University of Texas at San Antonio, I wish to thank the staffs of the Division of English, Classics, Philosophy, and Communication and the Office of Graduate Studies and to acknowledge the members of the Faculty Development Leave Committee for their support of this project. Guy Bailey, Interim Provost, has my lasting gratitude for his support of scholarship at UTSA and of my own in particular.

And of course, to John and John for all the time.

Part 1

THE SHORT FICTION

1. The Klondike

Away we went before the wind with a single reef in our sail. With clenched teeth sat the boat-steerer, grasping the steering oar firmly with both hands, his restless eyes on the alert—a glance at the schooner ahead, as we rose on a sea, another at the mainsheet, and then one astern where the dark ripple of the wind on the water told him of a coming puff or a large white-cap that threatened to overwhelm us. The waves were holding high carnival, performing the strangest antics, as with wild glee they danced along in fierce pursuit—now up, now down, here, there, and everywhere, until some great sea of liquid green with its milk-white crest of foam rose from the ocean's throbbing bosom and drove the others from view. But only for a moment, for again under new forms they reappeared. In the sun's path they wandered, where every ripple, great or small, every little spit or spray looked like molten silver, where the water lost its dark green color and became a dazzling, silvery flood, only to vanish and become a wild waste of sullen turbulence, each dark foreboding sea rising and breaking, then rolling on again.[1]

At the age of 17, Jack London wrote his first piece of fiction, "Story of a Typhoon Off the Coast of Japan," and submitted it to a literary contest held by the *San Francisco Morning Call*. To his surprise, he won. This little sketch, published November 12, 1893, tells of the death of a crew member aboard a sealing ship in the North Pacific. Written at the behest of London's mother for the purpose of winning the $25 prize, it already demonstrated London's facility with narrative, with its powerful visual description, emphasis on action, restlessness, and yoking together of intense physical and spiritual realities. It artfully combines adventure with romance and the macabre with sentimentality. It constructs a narrative voice rich in both naturalistic theme and metaphor. London would have an arduous apprenticeship before he would become the most widely read American writer in the world, but from his very first story he combined a keen gift for observation, a natural curiosity about other places and peoples, and a sense of the mythic dimensions of universal human experience.

By the end of his short career, London would be the highest-paid author of his day, credited as one of the inventors of American literary naturalism, and recognized as one of America's first modern literary celebrities. He would be author of short fiction, novels, drama, poetry, sociological treatises, political essays, war correspondence, children's literature, memoirs, and travel narratives. He would be known as a significant voice in American socialism and as an innovator in California horticulture. His life would be scrutinized in every imaginable detail, from his parentage to his very public divorce to his problematic death. London attained a mythic stature in the minds of his many admirers (and detractors) that still elicits a highly emotional personal response.

Not surprisingly for a native of San Francisco, the urban heart of America's western frontier, London led a life of adventure and rugged individualism but also a life of contradictions. His individualism was accompanied by his ardent socialism. He was quick to side with the underdog and generous with his time and fortunes for those who needed him, but he could be combative when provoked. Before writing his first story or essay, he spent years as a laborer, sailor, hobo (all before he attended high school), gold prospector, and college student. Like Mark Twain, London's varied background gave him both a sense of personal resilience and a broad sense of the varieties of American life. In addition to writing 50 books in 17 years, he carried on voluminous correspondence, handled his manifold business transactions, married and fathered children, covered the Russo-Japanese War, divorced and remarried, bought and ran a large ranch, sailed his boat the *Snark* through the South Seas, and traveled around the world. He died from a complex of ailments, exacerbated by previous tropical illnesses, on November 22, 1916, 23 years and 10 days after he published that first story.

Three recurring themes in London's short stories throughout his career are the role of the imagination, the desire for justice, and the longing for community. His interest in these can be traced to forces that shaped his psyche as a boy and young man. London's heroes in his Klondike stories have been described as merely survivors, succeeding through sheer strength and individual prowess—in other words, very limited examples of male naturalistic heroes. Although this sort of hero exists in London's work, he is doomed to failure. An example from the short stories is Axel Gunderson of "An Odyssey of the North." Such "inevitable white men" as Axel, as London called them, are often successful in dominating other people, and they seemed to stand for an idealized but also demonized Anglo-Saxon conqueror in London's mind. Such dualistic figures as the seemingly positive Scruff MacKenzie of "The Son of the Wolf" also come to mind, but more often these characters are also the corrupted colonizers of such South Seas stories as "Mauki," "The Chinago," "The Inevitable White Man," and "The House of Pride"—obverse views of the Kiplingesque white hero. The truer London hero is a balanced individual who exhibits the values of imagination, justice, and community and survives by them.

As a boy London was proud of his stepfather John London's Civil War and frontier experiences, and the young London identified himself as a son of the frontier, unaware that John London was not his real father. He learned that he was not John London's son but probably the son of an itinerant "professor," William Chaney, the common-law husband of Flora Wellman, London's mother, before she married John London. Chaney refused to admit his paternity, and this came as a terrible shock to young London. And given that Flora emotionally rejected her son, as London's biographers agree, it is not surprising that young "Johnny" was a quiet, lonely boy as the family moved from city to farm and back again—and again.[2] London conceived a dislike for the countryside that he would only overcome much later when he moved to the Sonoma Valley. But while the drudgery of farm work depressed him, he feared the city, too, especially the gangs he encountered, the grinding routine of child labor, and the bleakness of urban living conditions. When the family returned to the city, his mother supported the family by making their home a boardinghouse and conducting spiritualist seances, while John London's health steadily failed. Too infirm to pay much attention to his son, John London was able to give only a modicum of fatherly guidance to Johnny. Instead of relying on his parents for attention, Johnny turned to the nurturing of his stepsister, Eliza, who would become a lifelong emotional support, and, to a lesser but still important extent, to his former wet nurse, Virginia Prentiss, who loaned him money for his first boat and remained close to him and his family for life.

Johnny London graduated from Cole Grammar School in 1890, already seeking solace in books from the injustice of his de facto abandonment by all three of his parents—two fathers and a mother, as it were—and from the unstable, ugly economy of the life of the poor. Books afforded him the flights of imagination he craved. He wrote many years later to the Oakland Public Library librarian who had served him as a child—Ina Coolbrith, who would eventually become California's Poet Laureate—thanking her for her timely guidance:

The old Oakland Library days! Do you know, you were the first one who ever complimented me on my choice of reading matter. Nobody at home bothered their heads over what I read. I was an eager, thirsty, hungry little kid—and one day, at the Library, I drew out a volume on Pizzaro in Peru (I was ten years old). You got the book & stamped it for me. And as you handed it to me you praised me for reading books of that nature. Proud! If you only knew how proud your words made me. For I thought a great deal of you. You were a goddess to me. I didn't know you were a poet, or that you'd ever done such a wonderful thing as write a line. I was raw from a ranch, you see. But I stood greatly in awe of you—worshipful awe. In those days I named by adjectives. And I named you "Noble." That is what you were to me—noble. That was the feeling I got from you. Oh, yes, I got, also, the feeling of sorrow and suffering, but dominating them, always riding above all, was noble. No woman has so affected me to the extent you did. I was only a little lad. I knew absolutely nothing about you. Yet in all the years that have passed I have met no woman so "noble" as you.[3]

London made tremendous use of the library, as is clear from the allusions he employs in even his earliest short fiction.

In an interview with George Wharton James in 1912, London reflects upon the "contemplative spirit" he evolved: "I was a solitary and lonely child. Yet I was a social youngster, and always got along well with the other children. . . . I can now see that I lived a dual life. My outward life was that of the everyday poor man's son in the public school: rough and tumble, happy go lucky, jostled by a score, a hundred, rough elements. Within myself I was reflective, contemplative, apart from the kinetic forces around me." Ignoring his own Irish ancestry, he speaks of his fear of the "only other people of the neighborhood," Italians and Irish: "Ours was the only 'American' family." Having moved to the city, he again felt isolated:

> I clearly saw the futility of life in such a herd. I was oppressed with a deadly oppression as I saw that all the people, rich and poor alike, were merely mad creatures, chasing phantoms. . . . They had it in their own hands to remedy the evils that beset them, yet they were obsessed by the idea that their lot was God-ordained, fixed, immovable. How that cursed idea used to irritate me. How it fired my tongue. (James, 366–70)

London worked hard at two paper routes, on an ice wagon, in a bowling alley, and in factories; and his family often called upon him for help.

He was used to giving all of his earnings to his mother to support the family, and he also gave his bed to boarders. Following grammar school, he held odd jobs and did not even consider attending high school. Escape was to be found in the waters of the San Francisco Bay: As Franklin Walker notes, "One could sail on it unrestricted; one could sleep on it where one pleased; one could make a living on it by the use of brawn and cunning." London's wild adventures on the Oakland waterfront prompted Walker to add, "For most of four years Jack London was what today is termed a juvenile delinquent."[4] Heavy drinking and wandering as a hobo followed his oyster-pirating days. He took to the sea at the age of 16; returning from his sealing voyage, he found no jobs in the terrible times of economic panic that beset the nation in 1893, and so he took to "the Road."

London rode the rails east with the western contingent of Coxey's Army, a loose band of unemployed men who marched on Washington, D.C., to protest economic conditions. London left Coxey's band in Hannibal, Missouri, and, setting out on his own, was arrested and imprisoned as a vagrant for 30 days in Buffalo, New York. It was an experience he found so degrading that he could scarcely speak of it, but it prompted him to become a member of the Socialist Party and to try to express in his writing his newfound political awareness.

From Apprentice to "Vendor of Brains"

Reentering high school at age 19, London was hardly a traditional student. He had to work as a janitor in the new high school building to complete one year of regular curriculum. More important, he began to write. In 1895 he published nine stories and one essay in the Oakland High School magazine, *The Aegis*. The stories were mostly drawn from his experiences as a seal hunter and hobo and from his newly awakened interest in socialism, which was further sparked by his membership in the Henry Clay debating society. He crammed for university entrance exams and was admitted to the University of California, where he remained one semester. He withdrew because of lack of funds. But his education had only begun; feverishly, he read an array of writers, including Marx, Ruskin, and Morris, but also Kipling and Browning—from these latter he began to get ideas for his own writing. But his greatest discovery was the works of Herbert Spencer, whose *Philosophy of Style* London would admire for the rest of his career. He was especially drawn to Spencer's notion that progress was to be found not in theology but in the very laws of biology and physics themselves—it seemed a rational way of explaining his own desire for achievement. The social Darwinism that emerged with all its contradictions would appear throughout London's writings.

Awash in new ideas, London nevertheless was back on the streets looking for a job; he found one at the Belmont Academy (where Frank Norris had been a student) in the laundry room. This latest plunge into the world of the "work beast" was the real beginning of his apprenticeship as a writer, for here he was again, working desperately as a wage slave. His desire to escape into his writing prevailed, and despite all odds he began to write in earnest. As he states in his essay "What Life Means to Me,"

> I had been born in the working class, and I was now, at the age of eighteen, beneath the point at which I had started. I was down in the cellar of society, down in the subterranean depths of misery about which it is neither nice nor proper to speak. I was in the pit, the abyss, the human cesspool, the shambles and the charnel house of our civilization. This is part of the edifice of society that society chooses to ignore. . . . I was scared into thinking. I saw the naked simplicities of the complicated civilization in which I lived. Life was a matter of food and shelter. In order to get food and shelter men sold things. . . . Labor had muscle and muscle alone, to sell. . . . I learned further that brain was likewise a commodity. . . . So I resolved to sell no more muscle and become a vendor of brains.[5]

London goes on to describe his "frantic pursuit" of life as a "brain merchant," in which it was "inevitable that I should delve into sociology" (*Revolution*, 301). As a result, he relates, he discovered that he was simultaneously a writer and a socialist.

Although they originate in London's key ideas of the role of the imagination, the desire for justice, and the longing for community, the *Aegis* stories do not take on these concerns directly, instead depicting scenes of betrayal, despair, and even suicide with an aura of adolescent anxiety and extremity. Some also reveal London's class longing, especially what we may call his "frat boy" stories, such as one of his first published stories, "Two Gold Bricks," which is written in the spiffy tone of an imagined world of privileged youth. Thankfully, London left his yearning for this world behind once he moved into his Klondike phase.

Notable among the early stories is a trilogy about Japan: "Sakaicho, Hona Asi, and Hakadaki," "A Night's Swim in Yeddo Bay," and "O

Haru." These are indications of London's curiosity about ethnic and racial "others." They display only admiration for the Japanese. In "O Haru" the twin themes of gender and racial oppression are brought together when the heroine's lover spurns her for a Caucasian girl:

> She, the most beautiful of geishas, the most beautiful of all Japanese women, the personified ideal of the Japanese standard, was no longer beautiful to Toyotomi, her old-time lover. He would come home drunken and surly and criticize her walk, her carriage, her narrow hips, her flat breast, slim face and slanting eyes; then rave in ecstasies of delight over the Occident beauties. Buddha! That such could be! That her Toyotomi could admire those fierce, masculine creatures, that strode, long-stepping, like men; that had great hips and humps like actual deformities. Those repulsive creatures, with their large mouths, high noses, and eyes, deep-sunk in horrid sockets beneath fierce, heavy brows. Those creatures, so terrible, that when they looked on a Japanese baby it must burst into tears of fright. Those animals, who were so loathesome, disgustingly mouthing themselves and their men—Toyotomi called it kissing and had tried to teach her. Ach! How could it be!
>
> (*Complete*, 40)

"A Night's Swim in Yeddo Bay" (later rewritten as the more complex "In Yeddo Bay" [1902]), London's first frame story, relates an event of derring-do that happened aboard the *Sophia Sutherland*. London compares his fellow sailors' behavior unfavorably against the virtues of the Japanese.

To complement his exotic tales, London's "Who Believes in Ghosts!" (1895), "One More Unfortunate" (1895), "The Strange Experience of a Misogynist" (1897), "A Thousand Deaths" (1897), and "The Plague Ship" (1897) all utilize horror. In "Who Believes in Ghosts!," which takes place in a haunted house, two friends—a Damon and a Pythias—combat each other at chess, little realizing that they are repeating a fatal game played by another brother-against-brother pair; before they come to their senses, both are nearly destroyed. "One More Unfortunate" is one of several portrayals of suicide, and "The Strange Experience of a Misogynist" and "A Thousand Deaths" are bizarre and amusing tales combining elements of science fiction and fantasy.[6] In "The Strange Experience of a Misogynist," a woman-hating man falls asleep and dreams that when he wakes, all the women in the world have mysteriously vanished: "The immutability of natural law, the towering fabric of philosophic speculation, the dizzy atheistical negation of all supernaturalism, the adamantine division, between the knowable and the unknowable, of agnosticism; these, all these, and every system of thought and mode of action had been overthrown, confuted by this one fell blow" (*Complete*, 59). Step by step the world degenerates into brutality, alcoholism, suicide—a total collapse of the social fabric. When the dreamer awakens from his nightmare, he rushes off to propose to his girlfriend. More terrifying is "A Thousand Deaths," in which a young man lost at sea is rescued by a mysterious ship that just happens to be piloted by his long-lost father, a mad scientist who carries out a series of experiments on the captive young man, whom he does not recognize. The father is interested in what happens after death, and so he devises ways to repeatedly kill his subject and then revive him. Eventually the son devises a way to kill the father—and does not attempt to revive him. It is a gruesome tale that speaks to London's anxieties about his own role as a son. Immediately before composing this story London received two letters from Chaney, whom London had come to suspect was his father. Chaney bluntly denied his paternity, claiming impotence at the time of London's conception. Ironically, Chaney's cold refusal may have spurred on his son's career; London earned the serious sum of $40 from the *Black Cat* magazine for this very story.

"The Plague Ship" is also a grisly and puzzling sea story. A ship's doctor and nurse (with the name of Maud Appleton, echoing London's own early love interest, Mabel Applegarth) compete with one another in trying to cure the plague-stricken passengers and avert a riot by the Chinese workers on board. They fall in love in the process and then, surprisingly, do not marry each other. Instead they suddenly marry their patients. Perhaps London was privileging the need for power over the capacity to love, or simply parodying the reader's expectations about love stories. This tale has the unhappy distinction of containing London's first racial slur: "Among the Chinese were some of the most redoubtable high-binders and hatchet-men of the coast—mercenary and trained fighters for the societies to which they owed their allegiance. Unlike the average Chinese, they were not cowardly: murder and bloodshed was their profession" (90). As in the *The Sea-Wolf*, here the love element is combined with atavism and racialism. But London abruptly left the overheated temper of these earliest efforts for the icy grip of the Yukon.

The Northland

Jack London's real career began with his discovery of a real subject: the Northland and its effects on the men and women who braved it. It is startling to compare his earliest stories with those that were written barely a year and a half later set in the Klondike. Moreso, compare the following quotation from "The White Silence" with the one from "Story of a Typhoon Off the Coast of Japan" that opened this chapter:

> The afternoon wore on, and with the awe, born of the White Silence, the voiceless travelers bent to their work. Nature has many tricks wherewith she convinces man of his finity,—the ceaseless flow of the tides, the fury of the storm, the shock of the earthquake, the long roll of heaven's artillery,—but the most tremendous, the most stupefying of all, is the passive phase of the White Silence. All movement ceases, the sky clears, the heavens are as brass; the slightest whisper seems sacrilege, and man becomes timid, affrighted at the sound of his own voice. Sole speck of life journeying across the ghostly wastes of a dead world, he trembles at his audacity, realizes that his is a maggot's life, nothing more. Strange thoughts arise unsummoned, and the mystery of all things strives for utterance. And the fear of death, of God, of the universe, comes over him,—the hope of the Resurrection and the Life, the yearning for immortality, the vain striving of the imprisoned essence,—it is then, if ever, man walks alone with God. (143–44)

Admirable as "Typhoon" is, it cannot compare with the range of description and the profound sense of the complexities of human and divine existence that give "The White Silence" its haunting quality.

London's routine as a writer was established when *The Atlantic Monthly* agreed to publish "An Odyssey of the North" for $120. A book contract from Houghton Mifflin and an arrangement with *McClure's* to provide a series of Klondike stories quickly followed. Eventually London would publish in all of the major and many of the minor magazines of the day and would enter into a long-term agreement with George Brett of Macmillan for publication of his books. From this point on in London's career the sales pattern would be established: first publish the stories and novels in serial form (sometimes British and sometimes American) and then issue them as books.

On July 14, 1897, 40 passengers headed home from the Klondike disembarked from the *Excelsior* at San Francisco, none with less than $3,000 in gold nuggets and dust: "So heavy was the booty they carried in bags, tin cans, and valises that they chartered the Palace Hotel bus to take them directly to the mint," Franklin Walker writes (Walker, 44). The frenzy of the Klondike Gold Rush began on the spot. Thousands poured into San Francisco and Seattle from all over the world to outfit themselves with the one ton of supplies the Canadian Mounted Police required of all entrants into the Klondike. Bank clerks, policemen, firemen, teachers, farmers, doctors, ministers, missionaries, con men, and prostitutes packed their gear and headed north. Even the mayor of Seattle resigned on the spot and threw himself into the gold fever. "Prosperity is Here," boomed the *Seattle Post-Intelligencer*. Few realized the magnitude of the hardships they would face in the Yukon.

Ready to board the *Umatilla* for the Northland in less than a week, London did not know he would chronicle many of the experiences of the thousands of "passionate pilgrims" who made the terrible journey over the Chilcoot Pass and the brutal trail that lay beyond, but he later wrote:

> With heavy packs upon their backs men plunged waist-deep into hideous quagmires, bridged mountain torrents by felling trees across them, toiled against the precipitous slopes of the ice-worn mountains, and crossed the dizzy faces of innumerable glaciers. When, after incalculable toil they reached the lakes, they went into the woods, sawed pine trees into lumber by hand, and built it into boats. In these, overloaded, unseaworthy, they battled down the long chain of lakes. . . . At the rapids they ran the boats through, hit or miss, and after infinite toil and hardship, on the breast of a jarring ice flood, arrived at the Klondike. (*Revolution*, 153)

London should have added, Walker notes, that "they had to pack in everything they were going to wear, eat, or use; that they knew they would suffer through a severe Arctic winter as they huddled in inadequate shelters; that they planned to mine in perpetually frozen ground; and . . . that all the rich claims [had] already been staked. . . ." Indeed, the panicked mob from all over the world who took part in this "preposterous" adventure, "as insane a gamble for fortune, as perverse a movement toward the wilderness to escape a crowded world, as that world has known to date," made up the last grand trek of its kind across American wilderness (Walker, 13–14). But only a year later, London observed, a tourist could take a steamship and railway coach into this territory, "without having once soiled the lustre of his civilized footgear" (*Revolution*, 154).

London's time in the Klondike—and more important his literary use of his experiences—should be seen in an epic, Homeric light. Comparing Kipling to Homer in the essay "These Bones Shall Rise Again," London seems to describe his own goal: "That man of us is imperishable who makes his century imperishable. That man of us who seizes upon the salient facts of life, who tells what we thought, what we were, and for what we stood—that man shall be the mouthpiece to the centuries, and so long as they listen he shall endure. . . . Homer takes his place with Achilles and the Greek and Trojan heroes. Because he remembered them, we remember him." But "the romance of Homer's Greece is the romance of Homer's Greece," and in our "machine age" we must evolve our own romances (*Revolution*, 224).[7] London was the Homer of the Klondike. Like Homer's creation of the epic poem, on a more modest scale London's Northland fiction contributed a new form to the American short story—what Donald Pizer has termed the *naturalist fable*—which gave him his identity and enduring fame as a writer.[8] "It was in the Klondike I found myself. There you get your perspective," he said. "I got mine."[9] As London crafted his epic, he also crafted himself as a writer, and the conjunction of the two in his formative period is fundamental to understanding his life and work.[10]

London was a keen observer in the Klondike, keeping a detailed journal of his journey down the Yukon River, for example, and doing research on the Klondike upon his return (including first reading Harry De Windt's *Through the Gold Fields of Alaska*). His characters were often based on specific individuals and often not at all heroic or romantic. Nature is romanticized, not mankind. The all-seeing sun, which he calls "Old Sol," is one of nature's most significant presences. He derives nature, and this sun, remote from humankind but with its attention focused upon them, directly from Greek and Roman mythology.

Not until his exit from the Klondike—and, one surmises, his sense of the specter of family need at home awaiting him—did London conceive of a literary vision of the region. As Charmian London reports,

> Often I had heard Jack say that he had no idea of using the Klondike as a literary asset, until his dream of gold fell through and he was bound out of the country, penniless to all intents and purposes. It must have come suddenly to him that the adventure had been sufficient in itself, for he had been smitten with discouragement, before leaving home, as to any success in the coveted direction of a writing future. But now, floating half-frozen down the river of defeat, as the grey and white Yukon seemed to him in his predicament, his assertive buoyancy of brain could not help reviving what he had seen and done and felt in the year just past. Surely *something* could be realized out of it all, to enhance his chance of making a name, earning a voice in the affairs of men.[11]

He began a diary on the day he swung out on the current at Dawson toward home. In spite of some suffering he and his mates endured (including giant mosquitoes, lack of food, winter storms), there is only one reference to physical pain. Instead, he focuses on the sights of river and shore, on changeable currents and weather, on the overall strangeness of the landscape, and on the variety of Indians and whites he encountered as they went along. His ambition was first to get home and then only to write an article for *Outing Magazine* that would detail the "[b]eauty of the night—drifting down the river, midnight and broad daylight." But he also dwells on the landscape in its entirety: trade and settlements, dances in overheated log cabins, the ubiquitous Anglo-Saxon encountered up and down the river in all his doings. He is fascinated by Indian customs and villages, and he learned much from them, from how to make rope to how to hunt seal to how to tell a story (C. London, *Jack London*, 1:248–58).

Back at home in the summer and fall of 1898, London found his newly widowed mother living in a tiny cottage looking for rent. He performed odd jobs and studied for the civil service exam for the position of mail carrier. He also began to write anew. "[H]is life experience" now gave his work a freshness missing in the writers of the East, Charmian comments. Divorced from the commonplace by the Klondike experience, London relied on his "faculty of observation" to convey "vital, first-hand realities" in his fiction (258).

His vision of the Northland was of the wandering of an entire people. Like Odysseus, these modern argonauts were seeking "home"—or rather the means to make homes—but many found something different in the Northland than they intended. London introduced a New World saga of the white man in the Yukon, with its Indians and its testing of the white man's codes of behavior. In the Klondike London saw treasure and treachery; great beauty and horror; a code of brotherhood as well as stupid cruelties inspired by race hatred, ignorance, and cowardice. He unknowingly entered a true "far country" seeking treasure, an anti-Eden to be conquered but also a place where Greek virtues of comradeship, bravery, and humility in the face of awesome landscape could prevail over greed. London was able to narrate a personal and a national myth of the Northland that struck a deep chord.

Why did Homer affect London so? Since we do not know which translation(s) London read (he did not buy books as a rule during this early period but rather continued to make extensive use of the Oakland Public Library), we do not have marginalia or notes to draw upon.[12] The most popular translations of the day were by William Cowper, Samuel Butler, and William Morris; London could well have chosen Morris's colorful version, since he was an admirer of his other works. Whichever translation he chose, London clearly found Homer appealing because he chose to write about the archetypal young man's journey, the desire to experience adventures accompanied by the desire to find home, the saga of a people through the story of a strong leader, and the challenge of living by one's wits and facing numerous adversities in order to succeed. These themes emerge again and again in London's lifelong drive for adventure, especially in his intense curiosity about faraway places and peoples. London was an outsider, a fatherless, penniless outcast living at the edge of the West who could see things from an outsider's point of view. Inspired by journeyers such as Odysseus, he asked what it takes to belong, and this entailed, paradoxically, understanding multiple worlds and how they function. And Homer's plain, direct style evidently appealed to him. Neither Homer nor London tells us what to think; instead, they relate their tales objectively, relying upon the metaphysical dimension of things to provide frame and meaning. London praised *The Iliad* and *The Odyssey* as "human folk epics" (*Letters*, 1580).

Allusions of all kinds—classical, biblical, and literary from ancient times to his own contemporaries—are found in London's fiction right up until the Medusa image that closes one of his last stories, "The Red One." The importance of classical allusion in the Klondike stories is not just London's frequent usage, however, but how he encompassed the narrative structure and moral vision of the classics to build a framework for his early stories.

On September 17, 1898, London sent the following letter to the editor of the *San Francisco Bulletin*, laying out three features of a fictional framework he proposed:

> Dear Sir:—
> I have just returned from a year's residence in the Clondyke, entering the country by way of Dyea and Chilcoot Pass. I left by way of St. Michaels, thus making altogether a journey of 2,500 miles on the Yukon in a small boat. I have sailed and traveled quite extensively in other parts of the world and have learned to seize upon that which is interesting, to grasp the true romance of things, and to understand the people I may be thrown amongst.
> I have just completed an article of 4,000 words, describing the trip from Dawson to St. Michaels in a rowboat. Kindly let me know if there would be any demand in your columns for it—of course, thoroughly

understanding that the acceptance of the manuscript is to depend
upon its literary and intrinsic value.

Yours very respectfully,
Jack London (*Letters*, 18)

The editor scrawled across the bottom of London's letter: "Interest in
Alaska has subsided in an amazing degree. Then, again, so much has
been written, that I do not think it would pay us to buy your story."
(Charmian wrote at the top of the letter, "This is Jack's first letter to an
editor.") Nevertheless, London went on to mine his acute observations
of human survival and behavior in the frozen land of the "White
Silence," his imaginative insight into what the gold rush meant, and his
exhaustive reading and writing in order to create his Klondike saga.

London's apprenticeship as a writer in the late nineteenth century
occurred during a period of unprecedented fascination with the Greek
and Roman tradition, and the classics were often used as a basis for
understanding the relationship between the traditions of the past and
the ever-demanding present. Long seen as the ideal of liberal education, classics were viewed by many as examining two unified cultures
remote in time but timely in their cultural messages, cultures different
in outlook yet similar in social values, as attested by works such as Sir
James Frazer's *The Golden Bough*.

With its "subtly persuasive form of the loose, variegated, and often
contradictory intellectual tradition that shapes the modern spirit,"[13] as
John Vickery describes it, *The Golden Bough* proved to be a powerful influence on such figures as Matthew Arnold, William Morris, Algernon
Swinburne, T. H. Huxley, Ernest Renan, John Ruskin, and Joseph Conrad, all read by London. One reason for its appeal to such diverse readers is that "Frazer shows us the rational, evolutionary, historical, scientific temper conspiring with as well as opposing the imaginative,
spiritual, irrational, myth-making impulses of mankind." While on the
surface such notions as Mill's rationalism, Arnold's historical sense, and
Huxley's evolutionary outlook seem antithetical to the passion for the
classics shared by artists and their audiences, they "converge on an
impulse toward the release and expansion of the mind beyond the con-
fines of a constricting dogmatism" (Vickery, 14–15). Thus what Frazer
and London have in common with both the Utilitarian philosophers and
the artists of their day "is the ideal of the open, flexible mind, of reason
as man's best hope for reaching the truth and solving his problems"
(Vickery, 9). London's Darwinism must be seen in this progressive con-

text rather than as merely Spencerian, Marxist, or Freudian determinism. Vickery also suggests that "because the late nineteenth century saw clearly that it itself marked the transition from agrarian to industrial society it was easier to be concerned with other, vastly different societies, as *The Golden Bough* was. . . . As a political and social force imperialism obviously contributed to increased familiarity with remote and primitive countries" (Vickery, 36–37).

As a realist, London's habits and tools reflected his constant search for plots and patterns he could use in his writing; as archives at the Huntington Library and the Merrill Library at Utah State University attest, he read mountains of magazines and newspapers, carefully noting story ideas. But he read nearly everything else, too. In *"Tools of My Trade": Annotated Books in Jack London's Library*, David Mike Hamilton seeks to account for the enormous amount of reading London did in order to write. In his earliest years as a writer London read Shakespeare, Browning, Longfellow, Herrick, Tennyson, Rostand, Kipling, Keats, and others in addition to contemporary authors, philosophy, and science. He was particularly drawn to reading old travels, voyages, and historical tomes. In his excitement and industry he nearly read himself into nervous prostration.[14]

When the magazine *The Editor* asked him to contribute his opinions to an article of advice for young writers, London answered the question "Which is more acceptable, a well-told story with a weak plot or a poorly told story with a strong plot?" by unhesitatingly stating that the former was "vastly more acceptable" (*Letters*, 684). Another side of his orientation toward reading was revealed when he was also asked whether a young writer should study the old masters or the current styles to succeed with modern editors. He answered:

> I should advise the young story-writer to leave the old masters in literature alone, if he wishes to sell stories to the present-day magazines. I should advise the young story-writer to study the stories in the current magazines; in this case, if he has anything in him he will succeed in selling stories to the modern editors. But I must append this warning: HE WILL SUCCEED WITH THE EDITORS OF TO-DAY; BUT IN THE CENTURIES TO COME HE WILL NOT HIMSELF BE ACCREDITED AS A MASTER IN LITERATURE. (*Letters*, 684)[15]

The seriousness with which he took writing as a great tradition from the past and the sacrifices he made for his own calling to it are related quite powerfully in his early letters on the subject. On November 30, 1898, he wrote Mabel Applegarth of the difficulties of his childhood—including brutal labor and near-starvation—and describes her notion of "duty" as demonstrating no understanding of him or any "common ground." It is a letter that invokes both London's admiration for the literary past and his determination not to let his own past keep him from rising to it:

> If I had followed that ["duty"] from childhood, whose companionship would I be fitted to enjoy? Tennyson's, or a bunch of brute hoodlums on a street corner? . . . You cannot understand, nor never will. . . . I don't care if the whole present, all I possess, were swept away from me—I will build a new present; If I am left naked and hungry to-mor-row—before I give in I will go on naked and hungry; if I were a woman I would prostitute myself to all men but that I would succeed—in short, I will. (*Letters*, 25–26)

Fall of 1898 was the most critical season in London's entire career. While he was in the Klondike, his stepfather, John London, died, leaving him sole supporter of the family. Since he brought back less than $5 in gold dust from the Klondike, and was unable to find steady work, he was reduced to whatever odd jobs he could pick up. It was not an auspicious time to begin in earnest his writing career, and his clumsy typewriter was often in the pawnshop, along with just about anything else he owned. His desperation is reflected in his punishing schedule: no more than five hours of sleep per day and no less than 19 of work. At this early stage in his writing career he established the routine of one thousand words per day minimum, and he never ceased sharpening his literary skills, trying out new structures and ideas until he found those that worked for him, beginning with the formula story. He first used an essay-exemplum style in which a narrator offered background information on the setting and philosophized about the outcome of a story, and then a frame narrative that proved to be much more effective. But despite his steady work and his attention to the instructions offered by various theoreticians of the short story, he received not one penny writing during the year 1898. That year he had "the loneliest Christmas I ever faced" (*Letters*, 31–32). He collected 44 rejection slips and would collect 266 in 1899, but he was on his way.[16]

An important part of achieving success for London was integrating his reading with his writing, such as the deep layer of myth he constructed in "To the Man on Trail," following the tentative examples set in "Story of a Typhoon Off the Coast of Japan," the stories he published in *The*

Aegis, and the early Klondike tales written between the fall of 1898 and the spring of 1899. One finds Damon and Pythias; Chaldean necromancy; chimeras; "Heliobas the Second," which may be a means of Latinizing "Helios"; and scattered references to the Sphynx, Jove, Morpheus, Somnus, Lethe, the Three Graces, Mnemosyne, Scylla and Charybdis, and Olympus. From his very first Klondike story, "The Devil's Dice Box," to the one that finally brought him major recognition, "An Odyssey of the North," London integrated classical elements into his texts. Sometimes the motifs provide the structure for the tale; for example, "The Priestly Prerogative" is a retelling of the Medea story sympathetic to the woman and the conflicts created by opposing loyalties and oaths. London's development of a mythic superstructure is best observed through his use of Old Sol in his early Klondike stories. In "The Devil's Dice Box" (1878) London repeatedly uses the image of Old Sol. Old Sol also appears in "The Test: A Clondyke Wooing" (1898) and "The White Silence" (1898). Stories completed a bit later, such as "The Son of the Wolf" (1899), are similarly infused with the mythic structure of Old Sol. The landscape London creates through the welding of mythic patterns with the harsh terrain of the Northland in "The Devil's Dice Box" would provide the groundwork for "An Odyssey of the North," marking an end to London's own long winter of doubt and despair.

Sol is the Romanized Helios, the original Greek god of the sun. By the classical age, many of Helios's attributes had been assumed by Apollo, whose number was seven, possibly alluded to with the use of the seven male characters in "The Devil's Dice Box." Apollo was regarded as "the most Greek of all gods, in art the ideal type of young, but not immature manly beauty."[17] He is the model for the famed Colossus of Rhodes. Under Syrian influence in the time of the Emperor Aurelian (270–275 A.D.), the worship of "Sol Invictus" became the principal Roman cult until the rise of Christianity, with Sol retaining his minor Greek attributes, including the number seven, and acquiring new ones, such as the 25th of December as his designation day. The number seven and the Christmas Day setting also figure in "A Klondike Christmas" (1898), "To the Man on Trail" (1898), and "The Priestly Prerogative" (1899), all of which concentrate on oath-taking and breaking and contain numerous references to the all-seeing sun. From the earliest mention of Helios by Homer in the *Iliad* and *Odyssey*, his main role was witness to the actions and oaths of men for all the gods. Because Helios stresses personal responsibility, Homer calls him "Helios, who sees all things, and listens to all things."[18] Later Helios would figure prominently in Ovid's *Metamorphoses* as an observer of human frailties, and Tacitus would describe Sol as revealer of the crimes of men. Breaking an oath to a god, any god, was viewed as the cause of madness. Madness occurred when the furies came for vengeance, the most famous instance being Orestes chased by the furies for his revenge/murder of his mother, Clytemnestra. In Greek thought, Apollo made himself subject to the law that murder demands atonement and that this catastrophe could be overcome by expiation. Apollo particularly takes an interest in how men bury or fail to bury the dead. A person out of favor with him must himself discover the action that has brought about the god's displeasure and take steps to eliminate its miasma through renewed action.[19]

Later Greek poets did not distinguish between Helios, Apollo, and Sol. By the time Helios had been transformed into Sol, Sol combines all of Helios's and Apollo's attributes, including light as an emblem of knowledge, truth, moral purity, and justice. He even acquires twin Syrian "sun-dogs."[19] London uses all of these features in the Klondike tales, especially the sun-dogs, a rare occurrence in nature (although more common in the Arctic than elsewhere) in which two mock suns appear on either side of the real sun as part of an atmospheric effect caused by refraction and reflection of light through ice and snow crystals. In mythology, these figures are a curious feature of Sol's light. They originated in the East, but the Romans thought of them as aspects of Sol by the time of Cicero, who speaks in *On the Commonwealth* of "the second sun" reported in the Senate in 129 B.C., calling the phenomena "parhelia," or "sun-dogs."[20] Ancient sources tend to identify sun-dogs as harbingers of important events, as in Eusebius's *Life of Constantine*, which describes the cross Constantine is supposed to have seen in the sky upon his conversion to Christianity. Since sun-dogs appear in Syrian (or Chaldean) versions of Sol, they are perceived as figures from the strange lands of the seers to the east, territory never conquered by the Greeks and a problematic border for the Romans. In the Klondike stories, accordingly, travelers who trek to weird eastern regions risk their lives, and the sun-dogs appear to judge their struggles for survival. Perhaps the sun-dogs hint at some of the moral oppositions London poses for his characters afoot under the Arctic sky.

In "The Devil's Dice Box," seven males (Sol's number) and a female are staying together during the short days of December when a visitor from the east arrives with over one hundred pounds of gold on his sled. They are all curious about the gold, but he will not give them any information concerning its origin. After resting, the stranger's preparations to resume his journey on Christmas Day (Sol's day) are interrupted by his brother's arrival. In this scene brother squares off against brother:

> Never did Christmas Day look down on [a] stranger scene. It was high noon, and the upper rim of the sun, barely showing above the southern horizon, cast a blood-red streak athwart the heavens. On the other hand a sun-dog blazed, while the air was filled with scintillating particles of frost. A great silence prevailed. (*Complete,* 117–18)

The newly arrived brother kills his brother, the stranger from the east, and rides off, leaving the corpse. The whole death scene "happened in less than five minutes" (118), and the seven men are left with the dead body and the dead man's gold. Their first mistake is in deciding not to bury the stranger's body properly, merely abandoning it. Then the seven hold a council to decide what their next step should be. In the midst of this council, gold fever and greed overcome the men when the two 50-pound sacks of nuggets are emptied on the table. "[F]rom this moment the Madness began to grow" (118). The Madness grows because these men are not only breaking Northland codes but are offending Sol.

The seven decide to chase the murdered man's brother and take his gold. One of the seven, Charley, cannot keep up with the others. For the ancient Greeks, a brother who kills a brother is doomed, but this group, not yet completely seized by the Madness, is not necessarily doomed yet. It is possible that the gods will yet intercede depending upon whether the prospectors choose to continue their race or quit in order to save Charley:

> We found it impossible to get Charley up. His brain would rouse but his body could not respond. He was not sick, only exhausted. Rest was the only medicine for him, and we could not give it. . . . The sleds were loaded, the dogs were harnessed, but we waited and tried and tried in vain. As old Sol dipped over the horizon at meridian, we rose to our feet. The moment had come. We looked into each other's eyes coldly and without emotion. Lucy's face, though her throat was silent, voiced an eloquent appeal. The Madness was on us; we could not yield. The snapping whips and lunging dogs roused him, and by the look on his face, we knew he understood. It was a pious look—the look of a wounded doe or of a seal at the killing. So we left him because of the Madness, and small wonder that our gods forsook us as we forsook our comrade. (121)

Sol has witnessed their choice, and the gods—personified as "Fate"—do forsake the entire group, who die in their hellish mine pit. London's insertion of recognizable mythic imagery into this Northland setting suggests that the actions of the seven reflect an archetypal pattern of behavior. As this is London's first Klondike story, it is interesting to note that these seven, engaged in a struggle against their fellow man, nature, and the gods, will perish. London establishes in his first Klondike tale what will become a pattern in his stories—that those who foolishly pit themselves against community, nature, and/or the gods—that is, against justice—are punished by death. The epigraph to "The Devil's Dice Box," evidently composed by London for this tale, foreshadows this pattern with its Miltonian reference to Mammon:

> We worshipped at alien altars; we bowed our heads in the dust;
> Our law was might is the mightiest; our creed was unholy lust;
> Our law & our creed we followed—strange is the tale to tell—
> For our law & our creed we followed into the pit of hell.
> —*The Mammon Worshippers*

The story deserves the Miltonian reference in addition to the Greek allusions, since its image of the dice box is of a yawning pit of hell, a Satanic abyss holding both gold and skeletons. It is the site of the Fall, of the emergence of those negative values that lead to violence and death but (here) not to redemption, as brother murders brother and leaves the dead scattered about. It is a dice box in which everyone will lose every time the dice are thrown because in their pride they seek to outwit the gods—or the Devil—little suspecting that they themselves will become the dice.[21]

In contrast, "The Test: A Clondyke Wooing," is a retelling of the patient Griselda tale with Sol also serving as witness. It has a positive conclusion for characters who remain linked within a community, abiding by their oaths. It is interesting that London chose to retell an old story. "Patient Griselda"—the faithful wife who suffers the husband's cruel tests of her loyalty—first shows up as a distinct story in Bocaccio's *Decameron*, but its origins can be traced farther back, including to the Psyche/Cupid myth. For centuries, the Griselda story has provided a vehicle through which writers have worked out issues concerning oath-making and expressions of loyalty.

In London's version of Griselda, Lucille—with a forgotten and forgiven past—falls in love with London's version of the medieval husband, Walter, now called Jack Harrington. Jack wants proof that Lucille loves him and not his money, so he loses his fortune to see if she will still declare her love for him. She does. On the day they are to set up housekeeping, "Old Sol, attended by twin sun-dogs, has just cleared the southern horizon and pauses for a peep at the Northland Eldorado. Before he can slip behind the mountain over which he rose, he catches a glimpse of a scene, which all Dawson has turned out to behold" (129). Lucille and Jack will wed; both have remained true to their oaths. In this story, unlike "The Devil's Dice Box," Old Sol presides over a happy conclusion.

In "The White Silence," London uses the Sol image in a more subtle manner. Mason, mortally injured, exacts a terrible oath from Malemute Kid—to help him die, thus saving his wife and unborn child by taking them onward toward help. Malemute Kid strongly resists; he cannot leave Mason, but he does not want to administer the final death blow:

> An hour passed,—two hours,—but the man would not die. At high noon, the sun without raising its rim above the southern horizon threw a suggestion of fire athwart the heavens, then quickly drew it back. Malemute Kid roused and dragged himself to his comrade's side. He cast one glance about him. The White Silence seemed to sneer and a great fear came upon him. There was a sharp report; Mason swung into his aerial sepulcher; and Malemute Kid lashed the dogs into a wild gallop as he fled across the snow. (149)

Thematically "The White Silence" considers the relationship between man and his gods. London expresses the Greek notion that man struggles against the gods for his very existence. Man may be finite, but the gods are still jealous of his audacity. They do not want man to understand the "imprisoned essence" of reality, or solve "the mystery of all things [which] strive[s] for utterance" (144). The White Silence shrouds everything in an ominous silence, while man vainly tries to speak with his understanding. As characters in all three stories struggle for understanding, Old Sol is the silent observer, able to provide testimony concerning oath-keeping and breaking.

"The Son of the Wolf," with heavily nuanced folk origins, is perhaps a retelling of a trickster myth, structured around the presence or absence of the life-giving and all-seeing sun. Scruff MacKenzie journeys afar in the Northland in search of a wife. He heads into dangerous lands where he must use whatever is at hand to defend himself: "It required a deft hand and a deep knowledge of the barbaric mind effectually to handle such diverse weapons; but he was a past master in the art, knowing when to conciliate and when to threaten with Jove-like wrath" (196). Arriving in the village of Chief Thling-Tinneh, he mingles with the Indians, throws a potlatch, and joins in their games and sports while they "gave tongue to their folk-chants in honor of their guest" (196). Like Odysseus among the suitors, Scruff shows off his marksmanship, knowing he must best the young men of the tribe for the hand of the chief's daughter, Zarinska, whom he plans to marry and rename Gertrude. "[T]he camp rang with his plaudits when he brought down a moose at six hundred yards" (197), the young warriors mutter among themselves, and Scruff makes lavish gifts to the chief and asks the hand of his daughter. She, like Penelope before her, hides with her women and sews until her husband comes to claim her.

When Scruff brings Zarinska into the center of the camp, the Shaman curses him as the Son of the Wolf, the very Devil, who has no right to marry among "the children of Jelchs, the Raven, the Promethean fire-bringer" (202). With the White Silence "for the moment driven to the rimming forest, . . . ever crushing inward," and the stars dancing "with great leaps, as is their wont in the time of the Great Cold," the "Spirits of the Pole trailed their robes of glory athwart the heavens" (201). As the Shaman reviles him and all white men, calling upon the Indian god, the "Fire-Bringer," to punish him, "a great streamer of fire, the aurora borealis, purple, green, and yellow, shot across the zenith, bridging horizon to horizon" (203–4). But this is a false dawn, and its magic is no match for the Son of the Wolf's audacity and strength; Prometheus was only a stealer of fire, not the source himself, and he was defeated by the Olympians. Killing two of his foes, denouncing the Shaman, and making peace with the remainder, Scruff prevails and carries off his bride, making his oath to Thling-Tinneh that "[i]n the days to come thou shouldst journey to the Country of the Yukon, know thou that there shall always be a place and much food by the fire of the Wolf. The night is now passing into day" (208). In a sense, despite its use of Sol, "The Son of the Wolf" has a different tone within this group of stories. Although it lent its title to London's first collection, it is not as concerned—as are those tales that immediately precede and follow it—with the theme of preferring community over personal gain, a theme that resonates strongly in London's career from his socialist politics to his related ideas at every phase of his career. It is perhaps a case in which his shaping the folk tale itself overcame any conscious "theme" on the part of the writer, though it connects with the other stories in subtle ways.

The noonday night of winter is the setting for most of "In a Far Country," and although the protagonists endure the agonizing wait in the darkness for the return of the sun, they wait in vain, for they are incapable of keeping their oaths and the code of brotherhood. Two moral weaklings, Cuthfert and Weatherbee, winter together in a Klondike cabin because they were too lazy to make the journey out with their comrades. As they become progressively dispirited and turn against each other, each commits the seven deadly sins, ending in a ghastly double murder. The sun remains hidden, and their worst fears emerge out of the darkness, including shades of the dead who whisper evil thoughts and fan the flames of fear. To contrast this Hades-like gloom, Cuthfert muses that here "there were no lands of sunshine, heavy with the perfume of flowers. Such things were only old dreams of paradise. The sunlands of the West and the spicelands of the East, the smiling Arcadias and blissful Islands of the Blest,—ha! ha!.... There was no sun. This was the Universe, dead and cold and dark..." (218). When finally "a golden rim peeped over the mountain's snowy shoulder, smiled upon them an instant, then dipped from sight again, with tears in their eyes... they sought each other," experiencing a "strange softening" (220). But it is too late, for they have no faith. As they are dying together, one from a gunshot and the other from an ax blow to the spine, Cuthfert recalls that he had seen the sun, but realizes he cannot go and see it now. Fittingly, the story's last image is the two standing in front of the "great White Throne": "And God would judge them, God would judge them!" (223).[22]

The use of Old Sol becomes more subtle and more controlled as the Klondike stories progress. In "An Odyssey of the North," London transforms Sol using his own landscape of the Northland to retell Homer's *Odyssey*. Certainly the title itself suggests a comparison to Homer's tale, and when the basic structure of the *Odyssey* is compared to the structure of London's "Odyssey," they are remarkably similar. Homer's *Odyssey* is loosely framed in four sections: the adventures of Telemachos (I-IV); the homecoming of Odysseus (V-VIII and XIII.187); the retelling of his great wanderings (IX-XII); and Odysseus in Ithaka (XIII.187-XXIV.548). London's version begins with Malemute Kid, who assumes the role of Telemachos, and moves on to the homecoming of Naass, whom the Kid addresses as "Mr. Ulysses" (*Complete*, 234). Then Naass recounts his wanderings, and the tale ends with Naass back at the Kid's camp (Ithaka).

In addition to a similar frame and overarching themes of a hero's journey or trials that arise from an incident of host code-breaking, a violation of the Greek notion of the sacredness of hospitality, there are many other details in common between the stories. In both, the narrative order disagrees with the chronological order, which in the *Odyssey* covers about a 10-year span. Adding the eight years mentioned in one part of London's story to the time passed in the additional segments equates the time span of London version to Homer's. London's rhythmic use of language also echoes Homer's. London's repeated references to Naass as "He of the Otter Skins" (235) echoes Homeric formulas such as "Hektor, Breaker of Horses." But the most interesting commonalty is the ambiguity arising from the lack of moral conclusion in London's version, reflecting Homer's similarly problematic conclusion.

Like Telemachos, Malemute Kid finds his home invaded and himself welcomed by strangers—about a dozen or so who have taken over his home. Telemachos dreams before his journey, and the Kid dreams that "he, too, wandered through the white unknown, struggled with the dogs on endless trails, and saw men live, and toil, and die like men" (235). In addition, Malemute Kid recognizes Naass, which echoes Telemachos as the only one who knows Odysseus. Structurally it is important that in the *Odyssey* the theft of the Cattle of the Sun, which causes Helios to destroy Odysseus's men in retribution, occurs just before Odysseus's return to Ithaka. Thus the themes of oath-keeping and uprightness before the gods, of brotherly love, fatherhood, and the homecoming all are brought together, and London's tale echoes and reverberates with these structural and thematic patterns.

But the differences between London's version and Homer's illuminate London's own quest. One of the most significant differences is in London's choice of heroes: his leveling of Homer's class differences counters the typical Victorian reading of Homer's heroes. During this period, Homer was the darling of the imperialist upper classes. Homer's heroes were viewed as epic models for aristocratic young men to follow. Michael Wood describes Homer's influence at the time:

> The unrivaled popularity of Homer in the late Victorian and Edwardian imagination perhaps reflects the role of the *Iliad* in the English public-school system. At the height of the British empire Homer was perhaps the poet who spoke most feelingly to the British imperialists for his "gentlemanliness" and his "stiff upper lip" in the face of death . . . as much as for his glorification of courage in war . . . Homer evoked the

26

most powerful images in those brought up to believe to see themselves as the new Athenians.[23]

However, London viewed Homer's heroes very differently, moving his heroes from an aristocratic mode to a more egalitarian one. For instance, London's Odysseus is a mixed-blooded Indian, and the Malemute Kid's camp is surrounded by "these uncrowned heroes who had seen history made, who regarded the great and the romantic as but the ordinary and incidental in the routine of life" (*Complete*, 232). Malemute Kid passes his "precious tobacco among them with lavish disregard, and rusty chains of reminiscence were loosened, and forgotten odysseys resurrected for his especial benefit" (233). The odysseys they resurrect are a catalog of cultures including French romances, kings and queens, tales of Khartoum, Buffalo Bill's tour of Europe, and their own insurrection in the Northwest (232). London makes heroes commoners and invents American versions of classical heroes, the halfbreed Naass and Sitka Charley.

In addition to reworking Homer's class differences, London also reweaves the locale he constructed for "The Devil's Dice Box" into his version of *The Odyssey*. London's landscape is the fabled but ill-fated Eldorado into which Naass leads his Penelope. Here, during the fateful time when Axel Gunderson breaks the guest/host code, "the sun went away" (246). This allusion to Sol leads to the same problematic conclusion as in Homer's *Odyssey*. Many readers, including ancient Greeks, have questioned whether or not Penelope's suitors deserve their fate. Likewise, London's readers could question the justice of Unga and Axel's fate. Certainly, Prince calls Naass's actions "murder" (257). Malemute Kid turns aside Prince's reaction with his comment that "there are things greater than our wisdom, beyond our justice. The right and wrong of this we cannot say, and it is not answerable by humans" (258). Neither London nor Homer works out a moral solution as a response to Naass's and Odysseus's actions.

This sort of ambiguity was employed by London regularly throughout the rest of his career, and he also consistently returned to various mythic allusions derived from Greek and Roman sources, as evidenced in two of his final stories, "The Red One," with its Medusa, and "The Water Baby," with its references to Antaeus and other Greek motifs. London's early fascination with archetypal patterns in such works as *The Odyssey* and *Paradise Lost* and his knowledge of Greek and Roman myth enabled him later to absorb and use the myths of other cultures, including Polynesian.[24]

Occasionally the imagery of the sun and specifically Old Sol reappear in later Klondike stories, such as "The Sun-Dog Trail" (1905). After a hard day on trail, Sitka Charley and a companion sit smoking and contemplating the newspaper pictures pasted to the wall of the deserted cabin they occupy for the night. The first shows a man shooting another man; the second depicts the origins of Helen in a dramatization of "Leda and the Swan"; the third image is of a terribly ill child. Sitka Charley finds the pictures hard to understand since they have no beginning and no end, only a present reality; they are merely snapshots of life with no conclusion, hence no "meaning." The two men begin constructing their own picture of a dice game and explaining it, and then Charley is moved to recount a strange event in which he participated seven years before, in 1897, which he calls "The Sun-Dog Trail." He was hired for a huge sum by a lovely but mysterious white woman to take her to Dawson. They arrive in the last water before the freeze-up. A young man joins her and she then pays Charley more to take them to Circle City; they arrive on Christmas Eve and will not let Charley rest on Christmas Day. They plunge ahead into the bitter cold, wandering in a seemingly aimless fashion across the terrible waste, suffering from frostbite, starvation, and total exhaustion, but they will not stop. A one-eyed man brings them news but they will not tell Charley what it is; onward they go. Charley is reluctant and frightened, but has been bought: "They pay me seven hundred and fifty dollars each month. They are my masters. I am their man. If they say, 'Charley, come, let us start for hell,' I will harness the dogs. . ." (*Complete*, 977). As they pass the last outposts he notes that the sun only "looks at us for a moment over the hills to the south," and the "northern lights flame in the sky, and the sun-dogs dance, and the air is filled with frost-dust" (978). Sitka Charley knows they do not look for gold but for something else, and even he, born on the trail, begins to fail as the three crawl their way along, having eaten everything they have but their harnesses. The story has a strange repetitive quality as it recounts their journey in Charley's short, rhythmic sentences. Among the repeated references are the "sun-dogs flashing on either side" of the sun. At last the couple catch up with their prey, a frost-blackened, snarling, dying man, and the woman manages to shoot him. They then collapse. Though Charley never finds out why they did what they did, he saves their lives and takes them to board a steamer when they recover in St. Michaels: "They came into my life and they went out of my life, and the picture is as I have said, without beginning, the end without understanding" (985). Only the sun-dogs can know the meaning of these Furies' vengeance. London sought to convey "a piece of life" without undue authorial intrusion, and the classical stories provided a convenient and effective but multilayered way of doing this. In later works London would again structure his tale around an aloof, Homeric narrator who is immersed in an environment but not a part of it. This character is part of the culture he describes but also a viewer of it. In *The People of the Abyss* (1903), for example, though he is sympathetic to the slum dwellers of London, he describes them in a way that compares with Odysseus's horror and fascination at encountering strange creatures in the Aegean.

London's stories come to enact a metamorphosis of heroes, of culture, of *topoi*. At the beginning of his career London represented the Sun God as the eye of judgment. The naturalist world is looked down on by superior nature, that tip of the planet smitten by the cold of space described in "To Build a Fire." Later, the subject is the heroic young god, Martin Eden; Ernest Everhard; the young fighter in "The Night-Born"; or the boxer of *The Game*. But, finally, London supplements his fascination with the Sun God with other divinities, such as the trickster Maui, the Sea Mother, and, in the first paragraph of "The Red One," the pre-Olympian Titans and the cthonic figure of Medusa as an emblem of knowledge. Like many other ideas London encountered, even this obvious favorite, classical allusion, could not go unchallenged. Although Apollo remains the ideal of manhood, in the end, the author turns to Apollo's dark twins and exchanges, as it were, Hyperion for Medusa, the Sun God for the Red One, the Sky Father for the Water Baby in the age-old contest among the gods. By moving in this inward, questioning, dualistic direction, London makes his own myth, like Homer, Milton, and Blake before him. As London moved into subsequent Klondike and other stories, he joined the Greek value of justice with an insistence upon imagination and an even greater desire for community, especially as he deepened his socialist commitment.

The Klondike stories contain a great deal of action, of course, but they are also very conversational, with authentic voices and dialect. They are full of jokes, tricks (and tricksters), pranks, and games, but the stakes are higher than in the early stories. London characteristically presents ideas in pairs. Just as he struggled between extremes intellectually, so are his major ideas yoked to their opposites: adventure fiction versus stories of psychological insight, naturalism/romanticism, individualism/socialism, masculinity/femininity, the ancient world/the modern world, race difference/brotherhood. As we saw in the first few Klondike stories, the same topic may be treated from different points of view, often in stories written within days or weeks of each other, a habit that would persist for his entire career. As London continued to layer meaning in subsequent stories through the use of myth, he moved away from the Greek epic to biblical allusion and then to Jungian archetypes in the South Seas stories.

Other important techniques that were developed in the Klondike tales include experiments with subject matter, use of the frame story (sometimes with several layers and metafictive effects), exotic settings and powerful descriptions, language that is approachable but rich in vocabulary and allusion, interest in the macabre and science fiction, autobiography, and what appears to be firsthand knowledge of everything from gold prospecting to sailing to flying airplanes. This reflects London's own adventuring and experimenting as much as it does his capacity for research. With the overall emphasis upon character, the Klondike stories also exhibit recurring characters and character types, particularly the Northland code hero, who lives by the Code of the Northland and its insistence upon brotherhood and community. There are some stereotypes—the sociopath, the strong woman, trickster figures, the loyal Indian, the weakling, and many others—but three primary character types receive in-depth treatment in the Klondike tales: the Hero, the Indian, and the Woman. An examination of some of the most significant stories with these defining characters in mind reveals that they overlap in almost every one, with the greatest conjunctions occurring between the Indian and the Woman, yet each story tends to have an emphasis upon one or the other.

The Hero

In all the collections of Klondike stories, beginning with *The Son of the Wolf* (1900) and ending with *Smoke Bellew* (1912), the Klondike code hero is rugged and adept at survival in the frozen wilderness. He is usually a white man come to the North to prospect for gold, though he is nearly always immune to the gold fever, a *chechaqo* reformed. Sometimes, as in the case of Sitka Charley, he is an Indian. Holding a job, whether prospecting, serving as a trail guide, or carrying mail, does not consume his imagination; his love is the Northland itself. He is kind but tough on his dogs, a possessor of fine emotions, susceptible to falling in love, but reticent with his feelings. He often has a feminine quality or two about him, as Jack Westondale of "To the Man on Trail" who possesses, in addition to the "virtues of the lion," a "certain softness, the hint of womanliness, which bespoke the emotional nature" (159). With men he is a great companion and storyteller. He shoots straight and can live on chewed pack leather when he needs to. He is not exactly John Wayne, but he is not far from it. There is also a good deal of Leatherstocking and Huck Finn in him, as well as elements from Rudyard Kipling's free-booting adventurers and Bret Harte's frontiersmen. His cardinal virtues are honesty, fair play, and comradeship. He seems largely uninterested in personal gain as a life goal but rather demonstrates a strong social consciousness.

London observed the men and women around him and chose certain individuals to write about, such as his traveling companion, Merritt Sloper, who was the model for the Malemute Kid and who also appears under his own name in "In a Far Country." The Malemute Kid is London's most admirable Northland hero; he appears in nine stories, either as active participant in the plot or storyteller. In "The Men of Forty-Mile" (1898), he prevents two of his friends from entering into a murderous fight with each other by threatening to hang them both, demonstrating his resourcefulness, devotion to his companions, and integrity: they know he means it. The Malemute Kid is the possessor of the kind of imagination London deemed crucial to survival and understanding in life. London witnessed average men tested by extraordinary circumstances. As Walker notes,

> As with all random groups there were strong men and there were weaklings, there were novices right out of offices and experienced out-doorsmen who had followed gold before, there were homesick family men and there were restless wanderers who were happiest away from home. . . . London was seeing a male society living under difficult conditions, exhibiting the heights of resourcefulness and companionship and the depths of weakness and hostility which emerge in such situations. (Walker, 146)[25]

Yet much of London's information about the Klondike comes not from actual experience but from stories told to him by others. And those chroniclers who met him all mention similar things about him: his great propensity to tell stories himself, his zest for argument, and his insatiable curiosity about his environment. Some describe him deep in conversation with veteran sourdoughs in the Dawson bars, while others recall his frequent expostulations on Darwin and Spencer (Walker, 11, 135–36). When he was not doing all the talking, however, or reading *Paradise Lost* to bemused cabin mates, London picked up a wealth of information that would later allow him to people his Klondike stories; not only was the code hero constructed from these sources, but so, too, much of his information about the Indians of the Northland.

We have already examined several stories that emphasize the Klondike hero. This hero is a character London returned to many times; it should be kept in mind that just because he is a code hero he is not uniform, however. London's hero appears in many different manifestations and upholds the basic code by various means. In magazines like *Youth's Companion,* London found a ready market for tales of youthful heroism; he allowed plucky adolescents to exhibit their courage just as the older men. "The King of Mazy May: A Story of the Klondike," published in *Youth's Companion* in 1899, is an early example of a young hero whose adventures would culminate in those of *Tales of the Fish Patrol.* The boy, Walt Masters, makes his second appearance in "Chased by the Trail" (1900), in which he escapes the danger of the spring breakup of the Yukon River ice through teamwork and resourcefulness.

Another variation upon the code hero is the trickster, and he can be either good or bad. As he appears in the trickster traditions in American Indian, African American, Asian American, and Latina/o cultures, as well as in the lore of the American frontier, the trickster is a universal figure in society who calls hierarchies into question and overturns the everyday to bring us face to face with another dimension. One of London's best-known tricksters is Subienkow, the hero of "Lost Face" (1908), who fools his Indian captors into killing him quickly instead of torturing him over a period of time, as they have done to his companion. He fools them by pretending to make "medicine" that will deflect any blow; he applies it to his neck, inviting the chief to test it out. This trick is designed to embarrass the chief, who is forever after called "Lost Face." "This would not be nice" (*Complete,* 1418), the story opens, and it does indeed dwell upon the savagery of the setting, but the focus is on the whites' savagery as well as the Indians'. Whites are "fur thieves" without a trace of nobility: "Always it had been savagery—brutal, bestial savagery" (1420). But Subienkow himself is heroic because he is able to use his imagination. Other tricksters include characters such as Scruff MacKenzie, Porportuk, Lit-Lit, Scundoo, Thomas Stevens, and the Water Baby.

Sometimes the hero must undergo a major change in order to survive. Hay Stockard of "The God of His Fathers" (1899) kills the Indian followers of the halfbreed chief Red Baptiste in a futile attempt to defend his own wife, child, and the missionary party he is escorting, but in the end Stockard, not a Christian, dies for the faith while the missionary cowers and recants in the face of the chief. This story has Sol as observer of the deeds of the men, red and white, who struggle, but its moral perspective is cloudy and its irony bitter.

"Love of Life" (1903), the tale so admired by Lenin on his deathbed, is a grim, naturalist fable of survival at any cost. Suggested by a *McClure's* article about the experiences of one Charles Bunn, member of a small exploring party looking for mineral deposits in the Barren Lands of northern Canada during the summer of 1900, the tale is "a grim apotheosis of the struggle to survive"(Walker, 21). This tale displays London's strongest abilities as storyteller in an inch-by-inch saga of survival and its terrible costs. The protagonist is propelled by the life force itself, "some strange alchemy of soul" (*Complete*, 937). "Then why was he not content to die? . . . He, as a man, no longer strove. It was the life in him, unwilling to die, that drove him on. He did not suffer. His nerves had become blunted, numb, while his mind was filled with weird visions and delicious dreams" (933). Strong in naturalist elements, in the end the story's hero is described as a wormlike creature struggling up the beach.

"Was it reality, after all?" (934), the protagonist wonders. "Then he turned his gaze and slowly took in the circle of the world that remained to him now that Bill was gone . . . Everywhere was soft sky-line, . . . a tremendous and terrible desolation" (923). The landscape is a fitting backdrop for the desertion that has taken place; when his partner, Bill, leaves him, the man spends the first part of the story in total disbelief that betrayal could happen. The sun is there to witness the betrayal: "Near the horizon the sun was smouldering dimly, almost obscured by formless mists and vapors, which gave an impression of mass and density without outline or tangibility" (923). The ". . . dim ball of sun sank slowly into the northwest," but the sun also witnesses the fact that the man has "hope greater than knowledge and defying experience" (925). This story places value upon community by emphasizing the lack of it, and upon imagination and spiritual strength in their opposition to the White Silence—their "hope greater than knowledge." Although the sun remains hidden from the man for most of the story—"[t]here was no sun nor hint of sun" (926)—when he at last "awoke in his right mind," the sun "was shining bright and warm" (933). It continues to shine brightly until he reaches the ship. Why does he survive and Bill, who deserted him, turn into a pile of bones? The hero not only abides by the code but has imagination, although the code in this story is reduced to actions such as the hero not sucking Bill's bones, keeping his matches dry, leaving his gold behind when he needs to, and cleverly tricking the sick wolf that is pursuing him into succumbing to him for his grisly sustenance.

The hero must undergo a different kind of change in "The End of the Story" (1911), which at first appears to have the elements of the typical Klondike survival story: powerful descriptions of the effects of the great cold, gambling, yarn-spinning, and heroics on the trail. But it is a reworking of an earlier tale of a more ironic nature, "A Day's Lodging" (1907), in which a man has to stay overnight in a cabin with his former wife and the man for whom she left him.[26] " 'No one can explain love,' " comments Madge of "The End of the Story"(2105). Grant Linday, a doctor, must save Rex Strang's life and restore him to Madge: " 'He is my king, my lover' " (2101). But the woman's vision is clouded; her lover was hurt while foolishly toying with a panther. Rex himself is compared to a panther, but Grant, who thinks in more mechanical terms, plans to "reattach" the "wires" that hold Rex together. As in "To Build a Fire," here the drama of endurance is oddly reduced to the body as machine: As the sun dips at midnight for a few moments,

> Linday never let up on Strang. He studied his walk, his body movements, stripped him again and again for the thousandth time made him flex all his muscles. . . . But Linday was not yet satisfied. He put Strang through his whole repertoire of physical feats, searching him all the while for hidden weaknesses. He put him on his back again for a week, opened up his leg, played a deft trick or two with the smaller veins, scraped a spot of bone no larger than a coffee grain till naught but a surface of healthy pink remained to be sewed over with the living flesh. (2106)

This passage sounds uncomfortably like "A Thousand Deaths," and there is an undeniably peculiar tone to this entire story. The name "Strang" turns up again later as "Adam Strang," muscular hero of an important section of *The Star Rover* (1915). The oddness of the story is due to its unsettling combination of an assortment of competing elements: humanity and technology are opposed and accompanied by ideas from love and honor to the death wish and Dr. Frankenstein.

Sometimes the protagonist fails at being a hero, even though he sets out to be one. "The One Thousand Dozen" (1901) presents a hustler who has "one idea" (632), and that is to make a fortune by bringing eggs into Dawson. He struggles madly on the trail and nearly dies trying to get his sled of precious eggs into town. When he discovers that they are rotten, he hangs himself. His obsession with money has overcome any sense of practicality he may have had and makes his struggle, while arduous, anything but noble.

Sometimes the hero appears to be a criminal, but his true virtues are revealed—Jack Westondale of "To the Man on Trail" was a formative example. In "At the Rainbow's End" (1899), the Montana Kid, a speculator and gambler living off of the "passionate pilgrims" (349) of the Klondike, represents the spirit of the free man of the West who must live just outside the law and must move farther and farther west: ". . . the new territory was mostly barren; but its several hundred thousand square miles of frigidity at least gave breathing space to those who else would have suffocated at home" (349). After a struggle to escape being crushed by the spring breakup of the Yukon River, he eludes the police who have come to arrest him.

But of course there are also genuine criminals who are the antithesis of the hero. The most dramatic instance is the demonic man and dog pair of Black Leclere and Bâtard. In contrast to the man and dog in *The Call of the Wild*, the Darwinian tour de force "Bâtard" (1902) is a story of cruelty repaid, the evil of men visited upon them by the dogs they abuse. Bâtard is a product of "the fierceness and valor of the wolf" from his father and "the stealth and cunning of the husky" from his mother (730). But his character is actually molded by the cruelties of his human master:

> And then came Black LeClere, to lay his heavy hand on the bit of pulsating puppy life, to press and prod and mould till it became a big bristling beast, acute in knavery, overspilling with hate, sinister, malignant, diabolical. With a proper master Bâtard might have made an ordinary, fairly efficient sled-dog. He never got the chance: Leclere but confirmed him in his congenital iniquity. (730)

The greater Leclere's tortures, the stronger Bâtard's hatred and resolve:

> Often the man felt that he had bucked against the very essence of life—the unconquerable essence that swept the hawk down out of the sky like a feathered thunderbolt, that drove the great gray goose across

the zones, that hurled the spawning salmon through two thousand miles of boiling Yukon flood. At such times he felt impelled to express his own unconquerable essence; and with strong drink, wild music, and Bâtard, he indulged in vast orgies, wherein he pitted his puny strength in the face of things, and challenged all that was, and had been, and was yet to be. (737)

In the end, Leclere is punished for his misdeeds in a mock hanging; with his feet barely touching the box, he is left to ruminate his sins while the townspeople run off at the news of a new claim. Bâtard sees his chance, and takes it, tearing the flailing man to pieces at his leisure. "Bâtard" is a good example of London's skillful blending of a materialistic determinism (Leclere "moulds" Bâtard) and an equally strong sense of timeless moral justice (Bâtard destroys Leclere).

The villain of "Finis" (1906) is a fallen hero who hides out on the trail to kill a party loaded with gold as it comes by on Christmas Day. As he battles starvation and the killing frost, his thoughts turn not to his own death, as in "To Build a Fire," but to murder: "[T]he menace of death ... lurked in the form of a dying man beside the trail" (1175). In an eerie atmosphere of suspense, the reader must face the question, what *will* a person do to survive? His act—which takes place on Christmas Day—is successful, but a dog belonging to the victims' party, representing justice, slays him in revenge.

Christopher Bellew becomes the hero of a new Klondike bildungsroman, replacing the Malemute Kid of earlier stories. A pampered young man, he trades the indolence of the rich boy for manhood in the Klondike; he is a writer who has nothing to write about until he transforms himself into first "Kit" and then "Smoke" Bellew, but by then he is too busy having adventures to write. Smoke appears in dozens of stories. "The Taste of the Meat" (1911) begins the series; at the story's conclusion, his father is able to say, with some surprise, "You've made good, boy" (1797). Smoke's happiest moment in "The Taste of the Meat" is when he is able to compare his prowess at survival to that of the Indians—a reversal of the theme of white dominance that London employed in *The Son of the Wolf.*

The rest of *Smoke Bellew* traces Smoke's further adventures with his sidekick, Shorty, and the woman he strives to impress, the Klondike Princess, Joy Gastell. In "The Meat" (1911), Smoke and Shorty agree to act as guides to a party of well-to-do explorers, only to find them rather like Smoke himself when he was Christopher in his earlier incarnation:

" 'Oh, they are real hummers, your boss and mine, when it comes to sheddin' the mazuma an' never mindin' other folks' feelings,' " comments Shorty (1802). As in "In a Far Country," there are two "incapables," but here London makes class the issue, connecting with his more explicitly socialist stories. In contrast to the rich men, Smoke and Shorty respect and care for each other: " 'Well you're the real goods, at any rate. . . . It makes me respect God the more just to look at you,' " Smoke tells his friend (1802).

"The Stampede to Squaw Creek" (1911) focuses on Smoke the writer. A writer has to live what he writes, Smoke tells Shorty:

> "I've reconstructed every cell in my body since I hit the beach at Dyea. My flesh is as stringy as whipcords, and as bitter and mean as the bite of a rattlesnake. A few months ago I'd have patted myself on the back to write such words, but I couldn't have written them. I had to live them first, and now that I'm living them there's no need to write them." (1826)

He wishes to tell the tales of the Northland sourdoughs, who were "giants" and "heroes." They deserve some "reward" now that "thousands of green softlings, who haven't earned the right to stake anything" are crowding in on the strike (1829). Interestingly, developing the physique and skill for survival in the Northland is directly tied to developing the imagination and writing it.

Many of the Smoke Bellew stories partake of the trickster motif, as Smoke and Shorty outwit their competitors in gambling, love, and speculation. "The Race for Number Three" (1911) is a retelling of "A Daughter of the Aurora" (1899), and again the outcome of the manly contest is determined by a woman who sets it up, gets the hero involved, and then helps him at the finish line. Here Smoke races Big Olaf and Arizona Bill with the help of Joy Gastell, but it ends in a draw. In "The Stampede to Squaw Creek" (1911), Shorty and Smoke are trying to trick the *chechaquos* by leading them to a false claim—preserving the real claim for the sourdoughs—but in the end they miscalculate and lose their own claim. "The Man on the Other Bank" (1911), set at Surprise Lake and the McQuestion River, emphasizes Smoke's love of the "fine, wise, Spartan Northland," where he

> loved the life, the deep arctic winter, the silent wilderness, the unending snow-surface unpressed by the foot of man. About him towered icy

peaks unnamed and uncharted. No hunter's camp-smoke, rising in the still air of the valleys, ever caught his eye. He, alone, moved through the brooding quiet of the untraveled wastes; nor was he oppressed by the solitude. He loved it all, the day's toil, the bickering wolf-dogs, the making of the camp in the long twilight, the leaping stars overhead, and the flaming pageant of the aurora borealis.

Especially he loved his camp at the end of the day, and in it he saw a picture which he ever yearned to paint and which he knew he would never forget—a beaten place in the snow, where burned his fire; his bed a couple of rabbit-skin robes spread on fresh-chopped spruce-boughs; his shelter a stretched strip of canvas that caught and threw back the heat of the fire; the blackened coffee-pot and pail resting on a length of log, the moccasins propped on sticks to dry, the snow-shoes up-ended in the snow; and across the fire the wolf-dogs snuggling to it for the warmth, wistful and eager, furry and frost-rimed, with bush tails curled protectingly over their feet; and all about, pressed backward but a space, the wall of encircling darkness. (1852–53)

The Greek sense of justice under the gods has here been supplemented by a particular kind of "Spartan" enjoyment of the landscape itself. But Smoke and Shorty do find themselves as judges of the deeds of men, as in "The Mistake of Creation" (1911), in which a group of religious vegetarians is dying of scurvy. Smoke and Shorty help as many survive as they can, and uncover and punish a man who is hoarding potatoes, a cure for scurvy. The Code of North is superior to the selfishness of the "civilized." London is also able to satirize Smoke and Shorty's self-importance, however. In "A Flutter in Eggs" (1911), Smoke and Shorty are made fools in a scheme to corner the market on eggs—again, a woman sets them up. In "The Town Site of Tra-Lee" (1911), the partners plan their revenge on the town that embarrassed them, once more becoming tricksters themselves. This is an amusing story, especially as it portrays the townspeople's determination to sniff out the "plot" they believe will make Smoke and Shorty rich, but it raises some general questions about Smoke Bellew, such as whether these confidence games are worthy of the Northland Hero. Furthermore, in its exposure of the town's gold fever—"ain't folks fools?" Shorty giggles (2184)—and the near-riot that ensues, the joke goes too far.

The early Smoke Bellew stories sometimes have a silly and exaggerated quality, lack individuality, and are highly formulaic, although they provide good details of life in the Klondike gold rush, particularly of London's own experiences. In contrast to the earlier Klondike tales, which featured a middle-aged, fully developed hero in the Malemute Kid, Smoke matures over the course of the stories in which he is featured. His aging is a welcome thing: by the time of "The Little Man" (1911), near the end of the Smoke Bellew stories, the hero is shown expressing fear and doubting his abilities, a far cry from his earlier arrogance, and the focus of the story is not strictly on his prowess. The story reinforces the theme of community at the expense of individual heroics; its first line is Shorty's exclamation: " 'I wish you wasn't so set in your ways. . . . I'm sure scairt of that glacier. No man ought to tackle it by his lonely' " (2109).

But the two Klondike stories that succeed on the deepest level do not employ Smoke Bellew. They are "To Build a Fire" (1908) and the final Klondike tale, "Like Argus of the Ancient Times," which was written five years after all the others, in 1916. Examining them in the context of the Klondike tales as a whole reveals an important pattern in London's development: it seems he first visits a place and writes provocatively about it, changing his perspective, as in the Malemute Kid stories; he then revisits the scene for the purpose of serialization and the financial rewards that can bring, as with Smoke Bellew's adventures; and finally, he often has the opportunity to rethink the locale completely many years later, a process that results in his finest tales, and some of his most interesting depictions of heroes.

"To Build a Fire"

The 1908 version of "To Build a Fire" (the story appears in a very different, simplified 1902 version as well) is unquestionably London's masterpiece of short fiction, but the protagonist of "To Build a Fire" is the antithesis of the London hero. The story is also his most often cited example of literary naturalism, and yet its metaphysical insights do not seem in keeping with the sort of simplistic naturalism many students have been taught to associate with Jack London. These paradoxes and a fundamental irony in the central image of fire itself give the story its uncanny appeal.

That naturalism itself is more than merely materialistic determinism has long been recognized, thanks to the work of Donald Pizer and others. Pizer refers to naturalism's "affirmative ethical conception of life," noting that whether the naturalist depicts the new and discomforting truths discovered in the modern city or the dangers which are to be encountered in the natural world, he or she also portrays compensating humanistic values in the characters (Pizer, 12). Indeed, as June Howard has noted, the affirmative ethical and humanistic inconsistencies cited by Pizer and others are so common in naturalist works "that one begins to wonder just where one finds the novels that define the form."[27]

Given the general agreement upon this view of naturalism as a tension between environment and character, matter and spirit, it is odd that the best-known of all the naturalists has rarely escaped the most reductive sort of analysis in his best-known stories. Especially in analyzing stories of survival like "To Build a Fire," critics write Jack London's life as the naturalist saga he himself never wrote and then use that life story to read the works he did write; such autobiographical constructions have served to draw attention away from the writing that was always the central activity within his life. Portraying London as atavistic lone wolf, critics sell a version of London that silences the multitude of beliefs expressed in his work that "assert the value of all life" (Pizer, 12).[28]

London's naturalism consistently contains and implies manifold beliefs—transcendental, romantic, mythic, and religious—as well as deterministic. From his reading London evolved a scientific rationale for subscribing to a high order of "thought, mind, soul," as he called it, which has its place in the natural order (*Letters*, 164). Following Ernst Haeckel, he was thus able to reject a materialism that denied the existence of spirit and to reject spiritualism that dispensed with the notion of matter. "[M]atter cannot exist and be operative without spirit," wrote Haeckel, "nor spirit without matter."[29] This idea accounts, in James McClintock's words, for the "seemingly bizarre situation of a literary naturalist saying that, 'I am an agnostic, but with one exception: I do believe in the soul.' " This belief also helps account for the thread of optimism that runs through London's works.[30] Such dualistic thinking was typical of London's times and of naturalist writers.[31] Yet James G. Cooper misreads this as uncertainty: "London emerges as a classic case of the writer whose conscious mind says one thing while the reader, using the writer's work as the voice of his unconscious, hears just the opposite."[32]

Even in *John Barleycorn* (1913), his "Alcoholic Memoirs," when London describes one possible response to the White Silence, the "White Logic" brought on by alcoholism, as "the antithesis of life, cruel and bleak as interstellar space, pulseless and frozen as absolute zero, dazzling with the frost of irrefragable logic and unforgettable fact . . .," the response is critical:

I am aware that within this disintegrating body which has been dying since I was born I carry a skeleton; that under the rind of flesh which is called my face is a bony, noseless death's head. All of which does not shudder me. To be afraid is to be healthy. Fear of death makes life. But the curse of the White Logic is that it does not make one afraid. The world-sickness of the White Logic makes one grin jocosely into the face of the Noseless One and to sneer at all the phantasmagoria of living.[33]

But London's narrator enters into dialogue with this Noseless One, seeking to understand. He turns to his books as antidotes to hopelessness, even though the Noseless One scoffs at them as "Boglights, vapors of mysticism, psychic overtones, soul orgies, wailings among the shadows, weird gnosticisms, veils and tissues of words, gibbering subjectivisms, groupings and maunderings, ontological fantasies," mere "phantasms of hope" that "fill your bookshelves," the "sad wraiths of sad mad men and passionate rebels—your Schopenhauers, your Strindbergs, your Tolstois and Nietzsches." The White Logic would teach us that we may not understand anything of enduring value in human life, *or* represent it in art: life is simply "unthinkable." "Come," the White Logic murmurs, "Your glass is empty. Fill and forget" (*Barleycorn*, 329–30).

Every word London wrote was an attempt to combat the White Logic and reply to the White Silence; the belief in spirit (meaning) is in London's mind a belief first in himself and his efforts and second in humanity as a vast community spanning time and space, artist and audience in Whitman's "form, union, plan." When London insisted, "It was in the Klondike that I found myself," we may read this as finding a *voice*, a rejoinder to the awful White Silence within and without. Even in London's most "classic" naturalist story the three elements of justice, imagination, and community are represented as the search for spiritual as well as physical survival. "To Build a Fire" is a fine example. Despite what some critics have said, this tale is not London's most pessimistic story.[34] It is, however, one of his most ironic.

"To Build a Fire" operates as a grim contrast between the kind of knowledge the unnamed hero possesses and the kind he needs, a discrepancy that costs him his life. From the opening paragraph, the reader's imagination is invited to take an active role; through a negative building of suspense and through ambiguity, allusion, and symbolism the narrator guides the reader along the journey to knowledge. The hero, in contrast, is unknowingly embarked upon his journey. London weaves throughout the story the belief that finding a correct use of knowledge elevates an individual to the fullest human potential. Attaining knowledge alone will not lead to a higher quality of life, but the essential elements of character teach us that knowledge without the wisdom to apply it is useless. This philosophy survived all the intellectual conflicts that recurred throughout London's professional life. As he wrote to Anna Strunsky, "[M]ankind is my passion, and the search after potentiality and the realization thereof, my hobby" (*Letters*, 137).

In 1907, while sailing from San Francisco to Hawaii on the *Snark*, London completely revised and rewrote this story, going from the version published in *The Youth's Companion* (1902) to the infinitely richer tale that appeared in *Century* (1908) and then in *Lost Face* (1910). There is a sharp discrepancy between narrative style and epistemology: The much briefer 1902 version presents a prescriptive, univocal knowledge by having the narrator simply state its moral, "Never travel alone," whereas the 1908 story offers a very different hermeneutics. The reader's active role in the 1908 version works well with the key structural element lacking in the 1902 version: the *relationships* between the man and the dog, the man and "the boys" in the camp, and the man and the old timer on Sulphur Creek. These relationships deepen and complicate the theme of "man against nature" by redefining nature as human nature. The story is about human beings in nature and also in or out of community. Instead of a basic dichotomy between simply knowing and not knowing how to survive there are at least three separate forms of "survival knowledge" presented, and all of them involve the concept of knowing in relation to someone or something else: the protagonist's abstract theorizing about his environment, which fails at close observation; the dog's instinctual knowledge; and the old timer's wisdom. The man needs the other kinds of knowledge as well as his own, but he is "traveling alone" without them.

In the first two or three paragraphs, we have already left the realm of "pure" naturalism, for the narrator's language gives nature a human face: "the hair-line trail," the "intangible pall over the face of things," the sun a "cheerful orb" that will "peep" over the horizon. However, the man does not think of himself as quite human; that is, when he tires and has to pause for breath after climbing the snowbank, he "excus[es] the act to himself by looking at his watch" (*Complete*, 1301). His instinctual knowledge of survival in nature (his tired body warns him) and his civilized knowledge (what time it is) are in sharp contrast. The discrepancy illustrates both his prideful dishonesty with himself and his assumed distance from nature, which will bring about his downfall. Symbolically nature exhibits a sense of justice.

Community (or lack of it) is subtly invoked a few paragraphs later when the man crosses a "wide flat of niggerheads" (1303) and notes the layers of "snow-hidden ice-skin" (1304). The snow's "skin" is of course "pure white," "unbroken white" (1301). White—white and silent and solitary, like the "inevitable white man" after whom London titled a later story. The protagonist, we learn, is a *chechaquo*, out for gold. His alien Anglo-Saxon identity is not specifically an issue in the story, since there is no mention of the Indians who people most of London's other Klondike tales. But the association between whiteness and silence points away from the community of the living, rather in the way that the weird antarctic topography connotes death in Poe's *The Narrative of Arthur Gordon Pym of Nantucket*, a work that overtly invokes race. In London's story, when the snow-laden spruce branches release their burden above the man's fire, whiteness literally obliterates the protagonist's efforts to survive. The environment itself seems to reject the intruder.

The unnamed man may be said to reflect the Kiplingesque stereotype of the lone white man out to dominate the land and force it to produce for him, for his is the "insatiable blind will" of Nietzche's Übermensch, one who does not see himself in relation to the universe nor comprehend the value of adapting to a given universe instead of attempting to overcome it. At the man's side is the dog, whose aloof consciousness, as Arnold Chapman notes, provides a sense of what is enslaved as well as dramatic irony as the intruder is expelled.[35] London's explorer is doomed by his inability to place himself among the rest of us. How ironic that his desire to be among "the boys" in the camp is thwarted by his belief that he is better than they are.[36]

As in "In a Far Country," the theme of community in "To Build a Fire" is figured negatively, and the failure of community as well as survival is connected to a lack of imagination. For example, the man is as obsessed as Hemingway's heroes; a fixation with measurable details such as time and quantities is a clue to a character's allegiance to deterministic forces. The timeless quality of "To Build a Fire" is ironically counterpointed by its great attention to how many miles the man must travel, how cold it is, and what time of day it is. The story begins at 9 o'clock and pauses at 10. The zenith of the sun is noted, and the man pauses for lunch at 12:30, planning to be in camp by 6 o'clock. One of London's greatest strengths is his narration of action, but here, when the action is related from the protagonist's point of view, it is confined to what the man can measure (how many twigs, how many matches). Perhaps such a fixation is a defense against emotional contact with other people, and a futile defense against death itself. The irony of this is made clear when we read that the man builds his fire with "twigs the size of his finger" and then "branches the size of his wrist," having to look down to know whether he has hold of a twig or not, for "the wires were pretty well down between him and his finger-ends" (*Complete*, 1308). Although he may think in mechanical or technological images, he is not separate from nature and able to quantify it: his body *is* nature, twigs/fingers, branches/wrists.

In contrast to such epistemological confusion, the dog epitomizes instinctual knowledge. As Earle Labor and King Hendricks have noted, the dog is a *ficelle* that makes us see the protagonist as a "hollow man whose inner coldness correlates with the enveloping outer cold" and allows the "subtle counterpointing" between the dog's "natural wisdom" and the man's "foolish rationality."[37] The man's crystal beard of spittle and tobacco juice contrasts early in the story with the dog's "proper" wolf coat, and so his knowledge seems inferior to that of the dog, whose point of view, although not anthropomorphized, is presented as though he is a sentient character. The dog's instincts tell it that it is too cold to travel, and it feels the "vague but menacing apprehension" around the pair that the man ignores (*Complete*, 1303). All the dog's ancestry knew cold, "and it had inherited the knowledge." But because there is no intimacy between the dog and the man—the dog is the "toil-slave" of the man—the dog makes "no effort to communicate its apprehension" to him, and the man does not attempt to "read" the dog (1307). The man does not share the dog's instincts, and when his powers of observation and his theorizing fail him, he is resourceless. The man fails to capture the dog when he attempts to use its body to keep warm because he forgets how their relationship works (harsh words, erect posture).

Significantly, the man has chosen only a nonhuman companion, the dog, as his trail mate, and there is no love between them. Of course, since the man has his "muzzle of ice" and "crystal beard" the color of amber from the tobacco juice (1304), speech is impossible, even if there were anyone to talk to. He does, however, return again and again to one figure, the old timer on Sulphur Creek, who warned him, "Never travel alone." In effect the old timer is his companion, like the teller in the tale, sitting by his fire and relating his Northland lore. Unlike the man, the old timer does have imagination, and whereas the temperature strikes the man as "uncomfortable," but "did not lead him to meditate upon his frailty as a creature of temperature, and upon man's frailty in general, . . . and from there it did not lead him to the conjectural field of immortality and man's place in the universe" (1302), the old timer's wisdom must teach him otherwise. The man thinks, "Well, here he was; he had the accident; he was alone; and he had saved himself. . . . All a man had to do was to keep his head, and he was all right" (1308). The point is, of course, that his head is freezing! In using this image to emphasize isolation—and in dwelling in the same passage on the distance between the man and his control of his hands and fingers—London asks what is needed to compose identity. As the protagonist's body freezes, so his consciousness eventually undergoes a change; he first thinks that "the boys" will take care of him, but eventually, "[h]e did not belong with himself anymore, for even then he was out of himself, standing with the boys and looking at himself in the snow. It certainly was cold, was his thought" (1314).

In the end, losing control of his senses, the man runs blindly, like "a winged Mercury," unable to feel the ground (1313). From this trickster messenger of the gods, he learns that he is at last a man among other men, for when he finally decides to "take it decently," his notion of propriety resembles a social one. With his "new-found peace of mind" comes a final imaginative vision of the old timer "warm and comfortable, and smoking a pipe" (1315).

Of the half-dozen times the protagonist thinks of the wise old man on Sulphur Creek, all but once his specific thought is that the old man was right, that one should "never travel alone." The old man represents the wisdom that the man on the trail lacks; his power is most clearly alluded to by the several kinds of fire that accompany him: his warm fireside, his wreath of pipe smoke, his home at a place called "Sulphur" Creek. He is also connected to the "stars that leaped and danced" at the man's death, as the flame of the man's first fire earlier "danced." Life = fire; death = cold. But fire also = knowledge, especially the wisdom of the old timer, shared by the narrator and reader, who are listeners by the fireside. The vision of the old man replaces the hero's conscious knowledge of his surroundings, and he apologizes: " 'You were right, old hoss; you were right' " (1315). This unbidden image, with the statement made in response to it, is his last thought and his truest one. In spite of his arrogant determination to travel *his* way, the man at last has not traveled alone, if only in his dying moment. In this version of the story, no longer is there a simple moral; rather, one encounters the assertion of a relationship between hero and other, youth and old timer, and, in turn, of a collective knowledge that the narrator and reader share.

But the story is not that simple. The old timer's warning transcends the man's individual case and takes on a mythic dimension, characteristic of London in that it grows out of a naturalistic detail. Sulphur, or brimstone, is the stuff of hell, and after gold it is the "other" yellow mineral of the Northland. The burning brimstone flares up in the man's nostrils as he lights his second fire; when it happens, he immediately thinks, "The old timer on Sulphur Creek was right . . ." (1311). Later, when he picks up the entire 70 sulphur matches he possesses and scratches them against his leg, holding them until his flesh burns, he can feel it "deep down below the surface" (1311). Indeed, not unlike the damned "below the surface" in hell, despite his efforts he is isolated from the community of the blessed awaiting him at the camp.

The ancients believed sulphur to be the father of the elements. A telling reference occurs in *Paradise Lost*, where Mammon, one of the fallen angels in hell, is the leader of a band of "pioneers" who dig into the sulphuric earth for gold and other minerals from which to build Pandemonium:

> Mammon led them on:
> Mammon, the least erected Spirit that fell
> From Heav'n, for ev'n in Heav'n his looks and thoughts
> Were always downward bent, admiring more
> The riches of Heav'n's pavement, trodden gold,
> Than aught divine or holy else enjoyed
> In vision beatific: By him first
> Men also, and by his suggestion taught,
> Ransacked the center, and with impious hands
> Rifled the bowels of their mother earth
> For treasures better hid.
> (*Paradise Lost* 1.678–88)[38]

The word "Mammon" in Syriac meant "wealth" and became familiar in the New Testament through St. Matthew's use of it: "Thou canst not serve both God and Mammon" (Matt. 4:24). In Pandemonium, three plans are put forward: Moloch desires war, Belial hopes to stay "in peaceful sloth," and Mammon wants to build a rival kingdom:

rather seek
Our own good from ourselves, and from our own
Live to ourselves, though in this vast recess,
Free, and to none accountable, preferring
Hard liberty before the easy yoke
Of servile pomp.

                              (*Paradise Lost* 2.252–57)

To Mammon heaven is only a place of golden pavements and handsome, jewel-encrusted buildings; his eyes sparkle as he contemplates building his rival kingdom to be even more magnificent. The fallen ones can work with earth's resources and "thrive under evil and work ease out of pain / Through labor and endurance." "What can Heaven show more," he asks, than such self-sufficiency? "This desert soil / Wants not her hidden luster, gems and gold; / Nor want we skill or art . . ." (2.273).

As in "The Devil's Dice Box," these references in *Paradise Lost* would merely be interesting parallels to "To Build a Fire" were it not that *Paradise Lost* was one of three books London carried with him into the Klondike (Walker, 135).[39] These references clarify the symbolism of the old timer: He furnishes the thematic key to the story by warning against the entire enterprise of "traveling alone" in the White Silence—seeking Mammon. Is he one of the Fallen Ones who has made his peace, an Ancient Mariner who remains at home to counsel the unwary? His warning comes too late for the man, but not for the reader.

Yet why—if the old timer is associated so clearly with "the moral of the story"—is he connected to sulphur, the building block of Hell, at the same time as he is to fire, with his comforting images of pipe and fireplace? The answer lies in the true function of the central symbol of fire itself, manifested in so many ways in the story: the sun that peeps over the horizon, stars that dance, but, most important, the fire that the man *would* build. The fire in "To Build a Fire" is not the ultimate life-giving force, but rather an ironic comment on man's inability to see nature in all its dimensions. In this light, the old timer's wisdom can be seen as like that of the deceiver, Mammon himself. If the hero had been able to light a fire, he might have survived the cold, but he would not understand it. He would understand only his conquering of the cold. In his death, not his fire, is his victory—a strange paradox for a story supposedly predicated upon survival. Fire does not, it turns out, spell life; it consists only of another instance of the man's innate false pride in the face of nature and its inexorable judgment. The story is a brilliant instance of London's layering of meanings and his masterful use of irony.

With the dog by his side, the man dies, the occasion marked only by the dog's soft whines and throaty howls—recognition of the need it had of the man, if not true mourning. But the "stars that leaped and danced and shone brightly in the cold sky" (*Complete*, 1315)—a line repeated in other stories in a similar context—remind us that although nature seems far away and uncaring, *people* "leap" and "dance," not heavenly bodies, and not machines. Jack London's response to the White Silence of the Klondike was to abandon the search for Mammon there and to earn his gold by writing about it. There is no better example of the lack of imagination versus the absolute need for community than "To Build a Fire."

"Like Argus of the Ancient Times"
"Like Argus of the Ancient Times" is nearly as important to the Klondike fiction as "To Build a Fire," but it is much less known. Smoke's companion, Shorty, hummed the song "Like Argus of the Ancient Times" in earlier stories:

> Like Argus of the ancient times
> We leave this modern Greece,
> Tum-tum, tum-tum, tum-tum, tum-tum,
> To shear the golden Fleece.

In this tale, one of London's last three stories, the Klondike is once again seen as a classical landscape, but this time the heroes are the Argonauts searching for the Golden Fleece rather than Odysseus searching for home. As in earlier stories Christmas appears again, in the name "Father Christmas," nickname for the 70-year-old hero, Tarwater (2445), called "Santa Claus, Old Christmas, Whiskers, the Last of the Mohicans, and Father Christmas" (2457), as well as "Old Hero" (2458). (The number seven reappears in Tarwater's age of 70.) The real Tarwater was an old man from Santa Rosa who joined London's outfit after London's brother-in-law, Captain John Shepard, returned to California. The story relates how, against all odds, the old man's valor, wits, and sheer endurance allow him to find his treasure and return home a rich man. Again justice, coexisting with redemption, appears: Upon his return Tarwater is "a true prodigal grandfather for whom the fatted calf was killed and ready" (2459–60).[40] But this mythic tale of journeying for treasure, facing trials, coming near death, and finally arising into honor also tells us that gold fever never dies, whether the actions taken to win gold are admirable or not. The story contrasts Tarwater's friend Jack Liverpool (Jack London) with Clayton, a coward and traitor to the party, and the behavior of the men who team up in their voyage to the gold fields is judged depending upon how they treat one another, especially the "crazy" old man, Tarwater, who is only allowed to accompany them by serving as their cook. Driven by the desire for riches, through Tarwater's unexpected example they learn they can only attain them by discovering a different kind of treasure.

In Greek mythology, the name Argus occurs in two separate stories. Argus was a watcher with one hundred eyes, placed by Hera to watch over Zeus's beloved, Io. But allusion here is to Argus the Argonaut, who built Jason's ship, went with him to search for the Golden Fleece and helped Jason steal it from under the watchful eyes of a dragon. Both Jason and the ever-present sun also raise the moral theme, since although Jason was a hero and fought many monsters, he was also the betrayer of his lover Medea. As in earlier Klondike stories, the sun is mentioned in "Like Argus of the Ancient Times" as the watcher and judge and also as a representative of rebirth. Unlike the earlier Klondike stories that use Greek myths, London composed this one after reading Jung in 1916, and this lends to the mythic sources a deeper resonance. As he experiences the delirium of near-starvation, Tarwater has a vision of the treasure he seeks and the effect it will have upon him:

> And here, in the unforgettable crypts of man's unwritten history, unthinkable and unrealizable, like passages of nightmare or impossible adventures of lunacy, he encountered the monsters created of man's first morality that ever since have vexed him into the spinning of fantasies to elude them or do battle with them.
>
> In short, weighted by his seventy years, in the vast and silent loneliness of the North, Old Tarwater, as in the delirium of drug or anaesthetic, recovered, within himself, the infantile mind of the child-man of the early world. It was in the dusk of Death's fluttery wings that Tarwater thus crouched, and, like his remote forebear, the child-man, went to myth-making, and sun-heroizing, himself hero-maker and the hero in quest of the immemorable treasure difficult of attainment.
>
> Either must he attain the treasure—for so ran the inexorable logic of the shadow-land of the unconscious—or else sink into the all-devouring sea, the blackness eater of the light that swallowed to extinction the sun each night. . . . the sun that arose ever in rebirth next morning

in the east, and that had become to mean man's first symbol of immortality through rebirth. (*Complete*, 2454–55)

This evocative passage brings together major elements of the Klondike stories. Tarwater finds his Golden Fleece: "The sun smoldered on dully glistening yellow. He shook the handful of moss, and coarse nuggets, like gravel, fell to the ground. It was the Golden Fleece ready for the shearing" (2459). But his dark night of the soul makes him a new man, which is more important. He returns home to California a true hero.

The Other: The Woman, The Indian

As we have seen, London's Klondike code hero is a white male who has come to the region from elsewhere. But just as there is no single hero of this type, we should not make the mistake of thinking that he is the only or even the primary subject of the Klondike stories. In fact, nearly all of the tales are peopled by characters from the various Indian groups of the Northwest, from British Columbia to the Yukon and the Aleutian Islands. And the most prevalent Indian characters in the stories are women: London seems to have chosen to deal with race through gender in the Klondike, and vice versa.

Indeed, there are only a handful of stories that present white women as the main characters. In "The Scorn of Women" (1900), a comedy of class set in Dawson, we witness the clash of Freda Moloof, the Greek dancing girl, and Mrs. Eppingwell, the queen of white society. Both are "man-conquering, man-subduing machines, each in her own way." Freda "ruled down in the town" and Mrs. Eppingwell "in her own house, and at the Barracks, where were younger sons galore, to say nothing of the chiefs of the police, the executive, and the judiciary" (413). Although her station in life is a humble one, Freda is good-hearted and proud, and as Susan Ward points out, she is "possessed of a knowledge which [her] respectable sisters lack and which the dance hall girls often use to someone else's advantage."[41] Freda plots to help the rightful fiancé of a Bonanza King marry him, keeping the man away from the arms of a seductress by flirting with him herself. Mrs. Eppingwell misunderstands Freda's intentions and takes offense:

> It was another flashing, eternal second, during which these two women regarded each other. The one, eyes blazing, meteoric; at bay, aggres-

sive; suffering in advance and resenting in advance the scorn and ridicule and insult she had thrown herself open to; a beautiful, burning, bubbling lava cone of flesh and spirit. And the other, calm-eyed, cool-browed, serene; strong in her own integrity, with faith in herself, thoroughly at ease; dispassionate, imperturbable; a figure chiselled from some cold marble quarry. (*Complete*, 424)

Disguised in furs, Freda dances at the ball, the object of every eye, and the two women engage in a face-off. But all is worked out when the plot is revealed in the end:

On this day of the races, Mrs. Eppingwell, who had learned and unlearned numerous things, saw Freda for the first time since the night of the ball. "Publicly, mind you," as Mrs. McFee expressed it, "without regard or respect for the morals of the community," she went up to the dancer and held out her hand. At first, it is remembered by those who saw, the girl shrank back, then words passed between the two, and Freda, great Freda, broke down and wept on the shoulder of the captain's wife. It was not given to Dawson to know why Mrs. Eppingwell should crave forgiveness of a Greek dancing girl, but she did it publicly, and it was unseemly. (431)

Although the larger community sees this new relationship as "unseemly," it is in fact the model for a revised social system based on respect for the individual outside of social class.

"The Unexpected" (1905), with its evolutionary slant, is a more serious look at social norms. Described as "clear-eyed" (999), an allusion to Athena that London used in several of his stories about women, the British-born heroine, Edith Nelson, holds out for justice when a cabin mate inexplicably kills all the other gold prospecting partners but her and her husband:

The cabin epitomized the new world in which they must thenceforth live and move. The old cabin was gone forever. The horizon of life was totally new and unfamiliar. The unexpected had swept its wizardry over the face of things, changing the perspective, juggling values, and shuffling the real and the unreal into perplexing confusion. (1005)

An excellent example of London's ability to treat a female character with depth and respect, and an interesting comparison to "To Build a Fire," the story is a stirringly suspenseful tale as the three try to wait out the long winter together: the wife, Edith; the husband, Hans; and the prisoner, Dennin, bound to his bed and under the care of Edith. What to do when the unthinkable happens? Because "the effect of civilization is to impose human law upon environment until it becomes machine-like in its regularity, . . .[t]he objectionable is eliminated, the inevitable is foreseen. One is not even made wet by the rain nor cold by the frost; while death, instead of stalking about grewsome and accidental, becomes a prearranged pageant, moving along a well-oiled groove to the family vault, where the hinges are kept from rusting and the dust from the air is swept continually away" (998). Indeed,

> It is a simple matter to see the obvious, to do the expected. The tendency of the individual life is to be static rather than dynamic, and this tendency is made into a propulsion by civilization, where the obvious only is seen, and the unexpected rarely happens. When the unexpected does happen, however, and when it is of sufficiently grave import, the unfit perish. They do not see what is not obvious, are unable to do the unexpected, are incapable of adjusting their well-grooved lives to other and strange grooves. In short, when they come to the end of their own groove, they die. (998)

This tale is concerned with cultural relativism, adaptability, and codes of behavior, but its primary theme is justice, the "evolution of law" (1011). With no law present to guide them, the couple argue over what to do with their prisoner; Hans is in favor of instant execution, but Edith, who learned respect for the law in her English childhood, holds out for letting the authorities consider the matter. Finally, she realizes that she and her husband, snowed in as they are, must themselves act as the authorities, and she sets up a trial for the defendant that is as fair as she can devise. The verdict is death, but justice has been upheld. Using her imagination, Edith has learned to carve a new path between nature and civilization; law is inherited *and* invented. "With Hans's arm around her, supporting her weight and directing her helpless steps, she went off across the snow. But the Indians remained solemnly to watch the working of the white man's law that compelled a man to dance upon the air" (1016).

Even in these two stories, which do not have Indian women in them, ethnic difference is present, but in most of the other stories it is the main focus. Like the dance hall girls, the Indian common-law wives and mistresses are frowned upon by "respectable" women in the Klondike, but not by the men or the narrators of the stories. However, as Ward points out, London frequently portrays the abandonment of Indian wives by their white husbands when the men return to the United States, and his attitude toward this is ambivalent (Ward, 82–84). At times he condemns such behavior as cowardly, as in "The Wife of a King" (1899), in which the Malemute Kid and others help Madeline, an Indian girl, capture the heart of the Bonanza King Cal Galbraith by making her appear to be a lady. At other times, as in "The Story of Jees Uck" and "Siwash," despite the overall tone of tragedy, the actions of the men seem inevitable. The women, Ward emphasizes, are portrayed as "loyal, self-sacrificing, stoical in the face of pain or disappointment, and possessed of a natural sexuality which London does not allow to operate in 'respectable' white heroines. . . . They are loyal above the law of kind. . . . They are also possessed of a quality which London names 'elemental simplicity' " (84–85). Fred Lewis Pattee has observed that although London's Indian women are unquestionably idealized, "romanticized and overdrawn," they are "the most vital and convincing of all Jack London's characters," truly "additions to the gallery of original characters in American fiction."[42] London shows their virtues both upheld and betrayed.

London relies on three major types of Indian characters: the tribal elder mourning the loss of Indian lands, traditions, and daughters; the young male trying to negotiate both worlds in order to win a mate; and the young Indian wife. These figures are intimately related through their connections to the white invaders. Jonathan Auerbach has argued that "miscegenation lies at the very heart of London's early Northland narratives," particularly in the first and second collections, *The Son of the Wolf* and *The God of His Fathers*, but he asks, "Does London's primary identification between white men and the domineering Wolf make him a blatant racist?" The answer is no—for one thing, London was unusual for his day in "putting [the] dread of mixed blood in the mouths of Indians" instead of portraying the white men as concerned about intermarrying with Indians, thus making his white contemporaries "question some of their most basic assumptions about race." Auerbach also notes how London not only elevates the Indians' status in the stories but also makes the category of "whiteness" available to anyone, as with the so-called "white" Indian, Sitka Charley. He also senses the tragedy inherent in the portrayals of tribal elders in *Children of the Frost*, London's third Northland volume and his most compelling collection of Klondike stories. London shows "the tragic destruction of patriarchal law itself at the hands of the white race," viewing "these native fathers and daughters as unwilling actors in a larger historical process driven by the expansion of capital into foreign lands."[43]

We have already examined many of the stories of *The Son of the Wolf*. *The God of His Fathers* contains "Siwash" (1899), which perhaps most explicitly demonstrates both the virtues and the clearly subordinated position of the Indian woman in relation to the white master. In the story Tommy, Dick, and Molly are traveling companions on the trail. Observing Molly's pluckiness, Tommy tells Dick about his wife, Tilly, a Siwash Indian for whom he fought an entire tribe. During the seven years they were married, Tilly saved him many times, until she died in childbirth. "Siwash, Dick, but a woman. White, Dick, white, clear through" (*Complete*, 376). Dying, Tilly had made Tommy promise to marry a white woman, Tommy says. Just then Molly, who has been desperately trying to prove herself to the men by going out into the blizzard to retrieve their cache of food, comes back stumbling and frozen. Commenting on Molly's pluckiness, Dick observes, "But it's the edge that's her saving grace. . . . The edge that you and I've got, Tommy, and the edge of our mothers before us" (377). The story simultaneously seems to privilege women and to demean them, to privilege nonwhites and to condescend to them. It seems to be carrying on a debate with itself as to the relative merits of Indian versus white women, in the end characterizing the Indian as noble, self-sacrificing, and tragic, while the doughty white woman, with none of that depth of character, will prevail because she shares in the dominant characteristics of the white invaders of the land.

Similarly, in "Grit of Women" (1900), Sitka Charley remembers Passuk, his Indian woman, in reverent tones, with less of the racialist rhetoric:

> "Look you, brothers," broke in Sitka Charley from his seat on the grub-box. "Ye have spoken of the streak of fat that runs in big men's muscles, of the grit of women and the love, and ye have spoken fair; but I have in mind things which happened when the land was young and the finest of men apart as the stars. It was then I had concern with a big man, and a streak of fat, and a woman. And the woman was small; but her heart was greater than the beef-heart of the man, and she had grit. And we traveled a weary trail, even to the Salt Water, and the cold was bitter, the snow deep, the hunger great. And the woman's love was a mighty love—no more can man say than this." (462)

Passuk denies herself food to save Charley's life on the trail, and later she also denies food to her own brother in order to save Charley. She dies another sacrificial victim, and the allusions that surround her cast her as one of London's Greek heroes, a figure of legend: "It was midday. To the south, just clearing the bleak Henderson Divide, poised the cold-disked sun. On either hand the sun-dogs blazed. The air was a gossamer of glittering frost. In the foreground, beside the trail, a wolf-dog, bristling with frost, thrust a long snout heavenward and mourned" (471). The important thing is that Charley has to earn Passuk's love, so there was an act of judgment on her part, and now, in retrospect, Charley judges himself:

> "And she said: 'When first you came to the Chilcat, nor looked upon me, but bought me as a man buys a dog, and took me away, my heart was hard against you and filled with bitterness and fear. But that was long ago. For you were kind to me, Charley, as a good man is kind to his dog. Your heart was cold, and there was no room for me; yet you dealt me fair and your ways were just. And I was with you when you did bold deeds and led great ventures, and I measured you against the men of other breeds, and I saw you stood among them full of honor, and your word was wise, your tongue true. I grew proud of you, till it came that you filled all my heart, and all my thought was of you. You were as the midsummer sun, when its golden rail runs in a circle and never leaves the sky. And whatever way I cast my eyes I beheld the sun. But your heart was ever cold, Charley, and there was no room.'
>
> "And I said: 'It is so. It was cold, and there was no room. But that is past. Now my heart is like the snowfall in the spring, when the sun has come back. There is a great thaw and a bending, a sound of running waters, and a budding and sprouting of green things. And there is drumming of partridges, and songs of robins, and great music, for the winter is broken, Passuk, and I have learned the love of woman.' " (469)

Her death leads Charley, ever thoughtful, to muse on the meaning of life:

> "Life is a strange thing. Much have I thought on it, and pondered long, yet daily the strangeness of it grows not less, but more. Why this longing for Life? It is a game which no man wins. To live is to toil hard, and to suffer sore, till Old Age creeps heavily upon us and we throw down our hands on the cold ashes of dead fires. It is hard to live. In pain the babe sucks his first breath, in pain the old man gasps his last, and all

his days are full of trouble and sorrow; yet he goes down to the open arms of Death, stumbling, falling, with head turned backward, fighting to the last. And Death is kind. It is only Life, and the things of Life that hurt. Yet we love Life, and we hate Death. It is very strange." (468)

"Grit of Women" can be paired with "The Law of Life" (1900), written only three weeks earlier. One of London's best-known stories, it presents a picture of a tribe following the Eskimo custom of leaving the old and feeble behind to die on the trail. Old Koskoosh finds that his time to die has come and accordingly is left behind by his tribe. Dying, he remembers a youthful struggle with an old moose and sees himself in its place. An early instance of London's use of a limited third-person point of view, this somber narrative achieves its air of drama through its utter simplicity; everything is portrayed from the dying man's point of view. It furnishes a sense of inevitability and even nobility in the old man's death, although the naturalist elements are powerful. Wolves close in around him, and he fights for a while, but then gives in to the law of nature: "What did it matter after all? Was it not the law of life?" (450) The story should not only be compared with those that show the sacrifice of Indian women but also with the numerous stories that depict the defeat of the Indians in general. It is unfortunate that this story is so often reprinted in anthologies without any related London tales.

"Where the Trail Forks" (1900) tells of Sipsu, an Indian woman who is to be sacrificed in a tribal ritual but is saved by white men. Like "The Law of Life," the story presents a strong contrast between the Indian and the white way of seeing life:

> She was born of primitive stock, and primitive had been her traditions and her days; so she regarded life stoically, and human sacrifice as part of the natural order. The powers which ruled the daylight and the dark, the flood and the frost, the bursting of the bud and the withering of the leaf, were angry and in need of propitiation. This they exacted in many ways,—death in the bad water, through the treacherous ice-crust, by the grip of the grizzly, or a wasting sickness which fell upon a man in his own lodge till he coughed, and the life of his lungs went out through his mouth and nostrils. Likewise did the powers receive sacrifice. It was all one. And the witch doctor was versed in the thoughts of the powers and chose unerringly. It was very natural. Death came by many ways, yet was it all one after all,—a manifestation of the all-powerful and inscrutable. (515)

The white men tell Sipsu different beliefs. When she runs away with the whites the narrator compares it to the wolves interbreeding with whites' dogs, an analogy that will recur in other tales. (It is an analogy that may be helpful to readers of *The Call of the Wild* [1903], for London's totemic use of the wolf is enhanced by the role of the dog in these racial stories.) "But later, when all were gone, the shepherd dog crept back to the deserted camp, and all the night long and a day it wailed the dead. After that it disappeared, though the years were not many before the Indian hunters noted a change in the breed of timber wolves, and there were dashes of bright color and variegated markings and such as no wolf bore before" (522).

London's third story collection, *Children of the Frost*, is his strongest. Here he views the Northland through the eyes of the Indians, and although his firsthand knowledge of Indians was very limited, and although he persists in reductive racialism, idealizing certain Indian types and confusing the attributes of particular groups, he treats his characters with great emotional intensity and empathy. While he never gave up his love of a mythical Anglo-Saxon forebear, *Children of the Frost* demonstrates London's uniqueness among American writers of his day for his imaginative explorations of other cultures and ethnicities and for his ability to render the point of view of Indians and others. Even a glance at the works on race from a bookshelf at the turn of the century will illustrate the difference between London's curiosity about racial "others" in collections like this one and the attitude of many of his contemporaries.

Children of the Frost is also an artistic achievement. James McClintock finds the stories of *Children of the Frost* to be "dramatically and economically written and [capitalizing] upon the mellifluous style arising from the dignified language London associated with Indian speech" (McClintock, 100). He further points out that in contrast to many of the earlier Klondike tales, here "the demand for ideal characters is diminished. . . . The Indians in all of these stories had possessed all that London's white conquerors came to the Northland to find: individual dignity, courage, contact with and adjustment to the elemental strength of nature, and a sense of community within the tribe" (100-101). McClintock also praises London in these tales for having given up his earlier essay-exemplum narrative in favor of dramatic, visual scenes. The frame story meant that he could avoid "direct philosophical, social or psychological evaluations of character or setting in the voice of the narrator appealing directly to his audience. . . . The product of such a method would be similar to a painting, a pictorial representation of a situation" (27–28).

Several of the stories of *Children of the Frost* involve the loss of innocence of a young male Indian. "The 'Fuzziness' of Hookla-Heen" (1901), while not part of this volume, was written at the same time and parallels several tales in the collection, especially in its strongly visual character. Here, a white boy discovered with the Indians is "rescued" and brought back to live with the whites. Hookla-Heen has dreamt of words he used to know; the language of his white past has haunted him:

> It was the old sickness, *com-ta-nitch-i-wyan*, come back to him again—the dream-sickness, which he had thought outgrown. It was the sickness which, when a little boy, had made the children draw away from him in fear, and the tears come into the eyes of the squaws when they looked upon him. The dream-sickness—how it had made his childhood miserable!
>
> Of course all men dreamed, and even the wolf-dogs: but they dreamed with their eyes shut, and when they slept, and he had dreamed with eyes wide open, broad awake. And the men dreamed about things they knew, about hunting and fishing; but he had dreamed about things he did not know, and which nobody else knew. Haunting memories of things he could not express had come to him; and it seemed, if only he could think back, that all would be clear, only, try as he would, he could not think back. (*Complete*, 559)

The notion that racial identity persists as language appears in several other tales, including "Li-Wan the Fair" (1901), in which Li-Wan, like Hookla-Heen, was born white but was abandoned and taken in by the Indians. She, too, has inexplicable dreams and recalls strange words; she feels particularly drawn to a white woman, Mrs. Van Wyck, and she struggles to enunciate the half-remembered words. "Li-Wan" is a poignant but strained tale of racial confusion and nostalgia, compounded by the harsh treatment Li-Wan receives from her Indian husband, and contextualized by the social problem of being an "other." Interestingly, this story, along with one written just three weeks before it, "Nam-Bok the Unveracious," caused London to lose his contract with *McClure's* magazine—the stories were not deemed suitable for *McClure's* audience, and London was fired.

Perhaps the *McClure's* editors did not appreciate the fact that London wrote the story as an intentional satire in the mode of Plato's "Allegory of the Cave." Nam-Bok is the hero of this wry tale of lying versus truth-telling. While fishing as a boy, he is carried away from his primitive fishing village in Alaska by a storm and is picked up by an American ship. For years he lives among whites, and when he returns to tell the tale of the strange sights he has seen in San Francisco and elsewhere not only do his family and friends refuse to believe him, but they are terrified of him because they believe him to be an evil ghost (or "shadow" as in Plato). They run him off, even his own mother. The curiosity of the villagers is overcome by their need to remain whole. In the end, Nam-Bok is homeless despite his great knowledge. It is one of London's funnier stories but also quite sad—a tale of cultural homelessness that must have represented an all too common reality for many of the Indians who left home.

"Keesh, the Son of Keesh" (1901) carries the same theme as "Nam-Bok" but is far different in tone: It is a chilling and bloody story of the humiliation of a young Indian man by his beloved because of his contacts with the white man, and especially his Christianity—for the girl equates Christianity with loss of manhood. Her father berates Keesh:

> "Thy father, Keesh, was a mighty man. And he did love the song of the bowstring in battle, and these eyes have beheld him cast a spear till the head stood out beyond a man's body. But thou art unlike. Since thou left the Raven to worship the Wolf, thou art become afraid of blood, and thou makest thy people afraid. This is not good. For behold, when I was a boy, even as Kitz-noo there, there was no white man in all the land. But they came, one by one, these white men, till now they are many. And they are a restless breed, never content to rest by the fire with a full belly and let the morrow bring its own meat. A curse was laid upon them, it would seem, and they must work it out in toil and hardship." (566–67)

Ironically, the biblical reference to the expulsion from Eden here is offered unknowingly by the cursing father. Keesh protests that he can be a brave in the tribe and a Christian, but his beloved laughs and tells him that he must prove his worthiness to father her sons by bringing her three heads. He does. He brings her the heads of her father and brothers, and then takes her own. McClintock comments that the power of this story goes far beyond social criticism: "It arises from the tension between conflicting codes or value systems, each of which is unable to sustain positive human values. Neither the white man's way of life nor the Indian's code of honor leads to an integration of the spirit; instead, the one is hypocritical and, metaphorically, will not permit Keesh the basic privileges of a wife, children and honor, and the other is inhumanely grotesque" (McClintock, 102–3). In two trickster tales "The Story of Keesh" (1901), a prequel to the previous Keesh story, and "The Master of Mystery" (1901), London nostalgically recalls the days before the coming of the white men and of the violence of both Indians and whites. In the latter story, Jelchs the Raven appears as a benign trickster god, and the pattern of clever commoners tricking a shaman or missionary is repeated in other stories.

Many of the stories of *Children of the Frost* sound the note of nostalgia for the moral purity of the Indian way of life. "In the Forests of the North" (1901), which has some of the feel of an Edgar Rice Burroughs jungle tale, tells of a man named Van Brunt who goes to rescue his friend, Fairfax, who was lost in the wilderness and now is living with the Indians and his Indian wife. When "found," Fairfax at first doesn't want to leave:

> "Beastly life!" Van Brunt grimaced his disgust. "I suppose, after five years of it, civilization will be sweet? What do you say?"
>
> Fairfax's face took on a stolid expression. "Oh, I don't know. At least they're honest folk and live according to their lights. And then they are amazingly simple. No complexity about them, no thousand and one subtle ramifications to every single emotion they experience. They love, fear, hate, are angered, or made happy, in common, ordinary, and unmistakable terms. It may be a beastly life, but at least it is easy to live. No philandering, no dallying. If a woman likes you, she'll not be backward in telling you so. If she hates you, she'll tell you so, and then, if you feel inclined, you can beat her, but the thing is, she knows precisely what you mean, and you know precisely what she means. No mistakes, no misunderstandings. It has its charm, after civilization's fitful fever. Comprehend?
>
> "No, it's a pretty good life," he continued, after a pause; "good enough for me, and I intend to stay with it." (*Complete*, 659–60)

Fairfax decides to return when reminded of his white fiancé. In trying to escape, the entire party, whites and Fairfax's Indian wife, are killed by the outraged Indian village because he is abandoning her:

> A score of men hurled past on either side, and Fairfax, for a brief instant's space, stood looking upon her and her bronze beauty, thrilling, exulting, stirred to unknown deeps, visioning strange things, dreaming, immortally dreaming. Snatches and scraps of old-world

philosophies and new-world ethics floated through his mind, and things wonderfully concrete and woefully incongruous—hunting scenes, stretches of sombre forest, vastnesses of silent snow, the glittering of ballroom lights, great galleries and lecture halls, a fleeting shimmer of glistening test-tubes, long rows of book-lined shelves, the throb of machinery and the roar of traffic, a fragment of forgotten song, faces of dear women and old chums, a lonely watercourse amid upstanding peaks, a shattered boat on a pebbly strand, quiet moonlit fields, fat vales, the smell of hay. . . . (670)

Again, the white male's nostalgia is invoked, this time for both his old world and his new, and the Indian woman is exoticized. The male's attitude reveals a shallow sensibility that rings false in the face of the woman's "unknown deeps," but London simplifying of the Indians smacks of condescension.

At about the same time, London wrote "The Story of Jees Uck" (1902), published in *The Faith of Men* (1904), in which a brave Indian girl loves and saves a white man, living with him and bearing him a son. But he leaves her and does not return, marrying a white woman back in San Francisco. The man's loneliness at his remote station first drew him to the woman, Jees Uck, in whom he "found the youth of the world—the youth and the strength and the joy" (783). After he abandons her, Jees Uck faithfully journeys with their child to his home to find out what has happened to him, but she does not reveal herself to his wife as anything more than an acquaintance. She then returns north to carry out the work of "Alaskan education" and dies a respected leader of her people, her work supported by the philanthropy of the white couple. It is a story of almost incomprehensible sacrifice and jarring personal cruelty. "Jees Uck" was the name for Jesus among certain of the Northwest Indian groups, and this reference lends some needed dimension to the tale.

The story insists that Jees Uck's physical beauty and strength of spirit are the result of her racial mixing, which includes Eskimo, Innuit, Toyaat, Slav, and Siberian blood. The narrator carefully traces her ancestry back through several generations, as in a biblical genealogy, finding that her Russian ancestors intermarried with the "Deer People" and mingled with the "Sea People," which gives her "white" ancestry a different flavor. Jees Uck's "vagrant blood" makes the narrator think "what waifs of the generations we are, all of us, and the strange meanderings of the seed from which we spring" (774). The biblical allusions, only touched on here, will start to multiply as London leaves the Klondike stories and turns to tales of those who wander on the South Seas. There, as here, his sympathies will be with the racial "others" even as he adheres to his theories about racial "purity"—a rather glaring paradox. Although it is not an easy story to understand, "The Story of Jees Uck" brings together most of the important Klondike patterns—justice, race, sacrifice—but deepens their power and their mystery with the allusions to Christ.

The most powerful group of stories in *Children of the Frost* comprises the three that portray the sorrows of the tribal elders, "The Death of Ligoun" (1902), "The Sickness of Lone Chief" (1902), and "The League of the Old Men" (1902), all written within a month and a half of each other. "The Death of Ligoun" is told by a barfly, a story of the heroic past in the context of unheroic present. The hero of this tale within a tale, Ligoun, bravely stood up to his enemies and was killed; those in the bar who hear of it painfully recognize the distance between them and him. "The Sickness of Lone Chief" is another tale of Indian loss: ". . . having lived so long, they had fallen on evil days, these two old men, Lone Chief and Mutsak, and in the new order they were without honor or place. So they waited drearily for death . . ." (764). Lone Chief tells his companion of his exploits as a youth against a warring tribe, how he won his mate and saved his village. The story concludes: " 'And great honor was mine, and all men yielded me obedience.' 'Until the steamboat came,' Mutsak prompted. 'Ay,' said Lone Chief. 'Until the steamboat came' " (771).

London felt that "The League of the Old Men" was his finest story (James, 385). In it, a group of old Indians have turned terrorist to try to punish the whites for their ruination of the Indians' way of life. At his trial, old Imber, leader of the Whitefish people, tells his shocked audience through an interpreter why he and his companions have been randomly murdering white men. At first the reader, too, is repelled by this evil, but the story has the power to convince otherwise:

> And then began the story, the epic of a bronze patriot which might well itself be wrought into bronze for the generations unborn. The crowd fell strangely silent, and the square-browed judge leaned head on hand and pondered his soul and the soul of his race. Only was heard the deep tones of Imber, rhythmically alternating with the shrill voice of the interpreter, and now and again, like the bell of the Lord. . . ."I am Imber of the Whitefish people. . . . My father was Otsbaok, a strong man. The land was warm with sunshine and gladness when I was a boy. The people did not hunger after strange things, nor hearken to new voices, and the ways of their fathers were their ways. The women

found favor in the eyes of the young men, and the young men looked upon them with content. Babes hung at the breasts of the women, and they were heavy-hipped with increase of the tribe. Men were men in those days. In peace and plenty, and in war and famine, they were men. . . . It be true, we ate flour, and salt pork, and drank tea which was a great delight; only, when we could not get tea, it was very bad and we became short of speech and quick of anger. So we grew to hunger for the things the white men brought in trade. Trade! trade! all the time was it trade! One winter we sold our meat for clocks that would not go, and watches with broken guts, and files worn smooth, and pistols without cartridges and worthless. And then came famine, and we were without meat, and two score died ere the break of spring." (*Complete*, 816, 818)

The tale is one of the finest examples of London presenting the perspective of his native characters in their own voices. "The voices of millions are in the voice of old Imber," London wrote elsewhere, "and the tears and sorrows of millions are in his throat as he tells his story; his story epitomizes the whole vast tragedy of the contact of the Indian and white man."[44] Even though the Indians fail in their quest to preserve their lands and culture, their struggle is presented unambiguously in tragic terms:

> —"And yet, and here be the strangeness of it, the white men come as the breath of death; all their ways lead to death, their nostrils are filled with it; and yet they do not die. Theirs the whiskey, and tobacco, and shorthaired dogs; theirs the many sicknesses, the smallpox and measles, the coughing and mouth-bleeding; theirs the white skin, and softness to the frost and storm; and theirs the pistols that shoot six times very swift and are worthless. And yet they grow fat on their many ills, and prosper, and lay a heavy hand over all the world and tread mightily upon its peoples." (*Complete*, 819)

London simultaneously celebrates the strengths of white civilization and mourns the Indians' demise.

After *Children of the Frost*, London's Klondike stories of women and Indians are scattered throughout later collections. In them, he revisits—in both positive and negative portrayals—the themes of justice, community, and imagination he established in the Northland stories in general, and continues to explore the clash of cultures. He continued to focus upon such issues as trickery, language, and self-sacrifice on the part of Indian women. Cultural difference is vigorously asserted by an angry old Indian woman in "The White Man's Way" (1905), a counterpart to old Imber of "The League of the Old Men." In this black-humor tale of the unintentional trickery of cultural relativism, the question is again about interpretation of cultural signs, as it was in "The Sun-Dog Trail" and "Nam-Bok the Unveracious." An old couple present their argument to the narrator over how to decipher the codes of the white man: "Know, O White Man, that it is because of thy kind, because of all white men, that my man and I have no meat in our old age and sit without tobacco in the cold" (988), Zilla says. Her husband, Old Ebbits, tries to justify ways of white men:

> "Nay," old Ebbits interposed in kindliness, "the white man's is not a lying people. The white man speaks true. Always does the white man speak true." He paused, casting about him for words wherewith to temper the severity of what he was about to say. "But the white man speaks true in different ways. To-day he speaks true one way, to-morrow he speaks true another way, and there is no understanding him nor his way." (988–89)

The debate has arisen because an Indian struck a white man and was put in jail, where he was very happy and grew fat. He was never hurt and was thrilled by his journey far away to the white man's land. After his time was served, he was released. So the couple's son killed a white man so he could share that happy fate, but he was hung: ". . . the way of the white man . . . is without understanding and never twice the same," comments Ebbits (997).

London's awareness of and attraction to the mythic dimensions of the feminine matures in the later Klondike tales. In "The Marriage of Lit-Lit" (1903) and "The Wit of Porportuk" (1906), marriage again involves trickery, but the self-sacrificing quality of the women has been replaced by frank sexuality. Lit-Lit's father, Chief Snettishane, tries to extort his daughter's white husband, John Fox, by attempting to lure his daughter back home and demanding further payment for her. He tells her he will call to her as the Raven outside her house; for his trouble he is peppered with birdshot by her husband, to whom she has revealed the plot. After all is settled, Lit-Lit gives the "first new-woman lecture delivered north of Fifty-three" to her father (861). "The Wit of Porportuk" also has a folktale feel, but it is a grimmer version of the battle of wits. El-Soo's father is Klakee-Nah; he dies in debt to Porportuk. Porportuk buys El-Soo, but, young and swift of foot, she repeatedly runs away to her lover and mocks her aged husband. To exact justice from her, Porportuk gives her to her lover but shoots her in the ankles so she will never run again. Like Lit-Lit and Jees Uck, El-Soo is breathtakingly beautiful and different from the other Indian women in her independence; she was educated in a convent and holds herself above the other girls:

> But over all and through all poured the flame of her—the unanalyzable something that was fire and that was the soul of her, that lay mellow-warm or blazed in her eyes, that sprayed the cheeks of her, that distended the nostrils, that curled the lip, or, when the lip was in repose, that was still there in the lip palpitant with its presence. (1151–52)

But her undoing is her mocking of Porportuk; she has her own sense of right and wrong, to be sure, and defends her father's honor, but Porportuk, too, has his sense of justice. "It is just," say the old men (1169). In contrast to the earlier stories, it is significant that in this late story London has brought the young maiden and old father figure together only to war upon each other.

"Wonder of Woman" (1911) is the last Klondike story before London's final visit to the Northland in "Like Argus of the Ancient Times," and in it are all of the Northland themes and motifs, with the stress on the mystery and power of the feminine. The story is part of the *Smoke Bellew* volume and represents the final coming of age of that hero. The descriptions of its heroine, Labiskwee, are comparable to those of the goddesslike woman, Lucy, in "The Night-Born" (1911), written only a few months earlier:

> She was dressed entirely in skins, but such skins and such magnificently beautiful fur-work Smoke had never dreamed of. Her parka, the hood thrown back, was of some strange fur of palest silver. The mukluks, with walrus-hide soles, were composed of the silver-padded feet of many lynxes. The long-gauntleted mittens, the tassels at the knees, all the varied furs of the costume, were pale silver that shimmered in the frosty light; and out of this shimmering silver, poised on slender, delicate neck, lifted her head, the rosy face blonde as the eyes were blue, the ears like two pink shells, the light chestnut hair touched with frost-dust and coruscating frost-glints. (2207–8)

Labiskwee and her father, Snass, who are white, have been living with a tribe of Indians far to the east in the interior of Canada. Snass, a Scotchman by birth, is the "hi-yu, skookum top-chief" (2205). When Smoke and Shorty stray too close to the tribe's camp, they are captured and prohibited from ever leaving so that no other white man will ever find this frozen Shangri-la. Labiskwee falls in love with Smoke and helps them escape. Snass's name recalls Naass of "An Odyssey of the North," who also loses a woman and must undertake a terrible journey to regain her.

The Indians in this story are presented much more naturalistically than some of the previously idealized individuals. Smoke and Shorty must learn to emulate them in order to survive, and they boast to each other of the Indian ways they are learning. Once again, it is the Indians and their chief who resist the whites culturally, not the other way around. Labiskwee, while white, is used in the story to embody all of the virtues of the Indian women London has previously sketched—plus some of her own.

Smoke learns of "woman's purity" and "soul," and judging from his at-first simplistic idealization, he has a lot to learn: "For the first time in his life he was really learning woman, so clear was Labiskwee's soul, so appalling in its innocence and ignorance, that he could not misread a line of it. All the pristine goodness of her sex was in her, uncultured by the conventionality of knowledge or the deceit of self-protection." He concludes that "all woman-haters were sick men" (2215). Maturing under her eye, Smoke loves her "wild unearthly beauty," her exoticism: " 'I know what a woman is, now' " (2235). They escape together as lovers, as she, like Tilly and Passuk before her, tirelessly and faithfully helps him, and he continues to learn her complexity. Some of the formulaic elements of this story, including its racial and gender stereotyping, are offset by the strange power of Labiskwee and by the strangeness of the journey she and Smoke undertake. "Wonder of Woman" contains both Greek and biblical allusions, such as intriguing references to Jason and Medea and the sun-dogs, which appear and bring with them the "white death," a terrible mist of ice-crystals that blinds the pair as they struggle over the mountains. But when Smoke awakes to "another sun" after the blinding storm is over, Labiskwee dies, having starved because she saved back food for him, "crucifixions of life," the narrator calls it. In despair, he tosses the food away, but he must continue his journey west, forever changed by glimpsing the secrets of Labiskwee's heart.

2. Stories of Social Realism

One of Jack London's earliest insights was that "official" justice was fallible but an innate sense of justice was impossible to ignore. He related to George Wharton James how he felt very much alone as a child, and this fostered contemplation, which in turn led to analysis of his most fundamental relationship:

> I well remember how I used to look upon my mother. To me she was a wonderful woman with all power over my destiny. She had wisdom and knowledge, as well as power in her hands. Her word was my law. But one day she punished me for something of which I was not guilty. The poor woman had a hard life, and all her energies were spent in chasing the dollar that she might feed and clothe us, and she was worn out, nervous, irritable, and therefore disinclined to take the time and energy necessary to investigate. So I was punished unjustly. Of course I cried and felt the injustice. Now, had I had companions, it would not have been long before I should have found them, or they me, and we should have engaged in some fun or frolic, and my attention would have been diverted. I should soon have "laughed and forgot." But it was not so. I thought, and thought, and thought, and my brooded thought soon incubated. I began to see differently. I began to measure. I saw that my mother was not as large as I had thought. Her infallibility was destroyed. She had seen all there was to see. Her knowledge was limited, and therefore she was unjust. I can well remember that I absolved her from any deliberate intention to hurt me, but henceforth I decided for myself as to the right and wrong of things. (James, 365–66)

Several things about this passage are significant. London highlights his sense of isolation—a theme that also emerges in his sensitivity to class; and he describes his desire for community at the same time that he refers to his maturing ability to analyze right and wrong for himself in opposition to authority. That this passage appears in a section of the James interview describing Flora London's racism is also of interest in light of a racism directed at the family's neighbors, Greeks, Italians, and other immigrants, with whom she forbade young Johnny to play. Were London's later conflicting ideas about race in some way rooted in his relation to his mother and to the attendant issues of class and his evolving sense of justice?

Certainly the three aspects of social justice that London most vigorously examined throughout his career—race, gender, and class—are all heavily implicated in his origins, specifically what he was taught as a boy.[45] How does his relationship to the feminine intersect with his relationship to the racial "other" and with his class anxieties? We have seen some possible answers to this question in chapter 1 in the discussion of London's Indian women. London's sense of rejection by mother and father, and the class anxieties he picked up from Flora were a volatile combination, balanced only to some extent by the love he received from others—John London; Eliza; Virginia Prentiss; his second wife, Charmian; and his first wife, Bess, and daughters, troubled as their love was. If we picture a young boy, full of his own particular genius as Johnny London was, trying to understand how, despite his emotional rejection and poverty, he could allow himself to achieve at the level he felt drawn to, then it seems obvious the role *racialism* would have played vis a vis class—that is, the view that members of different races are fundamentally different from one other, as opposed to *racism*, implying dislike or hatred.[46] He could tell himself that his genius came not from his putative family but from his larger "family" of Anglo-Saxon overachievers, those swashbucklers he loved to read about as a child. Because this volume is neither a biography nor a psychological study, I will leave it for others to delve further into London's formative relationships. But in the following chapters we shall again encounter the intertwined issues of race, gender, and class. Following brief discussions of gender and race, I turn to the topic of class to focus closely on London's socialism. From near the beginning of his writing London identified himself as a socialist and did not resign from the Socialist Party until 1916. While one might speculate (as I have here) as to the psychological origins of London's commitment to social justice, the fact is that his devotion to socialism was a heartfelt and quite intellectually conscious, if not always consistent, lifelong commitment. That it was not one free of contradictions demonstrates London's complexity of ideas and leads us productively into a variety of related aspects of his writing.

Gender and Race: An Overview

As suggested above, perhaps the most striking feature of London's handling of gender is his constant search for connection with the "mother"—fertile ground for the artist's imagination. Certainly London sought both the mother and father in his writing, since he was in effect deprived of both. But the search for the mother persists in a way that the anxieties about the father do not—the latter were outgrown early on in his writing. From the very first Klondike stories with their self-sacrificing maidens to the very last novels, including *The Valley of the Moon* (1913), his heroes seek the healing that the woman as anima figure can bring. He tends to name this "soul-mate" character "Lucy"—perhaps a name derived from his second wife Charmian's nickname, "Lute," and also perhaps an allusion to St. Lucy as the *figura* of Light. He was fortunate enough to marry a soul mate in Charmian Kittredge, and her influence dramatically affected his view of women. As his "mate-woman," Charmian provided unqualified love and professional support but also, in her athleticism and adventurousness, the ideal androgynous companion.[47]

London tended to treat specifically feminist concerns in novels rather than short stories, but we will return to his handling of the feminine in chapter 3 when we turn to his experimentations with point of view, and in chapter 4 when we see how London used the insights of C. G. Jung to frame his inner quest for the feminine archetype in some of his most compelling Hawaiian stories.

In contrast, race tends to be addressed in the short fiction more than the novels, most often in the specific settings of the Klondike and the South Seas. As we have already seen, London's attitude toward racial "others" is anything but simple, since at times he displays the crudest possible views on white superiority and at others the most sensitive and imaginative insights into the point of view of the racial "other." His condescending portraits of Indians appear right alongside his deeply felt valorizations of them—and, more to the point, his realistic treatment of Indian characters. Surely one of the great appeals to his readers lies in his passionate attacks upon injustices committed in the name of racial superiority, and many of his most memorable and admirable characters are nonwhite—but for many readers detection of the opposite impulse in him is enough to dismiss him entirely. Still, there are a few fundamental features of his racial thinking that furnish means for sorting out some of the inconsistencies.

Not only were Flora's teachings important to his formation of racialist and racist ideas but the entire climate of working-class attitudes toward immigrants who arrived in greater and greater numbers in California during London's childhood naturally had its effect. Because the

whites felt their jobs threatened, labor unions and workingmen's societies practiced open racism against Asians, including organized beatings, lynchings, and attacks on neighborhoods. Even the socialists joined
in the hatred of nonwhites.[48] In addition, among many people, educated and uneducated, racialism was simply the rule of the day. The
white race was seen as superior to all others, as documented in "scientific" literature and taught in even the most socially liberal universities.
This laid the groundwork for what would become the legal doctrine of
racial segregation in America, the notion of "separate but equal." London read the works of Social Darwinists such as Herbert Spencer,
Thomas Henry Huxley, and David Starr Jordan, who spoke of eugenics
and of preserving "favored races" through natural selection; he read
Charles Darwin's *Origin of Species* and Ernst Haeckel's *History of Creation.*
He read popular works like James Hewitt's *The Ruling Races of Prehistoric
Times*, Alfred Schultz's *Race or Mongrel*, and Frank Roesler's *The World's
Greatest Migration: The Origin of the "White Man."* Haeckel, founder of the
philosophy of "monism" to which London subscribed—the attempt to
study the world and all its parts as an evolutionary whole—described
the "woolly-haired" Negroes as "incapable of a true inner culture and of
a higher mental development." Hewitt, following Hegel and other German Idealist philosophers, saw the older races, such as the Chinese, as
developmentally inferior in terms of the evolution of their society.
Schultz argued that Jesus Christ could not have been Jewish but must
have been Aryan, since he demonstrated "Aryan" characteristics.[49] Add
into this weird mix the "Americanization" movement and the U.S.
imperialism of the day, including waging war in the Philippines, Cuba,
and Mexico, and we begin to picture some of the influences on London's racial thinking. In light of the reading he was doing and the beliefs
of the day, it is astonishing that he was able to portray "alien" races sen-
sitively at all.

Finally, London's socialism seems powerfully at odds with his racialism—particularly when he harbored certain pet ideas regarding race
purity, which led him, for instance, to call the Mexican peons engaged
in the Mexican Revolution "mongrels" and "halfbreeds." (Hearing such
talk, sometimes the reader fears that he was thinking of his efforts at
horsebreeding, at which he was a master, for he writes unabashedly in
letters of the superiority of the Anglo-Saxon "breed" and of its eventual
domination.) McClintock reads race as the "dominant theme" of London's stories (McClintock, 96). By means of race theory, McClintock
argues, "London's impulse towards power and mastery could be joined

with his sense of insignificance and powerlessness since all individuals are impotent participants in the working out of inexorable natural law" (96, 98). McClintock's theory corresponds to the biographical context outlined earlier in this chapter. Scott Malcolmson takes a similar view, arguing that in his search for categorical certainty beyond class London thought he had found one in race, "an imaginary region at least as American as pitiless industrialism." London frequently made "his heroes' whiteness, their understanding of it and its requirements, the animating fact of their destinies." It is "an inexplicable tribal imperative and a historical force" that offered "the possibility of a worldview unlike that of socialism, one which accommodated both firm collective identities and human drama and tragedy on a global scale, without end. Life for London had to be a struggle; and racism, racial conflict, was full of promise." In the end, however, race did not deliver "the happy marriage of individual and collective destiny."[50]

Yet if London was always the racialist he was by no means always the racist. For example, when asked by a Japanese newspaper editor how Japan and the United States could foster among their children a desire for friendship between the two nations, London said, first, by stopping "the stupid newspaper from fomenting race prejudice," second, by educating their children "so that they will be too intelligently tolerant to respond to any call to race prejudice," and third, "by realizing, in industry and government, of socialism . . . the Brotherhood of Man." Only then, "just as boys grow up, so the races of mankind will grow up and laugh when they look back on their childish quarrels" (*Letters*, 1219). This is an interesting prescription, given that some of London's most racist discourse occurred in his newspaper journalism and was directed against the Japanese, but it does demonstrate unmistakable antiracist feeling.

What about these contradictions? As Andrew Furer has observed, London tended to sympathize with the underdog, but moreso to champion exceptional individuals of any race, such as Felipe Rivera of "The Mexican"; McCoy, the Christlike sailor who saves the ship in "The Seed of McCoy"; and the title characters of "Koolau the Leper" and "Chun Ah Chun." Furer acknowledges London's racism but examines numerous instances of his antiracism, including short stories and articles such as his coverage of the African American boxer, Jack Johnson. Furer identifies London's "fear of the horde" or "Yellow Peril," but also notes that "when London gives Asian and other non-white characters individuality accompanied by exceptional ability, his anxiety dissolves into admiration, and he begins to see numerous ways in which people of color are superior to Anglo-Saxons."[51]

There are also significant differences in London's handling of race depending upon which genre he was using. In the letters, essays, and, to a lesser extent, novels, he displayed his racist attitudes, as though he were on his soapbox as a public person and had to tell the crowds what would confirm their prejudices (and thus enhance his own status). However, in the short fiction, his largest body of work, where he invoked race it tended to be in terms of racialism rather than racism. In the short stories the focus is upon imagining *characters*—connecting with them as *people*—and while he tried to describe differences he did not necessarily claim superiority for white characters, especially in his South Seas work. This is London's best self—the imaginative artist at work.

As a writer traveling in the South Seas London enjoyed a somewhat privileged perspective on race, not sharing the greed of the white capitalists who were there to make their fortunes in the islands but at leisure to observe them and the native peoples they exploited. Indeed, his time in Hawaii seems to have been a turning point. Having moved from the pretensions of his Bay Area bohemian friends to ranch life with Charmian in the country, he was prepared to set sail on the *Snark* for Hawaii and points beyond freed from the old anxieties of life in the city and its memories of poverty and struggle. Only after the *Snark* voyage was London able to find his roots in Sonoma, building his 15,000-square-foot Wolf House to anchor himself to the land. London found on the seas a new arena and new experiences to fuel his thinking about civilization and social justice. His last years in Hawaii, where there was an easy mixing of the races at all levels, rich and poor, were especially significant, demonstrating a new model for social harmony.

But the most important aspect of London's vexing contradictions on race is the role of class. Throughout his life, London loved winners and hated (and feared) losers; from his early connection with the works of Nietzsche he sought intellectual justification for overcoming the life of the "work beast" that he had seemed destined to lead. Race was and is a key factor in class anxiety for many economically oppressed and socially irrelevant white working-class people, who often hang on to the thought that at least they are white. This feature of London's development emerges with startling clarity at certain moments, as when he served as a war correspondent in the Russo-Japanese War of 1904. Because his newly won status as well-known author of such works as *The*

Call of the Wild (1903) meant nothing to the officers of the Japanese army, with whom he marched into Korea, he responded in letters and dispatches with emotionally laden anti-Asian invectives. Reading those dispatches and letters is an exercise in observing a writer trying to construct himself *against* race. As we will see in chapter 4 in the analysis of race in the Pacific short stories, it took a great deal of success followed by a maturing sense of selfhood for London to readjust his views on race to conform to his socialistic ideals of what a community should be.

London's Socialism

Reading Karl Marx early on, and labeled the "boy socialist" by the Oakland newspaper for his curbside speeches, London ran twice for mayor of Oakland on the socialist ticket. His socialism was one of the factors that made him famous around the globe but which also turned many American critics of his day against him. He has long been the most popular American author in numerous communist and postcommunist nations as well as democratic countries, but only now is the subject of his left-wing politics attracting large numbers of American admirers from the ranks of the professoriate.

London claimed he believed in confronting life from a materialist standpoint, but he argued that "[t]o know the naked facts of life is not to be pessimistic" (*Letters*, 902). He explored socialist themes throughout his short fiction, although the materialistic monism he advocated in his speeches is less a factor in his fiction. It is surprising how few stories he wrote that are specifically politically "socialist," that is, overtly political and overtly concerned with issues of labor; only a handful qualify. Yet the themes that support socialism are everywhere in his work, and they take many forms. The Northland code of brotherhood and the three themes of the Klondike stories, imagination, justice, and community, are transformed in stories situated elsewhere—especially in urban landscapes—into sharply critical analyses of social ills and corrupt power systems.

Typical of London, within the socialist stories are elements that some readers might see as competing with a socialist politics and materialist world-view, including continued references to the Greek ideals so prominent in the Klondike stories, an upsurge of biblical allusions that climaxes in the late South Seas stories, and finally a turn inward toward resolving psychological issues rather than predominantly social ones. But London would argue that as a monist he could not separate earthly from spiritual concerns, especially when they related to social justice. His readers need to be constantly aware of this.

In such essays as "What Life Means to Me," "War of the Classes," "Revolution," and "Why I Became a Socialist," London detailed how his personal experiences led him to adopt socialism. Having left the university, London turned to socialistic meetings for intellectual stimulus, and, as he wrote in "What Life Means to Me,"

> Here I found keen-flashing intellects and brilliant wits; for here I met strong and alert-brained, withal horny-handed members of the working class; unfrocked preachers too wide in their Christianity for any congregation of Mammon worshippers; professors broken in the wheel of university subservience to the ruling class and flung out because they were quick with knowledge which they strove to apply to the affairs of mankind. Here I also found warm faith in the human, glowing, idealism, sweetness of unselfishness, renunciation and martyrdom—all the splendid, stinging things of the spirit. (*Revolution*, 302)

He went on to praise the "clean, noble" life he found amongst his comrades, "great souls who exalted flesh and spirit over dollars and cents; and to whom the thin wail of the starved slum child meant more than all the pomp and circumstance of commercial expansion and world-empire." London cast his socialist friends as new heroes to replace the Klondike code hero. He went so far as to see in their "nobleness of purpose" the "burning and blazing. . . Holy Grail, Christ's own Grail, the warm human, long-suffering and maltreated, but to be saved and rescued at the last" (*Revolution*, 302). This mingling of Christian imagery in London's socialistic writing is intriguing: he rejected the church because he perceived hypocrisy among its congregation, but the highest form of the good he could muster in this passage (and others like it) is the invocation of Christ.

In his 1915 novel *The Star Rover*, a searing indictment of the prison system, the largest section is made up of portions of London's unfinished "Christ novel," on which he labored intermittently for most of his writing career. Perhaps this interest arose in part from London's friendships with Christian socialists such as Frederick Irons Bamford. Such language appears again and again in his socialist writings. In "The Cry for Justice" London wrote, "He, who by understanding becomes converted to the gospel of service will serve kindness so that brutality will perish; will serve beauty to the erasement of all that is not beautiful. And he who is strong will serve the weak that they may become strong."[52] We should remember that in his day the socialists did not make an issue of eschewing religious imagery from their thought, as became more the case with the rise of world communism.

Substantiating his reading of theorists with shocking examples of the state of Chicago garment workers, the slums of Brooklyn, and the average yearly earnings of unskilled workmen in California, London pounded away in lectures and essays at his theme. In 1905 and 1906 he toured the East and Midwest for the Intercollegiate Socialist Society and drew huge crowds; he told the students of Yale University: "Fight for us or fight against us! Raise your voices one way or the other; be alive!" He challenged an audience of wealthy New Yorkers: "You have mismanaged the world, and it shall be taken from you! Look at us! We are strong! Consider our hands! They are strong hands, and even now they are reaching forth for all you have, and they will take it, take it by the power of their strong hands; take it from your feeble grasp." The former audience applauded; the latter did not.[53] But his socialist speeches and writings also tried to appeal to the capitalists' better instincts. The preface to *War of the Classes* states, "Socialism deals with what is, not what ought to be; and . . . the material with which it deals is the clay of the common road, the warm human, fallible and frail, sordid and petty, absurd and contradictory, even grotesque, and yet, withal, shot through with flashes and glimmerings of something finer and Godlike, with here and there sweetnesses of service and unselfishness, desires for goodness, for renunciation and sacrifice, and with conscience stern and awful, at times blazingly imperious, demanding the right— the right, nothing more nor less than the right."[54]

London learned not only from reading but also from watching the cruel machinery of the richest society in the world grind out its prosperity on the backs of manual laborers, such as himself. As Russ Kingman puts it,

> The men without trades were helpless cattle. If one learned a trade, he was compelled to belong to a union in order to work at his trade. And his union was compelled to slug it out with the employers in order to hold up wages or hold down hours. The employers likewise bullied and slugged. Jack couldn't see any dignity at all. And when a workman got old, or had an accident, he was thrown onto the scrapheap like any wornout machine. (Kingman, 46)

Facing the same labor conditions as his father before him, London saw around him over two million out of work. During the 1890s the nation was not only in the middle of a labor surplus but also facing the related problem of a crisis in currency that caused extreme variation in the quantity of money in circulation (Kingman, 46). The combination of a personal and national sense of the oppression of labor fueled London's socialism, especially in its angriest and most apocalyptic moments: "And far be it from me to deny that socialism is a menace," he wrote. "It is its purpose to wipe out, root and branch, all capitalistic institutions of present day society. It is distinctively revolutionary, and in scope and depth is vastly more tremendous than any revolution that has ever occurred in the history of the world" (*War of the Classes*, xiii).

Clearly the most emotionally significant factor in London's conversion to socialism was the time he spent at the Erie County Penitentiary, what he called his immersion in "a very nightmare of humanity, . . . unbelievable. . . unprintable . . . unspeakable."[55] Hitting the road again after his prison experience, he listened anew to the stories of his fellow tramps about how injuries, bad luck, or corruption had cost them their livelihoods and starved them and their families. As would later happen in the Klondike, he got his "perspective." As Kingman points out, "When Jack left Oakland, he was still a believer in Kipling's work ethic. He had believed the teachers and preachers who proclaimed the honor of work. Now he could see that hard labor was not as honorable as he had been told. . . . [And] his young muscles were strong, but they could earn only a pittance." Knowing firsthand the drawbacks to a life of crime, London decided "there would be no working life either. His only hope of ever escaping the 'trap' was to sell brains, and to do that he must get an education. He would 'open the books' " (Kingman, 59).

But despite the fervor of his belief in his new creed of socialism, and despite the powerful attacks on capitalism in his short fiction, London eventually resigned from the Socialist Party. On March 7, 1916, writing from Honolulu, he told the members of Local Glen Ellen that he was resigning from the party "because of its lack of fire and fight, and its loss of emphasis on the class struggle." He had believed "that the working class, by fighting, by never fusing, by never making terms with the enemy, could emancipate itself." He felt "the whole trend of socialism in the United States of recent years has been one of peaceableness and compromise," and "liberty, freedom, and independence, are royal things that cannot be presented to, nor thrust upon, races or classes. . . . [I]f such royal things are kindly presented to them by superior individuals, on silver platters, they will know not what to do with them, will fail to make use of them, and will be what they have always been in the past—

inferior races and inferior classes" (*Letters*, 1537–38). London's stated reason notwithstanding, this is a puzzling letter—it is not clear exactly what prompted London's resignation, and it sounds as if race is mixed up in things again. Particular events of the time, including the Mexican War, World War I, and alliances among socialist, progressive, and conservative political factions certainly played a role. Kingman argues that London's socialism "declined in almost direct proportion to the gradual takeover of socialist reform measures by other political parties," including abolition of child labor, better working conditions, job insurance, and community ownership of public utilities and transportation (Kingman, 11). These issues began to appear in the platforms of the two major parties to the detriment of the socialist vote. At the same time, London alienated himself from the socialists because of his position on the Mexican War; unlike the socialists, who believed that the war was a genuine political revolution, London did not. He took the side of the peons, but he believed they were exploited by their revolutionary leaders. London's references to the "breeds" of Mexico with their bombastic "*pronunciamentos*" mingled sympathy for the common people with a tone of disgust and, again, racism. The thesis-antithesis of his views on race and his socialism comes through repeatedly in his short stories.

The conflict between London's individualism and his socialism has been often explored by critics. For example, Katherine M. Littell notes that the apparent dichotomy between these philosophies forms a dialectic that illustrates "stages in London's development, which he subsequently synthesized in a philosophical perspective beyond both polarities,"[56] but a number of other readers of London have disagreed, seeing the opposition as irreconcilable and artistically damaging. From Nietzsche's *Thus Spoke Zarathustra* London got the idea of the "superman" who is perfect in mind and body, unmatched in strength and intelligence, and unencumbered by religious beliefs or social mores. London loved and hated this figure, as is apparent in characters like Wolf Larsen of *The Sea-Wolf*, at once compelling and doomed. London thought that both *The Sea-Wolf* and *Martin Eden* stood as indictments to the superman, but many readers have not read them that way. Similarly, his novel *The Iron Heel*, an all-out attack on the capitalist oligarchy, suffers from confusion because his hero, Ernest Everhard, is a "superman socialist" who, while he leads his comrades, denigrates the masses and seems aloof from them. Alfred Kazin explains such dissonance by arguing that "the clue to Jack London's work is certainly to be found in his own turbulent life, and not in his Socialism. He was a Socialist by instinct, but he was also a Nietzschean and a follower of Herbert Spencer by instinct. All his life he grasped whatever straw of salvation lay nearest at hand, and if he joined Karl Marx to the Superman with a boyish glee that has shocked American Marxists ever since, it is interesting to remember that he joined Herbert Spencer to Shelley, and astrology to philosophy, with as carefree a will."[57] And London did say: "I am first of all a white man and only then a Socialist" (Joan London, *Jack London and His Times*, 284).

Perhaps George Orwell best sums up the contradictory quality of London's adherence to socialism. London "was right where nearly all other prophets were wrong," in saying that "capitalist society would not perish of its 'contradictions,' but that the possessing class would be able to form itself into a vast corporation and even evolve a sort of perverted Socialism. . . ." London foresaw fascism because of his own "almost unconquerable preference for the strong man as against the weak man." London's outlook was "democratic in the sense that he hated exploitation and hereditary privilege," and he felt most comfortable in the company of people who worked with their hands. But London's "instinct lay towards acceptance of a 'natural aristocracy' of strength, beauty and talent." In much of his work "one strain in his character simply kills the other off: he is at his best where they interact, as they do in certain of his short stories," those in which his primary subject, the cruelty of (human) nature, is both accurately described and, without overt comment, bemoaned, as in "Just Meat" and "The Apostate." In the end, Orwell memorably characterizes London as a "Socialist with the instincts of a buccaneer and the education of a nineteenth-century materialist. . . . [His] better angel is his Socialist convictions, which come into play when he deals with such subjects as coloured exploitation, child labour or the treatment of criminals, but are hardly involved when he is writing about explorers or animals." But Orwell concludes that "if he had been a politically reliable person he would probably have left behind nothing of interest."[58]

Let us turn to the stories that deal with these many facets of social justice. We may approach London's stories of social realism by grouping them into four categories: Mad Masters, Workers United, The Sympathetic Hero, and The Ironic Narrator. These stories, mostly from the middle period of London's writing, are often described as socialist. Close reading of them will reveal, among other things, that no matter how appealing to the critic, no "theory" of London's on class, race, or society will always work when applied to actual stories. Like the sayings of famous people that are misquoted more often than not, London's stories surprise us in their variety of expression. They evince no one social theory but rather the less regular shape of an author's own intuited sense of justice and his fascination with human character.

Mad Masters

London's mad scientist in "A Thousand Deaths" is a foretaste of his Mad Masters stories, which continue with the two Thomas Stevens stories from the Klondike tales. These form a bridge between the scientists in his early work and his later world dictators. In "A Relic of the Pliocene" (1900) and "A Hyperborean Brew" (1900), submitted on the same day and published only months apart in 1901, we encounter the inveterate adventurer Stevens telling of his exploits within the frame structure. In the former tale, Stevens tells of chasing and killing a woolly mammoth that has miraculously survived in a remote valley. His wiles—he traps the animal in the valley and chases it until it dies of starvation and exhaustion—and his pride in his mammoth hide house shoes hardly make him an attractive hero, clever at survival though he is. But he comes off even worse in the companion story, subtitled, "The Story of a Scheming White Man among the Strange People Who Live on the Rim of the Arctic Sea," a nasty comedy of racial domination and humiliation. Stevens's imagination is again impressive, and his trickery is superior to that of the Indians, but his outwitting of the chief, medicine men, and villagers in the manufacture of "hootch," or liquor, and the pleasure he takes in beating a disloyal servant make the tone cruel and the character repugnant. The narrator praises Stevens's knowledge of the region but brands him a liar. Allusions to Apollo are to a god of wisdom made into a perpetrator of cheap tricks. The Hyperboreans were people living north of Greece who originated the worship of Apollo; these Hyperboreans, in contrast, receive an evil trickster god into their land.

Dualism is continued in portraits of world dictators. As Kazin and Orwell observed, London is both attracted to and repelled by mental giants, but three of his Mad Master stories, "The Minions of Midas" (1900), "Goliah" (1907), and "The Enemy of All the World" (1907), are critical of the dictators; any admiration for such supermen is more than offset by condemnation of their actions. Orwell may perceive fascistic elements in London's thought, but a careful reading of these tales reveals a sly and savage indictment of such "leadership." Although disillusioned with the pieties of "honest labor," that is, physical labor, London admired and elevated the value of real work, be it prospecting, sailing, or the efforts of a "brain merchant." Superman heroes are not real workers, and London classed them with the capitalists they think they oppose.

"The Minions of Midas," a macabre dystopian vision, was London's first socialist story. It hardly portrays socialism positively, however, although it conveys the collective power of the masses. An evil group of anticapitalists extort Mr. Eben Hale, Money Baron, by threatening to commit random murders unless he will pay them. They justify the random murders of innocent citizens by calling themselves the "intellectual proletariat" and by asserting that the "Money Baronage exploits the world by mastering and applying the world's economic forces. Brain, not brawn, endures; and those best fitted to survive are the intellectually and commercially powerful" (*Complete*, 435). They are organized to combat "wage slavery," and for a while it seems they are succeeding in getting the attention of the moneyed class. But Mr. Hale commits suicide, and the outcome of their terrorism only leads to more suffering. London's parable is a warning as to what could happen if the needs of the proletariat are not met and extremists come into power. Indeed, the "minions of Midas" are actually anarchists rather than socialists, and London had a great suspicion of anarchists; however, the casual reader is not apt to make the distinction.

"Goliah" was published in *Revolution and Other Essays* (1910), the only short story to be included in either of London's two books of socialist analysis (the second book is *War of the Classes* [1905]). It is the story of a madman who takes on the capitalist establishment and forces it to run the world his way. London satirized this utopian socialist impulse and may also have been satirizing his own grandiose ideas since the dictator, Goliah, bears some resemblance to his overdrawn portraits of himself in other works (such as "Planchette," "Bunches of Knuckles," and "The Kanaka Surf"). It is thus a warning about the abuse of intellectual power both politically and personally.

Goliah calls the businessmen, politicians, and scientists of the world to meet with him, but only the scientists listen to his ideas. In retaliation for being ignored by the others, Goliah commits atrocities like any modern terrorist—bombings with great loss of life. As he progresses in his dream of a world organized around his principles and grows in power, this mysterious figure with his awesome arsenal of unimaginable weapons—like another Connecticut Yankee[59]—frightens the world into submission. He addresses the world in letters that employ a formal, arrogant, inverted syntax—letters that at times sound a good deal like some of London's own epistolary diatribes.

As Goliah succeeds in intimidating the world to change government, labor, commerce, and every other aspect of human civilization and adopt his ideal of peaceful, productive rationality, the world he creates looks quite happy—people need rarely work, there is time for study and recreation, there is no war or class oppression. Goliah promises to provide "automatic" food and shelter to the world to obviate the need for material gain, and with that will pass away all evils: "With food and shelter automatic, the higher incentives will universally obtain—the spiritual aesthetic, and intellectual incentives that will tend to develop and make beautiful and noble body, mind, and spirit. Then all the world will be dominated by happiness and laughter. It will be the reign of universal laughter" (*Complete*, 1205). But this is a dystopia, built on terror and exploitation. For example, part of Goliah's plan involves kidnapping Africans and Orientals to force them to work for him on his Palgrave Island—the name alone signifying his deathly grip on the living. Goliah is a social engineer and he does not recognize what London's story subtly reinforces: that it is impossible to *make* people happy. Among other measures to ensure universal happiness is his plan to remove "all the extreme hereditary inefficients," who are "segregated and denied marriage" (1218); an "incurable" remnant are confined in asylums (1219). It may be true that "[h]e was a superman, a scientific superman" (1220), but the story's irony leaves no doubt as to his evil.

How do we know without a doubt that London was being ironic? First, from Goliah's name, both his given name, Percival Stultz, and his adopted name. "Goliah" is a variant of "Goliath," the Philistine behemoth slain by David. "Percival" is a name London used in several stories for very negative characters, including "In a Far Country" and "The House of Pride." Percival was introduced into Western literature by Chrétien de Troyes around 1200 as a country bumpkin who becomes the Grail hero. His mother kept Percival ignorant of chivalry (his father was a knight who was killed) but when he sees his first knight he disregards his mother's wishes that he remain safe at home and heads for Arthur's court, where he receives basic chivalric instruction. On his first adventure, he witnesses the Grail procession without knowing what he is seeing, and because he has been advised against asking too many questions, he fails to ask about what he has seen. Later he learns that had he questioned the significance of what he saw, he could have cured the ailing Fisher King and restored harmony and prosperity to the king's stricken lands. Percival the Knight was tainted by ignorance and lacked responsibility and understanding. In later versions of the myth he is shown to be a fool, as in *L'Morte d'Arthur* and in Wagner. London would probably have read the King Arthur tale via Howard Pyle, Sidney Lanier, or even Mark Twain, who used Malory. What does he make of this latter-day Percival? In "Goliah" Percival is a failure. Similarly, the last name, Stultz, can only associate him with stultification. Like Twain, London suggests through his allusions that the knights' dream of a utopian world in which the Grail would restore happiness was just that, only a dream, and that its hierarchical reality could ultimately mean a loss of freedom for its inhabitants.

Another way of judging Goliah a failure is through London's use of solar imagery. For example, "Energon," the mysterious force Goliah employs, is a power source manufactured from the light of the sun. But the sun's power—like that of "Apollo" in "A Hyperborean Brew"—is perverted in its use as an agent of destruction. The "famous Christmas letter" Goliah sends out that tells all the world to disarm describes Energon as "nothing more nor less than the cosmic energy that resides in the solar rays" (1216). More commandeering of divine attributes is revealed when Goliah names his massive palace "Asgard" and builds a statue of himself with an Ozymandias-like inscription: "ALL WILL BE JOY-SMITHS, AND THEIR TASK SHALL BE TO BEAT OUT LAUGHTER FROM THE RINGING ANVIL OF LIFE" (1221), as though joy can be "beat out" from life.

The last stroke of London's irony comes when we learn that the story is being told by a naive young student writing a school essay in a future still under Goliah's sway. Such a narrator, not revealed until the end, exposes Goliah, too, as like an adolescent totalitarian, although without saying so. An editor's note tells us:

> This remarkable production is the work of Harry Beckwith, a student in the Lowell High School of San Francisco, and it is here reproduced chiefly because of the youth of its author. Far be it from our policy to burden our readers with ancient history; and when it is known that Harry Beckwith was only fifteen when the foregoing was written, our motive will be understood. "Goliah" won the Premier for high school composition in 2254, and last year Harry Beckwith took advantage of the privilege earned, by electing to spend six months in Asgard. The wealth of historical detail, the atmosphere of the time, and the mature style of the composition are especially noteworthy in one so young. (1221)

I mentioned that "Goliah" may satirize both London himself (here as the young writer) and the ideas of reformers of his day. London signed his letters, "Yours for the Revolution," and Goliah signs his letters, "Yours for the reconstruction of society" (1202); and, like London the materialist, professes no "unscientific sentimentality about the value of human life" (1202). But this London-like sentiment is quickly replaced by a grimmer view of society, along the lines of Ayn Rand. Soon Goliah signs letters, "Mine is the power. I am the will of God. The whole world shall be in vassalage to me, but it shall be a vassalage of peace. 'I am Goliah' " (1208). The entire narrative ironically invokes the official biographies of dictators such as Adolf Hitler who carefully controlled their public images. For example, the narrator tells us that although Goliah was a world tyrant he "loved sweets, and was inordinately fond of salted almonds and salted pecans," but hated cats (1120). These distracting "facts" about the world ruler underscore the theme of needing to ask the right questions when presented with the history of Goliah.

"The Enemy of All the World" concerns an abused child, a "lonely, neglected" boy (1248) who becomes an anarchist and devises a way to make people shoot themselves, creating mass terror that affects everyone from the corner policeman to the members of the courts of Europe. The story is interesting to compare with "Goliah," with London's attack on child labor in "The Apostate" and with his workers' fantasy, "The Dream of Debs." As a parody of bildungsromane like *Oliver Twist* and *Great Expectations*, "The Enemy of All the World" concludes with irony: when the authorities finally track down the perpetrator of countless acts of sabotage and mayhem, they want to buy his contraption from him! Although some of the biographical overstatement again suggests self-parody, London also distanced himself from the story by casting it as a wild tale supposedly from a book called "Eccentricities of Crime," a device worthy of the authorial/editorial evasions of Hawthorne and Poe.

The extreme tone of the Mad Masters tales—their reliance upon horror and the macabre—may surprise us, but it is entirely in keeping with the extremities that filled the lives of laborers and the severity of the economic crises of London's day. As noted in chapter 1, from the 1870s until World War I, the nation experienced some of the worst excesses of economic panic and exploitation of labor. This was the age of robber barons, Molly McGuires, the Pinkerton National Detective Agency, strikes combatted by union infiltration, bullpens, bombings, and assassinations of capitalist overlords. In the newspapers, London would have read a daily fare of stories such as the 1907 trial of William D. "Big Bill" Haywood, accused of murdering a powerful mine owner in Idaho; he also followed the persecution of radicals such as Eugene V. Debs. Dark plots, violence, and class war were not the stuff of fantasy fiction—they were real. In the Mad Masters stories London employed the science fiction and dystopian fantasy genres to convey imaginatively the headlines' terrible truths.

Workers United

Not all of London's socialist stories were cast in such dark terms. To the contrary, of all of London's stories of social realism, the most consistently socialist—and some of the strongest—are those that portray the opposite end of the spectrum from the Mad Masters, casting an optimistic and positive light on the efforts of workers to free themselves from wage slavery. These are tales of workers united to overthrow their oppression with nonviolence and in a spirit of brotherhood. "The Dream of Debs" (1907) tells of a general strike from the point of view of a rich capitalist who must, in the end, accommodate the strikers. In college the wealthy narrator wrote an article on the "dream" of a general strike called "The Dream of Debs," but he is totally unprepared for what happens when a strike actually occurs. Like "The Minions of Midas," "Goliath," and "The Enemy of All the World," this is a fantasy story of outlandish proportions, but despite its exaggerations, it has a quality of verisimilitude missing in the previous tales. This is a story about labor, for a change without a superman; the laborers themselves get together and pull off the general strike on their own, cooperatively and carefully. And this time the scheme for justice works.

The story is pervaded by the themes that filled the Klondike stories, the importance of an imagination in making one able to adapt and survive, a sense of a code of justice, and, in the end, the assertion of community. The narrator, Bertie, answers the older men complaining in their club: "You've got labor down and gouged it, and now labor's got you down and is gouging you, that's all, and you're squealing. . . . [Y]ou're getting a taste of your own medicine" (1266–67). Just "leave morality out of it," he says, and "play the game" (1268), but his comments point to moral reversal. Like the other stories, this one contains persuasive irony, as in the scene of the refugee capitalists scouring the countryside outside San Francisco for food. They try to kill a cow to eat; they eventually mangle it to death and carry it in their car, but then lose it to a mob: "[W]e were unaccustomed to such work, and we bungled it" (1271). There is no lack of black humor as workers and capitalists fight bitterly in the road over the mutilated cow.

Scenes like this one highlight the naturalism of London's social critique: "Millionaires and paupers had fought side by side for food" (1276). Here, reality, it seems, is the foundation for behavior, not ideals; in the end, the strike over, the capitalist narrator has to let the servants come back to their jobs because he simply has no choice. He learns the rhetoric of how to talk about it, too: "The tyranny of organized labor is getting beyond human endurance. Something must be done" (1278). A strike by the rich, perhaps?

"A Curious Fragment" (1907) followed closely upon "The Dream of Debs." Typically, an editor's note explains the context: it is a tale told by slaves on a cotton plantation called "Hell's Bottom" in the twenty-sixth century. The slaves ask who controls history, education, codes? They are taught by a renegade slave that education is the key—they are asking the right questions and getting the truth. Part of London's socialist creed from the beginning—as we saw in the quotations from his socialist essays—was that whoever controls words, books, and stories will have power, and in this tale the stress is laid on the importance of keeping hold of one's stories. The narrator teaches the slaves that they are no different from the masters—he relates that master's family came from slaves—but it is the books they have to acquire. This tale's emphasis upon interpretation as a key to survival relates it to such Klondike tales as "The Sun-Dog Trail" and such Pacific stories as "Shin Bones."

"The Strength of the Strong" (1908) followed upon the heels of a series of stories about the "inevitable white man" in the Pacific and offers what is perhaps London's most effective version of the immorality of wage labor and ownership. Joan Hedrick says it is his "finest expression of his socialist consciousness."[60] The title's double meaning both praises collectively and is a warning against the strong man, even when he is a writer/propagandist who "gives us the words." Martin Eden was highly conscious of the writer's duty to the people, but here the writer, Bug, is a tool of the ruling class and little more than a propagandist.

In the story Old Long Arm tells of learning "to add our strength until our strength was the strength of all of us" (*Complete*, 1568), as he relates the story of how two tribes were formed, the Fish-Eaters and the Meat-Eaters. He argues that instead of squabbling with one another, the Fish-Eaters must stand united against the Meat-Eaters:

Part 1

So it was that the tribe was left without eyes or guards. We had not the strength of sixty. We had no strength at all. So we held a council and made our first laws. I was but a cub at the time, but I remember. We said that, in order to be strong, we must not fight one another, and we made a law that when a man killed another him would the tribe kill. We made another law that whoso stole another man's wife him would the tribe kill. We said that whatever man had too great strength, and by that strength hurt his brothers in the tribe, him would we kill that his strength might hurt no more. For if we let his strength hurt, the brothers would become afraid and the tribe would fall apart, and we would be as weak as when the Meat-Eaters first came upon us and killed Boo-oogh. (1569)

As with the insistence upon justice in the Klondike stories, in these men's hearts the law (and community) is stronger than any one man or interest—even the superman: "For we were the law, all of us, and no man was greater than the law." Yet ". . . it is not easy to make a tribe" (1570).

Bug is "singer of songs for the king." Bug is "small and ungainly of face and limb and excelled not in work or deed." But he loves the comforts of his position and sings for his snug place by the fire and the best marrow bones. Singing songs is "a way to do nothing and be fat" (1574). As an obverse of the honest Old Long Arm, Bug inspires and cajoles the tribe with his singing; when they grumble he sings new songs. The story brilliantly demonstrates how society and language develop in relation and opposition to each other. In the end, Bug's masters manage to quash opposition and make Old Long Arm and his friends pariahs, but the old man's nobility—like his story—outlives him.

The most important use of language as a political instrument is the social metaphor of the Bee. Bug's frenetic "Song of the Bees" incites the tribe to murder a dissenter, Split-Nose, who wants to stop fighting the Meat-Eaters and instead add that tribe's strength to their own. Bug, wasp, bee—how should people live? With Bug's masters in the ascendancy, London expresses pessimism about easy fixes to such an insect-like society's ills. In a letter to the Central Labor Council of Alameda County, he wrote that "[s]trength lies in comradeship and brotherhood, not in a throat-cutting struggle where every man's hand is against every man" (*Letters*, 515), but here the strength of the strong does not prevail as Old Long Arm hopes. What "the strength of the strong" really means is open to debate, since the insect metonymy calls into question the notion of the "tribe" over the individual.

London's best-known socialist story is "South of the Slot" (1909). Like the earlier story "The Benefit of the Doubt," this is a tale about trading places; it is also comparable to *The People of the Abyss*, as the hero, Freddie Drummond, a well-published college professor of sociology, goes slumming for his research on "the literature of progress" (*Complete*, 1580). Drummond enters a world that is at first strange, but he becomes part of it. Drummond leaves the upper class for the lower, becoming "Big Bill" Totts, labor leader (and an allusion to "Big Bill" Haywood). Drummond/Totts writes then lives, first writing favorably of business (progressivism); in contrast, London, one might say, lived then wrote, but, like Bill, spun discontent against political overlords of whatever stripe.

Drummond becomes astonished at "his own fluidity" as he enters the working-class world. "From doing the thing for the need's sake, he came to doing the thing for the thing's sake. . . . From acting outraged feelings, Freddie Drummond, in the role of his other self, came to experience genuine outrage" (1585). Adaptability, residing in the "other self" or dual personality, is related to London's interest in atavism, as in "When the World Was Young." Drummond illustrates London's characteristic notion that finding one's true self promotes the cause of justice. The story also argues that people can be educated to see the evils of capitalism around them. What changes Drummond, however, is more conventional than political: the love of a woman. Mary Condon engages the reader with London's romance tradition rather than keeping the emphasis upon Drummond's awareness of the class struggle.[61]

The Sympathetic Hero

"The Apostate" (1904) is London's most provocative story of social injustice, focusing upon child labor and the hero's eventual escape from servitude. Johnny is a starved, sickly boy who exists only to work in the garment factory in order to keep himself, his mother, and his youngest brother—who is spared Johnny's sacrifice—alive. In the end he becomes ill, and in the clarity illness briefly affords him, he sees the truth about his situation and flees into the countryside on a freight train. It is both a depressing portrait of the life-numbing reality of child labor as well as a romantic American escape from such slavery. In this tale an unbeliever in freedom becomes a believer in himself—but at the same time an apostate to the laws of wage slavery.

London valued hard work, but not the kind poor Johnny has to do; Johnny, to the reader's horror, is a little automaton:

Part 1

He was the perfect worker. He knew that. He had been told so, often. It was a commonplace, and besides it didn't seem to mean anything to him any more. From the perfect worker he had evolved into the perfect machine. When his work went wrong, it was with him as with the machine, due to faulty material. It would have been as possible for a perfect nail-die to cut imperfect nails as for him to make a mistake.

And small wonder. There had never been a time when he had not been in intimate relationship with machines. Machinery had almost been bred into him, and at any rate he had been brought up on it. Twelve years before, there had been a small flutter of excitement in the loom room of this very mill. Johnny's mother had fainted. They stretched her out on the floor in the midst of the shrieking machines. A couple of elderly women were called from their looms. The foreman assisted. And in a few minutes there was one more soul in the loom room than had entered by the doors. It was Johnny, born with the pounding, crashing roar of the looms in his ears, drawing with his first breath the warm, moist air that was thick with flying lint. He had coughed that first day in order to rid his lungs of the lint; and for the same reason he had coughed ever since.

He had a way of accepting things. (*Complete*, 1116)

Johnny's life is circumscribed by lack of sleep, lack of food, and endless toil:

There was no joyousness in life for him. The procession of the days he never saw. The nights he slept away in twitching unconsciousness. The rest of the time he worked, and his consciousness was machine consciousness. Outside this his mind was a blank. . . . He was a work-beast. He had no mental life whatever; yet deep down in the crypts of his mind, unknown to him, were being weighed and sifted every hour of his toil, every movement of his hands, every twitch of his muscles, and preparations were making for a future course of action that would amaze him and all his little world. (1124)

The story uses darkness throughout, and it focuses almost exclusively on eating and sleeping and working in darkness until the end when Johnny's sudden awareness of his situation hits like a thunderbolt. From being "one of a multitude that pressed onward through the dark" (1115), he turns unsentimental about his family, but romantic about nature, as symbolized by the lone tree he sees growing across the street—a metonymy for himself that represents hope. As he tells his mother that he is going to leave, "the tree across the street appeared with dazzling brightness on his inner vision. It seemed to lurk just under his eyelids, and he could see it whenever he wished" (1127). As he did in earlier tales, London used the sun here as an index of closeness to divine justice and rebirth.

Tom King in "A Piece of Steak" (1909) is only a slightly less sympathetic working-class hero. Based on a broken-down Australian boxer, Tom King is a deformed but tragic hero, an emblem of youth versus old age:

> But it was Tom King's face that advertised him unmistakably for what he was. It was the face of a typical prize-fighter; of one who had put in long years of service in the squared ring and, by that means, developed and emphasized all the marks of the fighting beast. It was distinctly a lowering countenance, and, that no feature of it might escape notice, it was clean-shaven. The lips were shapeless, and constituted a mouth harsh to excess, that was like a gash in his face. The jaw was aggressive, brutal, heavy. The eyes, slow of movement and heavy-lidded, were almost expressionless under the shaggy, indrawn brows. Sheer animal that he was, the eyes were the most animal-like feature about him. They were sleepy, lion-like—the eyes of a fighting animal. The forehead slanted quickly back to the hair, which, clipped close, showed every bump of a villainous-looking head. A nose, twice broken and moulded variously by countless blows, and a cauliflower ear, permanently swollen and distorted to twice its size, completed his adornment, while the beard, fresh-shaven as it was, sprouted in the skin and gave the face a blue-black stain. (1629)

Tom King is a "professional," and life is just a game to be played. He must play the game of survival, as he fights for meat "for his mate and cubs" (1630). Once King was on top; he was "Youth Eternal" (1635). But now he only has the "wisdom bred of long, aching fights" (1638). The story is somewhat understated, but King is still ennobled. One of his important attributes is that he feels pity for old "Stowsher Bill" who cried in the dressing room long ago when King was young. If Bill had had his epiphany sooner, perhaps he, like Johnny, could have escaped the "game" of exploitation.

The Ironic Narrator

In "Just Meat" (1906), a pair of down-and-dirty robbers and murderers play a game of survival as each plots to kill the other and take the haul of jewels: " 'Look here, Jim,' [Matt] snarled, 'You've got to play square.

If you do me dirt, I'll fix you. Understand? I'd eat you, Jim. You know that. I'd bite right into your throat an' eat you like that much beefsteak' " (*Complete*, 1193). They debate the value of jewels they have stolen: What is the value of something in the marketplace of the living? " 'Maybe stealin' won't be necessary in the life to come' " (1197), they muse, but there is no life to come in a world in which we are "just meat." Poisoning each other's food, they die together with spasms and accusations:

> He tried to soliloquize, to be facetious, to have his last grim laugh at life, but his lips made only incoherent sounds. . . . Another paroxysm had begun. And in the midst of the paroxysm, with his body and all the parts of it flying apart and writhing and twisting back again into knots, he clung to the chair and shoved it before him across the floor. The last shreds of his will were leaving him when he gained the door. He turned the key and shot back one bolt. He fumbled for the second bolt, but failed. Then he leaned his weight against the door and slid down gently to the floor. (1200)

The story works by drawing the irony of wanting a better life with the reality such an unchecked desire creates, worlds apart from the careful deliberations of social visionaries like the elders of the Northland Indian tribes or Old Long Arm. This street-level view of survival is as naturalistic as anything London ever set in the frozen Northland. The ironies of the "get-rich-quick" method of social advancement are wrenching indeed.

"The Unparalleled Invasion" (1907) must be recognized as one of London's most effective tales—*if* the irony is comprehended. The Western powers' foolhardiness and bloodthirstiness in deciding to use germ warfare against an ever-increasing Chinese population is treated with marked cynicism:

> And then began the great task, the sanitation of China. Five years and hundreds of millions of treasure were consumed, and then the world moved in—not in zones, as was the idea of Baron Albrecht, but heterogeneously, according to the democratic American program. It was a vast and happy intermingling of nationalities that settled down in China in 1982 and the years that followed—a tremendous and successful experiment in cross-fertilization. We know to-day the splendid mechanical, intellectual, and art output that followed.
>
> It was in 1987, the Great Truce having been dissolved, that the ancient quarrel between France and Germany over Alsace and Lorraine recrudesced. The war-cloud grew dark and threatening in April, and on April 17 the Convention of Copenhagen was called. The representatives

of the nations of the world being present, all nations solemnly pledged themselves never to use against one another the laboratory methods of warfare they had employed in the invasion of China. (1245–46)

"The Unparalleled Invasion" reflects some of the qualities London admired in Eastern peoples, and it further displays his suspicion of the Western governments' self-proclaimed humanistic values.

To illustrate the gap between East and West, London chose to dwell upon the fact that the two sides have no common speech:

> What they had failed to take into account was this: *that between them and China was no common psychological speech.* Their thought-processes were radically dissimilar. There was no intimate vocabulary. The Western mind penetrated the Chinese mind but a short distance when it found itself in a fathomless maze. The Chinese mind penetrated the Western mind an equally short distance when it fetched up against a blank, incomprehensible wall. It was all a matter of language. There was no way to communicate Western ideas to the Chinese mind. . . . Back and deep down on the tie-ribs of consciousness, in the mind, say, of the English-speaking race, was a capacity to thrill to short, Saxon words; back and deep-down on the tie-ribs of consciousness of the Chinese mind was a capacity to thrill to its own hieroglyphics; but the Chinese mind could not thrill to short, Saxon words; nor could the English-speaking mind thrill to hieroglyphics. The fabrics of their minds were woven from totally different stuffs. They were mental aliens. (1234–35)

Again the issue is speaking and reading: codes are different, and can be misread or misunderstood, as in so many of London's stories. This tale plays with the reader's expectations, for the focus on the dangers of China is shifted to the dangers presented by the West. London's story is a strident warning against race hatred and its paranoia, and an alarm sounded against an international policy that would permit and encourage germ warfare.[62] It is also an indictment of imperialist governments per se.

"The Princess" (1916) is one of the handful of tales that marked London's return to short story writing after a four-year hiatus. It is a late flowering both of London's capacity for social realism and his capacity for irony. Grotesquely funny, the story relates the degenerate lives and salvation of three one-armed stewbums, two of whom dream of a magical "Princess." Alcoholism is "the terrible one," but through their alcoholic communion comes their hope of companionship and hope of hope itself, even for misfits with "cave-man's weapons" (*Complete*, 2463) and terrible faces:

What was visible of the face looked as if at some period it had stopped a hand-grenade. The nose was so variously malformed in its healed brokenness that there was no bridge, while one nostril, the size of a pea, opened downward, and the other, the size of a robin's egg, tilted upward to the sky. One eye, of normal size, dim-drawn and misty, bulged to the verge of popping out, and as if from senility wept copiously and continuously. The other eye, scarcely larger than a squirrel's and as uncannily bright, twisted up obliquely into the hairy scar of a bone-crushed eyebrow. And he had but one arm. (2462)

London's understatement—saving the worst for last—is typical of the folktale quality of this story of "healed brokenness."

The men gathered around the crude campfire exchange draughts of "alki" and river water and pretend by turns to be of noble birth, telling their individual tales of degeneration. "Fatty," who says his real name is "Percival Delaney," proffers his claim of being of good family "not unknown at Oxford once upon a time," but he "played ducks and drakes at home and sported out over the world," engaging in polo, steeplechase, boxing, wrestling, and swimming. He describes himself as having been "some figure of a man before I lost my shape. Women turned their heads to look when I went by. The women! God bless them!" (2466). But he is a match for the others, including "Whiskers," whose people came "over with the Conqueror" and "Slim," who claims to be "Bruce Cadogan Cavendish" (2466), but who is the most menacing of the three.

Each man tells how he lost his arm; for the first two tellers, this involves a tale of a woman who almost saved him from his present life of ruin. Fatty goes first. While adventuring in the South Seas he came to Talofa, called "The Island of Love," and met Tui-nui, the only offspring of the aged king. He calls her a "goddess of love" worthy of Phidias or Praxiteles, and they inhabit a "sweet lover's inferno" during "swooning tropic nights" (2467). He wrestles with island champions to impress her and dives with her on the reef ten fathoms down to catch squid. He saves her from a ferocious tiger shark, losing his arm in the process but gaining her as his bride, until the day comes when he is thrust out by the French colonizers: "the wooden shoe going up and the polished heel descending" (2470), as he puts it.

Then we hear from Whiskers. Employing even more the tone of Twain's King and Duke, Whiskers relates how he came from a wealthy family that gave him every indulgence. He too found a Polynesian princess to marry, this time on Jolly Island, known by the locals as Manatomana (a nice joke of London's) or "The Island of Tranquil Laughter." Whiskers tells of the king, who has driven away the missionaries and traders, but finally invites everyone back for a "general love-fest" (2472) and proclaims religious liberty. Meanwhile, Whiskers has fallen in love with his "ethereal" daughter: "Hers was the sweetness of the mountain rose, the gentleness of the dove. And she was all of good as well as all of beauty, devout in her belief in her . . . worship." He is transformed by marriage with her from a drunk into a paragon of the church, but she dies tragically. After her death his rival attacks him with a cane knife but Whiskers survives, minus his arm, to mourn forever the "dear dust of my Princess" (2477).

Now it is Slim's turn. As the other two wait expectantly, he tells of his time on the island of Tagalag (westward of Manatomana) following his own devilish behavior at Oxford. He tells of running "blackbirds," or slaves, in his schooner in the South Pacific: "Beastly funny country over that way. . . . You've read this Sea-Wolf stuff—." After losing an entire cargo of four hundred natives in a typhoon, he and his companions are marooned on Tagalag. Maddened by their coconut-only diet, three of the men set off one at a time to the beach with some dynamite, hoping to dynamite some fish. When Slim only is left—the others having blown themselves up—he gives it a try, lighting his dynamite but throwing away the match instead of the stick.

> "Yes but . . ." Fatty suggested. "What happened then?"
> "Oh," said Slim. "Then the princess married me, of course."
> "But you were the only person left, and there wasn't any princess . . ." Whiskers cried out abruptly, and then let his voice trail away to embarrassed silence. (2483)

A social norm has been upset; an awful truth has been told. "That's right, Bruce Cadogan Cavendish, sneer as you like," Whiskers said earlier, "But I tell you that's love that I've been describing. That's all. It's love. It's the realest, purest, finest thing that can happen to a man. And I know what I'm talking about. It happened to me" (2476). This story must have meant something special to London. Here are to be found one after another of his characteristic social and psychological concerns wrapped in the guise of a joke: naturalistic depiction of class struggle and homelessness; adventure; romance; brotherhood; the saving feminine. Despite the horror of the hoboes' initial physical descriptions, the story preserves their dignity. London's punch line says it all: the two look at each other, and solemnly tie up and carry off their bundles, arm in arm. "Not until they reached the top of the embankment did they speak. 'No gentleman would have done it,' said Whiskers. 'No gentleman would have done it,' Fatty agreed" (2483).

3. Fictional Experimentation

Although he was a writer who knew "the writing game" and how to succeed at it, who made no secret of writing for cash, and who perfected certain formulas and subjects that were guaranteed to sell his books, Jack London was also one of the most radically experimental writers of his day. He wrote in virtually every genre imaginable, set his stories in far-flung locales, and invented characters of astonishing variety. What is more, through what London called his "impassioned realism"—a method Jacqueline Tavernier-Courbin has named his "naturalistic romance"—he invented a new American literary style.[63] Some of his experiments are bizarre: he was often well aware of the likelihood that a particular story would never be published, but he wrote it anyway and defended it against all comers. An excellent example is "Samuel," the story of the mysterious Margaret Henan of Island McGill, one of his most unusual and dramatic narratives. When finally published in *Bookman* in 1913 for $100, "Samuel" had been rejected by 14 other magazines, and was never placed with a British publication at all: "Why, the material in that story of 'Samuel' cost me at least $250 hard cash to acquire," he wrote John S. Phillips, "and 43 days at sea between land and land, on a coal-laden tramp-steamer. Also, it took me two weeks to write. And my wife threw in 43 days of her time helping me in making a study of the vernacular, and in writing it down and classifying it" (*Letters*, 894–95). In addition to writing the Klondike, South Seas, and socialist fiction, London also produced love stories, comedies, science fiction, fantasy, dialect tales, children's stories, even jokes, poems, and plays, as well as a variety of nonfiction. The radical experimentation came during the years 1910–1911, but there are samples of experiments throughout his story-writing career. This should not surprise us, for London's seemingly contradictory handling of such topics as race, gender, and socialism can be seen as evidence of his abiding desire to entertain conflicting points of view. He was especially interested in seeing things through the eyes of individuals different from himself, and this overcame his other inclination to present a fantasy figure of himself in his stories.

London's evolutionary philosophy helped create and support his urge to experiment in fiction. As he related to George Wharton James in an interview, commenting on his rejection of the "art for art's sake" credo of the day:

> I believe there are saints in slime as well as saints in heaven, and it depends how the slime saints are treated—upon their environment— as to whether they will ever leave the slime or not. People find fault with me for my "disgusting realism." Life is full of disgusting realism. I know men and women as they are—millions of them yet in the slime stage. But I am an evolutionist, therefore a broad optimist, hence my love for the human (in the slime though he may be) comes from my knowing him as he is and seeing the divine possibilities ahead of him. That's the whole motive of my *White Fang*. (James, 382)

Reviewing the stories published alongside London's in the magazines of the day is an exercise in extreme contrasts. London himself swore never to offer "mushy and inane" articles and stories but rather the "graphic, reportorial way I have of handling things" (*Letters*, 548–49). In a more personal moment, trying to connect more closely with his estranged daughters, he wrote Joan: "Remember that truth is the greatest thing in the world. If you will be great, you will be true. . . . Don't be afraid of being harsh. Don't be afraid of being true" (*Letters*, 1220).

His adventurous heroes and heroines and their dramatic natural settings, not to mention his frequent focus upon the brutal encounters with men and nature his characters face, drew sensationalistic attention from literary critics and newspaper reporters. Although he recognized that "I am generally accredited with exploiting brutality for brutality's sake," a view "of the reviewers and the public . . . hopeless to combat," he stated that his "really-and-truly-conscious aim . . . will be found woven into every bit of fiction I have written—the motif under the motif" (*Letters*, 496). But despite this symbolist effort, critics have never been comfortable with London's complexity; it is much more convenient to pigeonhole him. And he remains the object of our projections. Scholars who want to emphasize London as a figure of romantic nihilism are particularly prone to comical errors, as when Julian Symons writes in his foreword to the Penguin edition of *The Assassination Bureau* that London "died by his own hand in 1916 at his baronial California estate, Wolf House," when Wolf House had burned to the ground in 1913. Other distortions are more serious. For instance, Richard Gid Powers avers:

[London] was never able to root his ideas in his emotions; he never deepened attitudes into personality; he left his own soul unexamined while he mapped out the minds of others, until his life (with its sea voyages, alcoholism, and money grubbing) took on the aspect of an obsessive flight from self that he had never explored and that he finally came to fear and abhor. . . . London was a free thinker who raided the philosophies of Nietzsche, Spencer and Kidd as he once raided the oyster beds of San Francisco Bay. What he read he wrote, what he stole he sold, without any of the ideas he used tincturing his system; his mind was a faculty divorced from his personality, a sponge that he regularly squeezed for the popular magazines.[64]

London as the atavism is London as thief, brawler, drunk, sponge, money-grubber, obsessive, depressive: How, one wonders, did he ever manage to write? Although the critical tide has turned in London's favor in the last 20 years, new popular biographies continue the tradition of typecasting London as a brutish lout, sometimes proffering a sense of tragedy driven by incredulity at how the once-mighty could be brought so low. The idea that London's last years (or from 1910 on, by some accounts) were composed only of self-destruction, failure, and hack work is the biggest and most easily disproved falsehood about his career.

London's later career is hardly a vacuum—as even a cursory reading of the final few years of his fiction will show. But because an entire genealogy of biographies, beginning with Irving Stone's *Sailor on Horseback,* and to a lesser extent Joan London's angry version of her father's life, have perpetuated the myth of London as a cynical, self-destructive hack, for some of his biographers and critics he must at some point be made to seem artistically impotent. Following Stone, Andrew Sinclair, Christopher Wilson, and Kevin Starr have heavily influenced critics like Mark Seltzer and Jonathan Auerbach to perpetuate a particular reading of London: To be so successful, Jack London just couldn't have been anything—especially late in his career—other than a venal, calculating, self-created thing, someone who at the worst exhibited serious character flaws and at the best self-interest only—ALL of the time.[65] There is a strange chemistry between London and some of those who devote their careers to studying him—on the one hand a certain kind of hero worship, on the other a drive to exorcise him. Perhaps as a figure in certain imaginations he really is "too much with us."

But London was typecast in his own day, too, and he chafed at the pressure placed upon him first to conform to the tried and true formulas of romantic magazine fiction, and then later, when he was successful, to conform to the "Jack London" adventure formula. As Susan Ward points out, among the magazine editors of the day "fiction which did not follow one of the proper plot lines simply was not published. In general, popular authors of London's time had to bear in mind two fixed rules: love plots were by far the most popular, and very few plots could afford to end unhappily." Although London seemed to have gotten away with violating these rules, he was also constrained by them, as in *The Sea-Wolf*, when he was told to play up the "love interest" but play down the sex. Besides censorship—of everything from slang, portrayals of brutality, sexual innuendo, and politics—Ward notes that editors also decreed such elements as story length and level of vocabulary.[66] London complained of the "forces of suppression that so long made American literature sterile and artificial and so long fostered evil by keeping silence about it" (*Letters*, 1229–30). He was one of the writers of his day who led the revolt against sentimentalism and literary propriety; others included Edith Wharton, Frank Norris, Stephen Crane, and Theodore Dreiser. For these realistic thinkers, revolt against the genteel tradition took the form of what Van Wyck Brooks characterizes as "a vehement and even brutal affirmation of life."[67]

In *Martin Eden*, the writer-hero discovers the formula: "1) a pair of lovers are jarred apart; 2) by some deed or event they are reunited; 3) marriage bells."[68] Clearly a measure of Martin's disillusionment in the novel is because of the power such formulas have over his life. London begged Arthur T. Vance of *Woman's Home Companion*: "I'll deliver the goods, without swear-words (in the text), and do you fulfill your divinely appointed task of protecting your readers. But for goodness' sake don't turn all my good red blood to water" (*Letters*, 595). He had the occasional opportunity to protest the system, as when he was asked by the magazine *Editor* to provide advice to young writers and responded by advising them that greatness would not be achieved by merely pandering to current taste (*Letters*, 684). In a similar vein, he wrote to George Brett in defense of *The Road*, a book that Brett did not want to publish, that "IT WAS MY REFUSAL TO TAKE CAUTIOUS ADVICE THAT MADE ME" (*Letters*, 675). Thus with the limits of formula and the thrill of invention, London oscillated between conformity and experimentation. And as some of the stories discussed in this chapter demonstrate, he successfully escaped his own formulas as well as those of the editors—most of the time.

Writing by Formula

London took his writing as an art but also a craft, learned by hard apprenticeship, and developed further depth and complexity as the years went by. He worked to be a writer. His advice to fellow writers and would-be writers reflects some of the principles that shaped his own work. As an apprentice he consulted rhetorics and writing guides and had to learn grammar. He read professional journals such as the *Editor* as well as all the fiction he could. Like Martin Eden he strung ropes of vocabulary words across his room. He copied pages of successful writing by others. Once he developed his writing program, his hard apprenticeship paid off: rather than make several rough drafts, London seems to have composed his sentences in his head and revised minimally in manuscript and typescript and even less in proofs (see *Letters*, 115–17, 383–84). His casualness with regard to revision and his claim that once he finished a story he didn't see it again until it came out in print has given rise to the notion that he was a sloppy writer who didn't care about quality. His personal practice and his advice to young writers that fills much of his correspondence reveals the lie of such thinking. For example, he warned one young writer who believed he did not have to "plug" for as much as 19 hours a day:

> If you think you can jump in right now, without any apprenticeship, and lay bricks as well as a four, five, or six years' apprenticed bricklayer; if you think you can jump in on the floor and nail on shoes on ten horses as well as a man who has served a three, four, or five years' apprenticeship at shoeing horses on the floor; if you think you can jump in and nail laths, or spread plaster, or do concrete work, without previous experience. . . . [I]n short, if you think that a vastly better-paid trade than that, namely, the writing game, can be achieved in your first short story not yet written, or long story not yet written, why go ahead my boy and jump to it, and I'll pat you on the back—pat you on the back! the world will crush you in for the great genius that you are if you can do such a thing. In the meantime have a little patience and learn the trade. (*Letters*, 1239)

To another young writer he said, "Take your time. Elaborate; omit; draw; develop. Paint—paint pictures and characters and emotions—but paint, paint, draw, draw. And take your time. Spend a day on a paragraph, or on ten paragraphs" (*Letters*, 976). To Joseph Noel he wrote: "Let me tell you one thing, old man: A motif has got to stand on its own legs and deliver the goods in printed type. You talk about presenting it with warmth of argument, etc. But that's a case of hypnotism" (*Letters*, 875–76). And to his friend Blanche Partington he advised, "Rather than deal with your particular story (which I liked greatly) I'd like to give you one big general word of advice. If you are going to write at all, write regularly, every day. Work so long, or do so much, and do it every day. Or else leave it alone. Believe me, there is no other way" (*Letters*, 720–21). And despite his own willingness to experiment with characters as diverse as lepers and society matrons, London advised would-be writers to write about what they know, or rather not to write about what they don't know: "Just a word of advice," he wrote one correspondent, "do not laugh or sneer at love, because up to the present time evidently you have not been in love. Remember this also, and it is very important for one who wants to succeed at writing: No man can succeed who is not sincere in the things he is writing about. You cannot sneer at a thing and write about it successfully. You don't know love. Don't write about love until you do know love" (*Letters*, 1165).

London achieved great success by staying with the settings that he knew, by marketing such formula collections as *Tales of the Fish Patrol* (1905), *Smoke Bellew* (1912), and the David Grief stories of *South Sea Tales* (1911) and *A Son of the Sun* (1912), all built around a compelling central character. He planned several collections that did not come to pass, such as one he described in a telegram to Roland Phillips, of *Cosmopolitan*, in which he would take Smoke and Shorty into the South Seas and have them hunt for treasure (*Letters*, 1081). London's formula stories often suffer from having been written as a group, but they contain some undeniable gems. Further, in their *development* they nearly always evolve into the more complex forms of fully realized stories.

The version of formula writing that produced the worst results was London's portrayals of himself and Charmian as the super couple—smarter, stronger, more accomplished than anyone can possibly be. Even the most ardent of his fans blanch at some of his exaggerated portraits of himself and his wife. One of the most egregious examples is "Bunches of Knuckles" (1910), in which Boyd Duncan and his wife are "a royal pair of wanderlusters" (*Complete*, 1714) who are (perhaps justifiably) put over the side of their boat by their drunken, incompetent captain, whom Boyd plans to fire when they reach port. (Following the "Sol" pattern, it is Christmas day with the sun at high noon when this happens.)

Boyd Duncan was an original. At least that was the belief of his friends. Of comfortable fortune, with no need to do anything but take his comfort, he elected to travel about the world in outlandish and most uncomfortable ways. Incidentally, he had ideas about coral-reefs, disagreed profoundly with Darwin on that subject, had voiced his opinion in several monographs and one book, and was now back at his hobby, cruising the South Seas in a tiny, thirty-ton yacht and studying reef-formations.

His wife, Minnie Duncan, was also declared an original, inasmuch as she joyfully shared his vagabond wanderings. Among other things, in the six exciting years of their marriage, she had climbed Chimborazo with him, made a three-thousand-mile winter journey with dogs and sleds in Alaska, ridden a horse from Canada to Mexico, cruised the Mediterranean in a ten-ton yawl, and canoed from Germany to the Black Sea across the heart of Europe. (1713–14)

You would think that with all of the exciting and dangerous things Jack and Charmian *did* do, London wouldn't need to take things quite so far in this story. Boyd and Minnie float on a buoy in shark-infested waters for days before being rescued and meeting up with the captain in port. In the customs office, Boyd gives the captain what he has coming, "bunches of knuckles," to the delight of his wife. This sort of unpleasant self-glorifying is the result of London not taking his own advice, given to Cloudesley Johns and others, about keeping the author out of the story.

But more typical of his formula fiction are the thematic collections. We examined the "Smoke Bellew" stories in chapter 1 and will look at the David Grief tales in chapter 4. Here, let us take up the first of the collections that London built around a central character and wrote all of a piece: *Tales of the Fish Patrol*, whose hero, modeled on London, is based on a young boy working as a summer apprentice with the Shore Patrol of San Francisco Bay before continuing his schooling. The "Fish" Patrol, as he calls it in these stories, has chartered the boy's sloop, the *Reindeer*, and he accompanies Charley, the most daring of the patrol, on expeditions to capture pirates in the Bay. These stories connect with numerous facets of London's other work: seamanship, ecological preservation, interest in the diverse ethnic groups of the Bay area, the opposition of "sourdoughs" and "*chechaquos*," the privileging of brain over brawn— especially when it comes to tricking one's opponent instead of fighting with him—and the sense of boyish adventure mixed with real danger, as in the works of Robert Louis Stevenson. London once again succeeded with these stories partly because of the sense of authentic locale. His depiction of the many worlds of the Bay shows a strong sense of place and a fascination with the international scene, with its many competing ethnic groups.

The "Fish Patrol" stories were sold as a group to *Youth's Companion* and then Macmillan (see *Letters*, 348). Certainly they are something of a comedown after the more complex Klondike stories, and they are obviously aimed at juvenile readers in quest of manhood, but they teach the same codes of justice and imagination as the Klondike tales, although community is less easy to define in them. Law and order is the property of the whites in the stories; ethnic "others" are the criminals to be apprehended. But as in the Klondike stories, justice must be established over lawlessness in order that one community include everyone, despite nationality, for clearly a code is shared by police and criminals. The two groups have established certain rules pertaining to pursuit and capture that reveal a shared set of values, as in "The Siege of the 'Lancashire Queen,'" in which the code clearly forbids shooting at an unarmed opponent, no matter what the circumstances. This is illustrated also in "Demetrios Contos," when the narrator describes "a sort of tacit agreement. . . between the patrolmen and the fishermen. If we did not shoot while they ran away, they, in turn, did not fight if we once laid hands on them" (*Complete*, 877).

The first of the stories of *Tales of the Fish Patrol* openly plays the race card, announcing what will be a climactic theme. "White and Yellow" (1902) shows white men besting mutinous Chinamen in their fishing boat. They "break the spirit" of the Chinese, who are led by the evil Yellow Handkerchief, a harbinger of the dangers the narrator and Charley will face in later stories. Although racialism occupies some of the later plots, overt racism does not appear again until the last of the series, "Yellow Handkerchief." "The King of the Greeks" (1902), the second tale, tells of the capture of Big Alec, a Greek fisherman who wars with the Fish Patrol but who commands their complete respect.

In "A Raid on the Oyster Pirates" (1902) the heroes pretend to be oyster pirates and work the beds, but their real aim is to steal the pirates' boats and arrest them. Their clever masquerade is a lesson to young readers: " 'Now this illustrates the value of imagination,' " Charley was saying. " 'Taft has been trying for years to get them, but he went at it with a bull strength and failed. Now we used our heads . . .' " (841). Becoming "pirates" also underscores a theme introduced in this tale, the economic angle in which the corporations who own the beds are pitted against the fishermen who work them. "The Siege of the 'Lancashire Queen' " (1904) also involves trickery along with bravery, as the Fish Patrol tries to catch some miscreants hiding on a ship by getting a special speedboat of unheard power and luring them out: " 'Of course . . .it's the other fellow's imagination, but it did the work all the same' " (853). Similarly, in "Charley's Coup" (1903), they catch a pirate ship belonging to The Swede and haul it upriver. The law of the frontier is invoked when it has to be. To the young narrator, there at first seems to be no law in the Bay; they have to be clever enough to invent means to enforce one. Trying to capture the title character of "Demetrios Contos" (1903) nearly costs the narrator his life; he is saved by Demetrios, another "King" of the Greeks. In conformity with the shared code, the patrol pays Demetrios's fine. Like some of the others, this story explores the idea of civil disobedience, of private and public justice. This latter contrast, true to London's socialist instincts, allows him to handle "race" more critically than it may first appear.

Although the communities of the Bay compete for survival, their competition is handled more objectively than in the later novel *The Valley of the Moon*, which glorifies the Anglo-Saxon pioneer at the expense of others ("Japs," "Dagos," etc.). A community exists on the sea that is absent among the farmers of *The Valley of the Moon*, and racial attitude in the Fish Patrol stories is dependent not on the race of the other but whether or not he fits into the larger code of the community:

> It must not be thought, from what I have told of the Greek fishermen, that they were altogether bad. Far from it. But they were rough men, gathered together in isolated communities and fighting with the elements for a livelihood. They lived far away from the law and its workings, did not understand it, and thought it tyranny. Especially did the fish laws seem tyrannical. And because of this, they looked upon the men of the fish patrol as their natural enemies. (874)

But this antagonism is accompanied by a mutual respect for each other and for the wit and ingenuity—not to mention seamanship—that each side employs in order to do its business: " 'Imagination,' I answered. 'It's what you're always preaching—keep thinking one thought ahead of the other fellow, and you're bound to win out' " (878). These men share the love of the sea above all:

> I was as wildly excited as the water. The boat was behaving splendidly, leaping and lurching through the welter like a race-horse. I could

hardly contain myself with the joy of it. The huge sail, the howling wind, the driving seas, the plunging boat—I, a pygmy, a mere speck in the midst of it, was mastering the elemental strife, flying through it and over it, triumphant and victorious. (881)

This happy tone changes in the last story of the collection, as though the racial distastefulness of "White and Yellow" has been simmering uneasily all along. The title character of "Yellow Handkerchief" (1903) is the Chinese pirate of the first story who stalks the narrator in order to kill him in this last tale. The metonymy of the yellow handkerchief is a telling racial symbol, for it hides the man behind the stereotype. The narrator fears and hates the Chinese; they are wicked tricksters who try to "writhe and squirm out of [the] ropes with which they were bound" (891), tricksters of an entirely different order than the more Huck Finn-like tricks the narrator and Charley pull off. The chief pirate is a "yellow barbarian" (892) on the order of Stevenson's pirates in *Treasure Island*. But though we may see the Asians in this story as stereotypes out of juvenile fiction, they are part of London's pattern of often demonizing Asians: "[F]or the Chinese were a different race from mine, and from what I knew I was confident that fair play was no part of their make-up" (890), the narrator confides. "I was familiar enough with the Chinese character to know that fear alone restrained them. But what plan they offered in place of Yellow Handkerchief's murderous one, I could not make out." Thus if there is one major fault in the formula fiction, this story makes it dramatically apparent: anything that London handled clumsily elsewhere will be more clumsily handled in a set of stories bound together by a "sale"; that is, where London's racial views were most likely to be expressed crudely is here where his artistic judgment fell prey to his formulaic plans. This contrasts sharply with the experimental stories that followed later in his career.

The California Experiment

Even though London's life in the bucolic setting of Sonoma Valley may seem far from an experimental context, in fact his ranching innovations and his new approaches to writing went hand-in-hand. Branching out from his San Francisco and Oakland friends and following Charmian into the countryside was a tremendous step for London to take, and it is no accident that soon after buying his first pieces of land and settling into his new life he and Charmian conceived the idea of the *Snark* voyage.

This was not really an escape from the countryside but in a sense a continuation of the experimental impulse that led London out of his old life to Charmian and the Valley of the Moon. It was also, as his first mention of it to George Brett makes clear, a writer's decision: "I never more ardently desired to do anything in my life. I don't care very much for ordinary travel anyway, and this certainly would be anything but ordinary. And Lord! Lord! think of the chance to write without interruption when I am between-ports. First rattle out of the box, 2100 miles sailing from San Francisco to Honolulu, and then the long stretch down to the South Seas, and some time ultimately, the stretch across the Atlantic to New York City!" (*Letters*, 505). His search culminated in the Hawaiian stories of 1916. Like California, Hawaii[69] became a literal and spiritual home for London, a place where his imagination could work at its best. Following the *Snark* voyage, London returned to Glen Ellen in 1908 to recuperate from an assortment of tropical illnesses and begin ranching.

Visitors to London's Beauty Ranch near Glen Ellen, California, find this area of Sonoma Valley one of the most beautiful and tranquil places in the state, with its sweet, soft air; groves of olive trees and green and golden hillsides of grapevines; majestic forest of conifers, oaks, madrone, and manzanita scattered with the "fairy rings" of the Douglas firs; sparkling streams; and the ever-changing light and shadow of the surrounding mountains. Local legend has it that the Indians named this scenic area the Valley of the Moon; London was drawn to its natural beauties and to the languid, idyllic charm of its small villages. He eventually acquired 1,400 acres and in the space of five years built extensively on his property, vigorously experimenting with new growing methods for his crops, progressive methods of breeding and housing livestock, and an overall program of conservation and recycling of land and farm products. The Londons lived in the small cottage on the farm property until they built their rustic mansion, Wolf House, which burned to the ground in August 1913, shortly before they were to move in. Nevertheless, the Londons continued to live and entertain on the ranch as generously as they had before. As ranch foreman, London's sister, Eliza, provided invaluable assistance in maintaining London's plans; upon Charmian's death, the estate passed into the hands of Eliza's son, Irving Shepard. Today, London's heir and literary executor is I. Milo Shepard, Irving's son. Most of the ranch is now Jack London State Historic Park, which includes the buildings he used and erected, the cottage in which he lived for most of his time there—now newly restored and reopened, as well as the home Charmian built after her husband's death, The House of Happy Walls, now a museum. The rest is the Jack London Vineyards, a world-class vineyard operated by Shepard.

A trio of California stories expresses London's deep feelings for the countryside and his evolution of identity within it. "All Gold Canyon" (1905) is his first California pastoral story—and his strongest. The relation of human beings to the nature around them is the theme in this portrait of original sin. Into the garden of a valley in the Sierras come two men seeking gold. There is a murder. When the survivor departs, nature once again claims its valley. Only its mountain is scarred by a rough mine, and its tranquility is broken by the desperate act that has taken place in its heart. With the sound of his metal-trimmed boots clashing against the rocks, the hero, Bill, loudly singing a hymn, bursts through the "green screen" of the little valley (*Complete*, 1019) and into the clearing. London opened the story, however, with the scene a moment before Bill's invasion, a description full of feminine sexuality and fecundity that will be assaulted by the crudity of Bill's mission:

> It was the green heart of the canyon, where the walls swerved back from the rigid plan and relieved their harshness of line by making a little sheltered nook and filling it to the brim with sweetness and roundness and softness. Here all things rested. Even the narrow stream ceased its turbulent down-rush long enough to form a quiet pool. Knee-deep in the water, with drooping head and half-shut eyes, drowsed a red-coated, many-antlered buck.
>
> On one side, beginning at the very lip of the pool, was a tiny meadow, a cool, resilient surface of green that extended to the base of the frowning wall. Beyond the pool a gentle slope of earth ran up and up to meet the opposing wall. Fine grass covered the slope—grass that was spangled with flowers, with here and there patches of color, orange and purple and golden. Below, the canyon was shut in. There was no view. The walls leaned together abruptly and the canyon ended in a chaos of rocks, moss-covered and hidden by a green screen of vines and creepers and boughs of trees. Up the canyon rose far hills and peaks, the big foothills, pine-covered and remote. And far beyond, like clouds upon the border of the sky, towered minarets of white, where the Sierra's eternal snows flashed austerely the blazes of the sun. (1017)

The passage continues: "There was no dust in the canyon. The leaves and flowers were clean and virginal" (1017). But all this is to change. As Bill slowly and surely excavates a "V" shape into the face of the mountain, working to get closer and closer to its heart of gold, we begin to see that he is not necessarily the antithesis of the life of the canyon but is part of it, is "human" nature within the natural setting. His efforts are "natural" in that sense. Although he does not share in the canyon's "spirit of peace that was not of death, but of smooth-pulsing life, of quietude that was not silence, of movement that was not action, of repose that was quick with existence without being violent with struggle and travail," and does not know "the spirit of the peace of the living, somnolent with the easement and content of prosperity, and undisturbed by rumors of far wars," he does partake of the insistent life force that London paints so well in his descriptions of the setting (1017).

Unlike the man who sneaks up on him and tries to murder him, Bill is neither good nor evil. Although he despoils the lovely canyon, the story's conclusion makes it clear that the vegetation will grow back—is already starting to do so—and the life of the canyon will go on. London describes Bill as an Adam, an everyman, in his garden: "He stood erect, seeing wide-eyed the secrecy of the scene and sensuously inhaling the warm, sweet breath of the canyon-garden through nostrils that dilated and quivered with delight" (1020). He is also described as being like a shepherd, for "he herded his flock of golden specks so that not one should be lost" (1021). Singing his hymn about the "sweet hills of grace" and talking to himself and "Mr. Pocket," the mine, in a humorous dialect of mountain men, Bill goes about his work.

As in the Klondike stories, there is a great deal of attention paid to the movements of the sun; for instance, the sun witnesses the murder of Bill's assailant: "The sun was at its zenith when the man forced the horses at the screen of vines and creepers. . . . 'The measly skunk!' he said, and disappeared" (1033). Interestingly, in light of the patterns associated with the sun and judgment in the earlier tales, here the number seven reappears, with seven specks of gold in Bill's first pan. There are some other intriguing Greek references: the bees are called "Sybarites" (1018), who were a wealthy people defeated by the treachery of their neighbors, the Crotons, miners of silver who littered the formerly beautiful landscape of Sybaris with their slag heaps. Defeating the Sybarites, the Crotons plowed their land under with salt and redirected a river to flow through it, hoping to obliterate all traces of the once-pristine landscape. "All Gold Canyon" blends the Klondike themes of brotherhood (here presented negatively, as in "In a Far Country"), gold-hunting, and justice, resituated in the gentle California landscape.

"Planchette" (1905) has a totally different tone from "All Gold Canyon." It is a strange, unsatisfying story of the supernatural, "evil spirits," "obsession" (1047), and atavism ("man's inheritance from the wild and howling ages when his hairy, apelike prototype was afraid of the dark and personified the elements into things of fear" [1060]). Autobiographically it dwells on Jack and Charmian's decision to move to the country and marry. The protagonist, Chris Dunbar, is a personable, handsome young man, in love with Lute Story—but there is a problem. He won't marry her, and he won't say why. Although "[t]he mystery trembled for utterance" (1040), Chris will not reveal it. "Planchette" was written during London's divorce and just before his remarriage to Charmian. The story's mysteries have to be addressed within this biographical context. They have everything to do with London's own sense of his own "story."

The title refers to a ouijalike game of divining answers to questions from "spirits," which move the "planchette" to reveal what the players wish to know—or don't wish to know. As Chris, Lute, and Lute's Aunt Mildred and Uncle Robert—the latter two modeled on Roscoe and Ninetta Eames, Charmian's aunt and uncle—amuse themselves in the evenings with the game, it gets progressively more eerie, culminating in threats to Chris Dunbar's life from the ghost of Lute's father. London seems to be recalling his own family in these scenes, with the occult coming from Flora and the authoritative super-ego from Charmian's father. Like London, Chris and Lute think of themselves as progressive, twentieth-century people, and Chris scoffs at the planchette game as "medievalism" (1058). Lute, however, fears its truths, and through her London seems to be making a case for the power of the unconscious and the dangers of ignoring its promptings: For Lute the threat brings on a vision. While the rest argue pro and con and the air is filled with phrases—"psychic phenomena," "self-hypnotism," "residuum of unexplained truth," and "spiritism"—she revives mentally the girlhood pictures she had conjured of this soldier-father she had never seen (1059). She confesses to Chris, " 'I am not so sure. Science may be too dogmatic in its denial of the unseen. The forces of the unseen, of the spirit, may well be too subtle, too sublimated, for science to lay hold of, and recognize, and formulate.' " Chris responds, " 'I don't know all the mysteries of the mind. . . . But I believe such phenomena will all yield to scientific explanation in the not distant future' " (1063). Lute's devotion to Chris causes her to ignore her insights and go along with his version of things; her devotion to him, in a sense, kills him, although his egotism is as much to blame.

The story itself is a reenactment of Jack making up his mind to marry Charmian. With his divorce, he was breaking conventional codes and (as

107

revealed in letters between him and Carrie Sterling, wife of his friend George) was about to lose the respect of his friends for deserting Bessie and his children. Thus, he had to talk himself into Charmian and the countryside. In the story, the failure to honor love actually kills Chris Dunbar. Warned against riding his horse "Washoe Ban," the name of London's own horse, Chris is flung off and the horse breaks its spine. A few days later, riding toward Napa over Nun's Canyon, his new horse, Comanche, suddenly flings itself and its rider over a cliff in a suicidal plunge. Lute sees "her father dealing the spectral blow that had smashed Comanche down in mid-leap and sent horse and rider hurtling over the edge" (1071); she calls out hopelessly to her dead lover.[70]

Like a number of the stories written at this same time—"Goliah," "The Apostate," and "The Sun-Dog Trail"—"Planchette" poses a series of questions about interpretation, as when we reinterpret "Goliah" after discovering that a young boy has written it, or we find in "The Sun-Dog Trail" that one can't always really "interpret" a given picture. Through his inner struggles with identity and meaning, London was also evolving a more sophisticated set of questions about writing and a tendency not to draw clear conclusions. In "Planchette," he asks a lot of questions about his values, the value of his work, levels of meaning, self-reflexivity and reference, and authorial power. "Planchette" signals a new direction in his writing, a turn toward greater questioning of many generally accepted values and a turn inward toward the unconscious depths he would increasingly seek out.

"Brown Wolf" (1906), the third California story, reflects a sense of peace and of resolution between the male and female characters who represent Jack and Charmian, Walt and Madge Irvine, and appears to be a confirmation of the values decided upon in "Planchette." The key to "Brown Wolf" is the classical reference to Orpheus. Calling Brown Wolf, Walt says he outwhistles Orpheus (*Complete*, 1073), but at the end, when the dog's true owner appears to claim him, the dog departs with him for the Klondike and doesn't look back. Orpheus attracted and tamed wild beasts with his music but looked back upon retrieving his wife from Hades and lost her a second time. In this modern rendition of loss, Brown Wolf is reunited with gold prospector Skiff Miller, who offers only hard work, hard living, and none of the comforts the Irvines have showered upon the dog: for Brown Wolf the Irvines "were as dead" (1086).

This may seem to be merely a sentimental version of London's theme of atavism (since he had a dog named Brown Wolf), but like "Planchette" the story reveals London's important evolving attitudes toward his writing. Answering Madge's jibe that his whistling is less like Orpheus's than a "street-arab," Walt rejoins:

> "Poesy does not prevent one from being practical—at least it doesn't prevent *me*. Mine is no futility of genius that can't sell gems to the magazines."
>
> He assumed a mock extravagance, and went on:
>
> "I am no attic singer, no ballroom warbler. And why? Because I am practical. Mine is no squalor of song that cannot transmute itself, with proper exchange value, into a flower-crowned cottage, a sweet mountain-meadow, a grove of redwoods, and orchard of thirty-seven trees, one long row of blackberries and two short rows of strawberries, to say nothing of a quarter of a mile of gurgling brook. I am a beauty-merchant, a trader in song, and I pursue utility, dear Madge. I sing a song, and thanks to the magazine editors I transmute my song into a waft of the west wind sighing through our redwoods, into a murmur of waters over mossy stones that sings back to me another song than the one I sang and yet the same song wonderfully—er—transmuted." (1073–74)

Perhaps this confession points to London's desire to shed the tragic mode of his "Long Sickness" and get on with the business of living, into which writing fit nicely. In his new ranch life he would have refined and extended his materialist notion that beauty and utility are the same. But this story represents a questioning of this scheme, as though despite himself, London is still trying to refigure his life. The dog has utility to its real owner, not to the couple, for whom it only represents beauty. Labor is only what it buys, Walt thinks, but London questions that. Value lies in the work itself. The dog would much rather work hard than laze about. Separating the inherent good of work from the benefits it brings, Walt and Madge inhabit an Elysian Fields in which the offer of a life of ease, as in "Goliah," is really death. London is psychically on the trail with Skiff and Brown Wolf as much as he is at home in Glen Ellen, for that dualistic mode is the way his imagination characteristically works itself.

Experimental Point of View

As we have seen, one of the most engaging features of London's writing was his ability to enter into the minds of very different people and convincingly portray those minds in stories. Of all of London's experiments in fiction, these convincing portrayals are the most significant. His search for various views of the world included the "other" in gender, race, class, mental ability, morality, and philosophy: in ranging from character to character, he changed literary style, sometimes imitating literary forebears, other times his contemporaries, and still other times inventing new forms. These are the stories that cause novice readers of London to exclaim: "I didn't know he wrote something like this!"

"Moon-Face" (1902) is a black-humor tale in which the narrator tells how he tricks his neighbor into blowing up his dog; the narrator inexplicably hates this man, derisively calling him "moon-face" because of his happy and simple appearance. Like some of the early stories, this features another mad narrator who makes no attempt to justify or explain his sociopathic behavior. But London manages, like Edgar Allan Poe before him, to create a point of view that is persuasive and believable, if insane.

"The Madness of John Harned" (1909), while also focusing on a moment of insanity, could not be further from "Moon-Face" in development and tone. It is a richly layered, complex tale of cultural difference that interrogates both sides' presuppositions about the "other." In its cultural relativism, the story reveals the confusions of colliding beliefs and expectations between Latinos and Anglos, with the plot overlaid by a love triangle. John Harned is a wealthy American who is visiting Ecuador. He falls in love with the beautiful but remote Maria Valenzuela, who is also the object of interest for several of the Ecuadorians in the story. At a bullfight, John Harned argues with the Ecuadorians about the relative merits of bullfighting versus boxing. When one of the horses is gored, Harned seems to go berserk and starts a fight that results in his own death and the death of several soldiers.

The narrator of "The Madness of John Harned"—the talkative, self-justifying, self-interested Manuel Jesus de Patino—is one of London's best narrators. Through fine control of syntax and delivery that linguistically mimics Spanish as well as conveys de Patino's class and personality, London gives this unreliable perspective a lively and engaging, if not persuasive, voice: "I am Ecuadoriano, true, but I am Spanish. I am Manuel Jesus de Patino. I own many haciendas, and ten thousand Indians are my slaves, though the law says they are free men who work by freedom of contract" (1648). One wonders whom de Patino sees as his audience, since he uses markers of intimacy in his speech ("You know the way . . ."). He hints that his audience is Anglo— "Yes, I believe in God. I am not pagan like many of you English" (1648)—and he seems genuinely puzzled by Harned's behavior and by cultural differences in general, but he seems also to be addressing an audience of his peers.

De Patino is as fascinated with Maria as Harned is; on that the two men could agree. She is described with images of Cleopatra and Circe: "Women like Maria Valenzuela are born once in a hundred years. They are of no country and no time. They are what you call universal. They are goddesses" (1647). The opening images in general—of Pizzaro, slaves, savages, Cleopatra, Circe, damnation—reveal a deterministic universe of struggle with Maria as the prize at the top. De Patino sees this as the way things should be: "God is good. He made me an Ecuadoriano with ten thousand slaves. And when I die I shall go to God. Yes, the priests are right" (1648). But the outsider Harned sees things differently; his objection to bullfighting is that the bull "is compelled to fight" as the boxer is not, and he debates this with Maria.

> "He [the boxer] is the more brute therefore," said Maria Valenzuela. "He is savage. He is primitive. He is animal. He strikes with his paws like a bear from a cave, and he is ferocious. But the bull-fight—ah! You have not seen the bull-fight—no? The toreador is clever. He must have skill. He is modern. He is romantic. He is only a man, soft and tender, and he faces the wild bull in conflict. And he kills with a sword, a slender sword, with one thrust, so, to the heart of the great beast. It is delicious." (1648)

Who is a brute and who is "modern," boxer or bullfighter? For a sporting proposition the issue must be in doubt, according to Harned; it is "cowardly for five men to fight one stupid bull" (1656).

But there is another layer: the story is about the parallels between the bullfight and the game that is being played against Harned by the narrator and his friends, who deliberately bait him to make him look foolish in front of Maria. But the game turns into bloody, atavistic fighting among the men for the prize of the woman, and several people, including Harned (the "horned" one panned upon by his name), are killed. It ends with de Patino's puzzlement: "There is no understanding the Gringos. They are barbarians" (1659).

"The Mexican" (1911) is a good companion piece for "The Madness of John Harned." Both deal with cultural relativism and both oppose Latinos to Anglos. Once again London uses Spanish-sounding syntax and cadence to express the thoughts of Felipe and his friends. And like the prior story, "The Mexican" has a spare but symbolically effective

111

opening: "Nobody knew his history" (1983). This is the first thing we hear about the hero, Felipe Rivera, a Mexican boy who boxes for prize money in Los Angeles in order to send funds to the revolutionaries back in Mexico. What follows is a story of agonizing suspense—a classic fight story, a form that London helped invent—with a strong hero and provocative socialist message. The narrator clearly upholds the underdog by taking the side of the Mexican revolution. Although it is a fine example of London's abilities as a sports commentator, it is hardly objective sports writing, since London is so clearly on the Mexican fighter's side.

London relies upon powerful naturalistic imagery, accompanied by romantic and religious allusions: Felipe is the "breath of death" (1986), a "wild wolf," a "primitive" (1987), but also a "lamb led to slaughter" (1994). His eyes are described by one of his fellow revolutionaries as "savage as a wild tiger's." She feels that Felipe would kill her should she prove unfaithful to the revolution: "[H]e has no heart. He is as pitiless as steel, keen and cold as frost. He is like moonshine on a winter night when a man freezes to death on some lonely mountain top. I am not afraid of Diaz and all his killers; but this boy, of him am I afraid" (1985). Felipe has "a terrible passion," he is "the Revolution incarnate. . . . He is a destroying angel moving through the still watches of the night" (1987). But Felipe is noble in his motivations; he is contrasted with the baseness of the Anglo-Saxon champion Danny Ward and his handlers: " 'Why you dirty little greaser. . . . you little fool. . . . You're nobody. . . .' " (1993). " 'You little Mexican rat,' hissed from between Danny's gaily smiling lips, 'I'll fetch the yellow outa you' " (1997). Danny is "the popular hero who was bound to win" (1997), but the reader is allowed to hear what he says to Felipe under his breath as they clinch in the ring: while Danny "snarled insults unspeakable and vile in Rivera's ear" (2002), Felipe plays the "hated game of the hated Gringo" (1995) as a sacrifice for his people. Felipe is "more delicately coordinated, more finely nerved and strung than any of them. . . . The atmosphere of foredoomed defeat in his own corner had no effect on him. His handlers were Gringos and strangers. Also they were scrubs—the dirty driftage of the fight game, without honor, without efficiency" (1995).

One of the story's most effective features is its use of the flashback, as when Felipe's thoughts counterpose his mistreatment by the soldiers with his mistreatment by the boxer, Danny, and the other Anglos. Unlike Danny, who fights only for money, "the things Rivera fought for burned in his brain—blazing and terrible visions" of starving workers, a father murdered by the *jefes políticos*, his mother's body in a pile of bodies and himself slinking away "like some hunted coyote of the hills" (1996). Felipe is not an artist-hero himself, but it is significant that his father was a writer who set up his own revolutionary "printery" (1996). Like an artist, Felipe is motivated by the images he imagines as he fights; the story's cutting back and forth between past and present, inner and outer reality, and happy home memories and cruelties of Diaz is highly effective. As he fights Danny, Felipe thinks of how "the death-spitting rifles . . . seemed never to cease spitting, while the workers' wrongs were washed and washed again in their own blood" (1996). Images of the audience's brutality at the ring are juxtaposed with those of the revolution: " 'Kill'm, Danny, kill'm!' was the cry. Scores of voices took it up until it was like a war-chant of wolves. . . . The audience began to grow incensed with Rivera. Why didn't he take the licking that was coming to him?" (2001). It is important to remember that "The Mexican" was written at the same time as many of the South Seas stories such as "The Chinago" and "Mauki" that oppose young male heroes of diverse ethnicities to powerful whites who display shocking lapses of ethical and moral behavior.

"When the World Was Young" (1910) experiments with what is normal, but not in terms of insanity or cultural difference. It is the story of an atavism, a man who lives as a well-to-do businessman by day and who prowls the forest around his home by night, naked and savage, howling, running, and sleeping in the wild like his prehistoric forebears. Finally a blackmailer threatens to reveal the man's secret, and then he is transformed away from his night life by the love of a conventional woman. It is a weird tale of dual personality and of the split in class and gender: "For forty years he had tried to solve a problem that was really himself" (1695). James Ward begins to recover his "early self" through language, as he unconsciously speaks in an ancient Teutonic tongue—stretching the already taut credulity of the reader. London is having fun with the atavistic archetype, akin to Jekyll and Hyde and the werewolves of horror fiction, complete with the cliché that it is a woman who saves him. But certain elements of this story are a bit more troublesome than such formulaic genre devices suggest. For one thing, the juxtaposition of nature and capitalism in California is important in terms of London's socialism. Also, some of the images in the story are arresting enough to suggest deeper psychological explorations are going on than might first seem apparent: "The skin was smooth and hairless, but browned by sun and wind, while under it heavy muscles were knotted like fat snakes" (1690).

Another split personality is explored in "The Eternity of Forms" (1910), a story that recalls similar experiments of Poe, Hawthorne, James, and Gilman. Sedley Crayden kills his brother but does not seem to know it; he narrates the story of his own mental breakdown as he sees his brother's ghost sitting in his own chair. He keeps denying that he has killed his brother. Eventually, the narrator must sit in the chair all of the time to keep the brother's ghost away. As before, London experiments with the idea of the split personality, or the dark side of the mind. In order to reinforce the psychological complexity of his narrative, he gives us three layers of forms (texts) in the story's opening: the newspaper story on Sedley Crayden's death, a note from his personal servant, and a manuscript written by Sedley and arranged by the servant, Rudolph Heckler. Where is truth?

When both were alive, the brothers sparred with each other in philosophical arguments about what was real, whether one can make something out of nothing, the mutability of forms, and the reality of the imagination:

> I never killed my brother. Let this be my first word and my last. Why should I kill him? We lived together in unbroken harmony for twenty years. We were old men, and the fires and tempers of youth had long since burned out. We never disagreed even over the most trivial things. Never was there such amity as ours. We were scholars. We cared nothing for the outside world. Our companionship and our books were all-satisfying. Never were there such talks as we had. Many a night we have sat up till two and three in the morning, conversing, weighing opinions and judgments, referring to authorities—in short, we lived at high and friendly intellectual altitudes. (1752)

But now that his brother is dead, Sedley thinks, "I wish he would come back. Why did he go? Who can ever explain it?" (1753). Lonely and obsessed by terrors, he is sure that "form is mutable" and that "the dead do not come back," but nevertheless "I have had experiences here— here, in this very room, at this very desk, that—But wait" (1753). Even though someone is using his ink (not himself, he believes) and further tormenting him, Sedley denies that the imagination can create something out of nothing: "I never had any patience with philosophic idealists" (1755). He had made a "confession of faith" to his brother:

I assert, with Hobbes, that it is impossible to separate thought from matter that thinks. I assert, with Bacon, that all human understanding arises from the world of sensations. I assert, with Locke, that all human ideas are due to the functions of the senses. I assert, with Kant, the mechanical origin of the universe, and that creation is a natural and historical process. I assert, with Laplace, that there is no need of a hypothesis of a creator. And, finally, I assert, because of all the foregoing, that form is ephemeral. Form passes. Therefore we pass. (1755)

Sedley fears the notion that entities can be created by the mind, because if it is so, there could be a creator of all human minds. It is when his brother argued that forms are eternal, that "the human soul was itself a form, an eternal form," that Sedley picked up the poker and killed him (1756). When he comes to believe that his brother was right, he does wonder about the Creator, but jumps to the conclusion that he is a god because he has created! This story can be compared with some of London's socialist fiction that attacks the leisured class; here, two scholars have nothing better to do than debate their own existence. But it also raises questions relevant to London's own development of his artistic theory at this important time in his career. It was written a short time after the philosophical stories "When the World Was Young," "Under the Deck Awnings," and "To Kill a Man."

"War" (1910) is a little masterpiece; in its poignancy and naturalistic edge comparable to Ambrose Bierce's "An Occurrence at Owl Creek Bridge," with a tight control of style and a brevity that shocks us. The story of the death of a young soldier at the hands of an enemy soldier he has spared has a universal significance, and London wisely included no detail that would place the story in any particular national or historic context, although it has the feel of a Civil War tale. "War" opens at high noon, the time when, in the Greek tradition employed before, acts of humans take place on the stage watched over by the gods. Like "All Gold Canyon," the story sets the scene of people's acts of justice and injustice in a pristine natural setting, with brief but apt descriptions— like the "damp, fat soil" under their feet (1727). It effectively contrasts its lyrical descriptions of the natural environment that witnesses the death with the futility of the war itself. It presents a strong moral framework with its biblical references, especially the apples that the "red-cheeked" youth who is killed is gathering, alluding both to innocence and to sin (1730). Appalled at his loneliness, the youth fails to make his report; in contrast, the "ginger beard" who shoots him is surrounded by the laughter and applause of his companions, a powerful irony.

Surely one of London's unique experiments with point of view is "Told in the Drooling Ward" (1910), with its lively and personable narrator, a young mentally retarded man named Tom, who conveys the insider's view of the various inmates of "the Home," or Sonoma State Hospital: "Do you know what a micro is? It's the kind with the little heads no bigger than your fist. They're usually droolers, but they live a long time. The hydros don't drool. They have the big heads, and they're smarter. But they never grow up. They always die" (1764). Like Eudora Welty's "Sister," who tells the story of "Why I Live at the PO" and bears the ancestry of the great comic narrative voice of Huckleberry Finn, Tom is a strong, forceful, believable, likable, and all-too-human narrator. Although he is impaired, he has heart, will, compassion, and hope, the essential human moral qualities. Like Huck, his perspective reflects a wise innocence, although he is an outcast—fitting the pattern of London's portrayals of underdogs in this period. London eschews the atavism he employed so often in his portrait of Tom. Also, like Huck, Tom often says things that only the reader can fully appreciate. Don Graham calls this story "a totally original creation," and observes that except for a possible influence by Browning's dramatic monologues, "one looks in vain for analogues among American, English, and continental fiction prior to 1914."[71] Rather than treat this sort of material from the point of view of pathos, London launched out in a new direction that would not be fully exploited until the Benjy section of Faulkner's *The Sound and the Fury*, the portrayal of Lenny in Steinbeck's *Of Mice and Men*, and, above all, the "inverted world of the complete insane-asylum novel, Ken Kesey's *One Flew Over the Cuckoo's Nest*." It is "truly an anomaly in London's short fiction," for in no other work is he able to blend so successfully "three diverse elements: comedy, political commentary, and such familiar thematic matter as the search for gold" (Graham, 432–33). Graham challenges James McClintock's assertion that "London is not successful as a comic" (McClintock, 142).

Tom is a consummate storyteller, confiding that "I know a lot" (1764), and that includes a lot about the other inmates of the state asylum where he lives, the state hospital system, and the lives of the doctors and nurses. He possesses a fully realized moral sense about the outside world as well. He isn't really a "feeb," he tells us, but he is fortunate that he happens to look like one ("My mouth is funny, I know that, and it lops down, and my teeth are bad. You can tell a feeb anywhere by looking at his mouth and teeth" [*Complete*, 1764]). He can remain inside the safety of the hospital and not have to face the evils of the outside: "I'd sooner talk and be what I am" (1764). Although it is a very humorous story, in keeping with Tom's ironic construction of his feeble-minded mask, "Told in the Drooling Ward" contains serious criticism of what Tom calls "politics" in the hospital system. This is reflected in Tom's constant concern with social status within the institution, from his belief that one of the nurses wanted to marry him to his jockeying for position with the other "high-grade" feebs. Such rivalry emerges in exchanges like one with a "high-grade epilec": " 'Hello,' Joe said. 'How's droolers?' 'Fine,' I said. 'Had any fits lately?' " (1767). But despite his anxieties about his position, he shows nothing but gentle sympathy and care for those who are more "feeble" than he.

The plot of the story involves two escapes: one when Tom is placed in the home of Mr. and Mrs. Bopp, who treat him cruelly and from whom he cleverly escapes, and one when Tom and two of the "high-grade epilecs" sneak away from the hospital and set out to look for a gold mine, falling prey to the motivations of the larger society and its falsehoods. Leaving the home is an odyssey in the wilderness and a sly allusion to the Klondike tales. As in the Klondike stories, London's sympathies are with those who maintain a code of behavior in the wild, and the theme invokes the codes of justice and brotherhood, and the importance of the imagination. Upon initially leaving the asylum, Tom forgets "little Albert," the low-grade "feeb" he takes special care of, and he goes back to get him. But Albert isn't really little, and the three escapees take turns carrying him until they are exhausted. The scene in the woods around the hospital (the actual setting is in Glen Ellen, adjacent to the Beauty Ranch), causes us to question Tom's reliability, as admirable as he is, for he immediately and unthinkingly goes along with the gold mine idea, his innocence showing his vulnerability but only adding to his charm. His odyssey returns him home, where he is relieved to resume his important place in that community.

Jack and Charmian London help to get them home when they make an appearance in this story as the couple who ride by and laughingly question Tom and his friends. Amused by Tom's explanation, Mr. "Endicott," whom Tom identifies to the others as " 'the man who owns this ranch and writes books,' " wishes them luck and reminds them to " 'get back before dark.' " When Tom says, " 'But this is a real running away,' " the Endicotts laugh again, and Mr. Endicott says, " 'Good luck just the same. But watch out the bears and mountain lions don't get you when it gets dark' " (1768). Graham views the couple as representing "the unfeeling attitude toward the feeble-minded held by the general populace" (Graham, 432). But on the contrary, Endicott's good-natured warning provides the wise nudge that will send them back to where they belong in their little community. Tom remarks that "they rode away, laughing, pleasant like; but I wished he hadn't said that about the bears and mountain lions" (*Complete*, 1768), reflecting his thoughtfulness and his taking the cue. After a harrowing journey with the epileptics throwing fits, with hunger, and with night coming on, Tom must himself frighten his friends into going on: "Then I said I'd leave them and they'd get lost, and the mountain lions and bears would eat them" (1769). After that, there is no more refusal to carry Albert or move along, and the foursome make their way back to the home. In this way London reinforces his attachment to Tom's complex social and personal point of view and demonstrates both Tom's individual adaptability and care for his little community. Tom contemplates running away again for the adventure of it, but concludes that "I ain't going to run away. The drooling ward's a better snap than gold mines, and I hear there's a new nurse coming. Besides, little Albert's bigger than I am now, and I could never carry him over a mountain. And he's growing bigger every day. It's astonishing" (1770).

Difference and Community within the Feminine

From the Indian women of the Klondike stories on, London tended to see women as redemptive of men. This tendency comes to a climax late in his career in the Hawaiian stories' reliance upon the wisdom of native women and, in a different way, in the California novels' contrast of psychologically incomplete male characters with the women who try to redeem them. But London is not always certain that women possess any special moral qualities; on the contrary, he was capable of portraying women as demons. "Under the Deck Awnings" (1910) and "To Kill a Man" (1910) are tales of terrible women that were written one after the other. What sets the female characters in them apart from their good sisters who make up the majority of London's women is their membership in the upper class. Both of these stories are weirdly erotic, as the women make men perform for them out of cruelty and selfishness. The first story features a superwoman just as bad as some of London's supermen; she is the "universal woman" (1734), motivated by pride and thrill-seeking like the equally upper-crust Bertie in "The Terrible Solomons."

The story's arresting opening gets right to the point: " 'Can a man—a gentleman, I mean—call a woman a pig?' " (1732).

As the conversation continues "under the deck awnings" this question is answered. In their exploitation of the natives, the upper-class characters in the story are all worthy of the name "pig," but it is one woman in particular who stands as a metonymy for them all. Miss Caruthers, according to the narrator, is beautiful, athletic, and brilliant: "Men were wax in her hands. She melted them, or softly molded them, or incinerated them, as she pleased. There wasn't a steward, even, grand and remote as she was, who, at her bidding, would have hesitated to souse the Old Man himself with a plate of soup. You have all seen such women—a sort of world's desire to all men. As a man-conqueror she was supreme. She was a whip-lash, a sting and a flame, an electric spark. Oh, believe me, at times there were flashes of will that scorched through her beauty and seduction and smote a victim into blank and shivering idiocy and fear" (1734). This miracle of nature decides, in the time-honored custom of tourists, to amuse herself one day when the ship is in port by throwing coins into the sea so that native boys can dive for them. But there is a twist. A shark is in the water. They boys hang back, and her shipmates berate her, but she persists. One boy stares fascinated at the half-crown she holds up. She throws the coin, he dives, and "in the clear water, from the height we were above it, we saw everything. The shark was a big brute, and with one drive he cut the boy squarely in half" (1738). Despite her abilities, Miss Caruthers is without regard for humanity, and she is thus evil. Her portrait is a good counter-argument to the notion that London worshipped the superman or the superwoman.

"To Kill a Man" was finished six days after "Under the Deck Awnings" and is a fitting companion piece. Again the intersection between gender and class drives the story, this time in a game of wits between a burglar and the mistress of a house he is breaking into. Having cleverly tricked the intruder into remaining with her and talking until she can buzz for the police, the woman ends up being berated by him for her manipulation and trickery. He walks out of the door while her revolver is trained upon him. Earlier he tries to leave several times, but she promised that nothing would happen to him as she poured him drinks and asked him about his hard life. Like the Texan in "The Hobo and the Fairy," this criminal is a "man from the West" treated unfairly by the system, in this case her own husband's corporation. He gets the last word:

"You're sure bad, but the trouble with you is that you're weak in your badness. It ain't much to kill a man, but you ain't got it in you. There's where you lose out."

"Be careful what you say," she repeated. "Or else, I warn you, it will go hard with you. It can be seen to whether your sentence is light or heavy."

"Something's the matter with God," he remarked irrelevantly, "to be letting you around loose. . . . Ma'am, hell is full of women like you." (1743)

There are two sides to this woman—she is defending her life—like the protagonist of "When the World Was Young," but what finally defines her as wicked is not her actions but her obvious delight in planning to regale her friends with her trickery and her version of bravery: "To her it was an experience keen with enjoyment, and in her mind was the gossip of her crowd, and she saw notes in the society weeklies of the beautiful young Mrs. Setliffe capturing an armed robber single-handed. It would create a sensation, she was sure" (1748).

These two stories experiment by turning the tables on London's usual elevation of the feminine. Several other tales of women deepen and complete London's picture of the feminine, carrying out significant experimentation with subject matter as well as with form and technique.

"The Hobo and the Fairy" (1910) is one of London's most touching portraits of a young girl and the redemptive power of the feminine. It is also a highly experimental instance of shifting point of view. This story offers a strongly observer-based point of view, first from the perspective of the little girl, who discovers a broken-down hobo in the bushes near her home, and then from the perspective of the man himself, and we see them each through the other's eyes in the process. Beyond the initial emphasis upon the contrast of their appearances, the narrative reveals how they manage to see deeply into each other in the simplest possible way. A third character's point of view amplifies and completes the girl's and the hobo's visions of each other as members of a common human family—when the mother emerges from the house, showing no fear that her daughter is talking to the hobo, the man cannot believe he is treated so well. The story ends with the woman offering him a job, a chance to regain his livelihood and respect, and he is able to accept. The story is saved from pure sentimentality by its theme of justice, as we learn of the circumstances that have ruined the man's life. But the key is seeing the man through the eyes of the girl and the woman, a

sharp contrast to his own hopeless version of himself as he recalls his
prison days and the times that followed:

> He had known every infamy of human cruelty, and through it all he had
> never been broken. He had resented and fought to the last, until,
> embittered and bestial, the day came when he was discharged. Five
> dollars were given to him in payment for the years of his labour and the
> flower of his manhood. And he had worked little in the years that fol-
> lowed. Work he hated and despised. He tramped, begged, and stole,
> lied or threatened as the case might warrant, and drank to besotted-
> ness whenever he got the chance.
>   The little girl was looking at him when he awoke. Like a wild ani-
> mal, all of him was awake the instant he opened his eyes. The first he
> saw was the parasol, strangely obtruded between him and the sky. He
> did not start nor move, though his whole body seemed slightly to
> tense. His eyes followed down the parasol handle to the tight-clutched
> little fingers, and along the arm to the child's face. Straight and
> unblinking, he looked into her eyes, and she, returning the look, was
> chilled and frightened by his glittering eyes, cold and harsh, withal
> bloodshot, and with no hint in them of the warm humanness she had
> been accustomed to see and feel in human eyes. They were the true
> prison eyes—the eyes of a man who had learned to talk little, who had
> forgotten almost how to talk. (1774)

But the "Texan," as London calls him, is redeemed by the women's
innocence and compassion, and he is able to replace his prison memories with those of his upbringing by a pioneer-type mother. An intriguing biographical feature is that London names the little girl Joan.

The finest examples of London's experimentation with the feminine
are "Samuel" (1909) and "The Night-Born" (1910). "Samuel" is difficult to read and even more difficult to sort out thematically. Written in
a Hebrides dialect and told by a series of narrators, it poses the question, Is Margaret Henan admirable or not? Heroic or crazy? A rebel
against society and church or a lunatic? Margaret is a woman who had
many children, and when her boy named Samuel died, she had another,
then another, and called them by the same name. When the same fate
befell them, she once again, late in life, had a son and named him
Samuel. The villagers call her a witch, and gloat over the terrible result
of her pride: the last Samuel is an idiot, and because of his incessant
moaning and braying, his father goes mad and kills him and himself.
Margaret lives on, keeping to herself, but explaining in the end to the

narrator that she named them all Samuel because she liked the name. The narrator ponders:

> Was she a martyr to Truth? Did she have it in her to worship at so abstract a shrine? Had she conceived Abstract Truth to be the one high goal of human endeavor on that day of long ago when she named her first-born Samuel? Or was hers the stubborn obstinacy of the ox? the fixity of purpose of the balky horse? the stolidity of the self-willed peasant-mind? Was it whim or fancy?—the one streak of lunacy in what was otherwise an eminently rational mind? (1626–27)

The narrator is fascinated by "the marvel of it, the miraculous wonder of that woman's heroic spirit" (1623). The story charts his dialogues with the inhabitants of Island McGill, leading up to his final dialogue with Margaret. He burns to ask her the question, "Why," but unlike the knight Percival, he does ask, and he does find out the truth: beyond her simple assertion of "I like," the narrator learns and conveys with great subtlety her rebellion against the church. She named her first Samuel because she was memorializing her brother, whose marriage was annulled by the church based on a technicality; that Samuel died cursing the church.

To convey Margaret's archetypal quality as a Great Mother figure and her social role in her village, London relies on powerful imagery of her hands and eyes, which reflect her "muscular and spiritual determination" (1612). Her eyes and the allusions to the sacks of grain she carries connect her to Athena, a fitting emblem of her wisdom and mystery:

> The sunken cheeks and pinched nose told little of the quality of the life that flickered behind those clear blue eyes of hers. Despite the minutiae of wrinkle-work that somehow failed to wizen them, her eyes were clear as a girl's—clear-out-looking, and far-seeing, and with an open and unblinking steadfastness of gaze that was disconcerting. The remarkable thing was the distance between them. It is a lucky man or woman who has the width of an eye between, but with Margaret Henan the width between her eyes was fully that of an eye and a half. Yet so symmetrically molded was her face that this remarkable feature produced no uncanny effect, and, for that matter, would have escaped the casual observer's notice. . . .
>
> Again I was impressed by the enormous certitude of her. In this eternity that seemed so indubitably hers, there was time and to spare for safe-footing and stable equilibrium—for certitude, in short. No more in her spiritual life than in carrying the hundred-weights of grain

was there a possibility of a misstep or an overbalancing. The feeling produced in me was uncanny. Here was a human soul that, save for the most glimmering contacts, was beyond the humanness of me. (1612)

But the thrust of the story's allusions is biblical, beginning with the names Margaret, saint of women in childbirth, and Samuel, which means "beloved of God." This imagery helps identify Margaret's defiance of the church by honoring the divine sense within her, a sense of justice that bows to no man but only upholds her own sense of right and wrong: " 'I am beholden tull no one," she says; "I luv' wuth meself" (1613). Born on Good Friday, Margaret "paid her taxes, acknowledged her crowned rulers, and left the world alone; all she asked in return was that the world leave her alone" (1615).

Margaret Henan gives us a sense of the metaphysics of human choices and of the fundamental difference between God and a narrow, doctrinal conception of Him: " 'Do a wee but of a name change the plans o' God? .... Then wull you be thunkun' thot God thot directs the stars un their courses, an' tull whose mighty foot the world uz but a footstool, wull you be thunkun' thot he wull take a spite again' Margaret Henan an' send a bug wave off the Cape tull wash her son tull eternity, all because she was for namin' him Samuel?' " (1627). Margaret is true to herself ("I *like*" [1628]), despite her "life in tragic places," and the narrator can only respond "*Samuel!* There was a rolling wonder in the sound. Ay, there was!" (1628).

"The Night-Born" is told by another narrator amazed at the power of a woman. Trefethan tells the men gathered in the Alta-Inyo Club in San Francisco how the goldstead rotted him, and how his one chance to escape his disintegration was too much of a chance to take: "The good red blood is gone. I am a jellyfish, a huge, gross mass of oscillating protoplasm, a—a . . ." (1661). The story begins as the men talk of graft in the city government and of the death of a young prizefighter, O'Brien, "a beautiful young god" killed by the "grotesque sordidness and rottenness of man-hate and man-meanness" of the city (1660).

Middle-aged, Trefethan tells of a journey he once took to an unknown land in the North and seeking gold:

> It was a noble valley, now shut in by high canyon walls, and again opening out into beautiful stretches, wide and long, with pasture shoulder-high in the bottoms, meadows dotted with flowers, and with clumps of timber—spruce—virgin and magnificent. The dogs were packing on their backs, and were sore-footed and played out; while I was looking

for any bunch of Indians to get sleds and drivers from and go on with
the first snow. It was late fall, but the way those flowers persisted sur-
prised me. I was supposed to be in sub-arctic America, and high up
among the buttresses of the Rockies, and yet there was that everlasting spread of flowers. (1662)

Instead of the gold he had been seeking Trefethan finds a noble lady
ruling over a tribe of Indians; she tells him her story and asks him to be
her mate:

> And then I met her—Lucy. That was her name. Sign language—that
> was all we could talk with, till they led me to a big fly—you know, a
> half a tent, open on the one side where a campfire burned. It was all of
> moose-skins, this fly—moose-skins, smoke-cured, hand-rubbed, and
> golden-brown. Under it everything was neat and orderly, as no Indian
> camp ever was. The bed was laid on fresh spruce boughs. There were
> furs galore, and on top of all was a robe of swan-skins—white swan-
> skins—I have never seen anything like that robe. And on top of it, sit-
> ting cross-legged, was Lucy. She was nut-brown. I have called her a girl.
> But she was not. She was a woman, a nut-brown woman, an Amazon, a
> full-blooded, full-bodied woman, and royal ripe. And her eyes were
> blue.
>   That's what took me off my feet—her eyes—blue, not China blue,
> but deep blue, like the sea and sky all melted into one, and very wise.
> More than that, they had laughter in them—warm laughter, sun-warm
> and human, very human, and . . . shall I say feminine? They were.
> They were a woman's eyes, a proper woman's eyes. You know what that
> means. Can I say more? Also, in those blue eyes were, at the same
> time, a wild unrest, a wistful yearning, and a repose, an absolute
> repose, a sort of all-wise and philosophical calm. (1662)

As with Margaret Henan, it is Lucy's eyes that the narrator dwells upon:
"[T]hose were the most wonderful eyes I have ever seen—so very calm,
so very restless; so very wise, so very curious; so very old, so very young;
so satisfied and yet yearning so wistfully. Boys, I can't describe them.
When I have told you about her, you may know better for yourselves"
(1663). Frightened by Lucy's magnificence, Trefethan refuses her and
returns home, only to realize that he truly missed his chance at life in
rejecting her, his soul mate. But he wasn't up to it, and who would be,
one wonders? What *would* it take to live up to Lucy? Like Margaret
Henan, Lucy is a goddess; references to wheat tie her to Athena, while
swan skins connect her to Aphrodite. In her wanting to "run nights like

a wild thing, just to run through the moonshine and under the stars, to run white and naked in the darkness," she is also Artemis.

But Trefethan should have looked more closely; London does not allow Lucy's goddesslike demeanor to exist in a vacuum—she is a real woman as well as a fantasy. Her aura of divinity is cleverly counterpointed by her twanging accent, humanizing her, as her escape is set in the naturalistic context of wifely servitude in a hash house and the nitty-gritty life of the Indian camp. She is spirit and flesh, metaphysical and warmly graspable, but Trefethan cannot see both qualities at the same time. The power of "The Night-Born" is in its extraordinary amalgamation of the naturalistic and the mythic, though the weight of the story rests unmistakably in its paradisal myth of spiritual salvation.

Characteristic of such duality are the two textual sources London used for Lucy's story-within-a-story. There is the newspaper account of a woman who ran away to live with Indians that he used. London has Lucy inspired to flee by a quotation from Thoreau's "Cry of the Human":

> The young pines springing up in the corn field from year to year are to me a refreshing fact. We talk of civilizing the Indian, but that is not the name for his improvement. By the wary independence and aloofness of his dim forest life he preserves his intercourse with his native gods and is admitted from time to time a rare and peculiar society with nature. He has glances of starry recognition, to which our saloons are strangers. The steady illumination of his genius, dim only because distant, is like the faint but satisfying light of the stars compared with the dazzling but ineffectual and shortlived blaze of candles. The Society Islanders had their day-born and gods, but they were not supposed to be of equal antiquity with the . . . night-born gods. (1666)

"I knew that was where I belonged," Lucy says (1668). Knowing where you really belong is a goal London's heroes characteristically entertain, from Johnny in "The Apostate" to Bill Totts, Tom, Margaret, and Lucy, but in order to know they must be willing to throw off convention and seek self-knowledge before finding a true community with other individuals. Trefethan sadly confesses, "It would have been better had I stayed. Look at me" (1671).

4. The Pacific

"It is good to ride the tempest and feel godlike," London states in the foreword to *The Cruise of the Snark* (1908). But why would a man just married, just settled into the splendid surroundings of Sonoma Valley, who had an established and successful work life, throw caution and his bank account (at least $30,000 of it) to the winds and set out on a journey around the world in a 45-foot ketch? On April 23, 1907, just 10 years after his Klondike gold rush experience, Jack and Charmian did just that, setting sail from Oakland for Hawaii and the South Pacific. "I dare to assert," he said "that for a finite speck of pulsating jelly to feel godlike is a far more glorious thing than for a god to feel godlike. Here is the sea, the winds, and the waves of all the world. Here is ferocious environment. And here is the difficult adjustment, the achievement of which is delight to the small quivering vanity that is I. I like. I am so made. It is my own particular form of vanity, that is all."[72]

With the spontaneity of new lovers, Jack and Charmian had read Captain Joshua Slocum's book *Sailing Alone around the World* and talked over the prospect of doing the same thing. They asked Charmian's uncle, a yachtsman, to be their captain. They would defer all their plans for the ranch and, to the puzzlement of their friends, begin building a boat named for Lewis Carroll's poem "The Hunting of the Snark." Success, London believed, lay in the exaltation of such moments: "It is natural. It is a mere matter of satisfaction at adjustment to environment. . . . Life that lives life is successful, and success is the breath of its nostrils." When all about are "the great natural forces—colossal menaces, Titans of destruction, unsentimental monsters that have less concern for me than I for have for the grain of sand I crush under my foot, ... unconscious, unmerciful, and unmoral, ... the cyclones and tornadoes, lightning flashes and cloud-bursts, tide-rips and tidal waves . . . crushing humans to pulp or licking them off into the sea and to death," then "in the maze and chaos of the conflict of these vast and draughty Titans, it is for me to thread my precarious way" (*Snark*, 5–7).

But defying the titans of nature is not the only reason he and Charmian embarked on what would be a fundamentally life-changing journey; London also confesses in the foreword to *The Cruise of the Snark* that "there is another side. . . . Being alive, I want to see, and all the world is a bigger thing to see than one small town or valley" (*Snark*, 7). London planned to visit Hawaii, Samoa, New Zealand, Tasmania, Australia, New Guinea, Borneo, Sumatra, the Philippines, Japan, Korea, China, India, the Red Sea, and the Mediterranean. After two years his voyage was cut short by severe illness and he and Charmian returned to Glen Ellen. But although he did not visit all of the places he wanted to see, London's time in the South Seas and Hawaii was to be as profound an experience for his art as had been his time spent in the Klondike, and many of the same issues he addressed in the Klondike stories remained to be revisited in his stories of the Pacific. Some, perhaps, including his restless search for personal identity, may even have been solved. He had his "big moments of living," and he learned from them (*Snark*, 5–6). The stories and novels he produced are, as Thomas R. Tietze and Gary Riedl remark, "always entertaining, sometimes horrifying, magnificently colorful and usually bitingly satirical. All of them repay close reading."[73]

On the *Snark*, London found two Pacifics, one the Paradise Lost of Hawaii; the other the Inferno of the Solomon Islands and Melanesia. "When Hawaii was named the Paradise of the Pacific, it was inadequately named," London wrote: "The rest of the Seven Seas and the islands in the midst thereof should have been included along with the Pacific."[74] But as Labor et al. observe, "[I]t is in his Melanesian tales, rather than in his Klondike fiction, that we find London's bitterest naturalism" (*Complete*, xxxiv). Of Melanesia and its dissipations and diseases, London wrote, "If I were a king, the worst punishment I could inflict on my enemies would be to banish them to the Solomons. On second thought, king or no king, I don't think I'd have the heart to do it" (*Snark*, 282). London saw Hawaii's tragedy, "a lovely and loving land whose bountiful natural beauty had been commercialized, whose politics had been usurped, and whose inhabitants had been contaminated by the diseases of the 'civilized' *haoles*" (*Complete*, xxxiii). Nevertheless, in Hawaii London would come closest to resolution of his internal restlessness, and he would find a new way of looking at the old problem of racialism.

To trace these "two Pacifics"—and the culmination of London's career-long artistic interrogation of the value of community—we turn to the four collections of London's Pacific tales, moving from the early South Seas stories in *South Sea Tales* (1911), to the first Hawaiian stories of *The House of Pride* (1912), and then repeating the revision pattern with the formulaic David Grief stories of *A Son of the Sun* (1912) and the new views of the Pacific in the late Hawaiian tales of *On the Makaloa Mat* (1919). (Scattered South Seas stories also appear in the collections *When God Laughs* [1911] and *The Turtles of Tasman* [1916]). Cultural relativism and self-questioning crop up until the last story, "The Water Baby," as do London's characteristic themes of justice, community, and the imagination. London's racialism surfaces in its different forms: in Melanesia his worst fears of the limitations of race were confirmed in both the native islanders and the white colonizers, and the fiction he produced is full of violence and despair. But in London's Hawaiian fiction there is a change from this white versus black misery. The articulate, self-possessed, multicultural society of Hawaii at the turn of the century, in which people mingled their bloodlines and traditions, provided him a startling reeducation.

South Sea Tales

Both the exoticism of the South Seas and the horrors London encountered there drive the stories of *South Sea Tales.* One of London's motivations in undertaking the *Snark* voyage was his intense desire to visit Melville's Typee Valley in the Marquesas Islands. But as he relates in the "Typee" chapter of *The Cruise of the Snark,* when he arrived, he found that the Typeans of 1907 were no longer the magnificent race that Melville had described; no longer did they build the great stone walls and foundations. They dwelt in little straw huts and suffered from asthma, tuberculosis, and elephantiasis. Only a generation after Melville's visit in the 1840s their population had shrunk dramatically, victim of the white man's microbes, and London found only a dozen or so inhabitants of the valley, physically wrecked and spiritually without hope. London was deeply saddened by what he saw, and the experience would serve as a touchstone for much that would disillusion him about the South Seas (Kingman, 192). As David Moreland notes, "[T]he cruise of the South Pacific, which he had wistfully envisioned as an escape from mounting personal and financial concerns into a world typified by Melville's *Typee,* brought only a confirmation of his blackest fears."[75] "We are not in time," wrote Charmian; "the devastating civilizing years have preceded the *Snark* venture."[76]

But despite his disillusionment, "like Hemingway in the next decade," Moreland says, "London was concerned with telling the factual truth about the world he experienced, and he felt frustrated when he was dismissed as a writer of 'imaginative' fiction." He felt compelled, when years later he revisited the site of his South Seas stories in his book *Jerry of the Islands* (1917), to include in his preface a defense of his negative depiction of Melanesia. As Moreland notes, he cited "instances of decapitations, cannibalism, naval bombardments of native villages, the murders of friends . . . , and other horrors to dispel the misconception that his South Sea fiction was merely a 'highly credible effort of the imagination.' " London's aim was to dramatize Darwin's and Spencer's theories of the survival of the fittest, in addition to his "experiential level of truth." The islands' "elemental surroundings outside the mainstream of civilization" offered the writer a setting in which he could "graphically demonstrate the evolutionist's thesis which Bonapartes and sharks instinctively understand—the functional killer rules the world" (Moreland, "Violence," 2).

In "Make Westing" (1907) and "The *Francis Spaight*" (1908), both published in *When God Laughs,* London offers gruesome naturalistic portraits of the brutality of the seas that look back to his early horror fiction. He evidently remembered not only the exhilaration of surviving the typhoon from his *Sophia Sutherland* days but also the brutality of the life aboard ship. "Make Westing" is a somber story of a ship stuck at Cape Horn in a fog. Should the captain leave a man behind who has fallen overboard when the ship may be facing its last chance to escape destruction? Pledging himself to the Powers of Darkness, the captain leaves the sailor behind and writes up a false account of what happened in the log book. Although he boasts to himself that he has fooled God, the narrator conveys a Greek sense of the gods' jealousy at such hubris and forecasts the captain's doom. Written at about the same time as the second version of "To Build a Fire," the opening—"A gray gloom shrouded the world. . . while the snow-flurries were not white, but gray, under the somber pall of the heavens" (*Complete,* 1317)—conveys a similar sense of fatality.

"The *Francis Spaight*" is similar to the *South Sea Tales* story "The Whale Tooth," for in both a man is killed for principle, and cannibalism occurs. A crew is marooned on a drifting hulk, and the dying men revert to savagery. Because they are brutish and lazy, despite their physical strength they cannot get themselves out of their predicament. They turn on the boys as prey weak enough to be overcome and eaten. As in "The Whale Tooth," the theme is sacrifice, but this time of an even more horrific, meaningless nature. The lad they decide to kill, O'Brien, is so emaciated and dehydrated that as they saw away at his arm they cannot even draw blood. One sailor, Mahoney, protests, but despite O'Brien's shrieks they mangle him until they kill him, just when a ship comes into sight. It is not hard to see, reading this particular story, why some of London's readers felt that his use of violence was just for the shock value and served no other purpose than to terrify.

"The Whale Tooth" (1908), first published as "The Mission of John Starhust," employs violence for a more complex purpose. It is a black-humor tale told at the expense of a missionary, but it also reflects the savagery of the native rulers of the island. It combines conventional literary devices with what is obviously a folkloristic source. John Starhurst wants to go to the bush to convert the tribes; the chief on the shore with whom he first makes contact sends a man after him with a whale tooth and a request to the inland chiefs to kill the missionary, the rule being that if the chiefs take the gift of the whale tooth they have to carry out the request. They are too frightened to kill a white man, but finally chief Buli coldly murders Starhurst for the prize. "Forgive them, for they know not what they do," Starhurst says as he prays for "poor cannibal Fiji" (1499). This story recalls the Klondike theme of justice (as in "The God of His Fathers"), for here a brave man is killed for principle, and the man who has followed him to report back to the first chief hears himself called coward.

The most significant tie to the fiction of the Klondike in the South Seas stories is the theme of race. In many of London's South Seas stories, the same sense of the inevitability of racial contest emerges: "[T]he concept of racial mastery becomes more clearly defined and is mixed with evolutionary dogma," Moreland notes. "For better or worse, his heroes often carry the banners of their races. . . . [T]he yellow, black, brown, and white races clash and be tested. Almost forty years before the attack upon Pearl Harbor, London forecast a coming war between Japan and the United States for dominion in the Pacific" (Moreland, "Violence," 2–3).[77] But as Tietze and Riedl point out, London's South Seas fiction offered the large magazine readership of his day a revision of the idea of the "noble savage" of exotic lands, an idea that "only served to distance them from the real people who lived on these remote islands." London's stories "accurately and consistently showed the islanders as individuals who had to deal, in one way or another, with white intrusions: capitalist brutality, inhumane legal systems, foreign diseases, and racist social practices. Throughout, these tales stab, with an irony born of conviction, at the comfortable paternalism of whites toward people of color" (Tietze and Riedl, 1).

"The Heathen" (1908), which furnishes the Robinson Crusoe/Man Friday-like frontispiece to the volume *South Sea Tales*, is a story that can be read either as a testimony to London's questioning of imperialistic, racist ideas, or as his confirmation of them. Russ Kingman notes that London based the tale on his Tahitian crew member, Tehei, who is called Otoo in the story (Kingman, 202). In a story laden with Christian imagery, Otoo gives his life for his white brother, like Melville's Queequeg (who is probably an inspiration for "Otoo," since Otoo's name has a Melvillian echo itself). Although he knows nothing of Christian morality Otoo is a better Christian than any of the whites (*Complete*, 1510). Even small details of the story's language reinforce the theme of Christlike sacrifice, as in the opening description of the ship: "[S]he had no right to carry a tithe of the mob she had on board" and "[i]t was a miracle that the sailors could work her" (1501). As in the Klondike stories, here the theme of brotherhood, faith, and sacrifice is at the center of the tale, as the white master and native manservant even exchange names and identities, but biblical imagery supplants the Greek. Whites in the story are shown as dissipated and alcoholic, in strong contrast to Otoo's health and righteousness. Captain Oudouse kicks "the kanaka" and calls him "a black heathen" when they are shipwrecked, and the narrator cries out, " 'For two centimes I'd come over there and drown you, you white beast!' " (1507). The story relates how the narrator saves Otoo, and how Otoo later saves him, giving his life to the sharks to protect his beloved friend.

Like the character McCoy in "The Seed of McCoy," Otoo is somewhat feminized, an interesting intersection of race and gender. This intersection has the effect of making the narrator a better man, a strong parallel to the gender dynamics of London's Klondike stories and California novels. Otoo objects to gambling and drinking, and the narrator relates that "slowly I grew to comprehend the hurt I could inflict upon him by being anything less than my best" (1510). This relationship, again paralleling Ishmael and Queequeg, is described in even stronger terms in this passage: "And that was how Otoo and I first came together. He was no fighter. He was all sweetness and gentleness, a love-creature, though he stood nearly six feet tall and was muscled like a gladiator. He was no fighter, but he was also no coward. He had the heart of a lion; and in the years that followed I have seen him run risks that I would never dream of taking" (1507). Some readers have found this one of London's most moving portraits of interracial friendship, while others have objected to it as merely a "loyal darky" fable emphasizing the unquestioning devotion of the black servant. Probably the best way to go about addressing this disparity is to compare this one with its paired story, "The Terrible Solomons."

"The Terrible Solomons" (1908) contains a line critical to understanding London's emotional and moral attitude toward race struggle in the South Pacific, and, by inference, in any place. London's narrator defines what it takes to be a good racist:

> He must have the hall-mark of the inevitable white man stamped upon his soul. He must be inevitable. He must have a certain grand carelessness of odds, a certain colossal self-satisfaction, and a racial egotism that convinces him that one white is better than a thousand niggers every day in the week, and that on Sunday he is able to clean out two thousand niggers. For such are the things that have made the white man inevitable. Oh, and one other thing—the white man who wishes to be inevitable must not merely despise the lesser breeds and think a lot of himself; he must also fail to be too long on imagination. He must not understand too well the instincts, customs, and mental processes of the blacks, the yellows, and the browns; for it is not in such fashion that the white race has tramped its royal road around the world. (1519)

The importance of this passage lies in its Twainian tone. To miss that is to miss much of the satiric, ironic thrust of many of the South Seas stories. London may speak in glowing terms of the "race adventure" in his essays and some of his fiction, but he cannot sustain abstractions such as white supremacy in the face of his real experiences in the Pacific nor in the artistic practice of using his all-important imagination in creating and emotionally interacting with his characters.

The plot of "The Terrible Solomons" involves a lesson taught to an overweening youth, Bertie Arkwright, who desires to project himself into the savage environment of the Solomons and enjoy adventures that will make him the envy of those back home. He is handsome and much beloved of the lady tourists, who have nothing by which to judge save appearances. Bertie believes that the blacks are simply savages. He would agree that "their highest instinct of sportsmanship is to catch a man with his back turned and to smite him a cunning blow with a tomahawk that severs the spinal column at the base of the brain" (1519). But the narrator manages to paint the white characters in a light just as bad, and the story has much to do with such questions of appearance and reality: Bertie likes to play Russian roulette on a bet, a suicidal charade. Recognizing that Bertie's desire for adventure and his strong outward appearance are both falsehoods, his older companions set up some "experiences" for him that teach him what is real. London had in mind the many whites in the South Seas who came there as selfish thrill seekers—perhaps even himself and Charmian, who went on a "blackbirding," or slaving, expedition on the ketch *Minota* with Captain Jansen, who was recruiting for a Solomons plantation. The story engages in complex play with appearances; the situations in which Bertie finds himself—native revolts, for instance—are false, but the danger is always real. Bertie's "race adventure" ends with him as a consummate fool.

Two other stories, "Yah! Yah! Yah!" and "Mauki," were sent off to the magazines the same day as "The Terrible Solomons." They both take place on an atoll supposed to be Lord Howe Atoll, which the Londons visited. Along with the story "The Inevitable White Man" (1908), written a few months earlier, all four tales form a tightly knit group that explores the limitations of white ethics in the Pacific and the terror the white man can bring. "Yah! Yah! Yah!" develops the notion of white men taking revenge upon resistant natives. "White men are hell" (1551), the narrator, Oti, says, and the reader must agree. "What are you good for, anyway? I do not know, except to fight," he adds. Oti tells the story of the coming of McAllister, a white man who carries out the genocide of Oti's people on their once peaceful atoll. Every kind of death is represented by the inevitable white man, whom the natives can neither escape nor understand. Oti tries to explain why they tolerate the tyrant and never attempt to fight back any more. Much of the story's power lies in the islander speaking for himself rather than serving as the object of discussion by whites, although the narrator, who forms the frame for the story of Oti, is a white man, curious about the subservience of the native population—all five thousand of them—to a whiskey-guzzling old Scotsman. Oti relates how he participated in a raid on a schooner many years ago; its crew returned to punish the natives, killing all but three hundred of them. The title comes from the taunt that the mate of the avenging ship directs at the natives, along with dynamite, starvation, measles—intentionally introduced. This inarticulate hatred makes him a greater savage than the noble Oti, who tells his tale so movingly, marveling at the unbelievable evil of the white men. It is hard to see how London could have agreed with Benjamin Kidd, the race theorist London read, that what set the white man apart in his race adventure was his moral rectitude.

But one does hear Kidd's voice in the opening of "The Inevitable White Man" in Captain Woodward (a portrait of Captain Jansen), a battle-scarred veteran of native attacks, who remarks, " 'The black will never understand the white, nor the white the black, as long as black is black and white is white.' " The men sit in Charley Roberts's pub in Apia, Samoa: " 'Half the trouble is the stupidity of the whites,' said Roberts, pausing to take a swig from his glass and to curse the Samoan bar-boy in affectionate terms. 'If the white man would lay himself out a bit to understanding the workings of the black man's mind, most of the messes would be avoided' " (1557). The tone is ambiguous in this story, as it was in showing both Oti's fear and his admiration of the white man's power. The white man's stupidity leads to inevitability and to his success, but London seems to praise the white man in his domination of the world: " 'Just so,' said Roberts. " 'And somehow it doesn't seem necessary, after all, to understand niggers. In direct proportion to the white man's stupidity is his success in farming the world—' 'And putting the fear of God into the nigger's heart,' " Captain Woodward blurted out. 'Perhaps you're right, Roberts. Perhaps it's his stupidity that makes him succeed, and surely one phase of his stupidity is his inability to understand niggers. But there's one thing sure, the white has to run the niggers whether he understands them or not. It's inevitable. It's fate' " (1558–59). Roberts continues:

> "And of course the white man is inevitable—it's the niggers' fate, . . . Tell the white man there's pearl-shell in some lagoon infested by ten thousand howling cannibals, and he'll head there all by his lonely, with half a dozen kanaka divers and a tin alarm clock for chronometer, all packed like sardines on a commodious, five-ton ketch. Whisper that there's a gold strike at the North Pole, and that same inevitable white-skinned creature will set out at once, armed with pick and shovel, a side of bacon, and the latest patent rocker—and what's more, he'll get there. Tip it off to him that there's diamonds on the red-hot ramparts of hell, and Mr. White Man will storm the ramparts and set old Satan himself to pick-and-shovel work. That's what comes of being stupid and inevitable." (1559)

They talk of John Saxtorph, a New Englander incapable of any other work but marksmanship: " '[T]he most stupid man I ever saw,' " according to Charley, " 'as inevitable as death' " (1559). Like the mate in "Yah! Yah! Yah!," Saxtorph is another genocidal monster, shooting the fleeing islanders after a failed attack on his ship. His name gives pause: "Saxon" is a name and a "race" that London admired, and London's admiration for the whites' power is certainly there. The story's ambivalences are puzzling, but although it is hard to completely assess London's own feelings, the story makes clear enough that it is not about *farming* but *harvesting*, with no regard to the environment, human or otherwise. As Moreland remarks, although London sympathizes with Captain Woodward and feared the Melanesians, "[H]is positing of the abysmally stupid Saxtorph—whose one 'virtue' is a mastery of mindless slaughter—as the perfect farmer of the tropics is slim tribute to 'Mr. White Man,' " and London's praise of whites "is qualified almost to the point of extinction" (Moreland, "Violence,"15). Certainly London's ironic intentions become clearer if the story is paired with "Yah! Yah! Yah!," since it is an amplification that explains the former story, and also if we remember how important responsible farming was to London the rancher.

"Mauki" is without question the finest of these thematically interwoven tales. Max Bunster is another "inevitable white man," this time the owner and torturer of a Solomon Island youth named Mauki. Bunster is comparable to the mate of "Yah! Yah! Yah!" and to Saxtorph because he knows no other way of living than through violence, through inflicting pain and the taking of a life. Mauki is based upon a Solomon Island cook who worked for a Dutch trader and whom London met on Lord Howe Atoll, who was serving several sentences and undergoing numerous reprisals for committing various crimes, including murder, theft, and escape. The trader made a regular practice of cruelly beating his servants; Charmian remarked on the disparity between this young cook's crimes and punishments and his mild, even "deceptive weak prettiness" (C. London, *The Log*, 445).

The story of how Mauki finally does escape and his terrible revenge on his sadistic master, Max Bunster, is a hair-raising tale of brutality and grotesquerie. Although Mauki himself is described as grotesque, an emaciated, weak-chinned, jet-black teenager with his ears sprouting various cargo items including a can opener and teacup handle, his heart full of a murderous intent, London also gives us Mauki's innate nobility and admires both his crafty plot for revenge and his eventual wisdom in managing his people, for he returns home as a chief, although he was initially sold off as a slave by a conquering tribe.

The story works on powerful contrasts, such as the opening distinction between the white way of seeing Mauki and his own vision of himself: an identity as one who has three tambos (or taboos). There is no such inner and outer discrepancy between inner and outer points of view for Bunster; although his inner life is touched upon: "He was a strapping big German, with something wrong in his brain. Semi-madness would be a charitable statement of his condition. He was a bully and a coward, and a thrice-bigger savage than any savage on the island. Being a coward, his brutality was of the cowardly order" (*Complete*, 1539). We learn that "Bunster was a degenerate brute. But Mauki was a primitive savage. Both had wills and ways of their own. And Mauki soon learned that there were white men and white men" (1540). But Bunster, "offended with life" (1541), can learn nothing of it, and this is why he fails—not understanding a thing about Mauki-of-the-three-tambos. Like the doomed protagonist of "To Build a Fire," he is without imagination.

Symbolically speaking, Bunster punishes Mauki for his color; he takes a mitten made of ray fish skin the natives use to sand canoes and "strokes" Mauki's skin with it: "The first time he tried it on Mauki, with one sweep of the hand it fetched the skin off his back from neck to armpit. Bunster was delighted. He gave his [Polynesian] wife a taste of the mitten, and tried it out thoroughly on the boat-boys. The [Polynesian] prime ministers came in for a stroke each, and they had to grin and take it as a joke. 'Laugh, damn you, laugh!' was the cue he gave" (1542). In revenge, when Bunster falls ill to fever, Mauki is able to get the mitten and remove the white skin that has given Bunster his power, thus making Bunster the "other"—"a hideous, skinless thing" writhing on the beach (1544). At the story's close we see Mauki thoughtfully remove "its" head to take with him on his journey home.

In the end Mauki is a chief again, with wives, a fat belly, and captured heads all around him, including a certain blonde one he likes to contemplate at special times. He has killed the chief who enslaved him and has taken his place. Like Johnny in "The Apostate," Mauki runs away to define himself, each time losing years of his life, but gaining his soul. This demonstrates integrity. The ending tells us he is noble not because he gains a perfect revenge upon his oppressor but because politically he is a successful king, joining the bushmen and water people together to restore order and making a treaty with the white man's Moongleam Soap Company, which has held them all hostage so long.

Written in the same month, May 1908, "The Chinago" (included in *When God Laughs*) makes a fine companion story to "Mauki." It was written just after the Londons left Bora Bora in April, a place they agreed was a truly happy paradise with "the most thoughtful and generous people alive" (*Snark*, 210). That was where London met Tehei, the Tahitian who inspired the story "The Heathen." Set on a plantation in Tahiti, "The Chinago" offers finely tuned, wry, and ultimately tragic sensitivity in its narration of events from the title character's center of consciousness, making it one of London's finest uses of the Jamesian third-person narrative. Ah Cho, a meek young Chinese man, is serving a five-year indenture on a cotton plantation and is executed for a murder he did not commit. Through him London gives one of his most compelling, and effectively understated, attacks on white imperialism.

A masterpiece of atmosphere, suspense, and irony, "The Chinago" is similar to, but much richer than, "The Madness of John Harned." In its contrasting depiction of how competing cultures view one another—or fail to—the story presents tremendous irony in its portrayal of the inability of the Chinese and Europeans to see and hear each other:

> There was no understanding these white devils. Ah Cho pondered their inscrutableness as he sat in the court room waiting the judgment. There was no telling what went on at the back of their minds. He had seen a few of the white devils. They were all alike—the officers and sailors on the ship, the French officials, the several white men on the plantation, including Schemmer. Their minds all moved in mysterious ways there was no getting at. They grew angry without apparent cause, and their anger was always dangerous. They were like wild beasts at such times. There was a curtain behind the eyes of the white devils that screened the backs of their minds from the Chinago's gaze. And then, on top of it all, was that terrible efficiency of the white devils. (1408–9)

As in "The Unparalleled Invasion," the story enforces this distance by focusing specifically upon the distances created by language, as the opening line announces: "Ah Cho did not understand French" (1405). In an act that eventually results in Ah Cho's death, the coolies who have all either witnessed or participated in a deadly argument amongst themselves agree not to testify. Ah Cho, at first accused only of being in the fight, is mistaken for the man who actually did the killing, Ah Chow. Ah Cho doesn't speak up when the error is made because he thinks the French are stupid and should figure it out for themselves. Also, he is fatalistic: "And there was nothing he could do. He could only sit idly and take what these lords of life measured out to him. Ah Chow or Ah Cho—what did it matter which? They could never understand the white dogs any more than could the white dogs understand them" (1414). The French won't change the error because it is inconvenient and might give the wrong impression to the coolies. The gendarme,

Cruchot, like Bunster and Saxtorph, is as "slow-witted and stupid as in his peasant days" (1410). Neither he nor the Chinese seek to secure the truth, although for different reasons. Neither side tries to communicate because they both think there is no understanding the inscrutable "devils." But what sets Ah Cho apart is his idealistic musing upon his garden and the meaning of life he reads within it; at the end of the story, laying his head down for the guillotine, he sees something no one else does:

> Then he was aware that the board had come to rest. . . . He opened his eyes. Straight above him he saw the suspended knife blazing in the sunshine. He saw the weight which had been added, and noted that one of Schemmer's knots had slipped. Then he heard the sergeant's voice in sharp command. Ah Cho closed his eyes hastily. He did not want to see that knife descend. But he felt it—for one great fleeting instant. And in that instant he remembered Cruchot and what Cruchot had said. But Cruchot was wrong. The knife did not tickle. That much he knew before he ceased to know. (1417)

"The Seed of McCoy" (1908) is similar to "The Chinago" in the strength of its main character and the inner peace he maintains in the face of adversity, but the story is distinguished by a powerful reliance upon Christian imagery. A ship called the *Pyrenees*, loaded with wheat, has caught fire. Although the hold is sealed, danger is imminent as the wheat continues to smoulder and the decks grow hotter and hotter. Near the island of Pitcairn, home of the descendants of the *Bounty* mutineers, an old man comes aboard, calling himself the chief magistrate of Pitcairn and great-grandson of McCoy of the *Bounty*. He agrees to help the ship land on safe ground, but he emphasizes that he can only pilot the ship into a safe harbor, not steer into the harbor itself for the captain. Bringing food aboard, the strange man with the oddly soft and gentle voice and "liquid brown eyes [that sweep] over them like a benediction, soothing them, wrapping them as in a mantle of great peace" stays with the ship as it searches unsuccessfully from island to island for a safe berth (1358). As the men grow more and more terrified, McCoy becomes even more serene, promising salvation if they will only stay with him and believe him. He tells the frantic men, about to mutiny, of the terrible mutiny aboard the *Bounty*: They were very wicked. "God had hidden His face" from them (1377–78). After the first generation of *Bounty* mutineers had been succeeded on Pitcairn by their halfbreed children, a new beneficient Polynesian order slowly developed on the island, embodied in the Christlike McCoy himself. McCoy does save the ship, and the story ends with McCoy saying that he must get himself home.[78]

Despite his manliness there is a strangely childlike and feminine quality to McCoy, recalling the intersection of gender with race as seen in "The Heathen": here again, London loads this feminized, racially mixed hero with his most positive heroic traits, as he will also do to some extent in the men who encounter the feminine in the later California novels and are profoundly changed by it. As in "The Story of Jees Uck," mixed blood gives strength. In this regard the story also compares with "The House of Mapuhi," where good comes out of evil and faith endures when everything else is swept away in an apocalypse.

"The House of Mapuhi" (1908) is set in the Tuamotu Archipelago—also called the Paumotus—and is also loaded with biblical allusions, starting with the parables of the Pearl of Great Price and the building of one's house upon sand versus rock. Mapuhi has found a great pearl, greater than any he has ever seen. His family doesn't want money for it; they want a house and security. But since he owes money, Mapuhi must engage in a series of complicated deals in order to sell the pearl, and he is cheated. The deals then sink with the traders' ship as a terrible hurricane sweeps the island. In a brilliant panorama of islanders, white and native, captains and sailors, men and women, all trying to survive the avenging winds and lashing seas, London gives one of his most powerful descriptions of humans in the furious winds of chance. "So this was a hurricane," Alexandre Raoul, the pearl buyer, thinks to himself:

> It was a horrible, monstrous thing, a screaming fury, a wall that smote and passed on but that continued to smite and pass on—a wall without end. It seemed to him that he had become light and ethereal; that it was he that was in motion; that he was being driven with inconceivable velocity through unending solidness. The wind was no longer air in motion. It had become substantial as water or quick silver. He had a feeling he could reach into it and tear it out in chunks as one might do with the meat in the carcass of a steer; that he could seize hold of the wind and hang onto it as a man might hang on in the face of a cliff. . . . The wind strangled him. He could not face it and breathe, for it rushed in through his mouth and nostrils, distending his lungs like bladders. At such moments it seemed to him that his body was being packed and swollen with solid earth. Only by pressing his lips to the trunk of the tree could he breathe. Also, the ceaseless impact of the wind exhausted him. Body and brain became wearied. He no longer observed, no longer thought, and was but semiconscious. (1396)

London's effect grows out of his combination of tooth-rattling naturalism with a sense of heaven-directed fate. People clutch desperately to coconut trees, only to have them snapped away like matchsticks; the church is split in two and thrown from its foundation; children are snatched by the razor-sharp winds from their drowning mothers' arms. Mapuhi survives only by luck: It was ten miles across the lagoon to the farther ring of sand:

> Here, tossing tree-trunks, timbers, wrecks of cutters, and wreckage of houses, killed nine out of ten of the miserable beings who survived the passage of the lagoon. Half-drowned, exhausted, they were hurled into this mad mortar of the elements and battered into formless flesh. But Mapuhi was fortunate. His chance was the one in ten; it fell to him by the freakage of fate. He emerged upon the sand, bleeding from a score of wounds. Ngakura's left arm was broken; the fingers of her right hand were crushed; and cheek and forehead were laid open to the bone. He clutched a tree that yet stood, and clung on, holding the girl and sobbing for air, while the waters of the lagoon washed by knee-high and at times waist-high. (1397)

Maphui's mother is swept to sea and miraculously survives on a neighboring island. Without food or clothing or water, she is resigned to die, but she finds the pearl, stuck in the pockets of the cheating trader. She vows to live for the others and return home with the pearl so she can build her sturdy house with its octagon-drop-clock.

Most of the characters in the story disappear as the focus narrows on the mother. Many different classes and bloods are represented, but the mother comes to stand for all of them. As in "The Water Baby," here the Mother emerges from the sea, a shriveled, naked, brown little woman bearing the great treasure. Her victory is preposterous but entirely fitting.

The House of Pride

The stories of *The House of Pride* indicate a shift from the racial violence of *South Sea Tales*, but they continue the sense of irony at the pretensions of racial dominance. Several of the stories of this second collection offer native protagonists who command the reader's respect, but the general pattern, as it will be in *On the Makaloa Mat*, is of a *haole* (Caucasian) listener learning of the stories of the islands. London himself heard most of these stories in a similarly roundabout fashion; his tales of Hawaiian natives were told to him by his well-to-do *kama'aina haole* friends—that is, the descendants of the missionaries and traders, as well as less highly placed "locals." The well-born *kama'ainas* and other local people London knew were very often of mixed blood, however, as befits Hawaii, and they furnished him with new understandings of racial and cultural diversity.

First arriving in 1893 aboard the *Sophia Sutherland*, and anchoring the *Snark* for his first extended visit in 1907, over the years London found Hawaii a place to rest and allow his psyche room to examine itself. Yet although he was in "paradise," he was still on the streets, too, looking at urban life, labor, and politics in Honolulu, as well as natural beauty and unique features of the island. In every way Hawaii was fertile ground for the imagination, with much material to support his interest in the themes of justice, community, and the imagination.

Russ Kingman stresses that Hawaii, aside from providing a quiet life that fostered London's writing and affording an abundance of friendliness as well as enjoyment, also allowed London an escape from the "bickering, intrigue, and harassment" of his relations to fellow socialists on the mainland. He enjoyed Hawaii's exceeding hospitality and the convivial mixing of races: "He began to believe that a utopian society might come to pass without socialism. The lack of racial friction was a wonder to him. The patriarchal system of the Islands seemed to be satisfactory to worker and employer. Labor problems were few; everybody appeared to be happy and contented. The owners of the huge sugar and pineapple plantations were charitable and generous with their workers, and there was little poverty." Later, in 1915, revisiting Hawaii, London's impressions were confirmed, says Kingman: "[I]n Honolulu democracy and capitalism were working and bringing happiness to the majority without the poverty and suffering of exploited masses" (Kingman, 268). If Kingman paints too rosy a picture of the average level of content among Hawaii's workers, and I think he does, and if he is unnecessarily dismissive of London's commitment to socialism, he still points to an essential difference between Hawaii and most of the other places London had ever encountered. Its uniqueness had a defining impact on his thinking and his writing. London is buried with an ilima lei from Hawaii, and perhaps his most touching elegy was that expressed by a Hawaiian boy who played the ukulele at a San Francisco theater: "Better than any one, he knew us Hawai'ians . . . Jack London, the Story Maker . . . The news came to Honolulu—and people, they seemed to have lost a great friend."[79] His short stories set in Hawaii chart his growing awareness of what an alternative culture had to offer in many dimensions.

"The House of Pride" (1907), London's first Hawaiian story, is a well-chosen title story, for its themes and tone give shape to the entire book. First, in its portrait of the *hapa haole* (half Hawaiian, half Caucasian), Joe Garland, it reveals clearly London's sensitivity to the beauty of the Hawaiian people while simultaneously contrasting that natural beauty of body and spirit with the shriveled heart of race hatred, as represented by Joe's half brother, Percival Ford. Ford's betrayal of Joe is the primal ethical issue at the center of the story, with a revisioning of race and sex furnishing a complicating intersection and new moral vision.

Landed gentleman Percival Ford sees all sexes and races as bestial, but he discovers that his father, Isaac Ford, a famously devout New Englander who came to Hawaii, was a "beast" as well, enjoying a liaison with a Hawaiian woman that produced Joe Garland. But of course Percival is the real "beast," as he watches a dance going on and salaciously spies on the women's "challenging femaleness" and "essential grossness of flesh" (*Complete*, 1345). "His was a negative organism," the narrator says:

> His meagre blood had denied him much of life, and permitted him to be an extremist in one thing only, which thing was righteousness. Over right conduct he pondered and agonized, and that he should do right was as necessary to his nature as loving and being loved were necessary to commoner clay.
>
> He was thirty-five, and, having had no personal experience of love, he looked upon it, not as mythical, but as bestial. Anybody could marry. The Japanese and Chinese coolies, toiling on the sugar plantations and in the rice-fields, married. They invariably married at the first opportunity. It was because they were so low in the scale of life. There was nothing else for them to do. They were like the army men and women. But for him there were other and higher things. (1346)

London deftly controls point of view to reveal the truth about this missionary descendant so disgusted by the pattern of normal human evolution. Much of the story is a dialogue between Percival and the doctor, an interchange that shows Percival's failings as a human being: his judgment of Joe Garland as "immoral" and his own lack of love. London and the doctor frame the reader's judgment against Percival as an antihero like his knightly namesake who fails to understand what he sees:

> "No," was Percival Ford's answer. "That is what makes my position impregnable. I have no personal spite against him. He is bad, that is all. His life is bad—"

"Which is another way of saying that he does not agree with you in the way life should be lived," the doctor interrupted.

"Have it that way. It is immaterial. He is an idler—"

"With reason," was the interruption, "considering the jobs out of which you have knocked him."

"He is immoral—"

"Oh, hold on now, Ford. Don't go harping on that. You are pure New England stock. Joe Garland is half Kanaka. Your blood is thin. His is warm. Life is one thing to you, another thing to him. He laughs and sings and dances through life, genial, unselfish, childlike, everybody's friend. You go through life like a perambulating prayer-wheel, a friend of nobody but the righteous, and the righteous are those who agree with you as to what is right. And after all, who shall say? You live like an anchorite. Joe Garland lives like a good fellow. Who has extracted the most from life? We are paid to live, you know. When the wages are too meagre we throw up the job, which is the cause, believe me, of all rational suicide. Joe Garland would starve to death on the wages you get from life. You see, he is made differently. So would you starve on his wages, which are singing, and love—"

"Lust, if you will pardon me," was the interruption.

Dr. Kennedy smiled.

"Love, to you, is a word of four letters and a definition which you have extracted from the dictionary. But love, real love, dewy and palpitant and tender, you do not know. If God made you and me, and men and women, believe me he made love, too. But to come back. It's about time you quit hounding Joe Garland. It is not worthy of you, and it is cowardly. The thing for you to do is to reach out and lend him a hand." (1350)

But Percival is not able to feel anything for Joe: " 'Now I don't follow you,' Percival Ford answered. 'You're up in the air with some obscure scientific theory of heredity and personal irresponsibility. But how any theory can hold Joe Garland irresponsible for his wrongdoings and at the same time hold me personally responsible for them—more responsible than any one else, including Joe Garland—is beyond me' " (1351).

Percival Ford doesn't ask the right question, and like "Goliah," his totalitarian vision makes him a monster. London's biblical allusions reinforce his judgment against Percival Ford: " 'There's the machine,' Dr. Kennedy said, rising. 'I've got to run. I'm sorry I've shaken you up, and at the same time I'm glad. And know one thing, Isaac Ford's dab of unruly blood was remarkably small, and Joe Garland got it all. And one other thing. If your father's left hand offend you, don't smite it off.

Besides, Joe is all right. Frankly, if I could choose between you and him to live with me on a desert isle, I'd choose Joe.' " Unruly blood—what could this mean? Ford does not know—fears, but does not ask: It "was like learning suddenly that his father had been a leper and that his own blood might bear the taint of that dread disease. Isaac Ford, the austere soldier of the Lord—the old hypocrite! What difference between him and any beach-comber? The house of pride that Percival Ford had builded was tumbling about his ears" (1353–55). London's irony is that while the reader along with Ford's acquaintances sees history clearly, Ford himself is oblivious. He is doomed to commit the sin of banishing Joe from the garden without taking upon himself the sin of knowledge.

"Chun Ah Chun" (1908) is the story of an aged father who settles his accounts with his offspring and retires to the solitude of a garden back in his old country of China. Like London, Chun Ah Chun was "born to labor in the fields all his days like a beast" (1455) but he used his head to became wealthy. Chun Ah Chun succeeds because he is observant and perceives important details. Chun Ah Chun is one of Hawaii's success stories. He asks the right questions and is not afraid of the truth.

Chun Ah Chun is "undersized" and unimpressive: "The average tourist, casually glimpsing him on the streets of Honolulu, would have concluded that he was a good-natured little Chinese" (1455). Such a passage illustrates both the ignorance of *haoles* and also how London, now a part of the islands, is separated from such error. Like Ah Cho, the important thing for Chun Ah Chun is inner tranquillity and "poise of soul": "[H]e mastered problems such as are given to few men to consider" (1455). We learn that "[h]e was always the centre of his household and the head of his table. Himself peasant-born Chinese, he presided over an atmosphere of culture and refinement second to none in all the islands" (1459). Furthermore, "Ah Chun was a moral paragon and an honest business man" (1460). Despite all of this, Chun Ah Chun finds that it is hard to marry off his daughters to the sons of the *haole* businessmen who are his financial peers. But he cleverly solves the problem by attaching huge dowries to his girls; suddenly, racial and religious scruples evaporate as one stellar match after another is made. The narrator emphasizes the beauty of his own racially mixed children and of the grandchildren who come along:

> Thus, his children by Mrs. Ah Chun were one thirty-second Polynesian, one-sixteenth Italian, one-sixteenth Portuguese, one-half Chinese, and eleven thirty-seconds English and American. It might well

be that Ah Chun would have refrained from matrimony could he have foreseen the wonderful family that was to spring from this union. It was wonderful in many ways. First, there was its size. There were fifteen sons and daughters, mostly daughters. The sons had come first, three of them, and then had followed, in unswerving sequence, a round dozen of girls. The blend of the races was excellent. Not alone fruitful did it prove, for the progeny, without exception, was healthy and without blemish. But the most amazing thing about the family was its beauty. All the girls were beautiful—delicately, ethereally beautiful. Mama Ah Chun's rotund lines seemed to modify papa Ah Chun's lean angles, so that the daughters were willowy without being lanky, round-muscled without being chubby. In every feature of every face were haunting reminiscences of Asia, all manipulated over and disguised by old England, New England, and South of Europe. No observer, without information, would have guessed the heavy Chinese strain in their veins; nor could any observer, after being informed, fail to note immediately the Chinese traces.

He had furnished the groundwork upon which had been traced the blended patterns of the races. (1457–58)

Despite their racial harmony, the family members fight and argue with Ah Chun to make things more westernized in their lives, but he is a more clever labor boss than they are:

They had learned the virtues of the boycott as employed by organized labor, and he, their father, Chun Ah Chun, they boycotted in his own house, Mama Achun aiding and abetting. But Ah Chun himself, while unversed in Western culture, was thoroughly conversant with Western labor conditions. An extensive employer of labor himself, he knew how to cope with its tactics. Promptly he imposed a lockout on his rebellious progeny and erring spouse. He discharged his scores of servants, locked up his stables, closed his houses, and went to live in the Royal Hawaiian Hotel, in which enterprise he happened to be the heaviest stockholder. The family fluttered distractedly on visits about with friends, while Ah Chun calmly managed his affairs, smoked his long pipe with the tiny silver bowl, and pondered the problem of his wonderful progeny. (1459–60)

Ah Chun decides to distribute their inheritance among them and retire to a contemplative life: "He saw that there was no place for him amongst this marvellous seed of his loins, and he looked forward to his declining years and knew that he would grow more and more alien. He did not understand his children. Their conversation was of things that did not interest him and about which he knew nothing. The culture of the West had passed him by. He was Asiatic to the last fibre, which meant that he was heathen. Their Christianity was to him so much nonsense. . . . He was not slow in learning that the mind of each son and daughter was a secret labyrinth which he could never hope to tread. Always he came upon the wall that divides the East from West. Their souls were inaccessible to him, and by the same token he knew that his soul was inaccessible to them" (1461). In its keen ironies and graceful handling of both family conflicts and cultural difference, "Chun Ah Chun" pairs well with several stories, including "The Chinago," "Aloha Oe," and "On the Makaloa Mat."

"The Sheriff of Kona" (1908) is one of three stories London wrote about leprosy in Hawaii, and while he was the first American writer to address the issue of leprosy from a rational point of view, making the world recognize the humanity of the lepers, this caused him problems with his friends among the leaders of society and business in the islands.[80] Ironically, given the fuss that erupted over London's writing about lepers, his portrayals of them are anything but lurid—his aim was to humanize these outcasts and portray them with dignity. "It is not a nice thing to go into a man's house and tear away a father, mother, or child" (*Complete*, 1435), the narrator of "The Sheriff of Kona" tells us—for the law in the islands was that when someone became afflicted with leprosy he or she must go to live and die in the leper colony on the island of Molokai. In this story the white man who contracts the disease is treated well (he is spirited away to the Far East by his friends before he can be sent to Molokai), but he loses his beloved island home on the Kona coast. In "Koolau the Leper" (1908), however, the hero provides a contrast—he is deceived and then besieged by the law—but he dies a hero on his own island. The third story is called "Good-bye, Jack" (1908).'

Reinforcing the leprosy motif, there is a marked increase in biblical references in these stories, with phrases such as "the mark of the thing on his brow" (1431) and "[t]he mark of the beast was laid upon him" (1434). As was also the case in the stories of *South Sea Tales*, it seems as though London's increasing reliance upon biblical imagery indicates a fading of the Greek world view of the Klondike stories, with their reliance upon a Greek notion of justice, and working toward a new pattern. In his naturalistic style, London could not be content with depicting only the Edenic aspects of the Hawaiian Islands, turning instead to a fuller understanding of dark aspects as well. However, by no stretch of the imagination could London be thought of as a "Christian" writer or

146

even a religious writer; yet like Twain, he is invested in an encounter with belief. Perhaps because his own inner turn toward a more spiritual version of reality intersected at this particular time with his encountering simultaneously the Christian missionary frame of the Caucasian society in Hawaii and the power of the Hawaiian myths and legends, we see a redoubling of the biblical imagery used casually before. "The House of Maphui," "The Chinago," and "The Seed of McCoy" were written in the same five-month period as the stories of *The House of Pride*, as the heavy New Testament allusions underscore.

Was leprosy an ironic punishment to the paradise of Hawaii from a jealous God? London must have wondered, since he drew such stark contrasts between the beauty of the land and people of Hawaii and the horrifying deformities of leprosy, both physical and social. "Good-bye, Jack" turns the tables on the complacent bystander with a character who is something of a fantasy representation of the author:

> Jack Kersdale was one of these fellows. He was one of the busiest men I ever met. He was a several-times millionaire. He was a sugar king, a coffee planter, a rubber pioneer, a cattle rancher, and a promoter of three out of every four new enterprises launched in the islands. He was a society man, a club man, a yachtsman, a bachelor, and withal as handsome a man as was ever doted upon by mamas with marriageable daughters. Incidentally, he had finished his education at Yale, and his head was crammed fuller with vital statistics and scholarly information concerning Hawaii Nei than any other islander I ever encountered. He turned off an immense amount of work, and he sang and danced and put flowers in his hair as immensely as any of the idlers. (1475)

The story opens with the comment, "Hawaii is a queer place," but even so as it unfolds it seems that the descendants of the missionaries are punished for their crimes against the islands:

> The most ultra-exclusive set there is the "Missionary Crowd." It comes with rather a shock to learn that in Hawaii the obscure, martyrdom-seeking missionary sits at the head of the table of the moneyed aristocracy. But it is true. The humble New Englanders who came out in the third decade of the nineteenth century came for the lofty purpose of teaching the kanakas the true religion, the worship of the one only genuine and undeniable God. So well did they succeed in this, and also in civilizing the kanaka, that by the second or third generation he was practically extinct. . . . The missionary who came to give the bread of life remained to gobble up the whole heathen feast. (1474)

147

Although he is a far cry from the sheer malice of Percival Ford, Jack is a hypocrite who believes Molokai is fine for lepers until it is he who is exposed to leprosy by his girlfriend. This leads the narrator to meditate upon life and mourn the magnificent Lucy:

> I was oppressed by a heavy sadness. Life was a futile thing at best. A short two years and this magnificent creature, at the summit of her magnificent success, was one of the leper squad awaiting deportation to Molokai. . . .
> I recoiled from my own future. If this awful fate fell to Lucy Mokunui, what might not my lot be?—or anybody's lot? I was thoroughly aware that in life we are in the midst of death—but to be in the midst of living death, to die and not be dead, to be one of that draft of creatures that once were men, aye, and women, like Lucy Mokunui, the epitome of all Polynesian charms, an artist as well, and well beloved of men—. (1480)

As Jack watches Lucy loaded into the waiting steamer with the other deportees, he murmurs to himself, "I never knew" (1482). His panic is laced with mordent irony—unlike the narrator's philosophical musings, Jack's only concern is that he has had sexual relations with a diseased woman; his pity is for himself.

"Koolau the Leper" (1908) is London's best-known Hawaiian story and the most boldly articulated attack upon the authorities of the islands who used their power to exploit the native Hawaiians. In it he gives his finest portrait of a Hawaiian character.[81] The story powerfully evokes the natural beauties of the island of Kauai and dramatizes the heroism of the title character, one of the island's most revered heroes, close to Kauai's ancient kings in the hearts of the people. It is also a story of the onslaught of a terrible disease among a traditional people.

A turn-of-the-century field foreman who was diagnosed with leprosy and sentenced to life in the leper colony on the island of Molokai, Ko'olau was a respected member of his community and a devoted husband and father.[82] When the authorities reneged on their promise to let his wife, Pi'ilani, accompany him to Molokai as his *kokua*, or helper, he took her, their son, and a band of supporters and hid out in the deep green Na Pali valley of Kalalau, successfully fending off attacks (including shelling from the beach) by the local sheriff and police. Ko'olau eventually killed the sheriff, Louis Stoltz, in self-defense. Martial law was declared, but Ko'olau and his son died of leprosy in Kalalau. Pi'ilani later emerged from her hideaway to tell the story of her husband's resistance, which was published first in Hawaiian and later translated by historian Frances Frazier and published in English.[83]

London heard the story first from Bert Stoltz, crewman aboard the *Snark* and son of the murdered sheriff. He also heard it when he visited the islands on the *Snark* voyage. London's short story omits the wife and son and with them the strong love story element and the religious convictions that motivated Ko'olau and Pi'ilani—although both the romance and the religious sensibility are quietly retained in the Christian imagery used to describe Koolau. London focuses upon Koolau's betrayal by his followers and his heroic, lonely resistance to the *haole* authorities, the traders and descendants of the missionaries who, London has Koolau surmise, made "all the islands . . . theirs, all the land, all the cattle—everything. . . . They that preached the word of God and they that preached the word of Rum have foregathered and become great chiefs. They live like kings in houses of many rooms, with multitudes of servants to care for them. They who had nothing have everything, and if you, or I, or any Kanaka be hungry, they sneer and say, 'Well, why don't you work? There are the plantations'" (*Complete*, 1441).

Along with his admiration for Koolau and his compassion for his sufferings and those of his fellows, London's stunning descriptions of Kauai are justly admired:

> The far head of Kalalau Valley had been well chosen as a refuge. Except Kiloliana, who knew the back-trails up the precipitous walls, no man could win the gorge save by advancing across a knife-edged ridge. This passage was a hundred yards in length. At best, it was a scant twelve inches wide. On either side yawned the abyss. A slip, and to right or left the man would fall to his death. But once across he would find himself in an earthly paradise. A sea of vegetation laved the landscape, pouring its green billows from wall to wall, dripping from the cliff-lips in great vine-masses, and flinging a spray of ferns and air-plants into the multitudinous crevices. . . . [I]n every open space where the sunshine penetrated, were *papaia* trees burdened with their golden fruit. (1445)

Before he wrote this story London had not actually visited this magical place of waterfalls and unbelievably lush foliage—the beauty of which, convincing as London's descriptions are, would tax any writer. Even more surprising, given his having heard the story from Stoltz's own son and from the landowning class of *haoles* in Hawaii, is that he unambiguously takes Koolau's side in the matter. It is hard to overestimate the importance of the actual Ko'olau to the Kauaians, but it is London, a visitor, who made him known to the world and who, more than any other *malihini* (or newcomer), publicized the lives of the lepers of Molokai. Until recently, London scholars have never remarked on London's visit to Kauai at all.[84] London is an important figure in Kauai: according to travel books from the 1950s and 1960s, the Na Pali Coast, Kauai's most scenic attraction, was actually called "The Jack London Coast."

The splendor of the craggy green cathedrals of the Na Pali Coast and the magnitude of the moral struggle going on between his character Koolau and the authorities clearly heightened London's tendency toward biblical language, despite his dispensing with the direct religious ideas of Ko'olau and his wife. He engaged in heavy use of archaic syntax (Koolau calls his people "Brothers and Sisters"), sentences with lack of be-support, and inverted word order. There is other suggestive biblical language: "We have it from our fathers and our fathers' fathers"; ". . . upon them was placed the mark of the beast"; ". . . creatures that had been racked in millenniums of hell" (*Complete*, 1441–42). Koolau alludes to Ecclesiastes when he remarks, " 'Life is short, and the days are filled with pain' " (1444). The knife-edged terrain reinforces the idea that the way to heaven is narrow and steep. But most moving is the parallel to Christ: "His own people had betrayed him" (1451), "they hurled imprecations and insults at him as they went by" (1453). Koolau meditates upon his fate: "But how? Why? Why should the wholeness of that wild youth of his change to this?" (1454). Echoing Jesus ("Why hast thou forsaken me?"), Koolau is crucified for love of land and people, a real hero, while the white men are gods of madness who, with their terrible weapons, shred the jungle green and take "the envelope of the sky in their hands and [rip] it apart as a woman rips apart a sheet of cotton cloth" (1448).

Although London evidently agreed with the wisdom of confining carriers of the dread disease to Molokai, he used the episode of Koolau's resistance to make a broader statement about justice and a true community of all people:

> "Because we are sick they take away our liberty. We have obeyed the law. We have done no wrong. And yet they would put us in prison. Molokai is a prison. That you know. Niuli, there, his sister was sent to Molokai seven years ago. He has not seen her since. Nor will he ever

see her. She must stay there until she dies. This is not her will. It is not Niuli's will. It is the will of the white men who rule the land. And who are these white men?

"We know. We have it from our fathers and our fathers' fathers. They came like lambs, speaking softly. Well might they speak softly, for we were many and strong, and all the islands were ours. As I say, they spoke softly. They were of two kinds. The one kind asked our permission, our gracious permission, to preach to us the word of God. The other kind asked our permission, our gracious permission, to trade with us. That was the beginning. (1441)

As his story symbolically demonstrates, such resistance was the last that most Hawaiians would see of their traditional culture untainted by the "disease" of western civilization, a motif London would use again in the Hawaiian stories. Koolau's noble death—with the soft sound of rain around him as his fingerless hands clutch his Mauser—makes him a tragic revolutionary hero in a doomed but beautiful world.

A Son of the Sun

London intended to build another collection around a Smoke Bellew-sort of hero in *A Son of the Sun*, something as unified as *Tales of the Fish Patrol*, and he also hoped to create humorous tales like the earlier collection. The "stage" would be "all of the vast South Pacific," he stated. "I know this South Pacific. I sailed my boat, skipper and owner, through it for two years and a half. And remember, I was in the Klondike a few weeks less than one year all told. I couldn't write about the Klondike when I was there; but when I was far enough away from it, and had got my perspective, I picked it up in both my hands and wrote a score of books about it. I am confident, that I can skin my Klondike record in what I shall do with the South Seas" (*Letters*, 991–92). The impulse in *A Son of the Sun* is mightily different from that which fueled *The House of Pride*. Here, he seems out to "skin" his formula-producing record, and the stories of this volume are weaker, just as the Smoke Bellew stories are not London's best group of Klondike stories. And yet among the stories about the successful, strong, and upright hero David Grief are some gems. If Grief sometimes unintentionally amuses us with his bare-knuckled self-righteousness, then London surprises us—if such formula really was his goal—with some highly complex, highly ironic insights into race and power on the "stage" of the South Pacific. London is right that revisiting a locale for "perspective" pays off, as in the classic instance of "To Build a Fire."

"A Son of the Sun" (1911) is the lengthy introductory story that presents and defines David Grief. Grief's frequent allusions to the sun, and its appearance in a number of story titles, recalls the sun's role in the code of justice of the Northland. There are numerous mentions of the time of day being noon, or of the sun low on horizon. Someone navigating in a boat on the open sea would have frequent need to gauge the sun's position, and the white man in the tropics would need to take care of the sun's harmful rays, but the constant reference has a symbolic as well as literal function. "The little black boys, playing naked in the dazzle of sand and sun, were an affront and a hurt to the sun-sick man. He felt a sort of relief when one, running, tripped and fell on all-fours in the tepid sea-water" (*Complete*, 1886). This is a different sun than in the Klondike; there it witnessed and judged white men's deeds, but here it sickens white men and actually brings out their inherent cruelty:

> "Oh, I don't mind being caught in a dirty trick," Griffiths was saying defiantly. "I've been in the tropics too long. I'm a sick man, a damn sick man. And the whiskey, and the sun, and the fever have made me sick in morals, too. Nothing's too mean and low for me now, and I can understand why the niggers eat each other, and take heads, and such things. I could do it myself. So I call trying to do you out of that small account a pretty mild trick. Wisht I could offer you a drink. (1890)

But David Grief is a "true son of the sun" and is not corrupted or sickened by it (as London actually was):

> At least forty years of age, he looked no more than thirty. Yet beachcombers remembered his advent among the islands a score of years before, at which time the yellow mustache was already budding silkily on his lip. Unlike other white men in the tropics, he was there because he liked it. His protective skin pigmentation was excellent. He had been born to the sun. One he was in ten thousand in the matter of sun-resistance. The invisible and high-velocity light waves failed to bore into him. Other white men were pervious. The sun drove through their skins, ripping and smashing tissues and nerves, till they became sick in mind and body, tossed most of the Decalogue overboard, descended to beastliness, drank themselves into quick graves, or survived so savagely that war vessels were sometimes sent to curb their license. . . .
> He also arrived in a hurricane, the giant waves of which deposited him and yacht and all in the thick of a cocoanut grove three hundred

yards beyond the surf. Six months later he was rescued by a pearling cutter. But the sun had got into his blood. At Tahiti, instead of taking a steamer home, he bought a schooner, outfitted her with trade-goods and divers, and went for a cruise through the Dangerous Archipelago. (1894–95)

Upon his return from the *Snark* voyage, suffering from severe ultraviolet damage to his skin and body, London read with horror and relief Charles Woodruff's *The Effects of Tropical Light on White Men.* Thus David Grief is an anomaly of nature, a white man unaffected by the deleterious effects of the tropical sun, but subject to both the forces of nature (the hurricane) and heavenly judgment (the sun, the pearl). As will become clear, he is not only set apart from the other white men he encounters—nearly all morally as well as physically unfit—and a success in his trading and financial ventures in the region, but he is also connected to the native inhabitants of the Pacific Islands, whom, as the stories progress, he comes more and more to defend and admire.

The title story begins with a comparison of a grotesque fish to grotesque people (natives), both part of the natural environment. It then adds a grotesque view of a white character. People are deformed because of the environment of greed and opportunism around them. The narrator's description of the white character, the young German, is the most unattractive because it is not outward appearance that is ugly; that he has "the massive forehead of a scholar and the tumble-home chin of a degenerate" (1885) points to an inner moral lack. Grief himself is "a devil," but "straight" (1887) as his friends describe him; for London he is another superman, a boyish sort of rover:

The cheap undershirt and white loin-cloth did not serve to hide the well put up body. Heavy muscled he was, but he was not lumped and hummocked by muscles. They were softly rounded, and, when they did move, slid softly and silkily under the smooth, tanned skin. Ardent suns had likewise tanned his face till it was swarthy as a Spaniard's. The yellow mustache appeared incongruous in the midst of such swarthiness, while the clear blue of the eyes produced a feeling of shock on the beholder. It was difficult to realize that the skin of this man had once been fair. (1888)

Grief's real distinction from "degenerates" like the young German is less in his magnificent body, however, than in his behavior. The story contrasts his treatment of the black workers with others' treatment; the others beat and curse them but he does not. Now the judging eye of Old Sol is "ardent" in its contemplation of David Grief.

London's staunchly socialist readers will be troubled by the admiration he seems to have for Grief's capitalism:

> How many millions David Grief was worth no man in the Solomons knew, for his holdings and ventures were everywhere in the great South Pacific. From Samoa to New Guinea and even to the north of the Line his plantations were scattered. He possessed pearling concessions in the Paumotus. Though his name did not appear, he was in truth the German company that traded in the French Marquesas. His trading stations were in strings in all the groups, and his vessels that operated them were many. He owned atolls so remote and tiny that his smallest schooners and ketches visited the solitary agents but once a year.
>
> In Sydney, on Castlereagh Street, his offices occupied three floors. But he was rarely in those offices. He preferred always to be on the go amongst the islands, nosing out new investments, inspecting and shaking up old ones, and rubbing shoulders with fun and adventure in a thousand strange guises. He bought the wreck of the great steamship *Gavonne* for a song, and in salving it achieved the impossible and cleaned up a quarter of a million. (1893)

But the narrator follows this up with an amplification of Grief's personality that echoes Martin Eden's joy in the game, not the monetary prizes:

> As the golden tine burned into his face it poured molten out of the ends of his fingers. His was the golden touch, but he played the game, not for the gold, but for the game's sake. It was a man's game, the rough contacts and fierce give and take of the adventurers of his own blood and of half the bloods of Europe and the rest of the world, and it was a good game; but over and beyond was his love of all the other things that go to make up a South Seas rover's life—the smell of the reef; the infinite exquisiteness of the shoals of living coral in the mirror-surfaced lagoons; the crashing sunrises of raw colours spread with lawless cunning; the palm-tufted islets set in turquoise deeps; the tonic wine of the trade-winds; the heave and send of the orderly, crested seas; the moving deck beneath his feet, the straining canvas overhead; the flower-garlanded, golden-glowing men and maids of Polynesia, half-children and half-gods; and even the howling savages of Melanesia, head-hunters and man-eaters, half-devil and all beast. (1895)

What sets Grief apart from the other money grubbers in the South Pacific is his love of the seascape and the people—and his behavior toward them; the passage recalls the similar one in which Smoke Bellew meditates on the things he loves in the Northland scene. But this introductory story's plot concerns his setting right a man who cheated him, establishing the theme of justice and ethics that will concern the subsequent tales.

"The Proud Goat of Aloysius Pankburn" (1911) offers perhaps the most heavy-handed comedy of the David Grief stories, in which Grief literally beats a man out of his alcoholism. Although the tone is highly overstated and overdramatized, the theme, the reinforcement of individual dignity within the community, is one that London has used before, as in the Klondike code of brotherhood. Grief redeems his friend, the degenerate Pankburn, and thus in this and in other stories, Grief is not unlike a chief who faces "peril for the rest of the tribe" (1914), although it is a theme that will be presented in somewhat more broadly applicable instances than this private display of moral authority.

With "The Devils of Fuatino" (1911) the tone changes abruptly as Grief shifts from personal displays of righteousness to acting in the role of social reformer. He goes to save an occupied island from the white devils, the "robbers and pigs" (1926) who have taken it over and abused its inhabitants, as was the situation in "Yah! Yah! Yah!" The story is a suspenseful standoff of Grief and his native friends versus the pirates, dwelling upon the fearsome terrible practices of piracy in the South Pacific. As in all of these stories, the geography is very precise, lending verisimilitude to the sometimes fantastic goings-on. Fuatino is a sort of Bali Hai turned hell for the natives. One of Grief's allies in his tale is an interesting character called the Goat Man, the faun-like Mauriri, whose bravery is dwelt upon even more than Grief's, a welcome change. The focus is now on others—specifically on the native community—rather than just on Grief. It is as though, as with Smoke Bellew, London started out with a neat formula involving a fantastic hero, but as he worked with his locale and the hero's interactions with it (getting his "perspective," perhaps?) he found the exploration of the rest of the community—especially the nonwhites—more interesting and moved away from just using them as backdrops for his hero or as opponents. The same thing seems to have happened from the early stories of Smoke Bellew to the last appearances Smoke makes in "Wonder of Woman" and "Like Argus of the Ancient Times," in which other characters eclipse Bellew as the narrative focus shifts from being directed *on* him to being directed *by* him. This is a process of a character's maturing and becoming not an object of the author's vision but a wielder of it. By "The Devils of Fuatino," London was able to offer direct criticism of colonialism in the Pacific (of which Grief, of course, is a part) through the words of the pirate chief:

> "We are both strong men," Raoul said, with a bow. "We might have been fighting for empires a hundred years ago."
> It was Grief's turn to bow.
> "As it is, we are squalidly scrapping over the enforcement of the colonial laws of those empires whose destinies we might possibly have determined a hundred years ago."
> "It all comes to dust," Raoul remarked sententiously, sitting down. "Go ahead with your meal. Don't let me interrupt." (1937)

Grief responds:

> We've pretty well cleaned it out of the South Seas. But you are a—how shall I say? a sort of an anachronism. You're a throwback, and we've got to get rid of you. Personally, I would advise you to go back to the schooner and blow your brains out. It is the only way to escape what you've got coming to you." (1937)

The implied connection between white imperialism and piracy is intriguing, if understated.

The story's most interesting feature in regard to London's shifting allegiances in the Pacific is that Grief is clearly on the side of the natives, and he helps them sink the pirate ship and shoot pirates in the water. There is one detail that the race-conscious London could not have included without thinking about it: when the Raiatean sailors attack the pirates, and we are told that "[s]wimming swiftly, they singled out the blond heads and the brown" (1940). Up on the cliff from which they have been mounting their attack, watching his native allies strike the "blond heads and the brown," Grief thrills to the vantage point of another race.

"The Jokers of New Gibbon" (1911) is a very dark story that offers a wonderfully drawn native character in Koho, a "black Napoleon, a head-hunting, man-eating Talleyrand" (1942), who gets the last laugh on some whites who play a cruel practical joke on him:

> Nor did any of them notice the little black man who limped up the steps and stood looking on. Koho was a conservative. His fathers before

him had worn no clothes, and neither did he, not even a g-string. The many empty perforations in nose and lips and ears told of decorative passions long since dead. The holes on both ear-lobes had been torn out, but their size was attested by the strips of withered flesh that hung down and swept his shoulders. (1945)

Grief remarks, " 'How are the mighty fallen. . . .To think that used to be Koho, the fiercest red-handed murderer in the Solomons, who defied all his life two of the greatest world powers. And now he's going aboard to try and cadge Denby for a drink' " (1954). The story reveals itself as a human drama on top of the race drama, as Koho is finally able to wreak his revenge upon the men who laugh at him; it is also a message about the gravity of whites' situation among the people they try to exploit—they occasionally forget that they are in the midst of headhunters, who sometimes remember that white heads are not always taboo.

"A Goboto Night" (1911) was written just before "The Mexican," and it is comparable in its personalizing of cultural conflict. A "mecca of sprees" is Goboto, with "more cases of acute alcoholism than any other spot in the world"; it is a place where a dead man is pickled in a cask of rum to be sent back home (2006–7). The theme of gambling is a familiar one in both the Klondike and the South Seas stories, and here the theme of race is personified in Peter Gee, a Chinese trader being abused by drunken whites. Gee is a man who is portrayed as clearly superior. The whites pick on him for his "Chink blood" (2008), but the narrator goes on to say that it is his Chinese blood that gives him his integrity. Predictably, it falls to David Grief to straighten out the chief abuser, an Australian; he makes him memorize and a new credo and then gives him a job:

> "I must always remember that one man is as good as another, save and except when he thinks he is better.
> "No matter how drunk I am I must not fail to be a gentleman. A gentleman is a man who is gentle. Note: It would be better not to get drunk.
> "When I play a man's game with men, I must play like a man.
> "A good curse, rightly used and rarely, is an efficient thing. Too many curses spoil the cursing. Note: A curse cannot change a card sequence nor cause the wind to blow.
> "There is no license for a man to be less than a man. Ten thousand pounds cannot purchase such a license." (2018)

Part 1

The Australian admits in the end, "Maybe it was the whiskey, I don't know, but I'm an ass, a cad, a bounder—everything that's rotten" (2018), but he, too, is redeemed by Grief's code of justice.

"The Feathers of the Sun" (1911) brings together the major concerns of the David Grief stories, although Grief himself is as much observer as agent of change. He describes what he sees of the nations of the world scrambling for treasure in the South Seas: "It was like gamins scrambling for a penny. They got in one another's way" (2044). Japan, France, Germany, Britain, and the United States are locked in combat over the tiny island of Fitu-Iva. It is a comic version of "The Devils of Fuatino," in which a usurper is defeated by Grief, who restores order to the island. Fitu-Iva was the happiest of islands till an unscrupulous white man, Cornelius, calling himself "The Feathers of the Sun" came. He not only exploits the people and ruins their prosperous trading economy, but he blackmails the traders into paying huge fines. The speeches he gives make it sound as though all traders take advantage of natives; he is to be their "protector" and speaks of "white man's burden." The story ends with a hilarious trial scene in which Cornelius, despite his oily eloquence, is tricked by Grief and the fat, drunken King Tui Tulifau. He is humiliated by being beaten with a dead pig—a folk detail that sets the story squarely in the realm of the culture of the islanders, with the traditional (western) thematic center of Grief the hero and his righteousness accompanied by the indigenous comic traditions of the island.

On the Makaloa Mat

After "Wonder of Woman," finished November 25, 1911, London took a nearly five-year hiatus from short story writing, broken only by two minor and clumsy stories that recall his earliest efforts, one written in 1912 ("The Captain of the Susan Drew") and the other in 1914 ("Whose Business It Is to Live"). The hiatus ended in May 1916 with "The Hussy," closely followed by "The Red One," "Like Argus of the Ancient Times," "The Princess," and the stories of *On the Makaloa Mat*. Why this lapse from short stories, a central creative activity of his life? And why the sudden rebirth of powerful short stories?

Perhaps one of the last stories from the earlier period, "By the Turtles of Tasman," holds a clue. Finished July 31, 1911, and included in the collection *The Turtles of Tasman* (1916), it depicts a man's wrenching self-examination. The catalyst for his revision of identity is contact with a powerful woman. Two brothers, one carefree and one careful—a motif familiar to us from other pairs of similar stories, such as "When the World was Young" and "The Eternity of Forms"—face each other as the adventurous but irresponsible brother returns home to die. A prodigal son, Tom journeyed about the world leading a wild life of danger and excitement, while Frederick stayed home to mind the family fortunes. The title comes from the elegy for Tom delivered by an old friend of his, and it is a phrase that comes to haunt the surviving brother: " 'By the turtles of Tasman, he was a man' " (2088).

Tom's exotic daughter, Polly, also gives Frederick cause to doubt the wisdom of his stable existence:

> "You seem to value life in terms of profit and loss," she said. "I wonder if you have ever known love."
> The shaft went home. He had not kissed his woman. His marriage had been one of policy. It had saved the estate in the days when he had been almost beaten in the struggle to disencumber the vast holdings Isaac Travers' wide hands had grasped. The girl was a witch. She had probed an old wound and made it hurt again. He had never had time to love. He had worked hard. He had been president of the chamber of commerce, mayor of the city, state senator, but he had missed love. . . .
> In the moment following Polly's remark, he was aware of a great emptiness. It seemed that his hands had grasped ashes, until glancing into the other room, he saw Tom asleep in the big chair, very grey and aged and tired. He remembered all that he had done, all that he possessed. Well, what did Tom possess? (2075–76)

Suffering from increasing physical and spiritual afflictions, London himself was in the midst of a midlife crisis. What is to be valued in life? Polly says love, giving rise to a new theme in London's writing, or rather the revivifying of a theme. As the love stories of the California novels also attempt, "By the Turtles of Tasman" indicates the deep self-questioning the male psyche must undergo in order fully to appreciate the power of love. London even allows Polly to use the words of his own "credo": " 'When you are dust, my father will be ashes. That is the difference' " (2083).

There is no question that London was struggling in the seven months from May until November of 1916 when he entered into his last burst of short story writing, and no question that his struggle culminated in a series of epiphanies. That critics and biographers have assumed that, given his illnesses, he could not have been capable of grappling with serious issues in serious fiction indicates a surprising ignorance of what he actually was writing during the year of his death. Despite his kidney pain and the heavy doses of medication he was taking for it, he continued as ever his regular work schedule, traveling and also administering the many demands of the ranch. The longer works written toward the last years, including *The Star Rover* and the California trilogy, were fine works, but not up to the caliber of his best short fiction. One event that propelled a brilliant new burst of short story writing was his reading of Carl Jung's *Psychology of the Unconscious*, especially as it was juxtaposed with his deepening understanding of the myths and legends of ancient Hawaii. Although the duration of its direct influence was very short (a few months), Jung's is one of the most significant—and heavily annotated—volumes in London's huge library.

As the terrific imaginative impact of Homer and Milton upon London at the start of his career and his enthusiastic responses to the great theories of Darwin, Spencer, Marx, Nietzsche, and other major thinkers of his own age attest, he was always hungry for a world view that would "explain," and he leapt at what he learned in Jung. As a result, the process of self-examination he was already undergoing was accelerated and amplified, so that, in Jungian terms, he was able to approach the peace of an "individuated" (fully realized, psychically balanced) personality by the time of his death. But the brilliant stories of his last year, set in Hawaii, where he had returned for one last visit to rest and improve his health,[85] and collected in *On the Makaloa Mat* (1919), are ambiguous enough that the opposite could be argued as well: perhaps London only neared but never attained any fundamental sense of his own identity, never returned to Ithaka but only glimpsed it over the horizon.

One can tell from reading the letters of London's last year how sick he was, in both mind and body. Many of the letters of this time betray a weary, dull, and irritable mind, and there are dreadful exchanges with certain correspondents. London wrote a terrible letter to his 12-year-old daughter, Joan, notifying her of his disgust: "Unless I should accidentally meet you on the street, I doubt if I should ever see you again. If you should be dying, and should ask for me at your bedside, I should surely come; on the other hand, if I were dying I should not care to have you at my bedside. A ruined colt is a ruined colt, and I do not like ruined colts" (*Letters*, 1300–1301). Obviously London needed to recognize that his philosophical reliance upon materialism was not going to yield any further understanding of the meaning of his life and his relation to the lives of those around him, and having also failed to find answers in traditional religion, he turned to Jung's psychology of the unconscious.

Jung's version of the human soul offered London scientific support for the notion of free will, for, as Jung's translator Beatrice Hinkle puts it, Jung argues that a person "may to a certain extent become a self-creating and self-determining being" if he is able to "reflect upon himself and learn to understand the true origin and significance of his actions and opinions" through self-consciousness about previously buried unconscious motives and impulses. Rather than "a series of reactions to stimuli," an individuated person's behavior will reflect "the real level of his development" and he will no longer be "self-deceived." Charmian quotes from this very passage in Hinkle's introduction in the section of her biography that relates to London's discovery of Jung. Jack came in to Charmian, "all a tip-toe with discovery" at this "inkling free will." A few days later he told her, " 'For the first time in my life, . . . I see the real value to the human soul of the confessional. . . . I tell you I am standing on the edge of a world so new, so terrible, that I am almost afraid to look over into it.' "[86] That there could really be a realm beyond materialistic determinism came as an even greater revelation, and it allowed London to see anew the mythic archetypes he had worked with all along—from Sol to the Night-Born to the twinned dark and light "brothers."

Why did Jung in particular resonate so strongly for London? Jung and London were both representative of their time, the emergence of modernism, of internationalism, and of the astonishing changes that would be wrought with technology, including in war. As coevals—Jung was born on July 26, 1875, and London on January 11, 1876—these creative geniuses confronted many of the same great ideas and problems of their age, each in his way. Strangely, in a case of what Jung would call "synchronicity," they experienced their greatest crises in the same year, 1913, when London's Wolf House burned to the ground and Jung had his bitter split with Freud, who had once called him his "beloved son." There are other parallels—their peculiar mothers, their attraction/ repulsion to the ideas of Nietzsche, their interest in extraterrestrial life, their deep reading in ancient myth. Jungian analyst James Kirsch has remarked, "Jack London recognized that the archetypes are the factors which arrange and control our fate, and that by contacting them, we establish a relationship to our destiny and no longer remain mere objects of fate. He recognized his destiny, but also his inability to change his destiny at such late hour. . . . He was one of the great mythmakers of mankind." In stories like "The Red One," Kirsch notes, London does not describe his personal psychology, but gives "an accurate picture of American psychology and of Western man as a whole." Kirsch connects London's struggle to Nietzsche's and Jung's, and describes a modern world in "unrest" due to the modern contempt for the nonrational world of the unconscious Self.[87] This is a crucial point—London's interaction with Jung should be seen on a cultural and artistic rather than only on a personal level.

Two significant studies of London's identification with Jung's theories of the archetypes of the collective unconscious are Kirsch's and James McClintock's; they have influenced later scholars to revise the misconception of London's artistic decline. But of greatest importance has been Earle Labor, whose essays since the 1960s and whose 1974 Twayne's United States Authors Series volume, *Jack London*, insist upon the significance of London's reading of Jung,[88] as many references to him in these pages attest.

Kirsch gives an interesting and immediately recognizable analysis of London as though he is a patient. He calls London a "radiant, extraordinary human being," one who was "deeply and wildly in love with life" and who "lived it to the full, always risking himself and giving himself fully to life as he found it on the outside," but who also "gave himself to writing almost every day of his life." As a result, he was a man torn between his powerful extraversion and the introversion reflected in his books and stories. This conflict caught up with him following the loss of his dream house to fire, and he "was finally captured by the inner world. A profound and complete introversion began just when he was thirty-seven years of age, which was only occasionally interrupted by heavy drinking bouts and a few trips" (Kirsch, 137–39).

London's problem, according to Kirsch, was that since he denied the existence of the soul, "he did not notice that his prolific creative work came out of the Self," the "Self" being the term Jungians use for the center of the unconscious (the "ego" is the corresponding center of consciousness). London identified the ego with the Self, ignoring in his materialistic monism the tremendous creative energies of the Self. Although London stated that he had no patience with "fly-by-night" metaphysicians and believed that "when I am dead, I am dead," Kirsch comments that London also "wrote the most imaginative and lively stories we have known in American literature"; his true identity as a poet was lived with "incorruptible sincerity and unquestioned devotion in the service of his inner voice" (Kirsch, 140). "Yet London overestimated his stamina and powers, his physical and financial resources by far . . ."; he was "a tragic victim of the process of individuation." But he was ultimately not a failure, for "he lived his life fully and without reservation" and when the time came "courageously accepted the challenge of the Self" (Kirsch, 148).

McClintock is by far less certain that London achieved any hopeful insight from Jung in his last stories. Although there is no question of Jung's immediate and far-reaching impact on the writer, McClintock believes that London only glimpsed hope in the distance but could not overcome his innate pessimism and determinism in order to grasp it. Analyzing the Jungian story "Like Argus of the Ancient Times" and the five in *On the Makaloa Mat*, McClintock is most drawn to London's use of the hero archetype:

> According to Jung, a wandering hero, representing "ever-restless desire," undertakes a perilous "night journey" into a mysterious land, representing a subconscious secret, in search of the "treasure difficult to attain". . . . Late in the journey the sun-hero wanderer faces death, and this confrontation is, ironically, "the highest summit of life. . . ." Finally, the hero returns to water (the womb) and/or emerges in the east reborn. (McClintock, 156–57)

Somehow, McClintock says, beginning with the victory of the old "argonaut" Tarwater, "Jung's ideas had restored London's passion for adventure" and "rekindled" his ability "to assert positive values." In particular, Jung's concept of the libido allowed London to "resurrect his analogous concepts of 'true adventure' and 'imagination'—those prerequisite capacities for embracing the hardships in nature and wresting spiritual regeneration from a nightmarish encounter with the Arctic wasteland" (157). London read of the libido as "a hypothetical energy of life," as Hinkle puts it, "[a] cosmic energy or urge manifested in the human being [and like] the energy of physics" (in McClintock, 157–58). McClintock sees Tarwater, the "restless wanderer" driven by gold fever, as a figure Jung would identify as driven by the " 'unquenchable longing' of libido energy working within the sun-hero, making him continue his perilous journey" (158). This hero's eastward journey and his discovery of gold demonstrates Tarwater's success in revitalizing his libido energy. "[I]f one honors God, the sun or fire," Jung writes, "then one honors one's own vital force, the libido" (in McClintock, 158).

In addition to the male hero, the figures of the sexual and racial "other" had long been, as we have seen in this study, the subjects and objects of London's fictional work—Margaret Henan of "Samuel," Lucy of "The Night-Born," or Maphuhi's naked, brown mother diving for the Pearl of Great Price. With the Jungian framework of his last stories, these figures display at least some of their origination in his own unconscious. We must reread not only the sun-hero myth but also the racial and sexual "others" of London's fiction, since through these characters arise the major themes of justice, community, and imagination. From Sol as the figure of divine judgment, a Father Sky God who observes from afar, the sun in London's psyche transforms into the evanescent whole of the Red One buried deep in the jungle hell of Melanesia. What does his hero see in this new, this dark and bloody, sun?

"The Red One," written in May 1916, possibly just before London read Jung, represents London's characteristic themes and his favorite motifs of race, adventure, violence, facing death, and searching for a dimension beyond the materialist, naturalist universe. Lawrence I. Berkove has pointed out that London read Jung in June 1916, and "The Red One" was completed the month before. But Berkove notes that there were at least 15 other works of Jung's translated between 1907 and 1916. Although scholars do not know which if any of these London read, his lively interest in psychology (including his reading of Freud as early as 1912) and the widespread currency of Jung's ideas in America argue for his familiarity with Jung. "[I]t is not farfetched," Berkove writes, "to think that London had read the works of other psychologists as well, and that he read *Psychology of the Unconscious* when it first came out because he had encountered Jung's thought elsewhere." If the June encounter with Jung marked London's first, Berkove surmises, then "The Red One" "is even more remarkable because if it preceded London's contact with Jungian psychology then London would have had to arrive independently at some of the same insights as Jung."[89]

In March 1916, London wrote to George Sterling from Honolulu: "Do you remember that wonderful story you told me . . . ?—of the meteoric message from Mars or some other world in space, that fell amongst isolated savages, that was recognized for what it was by the lost explorer, who died or was killed before he could gain access to the treasure in the heart of the apparent meteor?" (*Letters*, 1542). Sterling's vignette prompted the competing elements of London's imagination to coalesce in one of his most unusual stories: a message from the stars, real *and* metaphysical; a lost explorer, dying but having seen the "treasure"; the "civilized" man among the "savages"; and the thrill of new, scientific knowledge falling amidst the primeval.

The story presents archetypes of the persona, shadow, anima, and wise old man in a tale of a scientist hunting a rare butterfly—a symbol of the soul—on a remote island. Although the scientist, Bassett, does not set out for a confrontation with the eternal, he finds himself over-come with fever and lost in the gloomy green of Guadalcanal, all the while pulled further into the interior of the island by a strange and pow-erful sound. He comes to find the source of the call, the "Red One," a giant sphere unearthed by the natives who worship and sacrifice to it. This sphere symbolizes wholeness, and it is specifically feminine, a Great Mother, a red bloody pearl of the earth, hollow like the womb, site of inscrutable blood mysteries. But because Bassett represents modern man's search for a soul, he believes it is a device from outer space, sent by intelligences far greater than our own but ironically fallen into a land of savages. Despite malaria, he is determined to find his way out and bring the Red One to the civilized world. According to Kirsch, "The Self truly inspired this story; there is not a superfluous word in it" (Kirsch, 143).

But driving himself harder and harder to write an "incredible amount of great and also mediocre stories, . . . always driven to over-demand himself," London strove for the impossible in everything, Kirsch says, "wantonly risking more than even his powerful organism could stand." Kirsch believes that the illnesses and personal disappointments that began to overtake London (the loss of Wolf House, his daughters' refusal to come live with him, and his loneliness in the midst of his many friends) were traceable to the long-lasting tropical illnesses he contracted on *Snark* voyage. He and Bassett are thus comparable. As Kirsch puts it, Bassett

> actually acquired his fatal illness practically at the instant at which he entered the jungle. And yet he did not die from his illness. His illness rather gave him the chance to expose himself once more to the great-est risk and grace which can be bestowed upon man. . . . It was a con-tract he made with the Self. At the last moment he was indeed tempted to cheat God but rejected it, because he acknowledged that the Self had played squarer than square with him. . . . Jack London's hero, in contrast, was true to himself to the end. He recognized that the Self had given him both spiritual and material riches, had played squarer than square with him and he, Jack London, must needs play fair as well with the Self to the end. (Kirsch, 146–47)

For his sacrifice, Bassett is granted "the vision of God" (Kirsch, 148).

Bassett keeps moving toward the "liberation" sound of the Red One, which the narrator compares to the trumpets of archangels and the sirens' call to Odysseus.[90] But the elevated imagery—from the Bible to Homer to Browning—used to describe the purity and beauty of the great voice of the Red One is accompanied by scenes of startling brutality, and each act of violence committed by Bassett in order to survive the jungle is followed by greater horrors.

And then he meets Balatta, a bushwoman who saves him from death and takes him back to her village. "And her face! A twisted and wizened complex of apish features, perforated by upturned, sky-open, Mongolian nostrils, by a mouth that sagged from a huge upper-lip and faded precipitately into a retreating chin, and by peering querulous eyes that blinked as blink the eyes of denizens of monkey-cages" (*Complete*, 2302). Ugly she may be—and to Bassett she is ugly insofar as she displays non-Caucasian features—but she is smart, curious, loyal, self sacrificing, and in her primitive way she loves him. But Bassett can only see her as grotesque, and he decides to use her to gain access to the Red One, which means certain death for her if she is caught. Summoning all his resolve, he takes her to the creek for a good scrubbing before making love to her "grotesque, female hideousness. . . ." Bassett, the narrator tells us, "was a fastidious man. He had never recovered from the initial horror caused by Balatta's female awfulness. Back in England, even at best, the charm of woman, to him, had never been robust. Yet now, resolutely, as only a man can do who is capable of martyring himself for the cause of science, he proceeded to violate all the fineness and delicacy of his nature by making love to the unthinkably disgusting bushwoman" (2307). As Moreland comments, Bassett's treatment of Balatta and his understanding that the entire population of the island could be destroyed if he sees the Red One and brings it back shows how he is "directed by a modern man's only moral guide—the end justifies the means," thus he is a forerunner of "the fathers of the mushroom cloud. . . . Could there be a more appropriate time for the expression of this theme than 1916, the year of Verdun and the Somme?" (Moreland, "The Quest," 66).

The shaman of the village is Ngurn, who is artful, intelligent, and fair, and whom the neo-colonialist Bassett vastly prefers to Balatta. He considers Ngurn a forerunner of civilization: "Head-hunting, cannibal beast of a human that was as much ape as human, nevertheless Old Ngurn had, according to his lights played squarer than square" (*Complete*, 2317). But Bassett does not listen to Ngurn, for Ngurn disputes Bassett's notion that the Red One came from the stars, describing it as being of another order entirely, one more in accord with the unconscious: "[W]hat were flame and blaze and glow when they had flamed, and blazed and glowed? Answer: memories, memories only, of things which had ceased to be, like memories of matings accomplished, of feasts forgotten, of desires that were ghosts of desires, flaring, flaming, burning, yet unrealized in achievement of easement and satisfaction. Where was the appetite of yesterday? the roasted wild pig the hunter's arrow failed to slay? the maid, unwed and dead, ere the young man knew her. A memory was not a star, was Ngurn's contention. How could a memory be a star? . . . . stars were fire, and the Red One was not fire—" (2305). Instead of going along with Bassett's theories, Ngurn looks forward to "curing"—the pun intended—Bassett's head.

The Red One recalls the Sol of the Klondike stories who judges the deeds of men, for it is called the "Sun-Singer" (2307) and knows a "cosmic secret" (2297): "No drop of red dew shaken from the lion-mane of some sun in torment was the sounding sphere" (2314). If it comes from "space," as Bassett wonders, is it less a "device" than a fallen sun? "At first he had fancied the Red One to be some colossal statue, like Memnon, rendered vocal under certain temperature conditions of sunlight. But when, after a war raid, a batch of prisoners was brought in and the sacrifice made at night, in the midst of rain, when the sun could play no part, the Red One had been more vocal than usual, Bassett discarded that hypothesis" (2308). A thing of light and reason is worshipped by evil savages in a bloody sacrificial pit in which evil deeds go unpunished and are even demanded by the Red One—this is Bassett's view. But the true subversion is different. The Red One is an *inner* sun that reveals who and what we are: "Truly had the bush-folk named themselves into the name of the Red One, seeing in him their own image which they strove to placate and please with such red offerings" (2312). If so, this is not so different from the role of Sol, since his presence causes men to reveal themselves. The other allusions to the divine—"Titan of the Elder World" (2296), "voice of God" (2317), "benediction" (2301), "the God-Voiced" (2304), and so forth—support the Sol connection, but the story constantly also reminds us of its (feminine) inversion.

As Bassett sits watching the "slow setting of the western stars beyond the black wall of jungle," it occurs to him that "all must obey, or compose, the same laws that ran without infraction through the entire experience of man" (2313). His plight is universal, but he must be dramatically shown the truth of his assertion that the laws of the universe are the same for all, in all times. His longing for psychological integration and individuation is manifested in his yearning for the source of the Red One, but he sees only man's escape from the "darkness and confusion" of the unconscious; he does not recognize that perhaps to include instead of exclude is the secret of the cosmos. The unity of the Red One still escapes him.

As the Southern Cross rises in the sky Bassett slowly fades: "Too long and too closely had life ebbed down in him to bite him with fear of his impending extinction. He continued to persist, alternating periods of unconsciousness with periods of semiconsciousness, dreamy and unreal, in which he idly wondered whether he had ever truly beheld the Red One or whether it was a nightmare fancy of delirium" (2315). Bassett loses control of his body until "he is scarcely aware of possessing one. Lightly indeed his flesh sat upon his soul, in its brightness and clarity, [that he] knew by its very clarity, that the black of cessation was near" (2315). Bassett's flesh is emaciated, but his soul, nearing its chance at transformation, burns ever brighter as he longs for "his final adventure in the quick of the flesh" (2315). Now is the time to look upon the Red One.

Turning his "clear, unfaltering, all-seeing eyes" upon the object of his search and moving "down the spiral path . . . encircling the sheening, glowing Red One that seemed ever imminent to iridesce from color and light into sweet singing and thunder," Bassett asks for "the wonder voice of the Red One" to sing in his ears as he dies, and Ngurn obliges, ordering the villagers to strike it with the giant key post. Its "abrupt and thunderous liberation" sounds once more, with its color "acrawl and tit-illant and vapourous" fusing with its sound, as symbolically all opposing elements are joined together. Significantly, as he peers into the bloody Pearl before him, Bassett sees there the "supermen of planets and other suns." Still, even in this extremity, he is unable to see beyond his construction of truth as rational, male, and scientific: "[T]he interstices of matter were his, and the interfusings and intermating transfusings of matter and force" (2317). Bassett's ecstasy is broken by an impatient movement of Ngurn, and, momentarily considering whether he should cheat Ngurn of his head, Bassett bends willingly to the ax:

—And Bassett, raising his hand in signal, bending forward his head as agreed so as to expose cleanly the articulation to his taut spinal cord, forgot Balatta, who was merely a woman, a woman merely and only and undesired. He knew, without seeing, when the razor-edged hatchet rose in the air behind him. And for that instant, ere the end, there fell upon Bassett the shadow of the Unknown, a sense of impending marvel of the rending of the walls before the unimaginable. Almost, when he knew the blow had started and just ere the edge of steel bit the flesh and nerves, it seemed that he gazed upon the serene face of the

Medusa, Truth—And, simultaneous with the bite of the steel on the onrush of the dark, in a flashing instant of fancy, he saw the vision of his head turning slowly, always turning, in the devil-devil house beside the breadfruit tree." (2317–18)

Bassett sees the last thing he must have expected to see: instead of the "supermen" from space revealing themselves in the depths of the Red One, it is a woman, a horrible woman, the most horrible woman who has ever lived—can this be Truth? His head and Medusa's coalesced, Bassett sees in the unknown a unity he has never known.

The choice of Medusa is significant: an evil creature of Greek mythology, Medusa was the daughter of two marine deities who were the children of Pontus (Sea) and Ge (Earth). She had a round, ugly face, snakes for hair, a belt of the teeth of a boar, and sometimes a beard, huge wings, and eyes that could transform people into stone. She may once have been an earth goddess, but as her story is usually told, she was loved by Poseidon but hunted and killed, with the aid of Athena, the hero Perseus; the head came to adorn the aegis of Zeus as well as that of Athena.[91]

For Bassett, Medusa is a dualistic figure. The rigidity associated with her is the rigidity of death, and her bloodthirstiness is the "horrors" he has encountered. Her grotesque femaleness links her to his disgust at Balatta, while the severed head connects her to Ngurn. But it is extremely important that what he sees in the Red One turns out to be female and "ugly," since those two traits reside in the one person in the story who is totally "other" to Bassett, Balatta. Although their very names echo one another, she is the gendered and racial opposite of the white male protagonist, and so, in the context of all of London's efforts at writing about racial and sexual others, we must take account of Medusa's peculiarly alien identity. She is Medusa, but she is also Truth—she thus reveals the integration Bassett has been seeking, but in the way he would least have imagined, in the "horror" of the feminine. Jung's warning seems appropriate: "Man would do well to heed the wise counsel of the mother and obey the inexorable law of nature which sets limits to every being. He ought never to forget that the world exists only because opposing forces are held in equilibrium. So, too, the rational is counterbalanced by the irrational, and what is planned and purposed by what is."[92] Penetrating his own unconscious, Bassett has passed through his "dark night of the soul" and may have achieved the momentous connection with the entirety of the soul's contents. As Erich Neumann explains, "Not only does the night, leading through death and sleep to healing and birth, renew the cycle of life; but, transcending earthly darkness, it sublimates the very essence of life through the eruption from the depths of those powers that, in drunkenness and ecstasy, poetry and illumination, manticism and wisdom, enable man to achieve a new dimension of spirit and light."[93] If only in his dying moment, Bassett may have seen and heard what he has quested for.

Any reading of "The Red One" ultimately depends on how one reads the Medusa at the end. Berkove finds only a sense of despair at the end of the story, the Medusa signaling hopelessness (Berkove, "The Myth," 215); Moreland says, "Death, the Noseless One, has the stage alone at the end," and that "London thought he had found a key to this mystery in the writings of Jung but the perplexities of John Lakana, Hardman Pool, Prince Akuli, and Bassett demonstrate that Truth still hid her face" (Moreland, "The Quest," 68). But perhaps Bassett's confrontation of the "Medusa, Truth" shows evidence of London's willingness to look within and face the darkness of his own unconscious, at least in the hopes of finding a solution. That willingness is not *about* hope; it *is* hope. "Sometimes I wonder if it can be possible, in the ponderings of the dying scientist, Bassett, that Jack London revealed more of himself than he would have been willing to admit—or else, who knows? more of himself than he himself realized," Charmian wrote (C. London, *The Book*, 2:334). Certainly looking at this story through the lens of Jung's relevance to London's own psyche is not the only way to read it and the related stories of *On the Makaloa Mat*, but it indisputably gives a defining structure to the story patterns and possible purpose.

The Hawaiian stories that follow "The Red One" share many of its attributes—especially the psychological underpinnings—but, with the exception of "Shin Bones," are generally simpler and brighter, more celebratory of "native" civilization. Their dialogic structure, most often involving a *haole* listener and native teller, and most often addressing the joint issues of race, gender, and class, lends them a pleasant air of "talk-story," as they say in Hawaii, amusing conversation to pass the time. But they also address key elements of life in Hawaii among people of different backgrounds and status. Not until the last story, "The Water Baby," did London again so nearly approach the ontological mysteries he gazed upon in "The Red One."

"On the Makaloa Mat," finished June 9, 1916, uses a Hawaiian cliché to frame the entire collection with its title: being "on the mat" in Hawaii means you belong, that you are *"kama'aina."* The story presents a "noble situation" as two Hawaiian sisters, Bella and Martha, sit under a magnificent hau tree and tell of love and of the past. The story shows great admiration for Hawaiians and their traditions and particular reverence for these noble ladies, "the sun-warm, love-warm heart of Hawaii" (*Complete*, 2321). The narrator confides:

> [A]s both sisters resumed their talk, an observer would have noted the striking resemblance of their pure, straight profiles, of their broad cheek bones, of their wide and loftly foreheads, of their iron-gray abundance of hair, of their sweet-lipped mouths set with the carriage of decades of assured and accomplished pride, and of their lovely, slender eyebrows arched over equally lovely long brown eyes. The hands of both of them, little altered or defaced by age, were wonderful in their slender tapering finger tips, love-lomi'd and love-formed while they were babies by old Hawaiian women like to the one even then eating *poi* and *iamaka* and *limu* in the house. (2329–30)

Fascinated with the unprecedented racial mixing in Hawaii, London relates in great detail the several bloodlines that Bella and Martha share. The body of the tale involves Bella's recalling her loveless marriage to a "gray," lifeless *haole* and her momentary escape into the arms of Lilolilo, a Hawaiian prince who dallies with her on one of his royal progressions and then abandons her, breaking her heart. It is a romantic tale demythologized by the woman's version of it, and it offers an inside look at her feelings that is remarkably fresh and natural for a male writer to have created.

"The Tears of Ah Kim," a love story told from an unusual angle, was completed June 19, 1916. It displays more overtly London's interest in Jung. Ah Kim has been tolerating the unprovoked beatings of his mother for years, and as a result has never married. He meets a woman, Li Faa, determined to save him from his fate, and he is finally able to escape his mother's wrath. It may seem like a thematically "eccentric" and "obscure piece of slapstick," McClintock notes, but "it is almost a programmatic presentation of specific symbols and themes discussed in *Psychology of the Unconscious*." The story reflects an oedipal complex and utilizes Jung's concept of "the sacrifice," in which the sexually maturing individual must find a "sexual object to replace the forbidden mother," whose punishments reinforce the individual's incestuous guilt. Freedom from the mother (symbolized by myths of death) results in a new, mature relationship with the sexual object (McClintock, 339–40). Ah Kim explains on his wedding night why he finally cried under his mother's last beating, after withholding his tears so long, and this broke the spell: " 'She no longer had strength enough to hurt me.' " His mother having lost her oedipal power, Ah Kim is free to enjoy Li Faa, "my Flower of Serenity, my Perfect Rest" (*Complete*, 184).

The story is also of interest because of its tongue-in-cheek handling of the racial and class changes that occur with immigration. It is odd, for example, that the mother uses a Hawaiian word, "*pake*," to describe Li Faa:

> "I will have no half *pake* daughter-in-law," his mother often reiterated to Ah Kim, *pake* being the Hawaiian word for Chinese. "All *pake* must my daughter-in-law be, even as you, my son, and as I, your mother. And she must wear trousers, my son, as all the women of our family before her. No woman, in the she-devil skirts and corsets, can pay due reverence to our ancestors. Corsets and reverences do not go together. Such a one is this shameless Li Faa. She is impudent and independent, and will be neither obedient to her husband nor her husband's mother. This brazen-faced Li Faa would believe herself the source of life and the first ancestor, recognizing no ancestors before her. She laughs at our joss sticks and paper prayers and family gods, as I have been well told." (2348)

For her part, "Li Faa would never come into Ah Kim's house as he thoroughly knew, and kowtow to his mother and be slave to her in the immemorial Chinese way. Li Faa, from the Chinese angle, was a new woman, a feminist, who rode horseback astride, disported immodestly garbed on Waikiki on the surf boards, and at more than one luau had been know to dance the hula with the worst and in excess of the worst to the scandalous delight of all. . . . [And] Ah Kim himself, a generation younger than his mother, had been bitten by the acid of modernity" (2349). Like most of the stories of *On the Makaloa Mat*, this one reflects ambiguity and thus shows maturity: " 'That will do for China. I do not know China. This is Hawaii, and in Hawaii the customs of all foreigners change,' " says Li Faa (2350). The cultural reversals going forward are amplified by the psychological dimensions of the story into a rich mix of conflicts.

"The Bones of Kahekili," completed July 2, 1916, has a darker tone than the two that preceded it. A wealthy *haole* landowner, Hardman Pool, likes to call together his Hawaiian sons and retainers and sit in judgment on them, answering their requests and generally bossing them around. One day he pries a sacred story out of an old retainer,

Kumuhana. The story involves the mandatory sacrifice of commoners upon the death of an *ali'i* (or lord) in Kumuhana's village. Kumuhana was chosen but escaped death in a grotesque accident. The arrogant Pool is not unlike the old chiefs who would sacrifice people to their whims: "He knew his Hawaiians from the outside and the in, knew them better than themselves—their Polynesian circumlocutions, faiths, customs, and mysteries" (2357). Pool also feels most men are fools, and this is why some rule and some follow: " 'All this is life for you, because you think but one day at a time, while we, your chiefs, think for you all days and far days ahead' " (2366). Despite his certainties, Hardman Pool is obsessed with the Maori death chants of Kumuhana: "But death is nothing new. / Death is and has been ever since old Maui died. / Then Pata-tai laughed aloud / And woke the goblin god, / Who severed him in two, and shut him in / So dusk of eve came on" (2372). As McClintock notes, "Maui the sun god of rebirth is dead. . . . The destructive 'goblin god' rules, bringing 'the dusk of eve' " (McClintock, 166). The story manages to place itself somewhere between the jaded truisms of the white patriarch and the memories of the old Hawaiian.

"Shin Bones" was finished on August 21, 1916. It relates the story of a young *ali'i* who has gone off to Oxford to be educated and has joined the modern world. To a *haole* companion, waiting with him and his broken-down car by the side of a road on his island of Lakanii, Prince Akuli recounts his experience journeying to a cave containing the bones of his ancestors. He tells the narrator how this experience changed his way of thinking. Prince Akuli is a modern Hawaiian trying to come to terms with his past. As he talks, an old lady sits and makes him a special lei of hala; out of her hearing he says, " 'It stinks of the ancient. . . . I stink of the modern' " (*Complete*, 2387). Ah Kim was "bitten by the acid of modernity," but what has happened to Akuli is much more profound:

> "I believe in no mystery stuff of old time nor the kahunas. And yet I saw in that cave things which I dare not name to you, and which I, since old Ahuna died, alone of the living know. I have no children. With me my long line ceases. This is the twentieth century, and we stink of gasoline. Nevertheless these other and nameless things shall die with me. I shall never revisit the burial place. Nor in all time to come will any man gaze upon it through living eyes unless the quakes of earth rend the mountains asunder and spew forth the secrets contained in the hearts of the mountains. . .
>
> "To them, those poor pathetic bones, I owe more than to aught else. I became possessed of them in the period of my culminating adoles-

cence. I know they changed the entire course of my life and trend of my mind. They gave to me a modesty and a humility in the world from which my father's fortune has ever failed to seduce me.

"And often, when woman was nigh to winning to the empery of my mind over me, I sought Laulani's shin bone. And often, when lusty manhood stung me into feeling overproud and lusty, I consulted the spearhead remnant of Keaho, one time swift runner, and mighty wrestler and lover, and thief of the wife of a king. The contemplation of them has ever been of profound aid to me, and you might well say that I have founded my religion or practice of living upon them." (2394)

Since Prince Akuli's mother bribed him to get the bones for her with the promise of an Oxford education, Moreland comments that "[i]ronically the Prince's journey into his past is his talisman into the future" (Moreland, "The Quest," 60).

The story's allusions point to its symbolic significances: the narrator is careful to point out that "Akuli" means "squid" in Hawaiian, an allusion to the deeps that Akuli must traverse in order to secure the treasure. There is a curious reference to "Don Juan Byron," who gave his grandmother a canopied four-poster bed, and mention of the story of King Arthur, Lancelot, and Guinevere. Lakanii is another allusion to the name of the author, and the landscape of the tale suggests the setting of London's earlier tale of freedom and identity, "Koolau the Leper," since the "Iron-Bound Coast" is supposed to the Na Pali Coast of Kauai where Koolau died. Akuli and Ahuna pass an old leper hiding in the bush—a self-reflexive allusion? The Jungian archetypes of the perilous journey, descent into water, and the cave are all aspects of the story's initiation theme. Alienated from the mythopoeic vision that gives meaning, modern man is both criticized in the story and sympathized with. Akuli and Ahuna personify the divergent visions struggling in the author's psyche: materialism versus faith.

Attaining the summit of the "Iron-Bound Coast," dropping down into a remote valley, and successfully swimming up a lava tube in pitch blackness, Akuli finds and moves about in the ancient burial cave of his ancestors, where his cynicism vanishes into an epiphany as he sees the remains of a famous royal love triangle and hears their tragic story from Ahuna:

> "And, Ahuna done, I could but gaze, with imagination at the one time
> sobered and fired. Old drunken Howard had lent me his Tennyson,

and I had mooned long and often over the 'Idyls of the King.' Here were the three, I thought—Arthur and Launcelot and Guinevere. This, then, I pondered, was the end of it all, of life and strife and striving and love, the weary spirits of these long-gone ones to be invoked by fat old women and mangy sorcerers, the bones of them to be esteemed of collectors and betted on horse races and ace-fulls or to be sold for cash and invested in sugar stocks. (2392)

Akuli recognizes for the first time what Gerard Manley Hopkins termed "the light man was born for," and he keeps two bones as *memento mori.* Moreland concludes: "Like Hardman Pool, Prince Akuli is wise, but the wisdom is bitter. . . . [M]oderation, resignation, and stoicism in the face of time and dissolution are his meagre substitutes for the customs, folklore, and beliefs that gave meaning to old Ahuna's life" (Moreland, "The Quest," 61). The events of this story make Akuli a man, but because he is also a modern, he is forever torn between Hawaii and the world, past and present, memory and reality.

"The Kanaka Surf" is the odd story out in *On the Makaloa Mat.* Completed August 22, 1916, and published with the ironical title "Man of Mine" in *Hearst's* in February 1917, it tells of a couple who face a love triangle and survive it; the husband, however, cruelly tests the wife's love by pretending to have a leg cramp as they swim beyond the reef off Waikiki Beach in order to see whether she will save him and stay with him. Then he really does get a leg cramp and they both nearly drown. It is different because it is more a Freudian story, and a reductive version of Freud at that, and it has an ugly tone that others in the volume do not. It looks back to London's occasional habit of glorifying the super couple, himself and Charmian, but this time, as in *The Little Lady of the Big House,* the warts are all we see, not what makes these people "super." Some of its unpleasantness resides in its tirades against those lesser mortals who cannot understand the "gloriousness" in Lee and Ida Barton. The opening dialogue is rather bad, with all the couple's strengths of body and mind grossly exaggerated. The protagonist, Lee, is suicidal and homicidal, addicted to alcohol and opium. But his worst trait is his unreasoned anger at women: *"[N]o woman, so beautiful as this one, should be permitted to show her beauty"* (2397) is a sentiment attributed to the onlookers but it is really a part of Lee's psyche.

The foregoing criticisms notwithstanding, "The Kanaka Surf" could be viewed, given its placement in the volume and the time at which it was written, as a satiric revision of the superman and super couple London portrayed in earlier stories such as "Bunches of Knuckles." That would comport with the irony of *The Little Lady of the Big House.* "The Kanaka Surf" is the dark side of London's soulful self-examination; his fantasy versions in "The Red One" and "The Water Baby" are easier to take because they are located in characters more clearly dissociated from the author. For readers "The Kanaka Surf" may represent self-loathing a little too close to home, but it helps make the argument for London's serious self-examination at the time these Hawaiian stories were written, since it indicates the scope of his self-criticism. One wonders what the recently bereaved Charmian made of the story when it was published the year after her husband's untimely death.

"When Alice Told Her Soul" followed "The Kanaka Surf" on September 15, 1916, and could not be further from it in tone, although it engages with one of Jung's most significant theses—the value of the confession—which, if we think about it, "The Kanaka Surf" absolutely is. But in "When Alice Told Her Soul" London has fun with confession instead of engaging in it himself.

Charmian states in her biography that in this story London was imaginatively recreating Jung's thesis that the libido can be released from the disturbing contents of the unconscious and can find creative outlets if the individual confesses his or her secrets (C. London, *The Book,* 2:355). But again history as an all-seeing eye that reveals and judges men's (and women's) deeds is humorously combined with the inner plot of self-examination. Honolulu is presented as a small town whose secrets are exposed, much to the embarrassment of the populace. Alice Akana is a madam who gets religion and confesses her sins publicly, in the meantime also confessing those of the powerful class who are her clients. Again London creates a powerful woman character, like Li Faa or Martha and Bella, to tell the history of Hawaii—or rewrite it. Although it is a comic story, it takes a serious look at the power structure of the islands and some of the underhanded ways people have acquired land and power; it satirizes religious fervor; and it points to an interesting intersection between sex and race in which all can mix in this new religion. Irony is provided in that preacher Abel Ah Yo manipulates racial issues in order to further his cause and thereby line his pockets. "When Alice Told Her Soul" probably did not please the already ruffled sensibilities of London's well-connected friends in Honolulu, some of whom appear here.

The very last story that London wrote was "The Water Baby," completed October 4, 1916. It has tremendous relevance to the circumstances in which it was written. Like "The Red One," it is the story of a dying man, "a Jungian parable," as A. Grove Day has said, of life and death (Day, 19). "The Water Baby" is a story about knowledge, about the kind of knowledge worth having, and it questions *all* of London's previous beliefs in knowledge systems that had failed to fulfill his longings for peace. Perhaps London finds himself—finally—at ease in "The Water Baby" with melding contradiction and complexity. At the end of the story the reader does not know whether the protagonist's mind has been changed, nor if limitations of his world view have been transcended—but the ambiguities are productive. It is not just that the story is ambiguous; it is that it is clever and witty as well as wise. London embraced a sophisticated and mature version of self-knowledge and knowledge of humanity.

The author steps through the fictive mask in this story as John Lakana, a *kama'aina haole* who goes out fishing one day with an old Hawaiian, Kohokumu. The names are significant: *Lakana* was London's Hawaiian name, and *Kohokumu* means "tree of knowledge." Weighted with conventional self-consciousness and burdened by illness and worldly cares, Lakana loses patience with Kohokumu's chanting of the deeds of Maui and his stories. One of the primary myths of Maui is that he snared the sun; here in London's last story of the Pacific the sun is significant as it was in his first story of the Klondike. As McClintock points out, "London explicitly links Kohokumu with the most common natural archetype which Jung identifies with the oedipal myths—that of the sun (the hero and libido energy) setting (dying) in the sea (the womb) and rising in the morning (being reborn)" (McClintock, 162). Kohokumu tells how Maui caught the sun to slow it down so that his mother's tapa cloth could dry, how he "fished up dry land from ocean depths with hooks made fast to heaven" (*Complete*, 2484); Lakana calls Maui a "Promethean demigod of Polynesia," but unlike Prometheus, who stole from heaven, Maui steals from the depths of the sea. While still involving the sun god, London thus privileges the depths, the unconscious, over the conscious light of rationality. Lakana's ire at Kohokumu is not really directed at the old man but at the old man's beliefs. Kohokumu sings, "Caught is the land beneath the water, / Floated up, up to the surface" (2486), as Lakana holds his head and moans: "My head ached. The sun glare on the water made my eyes ache, while I was suffering more than half a touch of mal de mer . . . . Lying back with closed eyes, I lost count of time." Lakana is startled awake "to the stab of the sun" when Kohokumu shouts, " 'Its a big one,' " having caught a huge squid. He places "his lean, hawklike face into the very center of the slimy, squirming mass, and with his several ancient fangs bit into the heart and life of the matter" (2486).

To Lakana's surmise that Kohokumu's beliefs are only "a queer religion," Kohokumu responds:

> "When I was young I muddled my head over queerer religions. . . . But listen, O Young Wise One, to my elderly wisdom. This I know: as I grow old I seek less for the truth from without me, and find more of the truth from within me. Why have I thought this thought of my return to my mother and of my rebirth from my mother into the sun? You do not know. I do not know, save that, without whisper of man's voice or printed word, without prompting from otherwhere, this thought has arisen from within me, from the deeps of me that are as deep as the sea. I am not a god. I do not make things. Therefore I have not made this thought. I do not know its father or its mother. It is of old time before me, and therefore it is true. Man does not make truth. Man, if he be not blind, only recognizes truth when he sees it. Is this thought that I have thought a dream?" (2488–89)

Lakana loses control of the narrative when Kohokumu forces him to hear the story of the Water Baby. As in "The Red One" and "Shin-Bones," the twentieth-century man both seeking and avoiding his identity confronts the secrets of the collective unconscious through contact with Kohokumu's tales of the Sea his Mother and the Sun his Father. Spiritually sterile, Lakana, like Bassett, is in need of what he hears, even though it comes in a form he is likely to reject. The last word in the story is Lakana's interjected "But—", so that the reader does not finally know what, if anything, he has learned.

The story of the Water Baby is a trickster tale that subverts Lakana's intellectual rigidity with its surprise ending. The Water Baby, with his knowledge of the language (and the social behavior) of sharks, tricks the sharks into attacking and eating the one among them with the shortest tail each time he wishes to enter the water. He tells them that the one with the shortest tail has betrayed them, and then he throws a lava rock into the ocean to distract them while he goes in and gets a lobster. The Water Baby's trick consists of telling them something they can "prove" to themselves each time. He always gets away, and their suspicions of betrayal thus seem well-founded, although their "evidence" bears no relation to the facts. The one with the shortest tail is there to blame, and blamed he is, until the 40 sharks are gone, the last having burst from eating the other 39! The voracious shark literally bursting with its proof is a brilliant symbol for the futility of relying only upon epistemological, materialistic knowledge.

At this point Lakana interrupts in disbelief but is silenced by Kohokumu, who regains his narrative and finishes with the proof: he himself has fished in that spot and seen the 39 rocks, and his grandfather knew the grandson of the Water Baby. Kohokumu's trick of using empirical knowledge to prove his story even when the story itself defeats all such designs has silenced Lakana, for after that, who is to say what is true and what is not? Two kinds of knowledge—conscious and unconscious, "factual" and mythic, epistemological and hermeneutic—are deftly shown as relative in Kohokumu's tale. (And are 40 sharks 40 years gone by?) The end of the story finds the reader in silent agreement, for Lakana's silence has allowed the reader a hermeneutical opening, just as the mystery of Bassett's vision allows the reader's imagination room to operate. The hermeneutical silence here is only fitting, because the Water Baby's secret is language: "[H]e was born with knowledge of the language of fishes" (2490).[94]

Conclusion

In "The Red One" and "The Water Baby" in particular, but in all the stories of *On the Makaloa Mat*, London dared to expose the wellsprings of the drive for knowledge of the Self. He extends his characteristic theme of brotherhood versus "man-hate and man-meanness" into the personal and interpersonal, a stage whereupon he could enact his most passionate inner necessities and yet continue to do what he had done so long: give the world a new portrait of its multifaceted character. He offers a writer's view of the burgeoning variety of peoples who would make up the population of the twentieth century and beyond; if many of his own anxieties and shortcomings are superimposed upon this vision, then he calls up even more effectively our own collective personal and transpersonal awareness of the modern world.

At the time of his death, London had been working on another attempt at analyzing cultural differences in his love story "Cherry" or "Eyes of Asia," the tale of a Eurasian girl's struggle for self-mastery. But a look at the files in the voluminous London Collection at the Henry E. Huntington Library in San Marino, California, also reveals dozens of other promising projects never to be completed. In 1913, London wrote a friend that "[i]f I live to be five hundred years I should never be able to do the work I have already mapped out and filed away. I have over 100 novels filed away on my shelves and possibly 500 short stories" (*Letters*, 1131–32).

Who could think in such huge terms? Whether this claim was more boast than anything else, it speaks of the ambition of London to write what was inside of him. This sort of life was that demanded by his famous credo:

> I would rather be ashes than dust!
> I would rather that my spark should burn out
>   in a brilliant blaze than it should be
>   stifled by dry-rot.
> I would rather be a superb meteor, every atom
>   of me in magnificent glow, than a sleepy
>   and permanent planet.
> The proper function of man is to live, not to
>   exist.
> I shall not waste my days in trying to prolong
>   them.
> I shall use my time.

On the night of November 22, 1916, after writing a letter making plans to see his daughters—ending a period of estrangement—London retired to his sleeping porch. The next morning, when his manservant, Sekine, attempted to wake him, he was in a coma. Charmian was summoned, and doctors rushed to his side, but to no avail. Despite repeated attempts to rouse him, he died without regaining full consciousness. The cause of death was listed as uraemia. Other evidence, however, suggests a massive stroke.

London kept on working to the end; Charmian notes that when Sekine gave her the ranch suit London had last worn, in its pockets were "a handful of keys, the dingy Klondike coin-sack of chamois, and a few stray notes, along with his usual notepad and pencil, which never left him" (C. London, *The Book*, 2:396). Considering the physical problems he was having, it is remarkable that he was working at all, that he wrote gems such as "Like Argus of the Ancient Times" and "The Princess," and especially that he was capable of such profound tales as "The Red One" and "The Water Baby." Like Shakespeare's Prospero, London's last protagonists make us wonder whether their creator sensed that he would soon have to "drown his book." But his energy seemed unabated; the tragedy is in contemplating what he could have produced given his new, more mature psychological and stylistic directions. What would his place have been among the modernists of the next generation? In all of his promise and contradiction perhaps Jack London should be seen specifically as a writer of the Pacific Rim, for it is in this cultural context that we can best appreciate his unique contributions to American literature. In his nearly two hundred short stories he explored new landscapes, characters, and subjects, in California, the Northwest, Japan, Korea, China, Mexico, and the South Pacific. At the same time, he probed the long-standing problems of everyday urban life in America. He troubled himself and continues to trouble his reader with the welter of contradictions he expressed with regard to such important modern and postmodern issues as gender equality, race, and class consciousness, while simultaneously working through timeless values of justice, community, and the social and personal roles of the imagination. He relied upon ancient sources—the learned archives of classical mythology as well as the intuited archetypes of the unconscious—even as he explored the startling new models of thinking available to him in science, anthropology, and politics. His vision was to the East and West, seeking new vistas but burdened with the restrictions of the place from which he gazed—and with those from within.

Notes to Part 1

1. Jack London, "A Typhoon Off the Coast of Japan," in *The Complete Short Stories of Jack London,* ed. Earle Labor, Robert C. Leitz, III, and I. Milo Shepard, 3 vols. (Stanford, Calif.: Stanford University Press, 1993), 2. Further references to London's short fiction are taken from this edition and will be cited in text as *Complete.*

2. See Jack London, quoted in George Wharton James, "A Study of Jack London in His Prime," *Overland Monthly* 68 (May 1917): 361–99. Hereafter cited in text as James.

3. Letter dated 15 December 1906 to Ina Coolbrith, in Jack London, *The Letters of Jack London,* ed. Earle Labor, Robert C. Leitz, III, and I. Milo Shepard, 3 vols. (Stanford, Calif.: Stanford University Press, 1988), 650. Further references to London's letters are from this edition and are hereafter cited in text as *Letters.*

4. Franklin Walker, *Jack London and the Klondike: The Genesis of an American Writer* (San Marino, Calif.: The Huntington Library, 1966; reprint with a foreword by Earle Labor, 1996), 18, 23. Hereafter cited in text.

5. Jack London, *Revolution and Other Essays* (New York: Macmillan, 1910), 299–301. Hereafter cited in text as *Revolution.*

6. Jacqueline Tavernier-Courbin offers readings of several of London's tales as science fiction, including "A Thousand Deaths," in "Jack London's Science Fiction," *Jack London Newsletter* 17 (September–December 1984): 71–78.

7. In other essays, London returns to Homer as an epic model: "What a tremendous affair it was, the world of Homer, with its indeterminate boundaries, vast regions, and immeasurable distances," he writes at the beginning of his 1899 essay "The Shrinkage of the Planet." "The Mediterranean and the Euxine were illimitable stretches of ocean waste over which years could be spent in endless wandering. On their mysterious shores were the improbable homes of impossible peoples." He lists major episodes of *The Odyssey,* from the Ethiopians in the east ("the most distant of men," Homer says) to the Cimmerians in the west ("covered with darkness and cloud," occupying the entrance to the underworld), from the land of the Lotus-eaters to the Island of the Sun. London's thesis is that "Homer's world, restricted to less than a drummer's circuit, was nevertheless immense, surrounded by a thin veneer of universe—the Stream of Ocean," although today it is "precisely charted, weighed, and measured," along with the rest of the planet, "gyrating to an immutable law through a universe the bounds of which have been pushed incalculably back." "There are no longer Cimmerians and Ethiopians, in widestretching lands," but on either hand humankind confronts "the naked poles, and they recoil from unnavigable space to an intenser struggle among themselves. And all the while the planet shrinks beneath their grasp." They "wrangle over the fragments" that are left, "like wolves at the end of a gorge." Much to mourn indeed if, London says, echoing Matthew Arnold, we merely privilege "the rise of the economic over the imaginative spirit" (all quotes from *Revolution,* 141–50). London took three volumes with him into the Klondike: a guidebook to the Yukon, Darwin's *Origin of Species,* and Milton's *Paradise Lost.* Charmian quotes fellow Klondikers who tell of London's nighttime reading aloud from classics. He even wrote a one-act verse play called "The Return of Ulysses—A Modern Version," submitted to *Collier's Weekly* in December 1898, and promptly rejected. As he wrote to his friend Mabel Applegarth, " 'Ulysses' came back like a shot, all the way from New York. . . . Needless to say, this Greek wanderer is abroad again" *(Letters,* 30). London retired the play after it was rejected by five other magazines.

8. Donald Pizer, *Realism and Naturalism in Nineteenth-Century American Literature,* rev. ed. (Carbondale: Southern Illinois University Press, 1984), 12. Hereafter cited in text.

9. Jack London, undated pamphlet, *Jack London by Himself.*

10. Glen P. Bush notes that like most American literature beginning with the Puritan journals of the seventeenth century, London's fiction opposes a pastoral ideal to violent reality, where the loss of innocence leads to being outcast. Bush notes Fred Lewis Pattee's formulation of London's American Arcadia as "the spirit of the new world beyond the Rockies, its magnificent distances, its recklessness and exaggeration, its adolescent dreams" (Fred Lewis Pattee, *The*

New American Literature 1890–1930 [New York: Cooper Square, 1968], 137). Comments Bush, "London replaces the shepherd with the trapper and the prospector; he replaces the warm hills and valleys of Arcadia with the rugged mountains and ice fields of the Klondike; and he replaces the grazing sheep with the herculean sled dogs. Tranquil Arcadia, in other words, has been replaced with the temperamental, and sometimes violent, North American wilderness" (Glen P. Bush, "The Pastoral and the Violent: Jack London's Literary Dialectic," *Jack London Newsletter* 20 [1987]: 52–53).

11. Charmian London, *Jack London*, 2 vols. (London: Mills & Boon, 1921), 1:247–48. Hereafter cited in text.

12. The 1885 shelf list for the Oakland Public Library includes no less than four separate translations of the *Odyssey* (Chapman, Pope, Bryant, Collins) as well as translations of the *Iliad* and various related books on Homer. Some of the more significant entries are *Thoughts of Aurelius* (ed. Long); Bulfinch's *Age of Fable*; Morris's translation of the *Aeneid* and of his *Earthly Paradise* and *Life and Death of Jason*; Longfellow's *Hyperion*; and Tylor's *Primitive Culture*. Numerous volumes were available with titles such as *Myths and Mythmakers* (Fiske), *Compendium of Classical Literature* (Cleveland), *Mythology of Greece and Rome* (Seeman), *Roman Legends* (Busk), *Greek Anthology* (Burges), and *Half Hours with Greek and Latin Authors* (Johnstone). London would have found upwards of 50 titles of these handy. There is a solid representation of Greek and Roman authors, including Aeschylus, Aristotle, Aristophanes, Julius Caesar, Catullus, Cicero, Euripides, Herodotus, Hesiod, Horace, Junius, Juvenal, Livy, Lucretius, Plato, Pliny, Seneca, Sophocles, Tacitus, and Virgil, many in several translations and multiple volumes.

13. John Vickery, *The Literary Impact of The Golden Bough* (Princeton, N.J.: Princeton University Press, 1973), 4–5. Hereafter cited in text.

14. David Mike Hamilton, *"The Tools of My Trade": Annotated Books in Jack London's Library* (Seattle: University of Washington Press, 1986), 11–13.

15. *The Editor* had requested a number of writers, including London, Mark Twain, Gertrude Atherton, Owen Wister, and Mary E. Wilkins Freeman, to answer questions on how young writers can best begin a successful writing career.

16. Russ Kingman, *A Pictorial Life of Jack London* (New York: Crown, 1979), 87. Hereafter cited in text.

17. N. G. L. Hammond and H. H. Scullard, eds., *The Oxford Classical Dictionary*, 2d ed. (Oxford: Clarendon Press, 170), s.v. "Apollo."

18. *The Odyssey of Homer*, trans. Richmond Lattimore (Chicago: University of Chicago Press, 1951), XI.109.

19. As Helios was initially a minor god of Indo-European origin and regarded as beneath Olympus, so too Apollo was probably a god from Lycia in Asia Minor, whose most important early rituals involved the initiation of young men. One of his most frequent epithets is Lykeios, or "the wolf-like." Another

version of his origins is the land of the Hyperboreans, a region north of Greece that sent offerings each year to his birthplace, Delos (Walter Burkert, *Greek Religion: Archaic and Classical*, trans. John Raffan[(New York: Blackwell, 1985], 144–45, 147; hereafter cited in text). London, known as "Wolf," may have also been interested in Apollo as a protector of artists.

20. Cicero also mentions sun-dogs in *de Divinatione* 1.43.97 and *de Republica* 2.5.14.

21. Milton makes Mammon one of the fallen angels in Hell. He figures prominently in *Paradise Lost* Books I and II, where he is the leader of a band of "pioneers" who dig into the sulphuric earth for gold and other minerals from which to build Pandemonium, a rival kingdom to Heaven. The word in Syriac meant "wealth" or "idol" and is most familiar to us through Matthew's use of it: "Thou canst not serve both God and Mammon" (4:24). I wish to thank Noël Mauberret and Christian Pagnard for directing my attention to the demonic aspects of this story.

22. London seems to have borrowed the major motif for "In a Far Country" from Joseph Conrad's story "An Outpost of Progress," published one year earlier. Conrad's story features two loafers, Carlier and Kayerts, confined to a lonely outpost in the Congo. They get along well at first, but rapidly degenerate into laziness and brutishness; they come to blows over their sugar supply, and one ends up killing the other and then succumbs to death himself. As London examines the effect of the gold fever on his two "Incapables," Conrad exposes the evils inherent in the spread of colonialism through the story of these isolated pilgrims within an incomprehensible wilderness. See Joseph Conrad, "An Outpost of Progress," in *Typhoon and Other Tales* (New York: Signet, 1962), 183–203. It is also inspired by the story of the prodigal son, as told in the Gospel of St. Luke, from which the title phrase is taken. Cuthfert and Weatherbee fighting over their "inheritance" represent two brothers of the story, but here is there no father to forgive them and welcome them home, only the distant Sol to judge them.

23. Michael Wood, *In Search of the Trojan War* (New York: New American Library, 1985), 34.

24. I am indebted to Gail Jones for several connections to *The Odyssey*, the Sol image, and to medieval literature. One would expect, given the setting of the Klondike stories and London's fascination with his "Teutonic" heritage, that there would be numerous allusions to Norse mythology; indeed, one might expect to find those instead of the Greek. But this is not the case. London does refer to Norse gods and heroes, but only sparingly. There is only one work cited in Hamilton that directly presents Norse material, a play called *Fenris, The Wolf* by Percy MacKaye (New York: Macmillan, 1905). London refers to "Mitgart" in a letter in July 1899 (*Letters*, 99), so he was familiar with the Poetic Eddas from some source or other, possibly William Morris's writings on Norse subjects. In

the Norse myths the sun is called Sunnâ and Sol (Old Icelandic) and most often portrayed as feminine. Though many versions of the story exist, at the time of Ragnarok, or the destruction of the gods, Fenris (or Fenrir) Wolf, the loathsome offspring of Loki, kills Odin, ruler of the gods; he is sometimes identified with Sköll, a wolf who devours the sun, and his sister with Midgard Serpent. The Roman and Norse "Sol" may be traceable to Indo-European roots.

25. Naturally, London also encountered some of the women who braved the Klondike, but Walker's point that it was really a male society is of course correct. For specific treatment of masculinity in London's work see Jonathan Auerbach, *Male Call: Becoming Jack London* (Durham, N.C.: Duke University Press, 1996).

26. In "A Day's Lodging," an ethical parable, the couple and their visitor play an ironic game of knowledge and concealment, until the wife begs her former husband to take her with him. The new husband pays him, but the hero abandons both wife and gold, throwing the dust down a river. The story is framed by the "Narrative of Shorty," who is to be a character in *Smoke Bellew* (1911), which relates how a stampede took place when the gold was discovered in the water.

27. June Howard, *Form and History in American Literary Naturalism* (Chapel Hill: University of North Carolina Press, 1985), 37.

28. One of the most egregious examples of a reading of London that seeks to typecast his fiction is Mark Seltzer's *Bodies and Machines* (New York: Routledge, 1992), which includes a chapter on London called "Men in Furs." Seltzer sees London's writing as a "naturalist machine" operating, in this case, at the behest of a homoerotic drive, and evidently sees nothing in the stories beyond the objectification of the male body.

29. Ernst Haeckel, *The Riddle of the Universe*, trans. Joseph McCabe (New York: Harper & Brothers, 1900), 20–21.

30. James I. McClintock, *White Logic: Jack London's Short Stories* (Cedar Springs, Mich: Wolf House Books, 1976), 44–45. Hereafter cited in text. McClintock's book has recently been reissued as *Jack London's Strong Truths* (East Lansing: Michigan State University Press, 1997) with a new introduction by Sam S. Baskett.

31. Numerous critics, including Earle Labor, Charles N. Watson Jr., Jay Gurian, and Terry Whalen, have underscored the profound dualities in London's thought, especially his dialogic treatment of spirit and matter. See Earle Labor, "Jack London's Symbolic Wilderness: Four Versions," *Nineteenth-Century Fiction* 17 (September 1962): 149–61; Charles N. Watson Jr., "Jack London: Up from Spiritualism," in *The Haunted Dusk: American Supernatural Fiction, 1820–1920*, eds. Howard Kerr, John W. Crowley, and Charles Crow (Athens: University of Georgia Press, 1983), 195–205; Jay Gurian, "The Romantic Necessity in Literary Naturalism: Jack London," *American Literature* 38 (March 1966): 112–30; and

Terry Whalen, "Roberts and the Tradition of American Naturalism," in *The Sir Charles G. Roberts Symposium*, ed. Glenn Clever (Ottawa: University of Ottawa Press, 1984), 127–42. Whalen emphasizes London's capacity for "primordial wonder," which allowed him to represent the ambiguity inherent in the act of apprehending the wilderness, and calls his style "an index of his religious dimension as a writer who seeks to unmask the face of the god behind the physical world he observes." Whoever is not alert to the "mysterious presence of the physical world" is "limited, narrow, and morally dangerous" (133–35).

32. James G. Cooper, "The Summit and the Abyss: Jack London's Moral Philosophy," *Jack London Newsletter* 12 (January–April, 1979): 24–27.

33. Jack London, *John Barleycorn* (New York: Century, 1913), 315, 318. Hereafter cited in text.

34. According to Lee Clark Mitchell, the story's determinism makes the status of narrator and protagonist "of little or no concern" since there are no "card-carrying persons" (*Determined Fictions: American Literary Naturalism* [New York: Columbia University Press, 1989], 52–53). Similarly, Charles E. May argues that London, "like his protagonist, is without imagination in this story, because he too is concerned here only with the things of life and not with their significance. . . . [N]othing in the story leads . . . [the reader] to the metaphysical conjectural field of immortality and man's place in the universe" (" 'To Build a Fire': Physical Fiction and Metaphysical Critics," *Studies in Short Fiction* 15 [1978]: 22–23).

35. Arnold Chapman, "Between Fire and Ice: A Theme in Jack London and Horacio Quiroga," *Symposium* 24 (Spring 1970): 20–24.

36. Toni Morrison has recently examined this sort of exclusivity implicated in the image of "whiteness" in American literature and its relation to literary "blackness." These opposed figurations, she argues, are present even in works that understand themselves to be "universal" or "race-free." In the writings of Melville and Hawthorne "blackness" is racialized in the sense that the American imagination played upon an enslaved population in order to project its fears of boundarylessness, of "nature unbridled and crouched for attack." And later artists such as Twain, Faulkner, and Hemingway also "transferred internal conflicts to a 'blank darkness.' " Images of blackness, Morrison concludes, are self-reflexive; they can be "evil and protective, rebellious and forgiving, fearful and desirable—all of the self-contradictory features of the self." But in contrast, in works such as *Absalom, Absalom!* and "The Snows of Kilimanjaro," "whiteness, alone, is mute, meaningless, unfathomable, pointless, frozen, veiled, dreaded, senseless, implacable"—it is "inarticulate" (*Playing in the Dark: Whiteness and the Literary Imagination* [Cambridge, Mass.: Harvard University Press, 1992; New York: Vintage, 1993], xii, 5, 33–37, 58–59). Although not discussed by Morrison, racialized possibilities of "To Build a Fire" are powerfully implicated in the story's overall exploration of the theme of community. This emphasis is also present elsewhere in London's corpus, as in the working out of the binary opposi-

tion of slavery and freedom in *The Call of the Wild, White Fang,* "Batârd," *The Sea-Wolf,* and *The House of Pride,* to name but a few.

37. Earle Labor and King Hendricks, "London's Twice-Told Tale," *Studies in Short Fiction* 4 (1967): 335.

38. John Milton, *Paradise Lost,* ed. Scott Elledge, 2d ed. (New York: W. W. Norton & Co., 1993). Line references cited in text.

39. And Milton remained a favorite. London wrote in 1916: "I can still fall for the rolling wonder of the music of *Paradise Lost.* Intellectually, it has always affected me as would affect me the reading of a sort of modernized version of an ancient sun myth" (*Letters,* 1580).

40. Compare this happy outcome with the understanding and forgiveness attained by the surviving brother in "By the Turtles of Tasman"; contrast it with the dark outcome of the other prodigal son stories, "In a Far Country" and "The House of Pride."

41. Susan Ward, "Jack London's Women: Civilization vs. The Frontier," *Jack London Newsletter* 9 (May–August 1976): 82. Hereafter cited in text.

42. Fred Lewis Pattee, "The Prophet of the Last Frontier," in *Side Lights on American Literature* (New York: Century, 1922), 123–24.

43. Jonathan Auerbach, introduction to *Northland Stories,* by Jack London, ed. Auerbach (Harmondsworth, U.K.: Penguin, 1997), xiv-xx.

44. Jack London, "My Best Short Story," *The Grand Magazine* (London, England), August 1906. MS in Henry E. Huntington Library; quoted in Walker, 222.

45. For insights into what London learned from Virginia Prentiss, see Eugene P. Lasartemay and Mary Rudge, *For Love of Jack London: His Life with Jennie Prentiss—A True Story* (New York: Vantage, 1991). There is no definitive work to date on London's relation to his mother or Eliza, although both relationships are crucial to understanding London's development. For his daughters' perspectives, see Joan London, *Jack London and His Daughters* (Berkeley, Calif.: Heyday Books, 1990); Joan London, *Jack London and His Times* (New York: Doubleday, 1939; Seattle: University of Washington Press, 1968; hereafter cited in text); Becky London, "Memories of My Father, Jack London," *The Pacific Historian* 18 (Fall 1974): 5–10; and Becky London, "My Jack London: A Daughter Remembers," American Literature on Video Series, Films for the Humanities, 1988. The two daughters offer totally different views of their father. Another interesting source is *With a Heart Full of Love: Jack London's Presentation Inscriptions to the Women in His Life,* ed. Sal Noto (Berkeley, Calif.: Twowindows Press, 1986).

46. For clarification of the differences between these terms, see Henry Louis Gates Jr., ed., *"Race," Writing, and Difference* (Chicago: University of Chicago Press, 1986).

47. For treatment of Charmian's influence on Jack, see Clarice Stasz, *American Dreamers: Charmian and Jack London* (New York: St. Martin's Press, 1988).

48 See Alexander Saxton, *The Indispensable Enemy: Labor and the Anti-Chinese Movement in California* (Berkeley: University of California Press, 1971). Also see Mark Pittenger, *American Socialists and Evolutionary Thought, 1870–1920* (Madison: University of Wisconsin Press, 1993).

49. Ernst Haeckel, *History of Creation* (New York: D. Appleton, 1876); James Francis Katherinus Hewitt, *The Ruling Race of Prehistoric Times* (Westminster: Archibald Constable & Co., 1894); Alfred Paul Karl Edward Schultz, *Race or Mongrel: A Brief History of the Rise and Fall of the Ancient Races of Earth: A Theory That the Fall of Nations Is Due to Intermarriage with Alien Stock* (Boston: L. C. Page & Co., 1914); Frank Emile Roesler, *The World's Greatest Migration: The Origin of the "White Man"* (Kansas City, Mo.: F. E. Roesler, 1913).

50. Scott L. Malcolmson, "The Inevitable White Man: Jack London's Endless Journey," *Voice Literary Supplement*, February 1, 1994, 10–12.

51. Andrew Furer, " 'Zone-Conquerors' and 'White Devils': The Contradictions of Race in the Works of Jack London," in *Rereading Jack London*, ed. Leonard Cassuto and Jeanne Campbell Reesman (Stanford, Calif.: Stanford University Press, 1996), 163.

52. Quoted in Upton Sinclair, "About Jack London," *The Masses* 10, nos. 1, 2 (November–December 1917): 20.

53. See "Jack London to Yale Men," *Yale Alumni Weekly* 15 (January 31, 1906), 344; also see Joan London, *Jack London and His Times*, 301, 308–09.

54. Jack London, *War of the Classes* (New York: Macmillan, 1905), xvi. Hereafter cited in text. Having glimpsed the heights to which socialism can lead humanity, London goes on in "What Life Means to Me" to describe his decision to return to the "foundation" of society in the working classes and "crowbar in hand, shoulder to shoulder with intellectuals, idealists and class-conscious workingmen, getting a solid pry now and again and setting the whole edifice rocking." He looks forward to a future day when "there will be a finer incentive to impel men to action than the incentive of to-day, which is the incentive of the stomach." Then "spiritual sweetness and unselfishness will conquer the gross gluttony of to-day" and the "nobility and excellence" of humankind will prevail. London's turn-of-the-century thought is fascinating in its conglomeration of ideas from many sources; here the influence of Victorian thinkers such as Arnold and Carlyle is apparent (*Revolution*, 308–9).

55. Jack London, *The Road* (New York: Macmillan, 1907), 106–7.

56. Katherine M. Littell, "The 'Nietzschean' and the Individualist in Jack London's Socialist Writings," *Jack London Newsletter* 15, no. 2 (1982): 76.

57. Alfred Kazin, "Progressivism: The Superman and the Muckraker," in *On Native Grounds: An Interpretation of Modern American Prose Literature* (New York: Reynal & Hitchcock, 1942) 112–13. William Cain is even more explicit than Kazin in his critique of London's socialism. He finds London's racism to be "pervasive and troubling" enough to discount him as a "stalwart socialist": London saw socialism "as for whites only." Cain continues: "The day of the classless

society—a racially pure economic equality—will begin to dawn, London contends, when whites have beaten back the other races and forced them to accept their absolute inferiority. White workers will no longer feel blood loyalty to their white masters and can wrest power from them" ("Socialism, Power, and the Fate of Style: Jack London in His Letters," *American Literary History* 3, no. 3 [1991]: 604).

58. George Orwell, introduction to *Love of Life and Other Stories*, by Jack London, rpt. in *In Front of Your Nose, 1945–1950*, vol. 4 of *The Collected Essays, Journalism and Letters of George Orwell*, ed. Sonia Orwell and Ian Angus (New York: Harcourt, Brace & World, 1968), 24–29.

59. Debbie López first drew this connection in her paper presented at the American Literature Association Conference, San Diego, June 1996, entitled "Once and Future Bosses: Twain's Connecticut Yankee and London's Goliah."

60. Joan Hedrick, *Solitary Comrade: Jack London and His Work* (Chapel Hill: University of North Carolina Press, 1982), 265.

61. For an examination of the many dualities of "South of the Slot" see Christopher Gair, "Hegemony, Metaphor, and Structural Difference: The 'Strange Dualism' of 'South of the Slot,' " *Arizona Quarterly* 49, no. 1 (Spring 1993): 73–97.

62. The most insightful treatment of London's irony in this tale is Lawrence I. Berkove's "A Parallax Connection in London's 'The Unparalleled Invasion,' " *American Literary Realism* 24, no. 2 (Winter 1992): 33–39.

63. See Jacqueline Tavernier-Courbin, *The Call of the Wild: A Naturalistic Romance* (New York: Twayne, 1994).

64. Richard Gid Powers, ed., introduction to *The Science Fiction of Jack London* (Boston: Gregg Press, 1975), vii–xxiv.

65. Irving Stone, *Sailor on Horseback: The Biography of Jack London* (Cambridge, Mass.: Houghton Mifflin, 1938); Joan London, *Jack London and His Times*; Andrew Sinclair, *Jack: A Biography of Jack London* (New York: Harper & Row, 1977); Christopher Wilson, *The Labor of Words: Literary Professionalism in the Progressive Era* (Athens: University of Georgia Press, 1985); Kevin Starr, "The Sonoma Finale of Jack London, Rancher," in *Americans and the California Dream* (New York: Oxford University Press, 1973), 210–38; Seltzer, *Bodies and Machines*; Auerbach, *Male Call: Becoming Jack London*. The latest entrant into this field is the nonscholarly biography by Alex Kershaw, *Jack London: A Life* (New York: HarperCollins, 1997), which is so embarrassing in its inaccuracies and exaggerations that it makes Stone seem a model of biographical responsibility.

66. Susan Ward, "Jack London and the Blue Pencil: London's Correspondence with Popular Editors," *American Literary Realism, 1870–1910* 14, no. 1 (Spring 1981), 16–18.

67. Van Wyck Brooks, *The Confident Years, 1885–1915*, vol. 5 of *Makers and Finders: A History of the Writer in America, 1800–1915*, (New York: E. P. Dutton, 1952), 231.

68. Jack London, *Martin Eden* (New York: Macmillan, 1909).

69. I have chosen to use "Hawaii," and the names of individual Hawaiian islands without the glottal stop (*okina*) even though that is how the words are written today. My decision is merely to use the names as London used them, to avoid confusion.

70. The definitive essay on "Planchette" is Earle Labor's study of the story's relation to biographical data. Labor points to certain diary entries of Charmian's of this time, noting one in particular on March 11: "Mate returned [to] Napa—I rode with him over Nun's Canon into Napa Co. Raining. Mate decided to come here April 1st" (Jack London Collection, Henry E. Huntington Library). Charmian records his anxiety about this move in her biography of London: When Netta Eames invited him to work in one of her cottages, "[t]he eyes he raised to her face were as of some creature hunted. He shifted uneasily, almost as if embarrassed, and the corners of his mouth drooped like a child's on the verge of tears. Yet when he replied it was with a tinge of impatience, though a pitiful tiredness lay under the tone: 'Oh, Mother Mine—thank you . . . . You're kind. . . . But . . . but I think that the very quiet would drive me crazy' " (C. London, *The Book*, 2:29–30). Labor associates London's reluctance with the "deep unconscious childhood association of the country with loneliness" of twenty years earlier in San Mateo and Livermore, and points to an essential paradox in London's complex nature: "He needed solitude not only to do his creative work, but also to cope with the myriad personal and professional problems which had plagued the years of his manhood. He had been on the verge of hysteria, in danger of a nervous breakdown, when he arrived at Wake Robin . . ." (Earle Labor, "Jack London's 'Planchette': The Road Not Taken," *Pacific Historian* 21, no. 2 [Summer 1977], 140). London described this period as his "Long Sickness," and although he needed to get away from people, he resisted commitment to a new marriage and the country: "I don't seem to care for anything," he told Charmian. "This doesn't seem to be what I want. I don't know what I want. Oh, I'm sorry—I am, I am; it hurts me to hurt you so. But there's nothing for me to do but go back to the city. I don't know what the end will be" (C. London, *The Book*, 2:31). Charmian's response was the same as Lute's: she told him he must do as he felt best, which was exactly the right response. That night changed everything, Labor asserts. London slept soundly—which he had thought was a thing of the past—and arose "a changed person: no longer a Chris Dunbar doomed to martyrdom on the cross of his own egotistical ambivalence, but a man capable of seeing the road he must take" (Labor, "Jack London's 'Planchette'," 146).

The story contains an important classical allusion that connects it to the theme of justice of the Northland tales: Lute meditates upon woodland flowers called Diogenes' lanterns; the allusion connects the biographical parallels to the story's theme of self-knowledge. The Greek Cynic Diogenes believed that happiness was to be attained by satisfying one's natural needs; unnatural conventions are unhealthy insofar as they interfere with natural good. Diogenes' wandering around with a lantern looking for an honest man was a product of his belief that what is natural is neither dishonorable nor indecent and should be performed in public. "Diogenes" is related to the notion that truth must emerge unfettered by habit or what Labor calls "egotistical ambivalence" (Labor, "Jack London's 'Planchette'," 139).

71. Don Graham, "Jack London's Tale Told by a High-Grade Feeb," *Studies in Short Fiction*, 15, no. 4 (Fall 1978), 429. Hereafter cited in text.

72. Jack London, *The Cruise of the Snark* (New York: Macmillan, 1911), 7. Hereafter cited in text as *Snark*.

73. Thomas R. Tietze and Gary Riedl, "Jack London and the South Seas," Jack London Collection, Sunsite Digital Library, University of California, Berkeley (Sunsite.Berkeley.EDU/London/Essays/southseas.html), page 1. Hereafter cited in text. See also their article " 'Saints in Slime': The Ironic Use of Racism in Jack London's South Seas Tales," *Thalia: Studies in Literary Humor* 12 (1992): 59–66. One of the most signficant chapters of *The Cruise of the Snark* brought worldwide attention to an aspect of Hawaii that the ruling class in Hawaii did not appreciate: "The Lepers of Molokai," chapter 7, allowed an American writer to speak out for the first time to debunk the many terrifying myths that surrounded leprosy; London wrote a scientifically well-researched, balanced portrait of the real lives of the lepers of Molokai and confidently predicted a total cure. He was anxious to represent the lepers in the way they would like to be represented, without the stereotyping and lurid sensationalism of other journalists. For a helpful discussion of many of the important features of *The Cruise of the Snark*, see David A. Moreland, "The Author as Hero: Jack London's 'The Cruise of the Snark,' " *Jack London Newsletter* 15, no. 1 (January-April 1982): 57–75.

74. Jack London, "My Hawaiian Aloha," in *Our Hawaii*, by Charmian London, rev. ed. (New York: Macmillan, 1922), 18.

75. David Moreland, "Violence in the South Sea Fiction of Jack London," *Jack London Newsletter* 16, no. 1 (January–April 1983): 2. Hereafter cited in text as "Violence."

76. Charmian London, *The Log of the Snark* (New York: Macmillan, 1915), 90. Hereafter cited in text as *Log*.

77. Moreland notes the influence of Benjamin Kidd's theory of the tropics on London's thinking. Kidd argued that because the natives of this potential breadbasket of the world were constitutionally unfit to develop the rich resources around them, it was the white man's duty to "farm the tropics." If the native inhabitants suffered in the process, that was regrettable but necessary for the greater good of mankind. London seems to have accepted this idea in his essays and letters, arguing for the moral superiority of the white man. "No great

race adventure," he said, "can go far nor endure long which has no deeper foundation than material success, no higher prompting than conquest for conquest's sake and mere race glorification. To go far and endure, it must have behind it an ethical impulse, a sincerely conceived righteousness." Moreland compares this sentiment to Marlow's comment in *Heart of Darkness*: "The conquest of the earth, which mostly means the taking it away from those who have a different complexion or slightly flatter noses than ourselves, is not a pretty thing when you look into it too much. What redeems it is the idea only. An idea at the back of it; not a sentimental pretense but an idea; and an unselfish belief in the idea—something you can set up, and bow down before, and offer sacrifice to. . . ." Moreland rightly notes that, fortunately, London did look into the "idea" critically and saw the reality of imperialism during the *Snark* voyage, "and the tension created by the discrepancy between idea and actuality produced some of his better tales of the South Pacific" (Moreland, "Violence in the South Sea Fiction of Jack London," 2, 8–9; Jack London, "The Yellow Peril," in *Revolution*, 288; Joseph Conrad, *Heart of Darkness*, in *Tales of Land and Sea* [Garden City, NY: Hanover House, 1953], 37).

78. Intermittently London worked on a "Christ" novel, allowing it to surface finally in the Passion scenes of *The Star Rover*—but this is only one example of the heavy use of the Bible London made in the Pacific stories. See Dennis Hensley for London's reliance upon biblical language, including vocabulary, metaphor, word order, pace, and punctuation ("Jack London's Use of the Linguistic Style of the King James Bible," *Jack London Echoes* 3, no. 3 [July 1983]: 4–11).

79. Quoted in A. Grove Day, introduction to *Stories of Hawaii*, by Jack London, ed. A. Grove Day (New York: Appleton-Century, 1965), 19.

80. An exchange of letters with his close friend, Honolulu businessman and journalist Lorrin A. Thurston, illustrates the fury of the Honolulu business establishment at London for drawing attention to a less-than-attractive feature of their budding tourist destination, and also London's deep feeling for Hawaii and its people. Thurston's attack on London, in which he calls him a "sneak of the first water, a thoroughly untrustworthy man, and an ungrateful and untruthful bounder," was published in the *Honolulu Advertiser*, as was London's reply (*Letters*, 859–61). In a private letter, London berated Thurston for not understanding that "[t]o know the naked facts of life is not to be pessimistic. Your contention that we must ignore certain unpleasant facts, and dwell upon the nice facts, is a sign that you are afraid of a portion of life. And insofar as you run away from a portion of life, by that much will you be ignorant of life. As a man thinks, he is." Thurston, not London, is "abnormal" and "morbid": "Think only of the bright things. Well, a nice squint-eyed vision of life such a lopsided man must see" (*Letters*, 902).

81. The most in-depth study of London's feeling for Hawaiians in this story is James Slagel's "Political Leprosy: Jack London the Kamaʻāina and Koolau the Hawaiian," in *Rereading Jack London*, 172–91.

82. I shall refer to the real Koʻolau using the glottal stop marker but London's character without it, since that is how London wrote the name.

83. "The True Story of Kaluaikoʻolau or Koʻolau the Leper," *Hawaiian Journal of History* 21 (1987): 1–41.

84. Kingman has the Londons, while visiting the islands, journeying to Hilo on May 12, 1915, where Jack sailed with a Congressional party on the *Mauna Kea*. Kingman notes that on May 14 Charmian left for Honolulu on the *Kilauea* and that she met Jack when he arrived there on May 15. Jack's time is unaccounted for (Russ Kingman, *Jack London: A Definitive Chronology* [Middletown, CA: David Rejl, 1992]). But according to Kauai newspaper accounts and private papers of those he visited, London and the Congressional party spent May 13–15 visiting Kauai.

The *Garden Island* (Kauai's local paper) reported in its May 18, 1915, issue on a reception held in Lihue for the Congressional party at which various senators held forth on such subjects as harbor-building and other topics of local interest. The paper noted, "One of the interesting features of the evening was the presence of Jack London, the famous novelist, who, however, is so unobtrusive and retiring, and so averse to speech making that he escaped as early as he could. Privately he expresses himself as delighted with the island and promises himself a more extended visit in a few weeks, with Mrs. London." (This visit did not take place.) The newspaper account itself is evidence of London's worsening illness that made him return to Hawaii; who could imagine him "unobtrusive and retiring," and "averse to speech making," let alone retiring early? (*Early Days of Kalalau under the Old Kingdom*, Kauai Historical Society Manuscript Collection: The Kauai Papers, vol. 3, pp. 19–20). On Kauai London stayed with the missionary and ranching family of the Rev. J. M. Lydgate, signing the guest book, as his son noted in his memoirs, with "a bold and masculine hand," writing opposite, "Valley of the Moon, California, May 13/15" ("A Life" by William A. Lydgate, private printing, 1985). London was interviewed by the Rev. Lydgate in the *Garden Island* (May 25, 1915).

85. After his lengthy visit in early 1915, London once again went to Hawaii in December 1915, remaining until July 26, 1916.

86. Beatrice M. Hinkle, introduction to *Psychology of the Unconscious*, by C. G. Jung, trans. Beatrice M. Hinkle (New York: Moffat, Yard and Co., 1916), as quoted in Charmian London, *The Book of Jack London*, 2 vols. (New York: Century, 1921), 2:367, 359, 322–23. Hereafter cited in text as *The Book*.

87. James Kirsch, " 'The Red One,' " *Psychological Perspectives* 11, no. 2 (1980): 152–54. Hereafter cited in text.

88. See Kirsch, 137–54; McClintock; and Earle Labor and Jeanne Campbell Reesman, *Jack London: Revised Edition* (New York: Twayne, 1994). See also Earle Labor, "The Archetypal Woman as 'Martyr to Truth': Jack London's 'Samuel,' " *American Literary Realism* 24, 2 (Winter 1992): 23–32; Jeanne Camp-

bell, "Falling Stars: Myth in 'The Red One,' " *Jack London Newsletter* 11 (May-December 1978): 87–101; and Jeanne Campbell Reesman, "The Problem of Knowledge in 'The Water Baby,' " *Western American Literature* 22, no. 3 (Fall 1988): 201–118.

89. Berkove finds that despite the promise Jung's ideas held out to London, in the end London's vision—as manifested in "The Red One"—is one of despair and disillusion: " 'The Red One' . . . represents his fear that the growth of human intelligence divorced from other humane qualities would lead to the bleak alternative that strife is life, and to a pitiliess process of random natural selection that is equivalent to human regression" (Lawrence I. Berkove, "The Myth of Hope in Jack London's 'The Red One,' " in *Rereading Jack London*, 205; hereafter cited in text as "The Myth.") For Jung's publications, see *General Bibliography of C. G. Jung's Writings*, Bollingen Series 20 (Princeton, N.J.: Princeton University Press, 1979). For London's reading of Freud, see Hamilton, 129.

90. Moreland, "The Quest That Failed: Jack London's Last Tales of the South Seas," *Pacific Studies* 8 (Fall 1984): 63. Hereafter cited in text as "The Quest."

91. *Oxford Classical Dictionary*, ed. N. G. L. Hammond and H. H. Scullard (Oxford: Clarendon Press, 1977), s.v. "Gorgo or Medusa."

92. C. G. Jung, *The Archetypes and the Collective Unconscious*, Bollingen Series 20, vol. 9, pt. 1, (Princeton, N.J.: Princeton University Press, 1968), 94.

93. Erich Neumann, *The Great Mother: An Analysis of the Archetype*, trans. Ralph Manheim, Bollingen Series 47 (Princeton, N.J.: Princeton University Press, 1955), 291.

94. McClintock's conclusion that "London's use of Jungian conceptions . . . turned from a celebration of life's vitality to a final pessimistic preoccupation with death" is an influential view, but a wrong one. McClintock's thesis is based upon his considering "The Bones of Kahekili" London's "last Jungian Hawaiian story" (165). "The Water Baby" is London's last Hawaiian story; "Kahelili" was completed July 2, and "The Water Baby" October 4.

Part 2

THE WRITER

Introduction

Jack London wrote several essays on writing containing the story of how he himself struggled to succeed as an author and advising young writers engaged in their own struggles. The piece excerpted here, "The Terrible and Tragic in Fiction," argues for publishing more "terrible" and "tragic" fiction—whether naturalistic, horror, or romantic fiction. Frustrated by the squeamishness of magazine editors, London wished to point out the value of such work by referring to Edgar Allan Poe as a model. It is an interesting instance of London's attempting to contextualize his own work. When this essay was written London had already written a handful of horror tales, and a sociological horror story in *The People of the Abyss* (1903), and he would soon produce a tale of terror on the high seas, *The Sea-Wolf* (1904), along with several varieties of horror fiction more complex than his early stories, such as "Goliah," "Moon-Face," and "The Red One." For a collection of London's writing about writing, the best source is *"No Mentor but Myself": A Collection of Essays, Reviews, and Letters on Writing and Writers,* edited by Dale L. Walker.[1]

In the sections reprinted here from *Martin Eden* (1909) and *John Barleycorn* (1913), London gives us himself as a neophyte—both works follow a similar trajectory of struggle rewarded by success and followed by disillusionment, leaving the reader wondering just how closely these semiautobiographical books mirrored London himself. As a portrait of the writer and his passion for his craft they are uniquely revealing.

London was a prolific letter writer, and with the 1988 publication by Stanford University Press of *The Letters of Jack London* in three volumes, the letters were made available to scholars around the world. They, too, are highly revealing, covering a range of subjects including his reading, advice to writers, observations of the various locales in which he traveled, details of business arrangements with Macmillan and other publishers, literary friendships, love letters, and self-portraiture. The excellent introduction to *Letters* by editors Earle Labor, Robert C. Leitz III, and I. Milo Shepard is an invaluable guide. The letters presented here

range from warnings to recalcitrant editors to advice to a young author
to an exchange with Joseph Conrad.

Notes

1. Dale L. Walker, ed., *"No Mentor but Myself": A Collection of Articles, Essays, and Letters on Writing and Writers* (PortWashington, N.Y.: Kennikat Press, 1979).

From *John Barleycorn*

Unskilled labor is the first to feel the slackness of hard times, and I had no trades save those of sailor and laundryman. With my new responsibilities I didn't dare go to sea, and I failed to find a job at laundrying. I failed to find a job at anything. I had my name down in five employment bureaus. I advertised in three newspapers. I sought out the new friends I knew who might be able to get me work; but they were either uninterested or unable to find anything for me.

The situation was desperate. I pawned my watch, my bicycle, and a mackintosh of which my father had been very proud and which he had left to me. It was and is my sole legacy in this world. It had cost fifteen dollars, and the pawnbroker let me have two dollars on it. And—oh, yes—a water-front comrade of earlier years drifted along one day with a dress suit wrapped in newspapers. He could give no adequate explanation of how he had come to possess it, nor did I press for an explanation. I wanted the suit myself. No; not to wear. I traded him a lot of rubbish which, being unpawnable, was useless to me. I peddled the rubbish for several dollars, while I pledged the dress suit with my pawnbroker for five dollars. And for all I know, the pawnbroker still has the suit. I had never intended to redeem it.

But I couldn't get any work. Yet I was a bargain in the labor market. I was twenty-two years old, weighed one hundred and sixty-five pounds stripped, every pound of which was excellent for toil; and the last traces of my scurvy were vanishing before a treatment of potatoes chewed raw. I tackled every opening for employment. I tried to become a studio model, but there were too many fine-bodied young fellows out of jobs. I answered advertisements of elderly invalids in need of companions. And I almost became a sewing machine agent, on commission, without salary. But poor people don't buy sewing machines in hard times, so I was forced to forego that employment.

From Chapters 25 and 26 of *John Barleycorn* by Jack London (New York: Century Co., 1913).

Part 2

Of course, it must be remembered that along with such frivolous occupations, I was trying to get work as wop, lumper, and roustabout. But winter was coming on, and the surplus labor army was pouring into the cities. Also, I, who had romped along carelessly through the countries of the world and the kingdom of the mind, was not a member of any union.

I sought odd jobs. I worked days, and half-days, at anything I could get. I mowed lawns, trimmed hedges, took up carpets, beat them, and laid them again. Further, I took the civil service examinations for mail carrier and passed first. But alas, there was no vacancy, and I must wait. And while I waited, and in between the odd jobs I managed to procure, I started to earn ten dollars by writing a newspaper account of a voyage I had made, in an open boat down the Yukon, of nineteen hundred miles in nineteen days. I didn't know the first thing about the newspaper game, but I was confident I'd get ten dollars for my article.

But I didn't. The first San Francisco newspaper to which I mailed it never acknowledged receipt of the manuscript, but held on to it. The longer it held on to it, the more certain I was that the thing was accepted.

And here is the funny thing. Some are born to fortune, and some have fortune thrust upon them. But in my case I was clubbed into fortune, and bitter necessity wielded the club. I had long since abandoned all thought of writing as a career. My honest intention in writing that article was to earn ten dollars. And that was the limit of my intention. It would help to tide me along until I got steady employment. Had a vacancy occurred in the post office at that time, I should have jumped at it.

But the vacancy did not occur, nor did a steady job; and I employed the time between odd jobs with writing a twenty-one-hundred-word serial for the *Youth's Companion*. I turned it out and typed it in seven days. I fancy that was what was the matter with it, for it came back.

It took some time for it to go and come, and in the meantime I tried my hand at short stories. I sold one to the *Overland Monthly* for five dollars. The *Black Cat* gave me forty dollars for another. The *Overland Monthly* offered me seven dollars and a half, pay on publication, for all the stories I should deliver. I got my bicycle, my watch, and my father's mackintosh out of pawn and rented a typewriter. Also, I paid up the bills I owed to the several groceries that allowed me a small credit. I recall the Portuguese groceryman who never permitted my bill to go beyond four dollars. Hopkins, another grocer, could not be budged beyond five dollars.

And just then came the call from the post office to go to work. It placed me in a most trying predicament. The sixty-five dollars I could earn regularly every month was a terrible temptation. I couldn't decide what to do. And I'll never be able to forgive the postmaster of Oakland. I answered the call, and I talked to him like a man. I frankly told him the situation. It looked as if I might win out at writing. The chance was good, but not certain. Now, if he would pass me by and select the next man on the eligible list, and give me a call at the next vacancy—

But he shut me off with: "Then you don't want the position?"

"But I do," I protested. "Don't you see, if you will pass me over this time—"

"If you want it you will take it," he said coldly.

Happily for me, the cursed brutality of the man made me angry.

"Very well," I said. "I won't take it."

. . . Having burned my one ship, I plunged into writing. I am afraid I always was an extremist. Early and late I was at it—writing, typing, studying grammar, studying writing and all the forms of writing, and studying the writers who succeeded in order to find out how they succeeded. I managed on five hours' sleep in the twenty-four, and came pretty close to working the nineteen waking hours left in me. My light burned till two and three in the morning, which led a good neighbor woman into a bit of sentimental Sherlock Holmes deduction. Never seeing me in the daytime, she concluded that I was a gambler, and that the light in my window was placed there by my mother to guide her erring son home.

The trouble with the beginner at the writing game is the long, dry spells, when there is never an editor's check and everything pawnable is pawned. I wore my summer suit pretty well through that winter, and the following summer experienced the longest, dryest spell of all, in the period when salaried men are gone on vacation and manuscripts lie in editorial offices until vacation is over.

My difficulty was that I had no one to advise me. I didn't know a soul who had written or who had ever tried to write. I didn't even know one reporter. Also, to succeed at the writing game, I found I had to unlearn about everything the teachers and university had taught me. I was very indignant about this at the time; though now I can understand it. They did not know the trick of successful writing in the years of 1895 and 1896. They knew all about "Snow Bound" and "Sartor Resartus"; but the American editors of 1899 did not want such truck. They wanted the 1899 truck, and offered to pay so well for it that the teachers and professors of literature would have quit their jobs could they have supplied it.

I struggled along, stood off the butcher and the grocer, pawned my watch and bicycle and my father's mackintosh, and I worked. I really did work, and went on short commons of sleep. Critics have complained about the swift education one of my characters, Martin Eden, achieved. In three years, from a sailor with a common school education, I made a successful writer of him. The critics say this is impossible. Yet I was Martin Eden. At the end of three working years, two of which were spent in high school and the university and one spent at writing, and all three in studying immensely and intensely, I was publishing stories in magazines such as the *Atlantic Monthly*, was correcting proofs of my first book (issued by Houghton, Mifflin Co.), was selling sociological articles to *Cosmopolitan* and *McClure's*, had declined an associate editorship proffered me by telegraph from New York City, and was getting ready to marry.

From *Martin Eden*

He read to her a story, one that he flattered himself was among his very best. He called it "The Wine of Life," and the wine of it, that had stolen into his brain when he wrote it, stole into his brain now as he read it. There was a certain magic in the original conception, and he had adorned it with more magic of phrase and touch. All the old fire and passion with which he had written it were reborn in him, and he was swayed and swept away so that he was blind and deaf to the faults of it. But it was not so with Ruth. Her trained ear detected the weaknesses and exaggerations, the overemphasis of the tyro, and she was instantly aware each time the sentence-rhythm tripped and faltered. She scarcely noted the rhythm otherwise, except when it became too pompous, at which moments she was disagreeably impressed with its amateurishness. That was her final judgment on the story as a whole—amateurish, though she did not tell him so. Instead, when he had done, she pointed out the minor flaws and said that she liked the story.

But he was disappointed. Her criticism was just. He acknowledged that, but he had a feeling that he was not sharing his work with her for the purpose of schoolroom correction. The details did not matter. They could take care of themselves. He could mend them, he could learn to mend them. Out of life he had captured something big and attempted to imprison it in the story. It was the big thing out of life he had read to her, not sentence-structure and semicolons. He wanted her to feel with him this big thing that was his, that he had seen with his own eyes, grappled with his own brain, and placed there on the page with his own hands in printed words. Well, he had failed, was his secret decision. Perhaps the editors were right. He had felt the big thing, but he had failed to transmute it. He concealed his disappointment, and joined so easily with her in her criticism that she did not realize that deep down in him was running a strong undercurrent of disagreement.

"This next thing I've called 'The Pot'," he said, unfolding the manuscript. "It has been refused by four or five magazines now, but still I

From chapter 14 of *Martin Eden* by Jack London (New York: Macmillan, 1909).

think it is good. In fact, I don't know what to think of it, except that I've caught something there. Maybe it won't affect you as it does me. It's a short thing—only two thousand words."

"How dreadful!" she cried, when he had finished. "It is horrible, unutterably horrible!"

He noted her pale face, her eyes wide and tense, and her clenched hands, with secret satisfaction. He had succeeded. He had communicated the stuff of fancy and feeling from out of his brain. It had struck home. No matter whether she liked it or not, it had gripped her and mastered her, made her sit there and listen and forget details.

"It is life," he said, "and life is not always beautiful. And yet, perhaps because I am strangely made, I find something beautiful there. It seems to me that the beauty is tenfold enhanced because it is there—"

"But why couldn't the poor woman—" she broke in disconnectedly. Then she left the revolt of her thought unexpressed to cry out: "Oh! It is degrading! It is not nice! It is nasty!"

For the moment it seemed to him that his heart stood still. *Nasty!* He had never dreamed it. He had not meant it. The whole sketch stood before him in letters of fire, and in such blaze of illumination he sought vainly for nastiness. Then his heart began to beat again. He was not guilty.

"Why didn't you select a nice subject?" she was saying. "We know there are nasty things in the world, but that is no reason—"

She talked on in her indignant strain, but he was not following her. He was smiling to himself as he looked up into her virginal face, so innocent, so penetratingly innocent, that its purity seemed always to enter into him, driving out of him all dross and bathing him in some ethereal effulgence that was as cool and soft and velvety as starshine. *We know there are nasty things in the world!* He cuddled to him the notion of her knowing, and chuckled over it as a love joke. The next moment, in a flashing vision of multitudinous detail, he sighted the whole sea of life's nastiness that he had known and voyaged over and through, and he forgave her for not understanding the story. It was through no fault of hers that she could not understand. He thanked God that she had been born and sheltered to such innocence. But he knew life, its foulness as well as its fairness, its greatness in spite of the slime that infested it, and by God he was going to have his say on it to the world. Saints in heaven— how could they be anything but fair and pure? No praise to them. But saints in slime—ah, that was the everlasting wonder! That was what made life worth while. To see moral grandeur rising out of cesspools of iniquity; to rise himself and first glimpse beauty, faint and far, through mud-dripping eyes; to see out of weakness, and frailty, and viciousness, and all abysmal brutishness, arising strength, and truth, and high spiritual endowment—

He caught a stray sequence of sentences she was uttering.

"The tone of it all is low. And there is so much that is high. Take 'In Memoriam.' "

He was impelled to suggest "Locksley Hall," and would have done so, had not his vision gripped him again and left him staring at her, the female of his kind, who, out of the primordial ferment, creeping and crawling up the vast ladder of life for a thousand thousand centuries, had emerged on the topmost rung, having become one Ruth, pure, and fair, and divine, and with power to make him know love, and to aspire toward purity, and to desire to taste divinity—him, Martin Eden, who, too, had come up in some amazing fashion from out of the ruck and the mire and the countless mistakes and abortions of unending creation. There was the romance, and the wonder, and the glory. There was the stuff to write, if he could only find speech. Saints in heaven!—They were only saints and could not help themselves. But he was a man.

From "The Terrible and Tragic in Fiction"

I am anxious that your firm should continue to be my publishers, and, if you would be willing to bring out the book, I should be glad to accept the terms which you allowed me before—that is, you receive all profits, and allow me twenty copies for distribution to friends.

So wrote Edgar Allan Poe, on August 13, 1841, to the publishing house of Lee & Blanchard. They replied:

We very much regret to say that the state of affairs is such as to give little encouragement to new undertakings. . . . We assure you that we regret this on your account as well as our own, as it would give us great pleasure to promote your views in relation to publication.

Five years later, in 1846, Poe wrote to Mr. E. H. Duyckinck:

For particular reasons I am anxious to have another volume of my tales published before the first of March. Do you think it possible to accomplish it for me? Would not Mr. Wiley give me, say $50, in full for the copyright of the collection I now send?

Measured by the earnings of contemporaneous writers, it is clear that Poe received little or nothing for the stories he wrote. In the autumn of 1900, one of the three extant copies of his *Tamerlane and Other Poems* sold for $2050—a sum greater, perhaps, than he received from the serial and book sales of all his stories and poems. . . .

Though his stories threw people into "most admired disorders" and scared men in broad day in "Turkey blinds," and though his stories were read, one might say, universally, there seemed at the time a feeling against them which condemned them as a class of stories eminently repulsive and unreadable. The public read Poe's stories, but Poe was not

From Jack London, "The Terrible and Tragic in Fiction," *The Critic* 42 (June 1903): 542–49.

in touch with that public. And when that public spoke to him through the mouths of the magazine editors, it spoke in no uncertain terms; and, rebelliously aspiring, he dreamed of a magazine of his own—no "namby-pamby" magazine, filled with "contemptible pictures, fashion-plates, music, and love-tales," but a magazine which uttered the thing for the thing's sake and told a story because it was a story rather than a hodge-podge which the public might claim it liked. . . .

. . . [T]he writer-men of that day, who wrote the popular stories and received readier sales and fatter checks, are dead and forgotten and their stories with them, while Poe and the stories of Poe live on. In a way, this side of Poe's history is a paradoxical tangle. Editors did not like to publish his stories nor people to read them, yet they were read universally and discussed and remembered, and went the round of the foreign newspapers. They earned him little money, yet they have since earned a great deal of money and to this day command a large and steady sale. It was the common belief at the time they appeared that they could never become popular in the United States, yet their steady sales, complete editions, and what-not, which continue to come out, attest a popularity that is, to say the least, enduring. The sombre and terrible "Fall of the House of Usher," "Ligeia," "Black Cat," "Cask of Amontillado," "Berenice," "Pit and the Pendulum," and "Masque of the Red Death" are read today with an eagerness as great as ever. And especially is this true of the younger generation, which ofttimes places the seal of its approval on things the graybeards have read, approved, forgotten they have approved, and finally censured and condemned.

Yet the conditions which obtained in Poe's time obtain just as inexorably today. No self-respecting editor with an eye to the subscription-list can be bribed or bullied into admitting a terrible or tragic story into his magazine; while the reading public, when it does chance upon such stories in one way or another—and it manages to chance upon them somehow—says it does not care for them.

A person reads such a story, lays it down with a shudder, and says: "It makes my blood run cold. I never want to read anything like that again." Yet he or she will read something like that again, and again, and yet again, and return and read them over again. Talk with the average man or woman of the reading public and it will be found that they have read all, or nearly all, of the terrible and horrible tales which have been written. Also, they will shiver, express a dislike for such tales, and then proceed to discuss them with a keenness and understanding as remarkable as it is surprising.

When it is considered that so many condemn these tales and continue to read them (as is amply proved by heart-to-heart experience and by the book sales such as Poe's), the question arises: Are folk honest when they shudder and say they do no care for the terrible, the horrible, and the tragic? Or are they afraid that they do like to be afraid?

Deep down in the roots of the race is fear. It came first into the world, and it was the dominant emotion in the primitive world. Today, for that matter, it remains the most firmly seated of the emotions. But in the primitive world people were uncomplex, not yet self-conscious, and they frankly delighted in terror-inspiring tales and religions. Is it true that the complex, self-conscious people of today do not delight in the things which inspire terror? or is it true that they are ashamed to make known their delight?

What is it that lures boys to haunted houses after dark, compelling them to fling rocks and run away with their hearts going so thunderously pit-a-pat as to drown the clatter of their flying feet? What is it that grips a child, forcing it to listen to ghost stories which drive it into ecstasies of fear, and yet forces it to beg for more and more? Is it a baleful thing? A thing his instinct warns him as unhealthy and evil the while his desire leaps out to it? Or, again, what is it that sends the heart fluttering up and quickens the feet of the man or woman who goes alone down a dark hall or up a winding stair? Is it a stirring of the savage in them?—of the savage who has slept, but never died, since the time the river-folk crouched over the fires of their squatting-places, or the tree-folk bunched together and chattered in the dark?

Whatever the thing is, and whether it be good or evil, it is a thing and it is real. It is the thing Poe rouses in us, scaring us in broad day and throwing us into "admired disorders." It is rarely that the grown person who is afraid of the dark will make confession. It does not seem to them proper to be afraid of the dark, and they are ashamed. Perhaps people feel that it is not proper to delight in stories that arouse fear and terror. They may feel instinctively that it is bad and injurious to have such emotions aroused, and because of this are impelled to say that they do not like such stories, while in actuality they do like them. . . .

Long ago, Ambrose Bierce published his *Soldiers and Civilians*, a book crammed from cover to cover with unmitigated terror and horror. An editor who dared to publish one of these tales would be committing financial and professional suicide; and yet, year after year, people continue to talk about *Soldiers and Civilians*, while the innumerable sweet and wholesome, optimistic, and happy-ending books are forgotten as rapidly as they leave the press. . . .

Of two collections of tales recently published, each of which contained one terror-story, nine out of ten reviewers, in each instance, selected the terror-story as worthy of most praise, and, after they had praised, five out of the nine of them proceeded to damn it. Rider Haggard's *She*, which is filled with grewsome terror, had a long and popular vogue, while the *Strange Case of Dr. Jekyll and Mr. Hyde* achieved, if anything, a greater success and brought Stevenson to the front.

Putting the horror-story outside the pale, can any story be really great, the theme of which is anything but tragic or terrible? Can the sweet commonplaces of life be made into anything else than sweetly commonplace stories?

It would not seem so. The great short stories in the world's literary treasure-house seem all to depend upon the tragic and terrible for their strength and greatness. Not half of them deal with love at all; and when they do, they derive their greatness, not from the love itself, but from the tragic and terrible with which the love is involved. . . .

The *Fall of the House of Usher* depends upon all that is terrible for its greatness, and there is no more love in it than in Guy de Maupassant's "Necklace," or the "Piece of String," or in "The Man Who Was," and "Baa, Baa, Black Sheep," which last is the most pitiful of all tragedies, a child's.

The editors of the magazines have very good reasons for refusing admission to the terrible and tragic. Their readers say they do not like the terrible and tragic, and that is enough, without going farther. But either their readers prevaricate most shamelessly or delude themselves into believing they tell the truth, or else the people who read the magazines are not the people who continue to buy, say, the works of Poe.

In the circumstance, there being a proved demand for the terrible and tragic, is there not room in the otherwise crowded field for a magazine devoted primarily to the terrible and tragic? A magazine such as Poe dreamed of, about which there shall be nothing namby-pamby, yellowish, or emasculated, and which will print stories that are bids for place and permanence rather than for the largest circulation?

On the face of it two things appear certain: that enough of that portion of the reading public which cares for the tragic and terrible would be sufficiently honest to subscribe; and that the writers of the land would be capable of supplying the stories. The only reason why such stories are not being written today is that there is no magazine to buy them, and that the writer-folk are busy turning out the stuff, mainly ephemeral, which the magazines will buy. The pity of it is that the writer-folk are writing for bread first and glory after; and that their standard of living goes up as fast as their capacity for winning bread increases—so that they never get around to glory—the ephemeral flourishes, and the great stories remain unwritten.

Selected Letters

To Cloudesley Johns [Excerpt]

1130 East 15th st.,
Oakland, Calif.,
June 16, 1900.

Dear Cloudesley:

... You are handling stirring life, romance, things of human life and death, humor and pathos, etc. But God, man, handle them as they should be. Don't you tell the reader the philosophy of the road (except where you are actually there as participant in the first person). Don't you tell the reader. Don't. Don't. But HAVE YOUR CHARACTERS TELL IT BY THEIR DEEDS, ACTIONS, TALK, ETC. Then, and not until then, are you writing fiction and not a sociological paper upon a certain sub-stratum of society.

And get the atmosphere. Get the breadth and thickness to your stories, and not only the length (which is the mere narration). The reader, since it is fiction, doesn't want your dissertations on the subject, your observations, your knowledge as your knowledge, your thoughts about it, your ideas—BUT PUT ALL THOSE THINGS WHICH ARE YOURS INTO THE STORIES, INTO THE TALES, ELIMINATING YOURSELF (EXCEPT WHEN IN THE FIRST PERSON AS PARTICIPANT). AND THIS WILL BE THE ATMOSPHERE. AND THIS ATMOSPHERE WILL BE YOU, DON'T YOU UNDERSTAND, YOU! YOU! YOU! And for this, and for this only, will the critics praise you, and the public appreciate you, and your work be art. In short, you will then be the artist; do not do it, and you will be the artisan. That's where all the difference comes in. Study your detestable Kipling; study your Beloved's[1] *Ebb Tide*. Study them and see how they eliminate themselves and create things that live, and breathe, and grip men, and cause reading lamps to burn overtime. Atmosphere stands always for the elimination of the artist, that is to say, the atmosphere is the artist; and when there is no atmosphere and the artist is yet there, it simply means that the machinery is creaking and that the reader hears it. . . .

Do the wheels in Shakespeare creak? When Hamlet soliloquizes, does the reader think at the time that it is Shakespeare? But afterwards, ah afterwards, and then he says, "Great is Shakespeare!" . . .

Jack London.

Notes

1. Robert Louis Stevenson.

To Madge Selinger

Glen Ellen, Calif.
Jul 1 1906

Dear madam:

I have learned that I am a personal friend of yours, and that you have known me for a number of years. I have learned also of a remarkable attachment of mine for a Mrs. Stenberg, formerly of Fresno, now of Sacramento. I have learned that you have been a sort of go-between between us. I have learned a great many things also, about the Hindoo, and his and my persecution of Mrs. Stenberg through you.

Now I am writing to you for information. I am the real Jack London. I don't know you. I don't know the Hindoo. I don't know Mrs. Stenberg, much less love her. Was this all a concoction of yours, or did you really know some fellow who claimed that he was Jack London? I should be very grateful for a reply at your early convenience.

Very truly yours,
Jack London

To the Editor, *Cosmopolitan*

[Glen Ellen]
November-24-1906-

Dear sir:—

I have just seen the Christmas number of *The Cosmopolitan*. You got the article[1] out beautifully, and you are featuring it splendidly, for which two things you have my congratulations and thanks. But on top of that, I have a howl coming—the regular long wolf-howl. I don't like the way you have taken liberties with my copy. Any tyro can cut a manuscript and feel that he is the co-creator with the author. But it's hell on the author. Not one man in a million, including office-boys, is to be found in the magazine offices, who is able properly to revise by elimination the work of a professional author. And the men in your office have certainly played ducks and drakes with the exposition in the first half of my first boat-article.

The men in your office are certainly most unfit for such work. For instance, I have just finished reading the proofs of "Just Meat." In one place I have my burglar say, "I put the kibosh on his time." Some man in your office changed this to, "I put a crimp in his time." In the first place, "crimp" is incorrect in such usage. In the second place, there is nothing whatever in the connotation of "kibosh" that would prevent its appearing in the pages of your magazine. "Kibosh" is not vulgar, it is not obscene. Such an action is wholly unwarranted and gratuitously officious. Did this co-creator of mine, in your office, think that he knew what he was doing when he made such a ridiculous substitution? And if he does think so, why in the dickens doesn't he get in and do the whole thing himself?

In our Contract, I take your right of revision to consist in rejecting an article as a whole, or in eliminating objectionable phrases. Now I have no objection to that. I have no objection to your truckling to Mrs. Grundy, when, for instance, you cut out swear-words or change "go to hell" to "go to blazes." That's the mere shell. In that sort of revision you can have full swing; but that is a different matter from cutting the heart out of my work, such as you did in my first boat-article. You made my exposition look like thirty cents.

I WEAVE my stuff; you can cut out a whole piece of it, but you can't cut out parts of it, and leave mutilated parts behind. Just think of it. Wading into my exposition and cutting out the premises or proofs or anything else just to suit your length of an article, or the space, rather, that you see fit to give such article. Who in the dickens are you, any of you, to think that you can better my work! Don't you see my point? If the whole woven thing—event, narrative, description—is not suitable for your magazine, why cut it out—cut out the whole thing. I don't care. But I refuse to contemplate for one moment that there is any man in your office, or in the office of any magazine capable of bettering my art, or the art of any other first-class professional writer.

213

Now I want to give warning right here: I won't stand for it. Before I'll stand for it, I'll throw over the whole proposition. If you dare to do it with my succeeding articles (and I'll know shortly after the article in which you do it is published) I'll not send you another line. By golly, you've got to give me a square deal in this matter. Do you think for one moment that I'll write my heart (my skilled, professional heart, if you please) into my work to have you fellows slaughtering it to suit your journalistic tastes? Either I'm going to write this set of articles, or you're going to write it, for know right here that I refuse definitely and flatly, to collaborate with you or with any one in your office.

In order that this letter may not go astray, I am sending copies to each of the three men who, in my present hypothesis, I think may possibly be editor of *The Cosmopolitan*.[2]

And I want, at your earliest convenience, an assurance that the sort of mutilation that I am complaining about, will not occur again.

Sincerely yours,
Jack London

Notes

1. "The Voyage of the *Snark*."
2. London sent copies of this letter to Perriton Maxwell, Bailey Millard, and John Brisben Walker.

To Max E. Feckler

[Oakland]
October 26, 1914

Dear Max Feckler:—

In reply to yours of recent date undated, and returning herewith your Manuscript.[1] First of all, let me tell you that as a psychologist and as one who has been through the mill, I enjoyed your story for its psychology and point of view. Honestly and frankly, I did not enjoy it for its literary charm or value. In the first place, it has little literary value and practically no literary charm. Merely because you have got something to say that may be of interest to others does not free you from making all due effort to express that something in the best possible medium and form. Medium and form you have utterly neglected.

Anent the foregoing paragraph, what is to be expected of any lad of twenty, without practice, in knowledge of medium and form? Heavens

214

on earth, boy, it would take you five years to serve your apprenticeship and become a skilled blacksmith. Will you dare to say that you have spent, not five years but as much as five months of unimpeachable, unremitting toil in trying to learn the artisan's tools of a professional writer who can sell his stuff to the magazines and receive hard cash for same? Of course you cannot; you have not done it. And yet, you should be able to reason on the face of it that the only explanation for the fact that successful writers receive such large fortunes, is because very few who desire to write become successful writers. If it takes five years work to become a skilled blacksmith, how many years of work intensified into nineteen hours a day, so that one year counts for five—how many years of such work, studying medium and form, art and artisanship, do you think a man, with native talent and something to say, requires in order to reach a place in the world of letters where he received a thousand dollars cash iron money per week?

I think you get the drift of the point I am trying to make. If a fellow harnesses himself to a star of $1000 a week, he has to work proportionately harder than if he harnesses himself to a little glowworm of $20.00 a week. The only reason there are more successful blacksmiths in the world than successful writers, is that it is much easier, and requires far less hard work, to become a successful blacksmith than it does to become a successful writer.

It cannot be possible that you, at twenty, should have done the work at writing that would merit you success at writing. You have not begun your apprenticeship yet. The proof of it is the fact that you dared to write this manuscript, "A Journal of One Who is to Die." Had you made any sort of study of what is published in the magazines you would have found that your short story was of the sort that never was published in the magazines. If you are going to write for success and money, you must deliver to the market marketable goods. Your short story is not marketable goods, and had you taken half a dozen evenings off and gone into a free reading room and read all the stories published in the current magazines, you would have learned in advance that your short story was not marketable goods.

Dear lad, I'm talking to you straight from the shoulder. Remember one very important thing: Your ennui of twenty, is your ennui of twenty. You will have various other and complicated ennuis before you die. I tell you this, who have been through the ennui of sixteen as well as the ennui of twenty; and the boredom, and the blaseness, and utter wretchedness of the ennui of twenty five, and of thirty. And I yet live, am growing fat, am very happy, and laugh a large portion of my waking hours. You see, the disease has progressed so much further with me than with you that I, as a battle-scarred survivor of the disease, look upon your symptoms as merely the preliminary adolescent symptoms. Again, let me tell you that I know them, that I had them, and just as I had much worse afterward of the same sort, so much worse is in store for you. In the meantime, if you want to succeed at a well-paid game, prepare yourself to do the work.

There's only one way to make a beginning, and that is to begin; and begin with hard work, and patience, prepared for all the disappointments that were Martin Eden's before he succeeded—which were mine before I succeeded—because I merely appended to my fictional character, Martin Eden, my own experiences in the writing game.

Any time you are out here in California, I should be glad to have you come to visit me on the ranch. I can meet you to the last limit of brass tacks, and hammer some facts of life into you that possible so far have escaped your own experience.

Sincerely yours,
Jack London

Notes

1. Along with his undated letter to Jack London (Jack London Collection, Huntington Library), Feckler sent the manuscript "A Journal of One Who Is to Die."

To H. G. Wells*

Glen Ellen, Calif.
Mar 23 1913

Dear sir:—
I live in California—when I am not farther afield. I have published thirty-three books, as well as an ocean of magazine stuff, and yet I have never heard the rates that other writers receive.

*Identical letters were sent to George Bernard Shaw; Winston Churchill (1871–1947), American novelist; Robert W. Chambers (1865–1933), American novelist; Samuel Lloyd Osborne (1868–1947), San Francisco novelist and playwright and stepson of Robert Louis Stevenson, with whom he co-wrote *The Ebb Tide;* and Owen M. Johnson (1878–1952), American author of popular novels about boys and son of Robert U. Johnson.

If it is not asking too much, may I ask you to tell me (confidentially, of course) what top rates, average rates, and minimum rates, you receive from (1) English magazines, (2) American magazines, (3) English book-publishers, (4) American book-publishers.

Sincerely yours,
Jack London.

To Joseph Conrad

Honolulu, T.H.
June 4, 1915.

Dear Joseph Conrad:
The mynah birds are waking the hot dawn about me. The surf is thundering in my ears where it falls on the white sand of the beach, here at Waikiki, where the green grass at the roots of the coconut palms insists to the lip of the wave-wash. This night has been yours—and mine.

I had just begun to write when I read your first early work. I have merely madly appreciated you and communicated my appreciation to my friends through all these years. I never wrote you. I never dreamed to write you. But *Victory* has swept me off my feet, and I am inclosing herewith a carbon copy of a letter written to a friend at the end of this lost night's sleep.

Perhaps you will appreciate this lost night's sleep when I tell you that it was immediately preceded by a day's sail in a Japanese sampan of sixty miles from the Leper Settlement of Molokai (where Mrs. London and I had been revisiting old friends) to Honolulu.[1]

On your head be it.

Aloha (which is a sweet word of greeting, the Hawaiian greeting, meaning "my love be with you").[2]

Jack London

Notes

1. The Londons sailed for Molokai on the *Likelike* on May 25. They visited the leper colony and Edward Goodhue on May 28 and 29 and returned to Honolulu on May 31.

2. Joseph Conrad responded in a letter to London of September 10, 1915: "I am immensely touched by the kindness of your letter—that apart from

intense satisfaction given me by the approval of an accomplished fellow-crafts-man and a true brother in letters—of whose personality and art I have been intensely aware for many years. A few days before it reached me Percival Gibbon (a short-story writer and a most distinguished journalist and war corresp.) and I were talking you over endlessly, in the quiet hours of the night. Gibbon, who had just returned after 5 months on the Russian front, had been taking you in bulk, soaking himself in your prose. And we admired the vehemence of your strength and the delicacy of your perception with the greatest sympathy and respect. I haven't seen your latest yet. The reviews such as come my way are enthusiastic. The book is in my home but I wait to finish a thing (short) I am writing now before I sit down to read you. It'll be a reward for being a good industrious boy. For it is not easy to write here nowadays. At this very moment there is a heavy burst of gunfire in Dover. I can hear the quick firers and the big guns—and wonder what it is. The night before last a Zep passed over the house (not the first time) bound west on that raid on London of which you would have read already in your papers. Moreover I've just now a quonty wrist. This explains my clumsy handwriting. And so no more—this time. Keep me in your kind memory and accept a grateful and cordial handgrasp. (Jack London Collection, Henry E. Huntington Library.)

To Mary Austin

Glen Ellen, California
November 5, 1915.

Dear Mary Austin:[1]
In reply to yours of October 26, 1915:
   Your letter strikes me that you are serious. Now, why be serious with this bone-head world? Long ere this, I know that you have learned that the majority of the people who inhabit the planet Earth are bone-heads. Wherever the bone of their heads interferes there is no getting through.
   I have read and enjoyed every bit of your "Jesus Christ" book as published serially in the *North American Review*. What if it does not get across?[2]
   I have again and again written books that failed to get across. Long years ago, at the very beginning of my writing career, I attacked Nietzsche and his super-man idea. This was in *The Sea Wolf*. Lots of people read *The Sea Wolf*, no one discovered that it was an attack upon the superman philosophy. Later on, not mentioning my shorter efforts, I wrote another novel that was an attack upon the super-man idea, namely, my *Martin Eden*. Nobody discovered that this was such an

attack. At another time I wrote an attack on ideas brought forth by Rudyard Kipling, and entitled my attack "The Strength of the Strong." No one was in the slightest way aware of the point of my story.

I am telling you all the foregoing merely to show that it is a very bonehead world indeed, and, also, that I never bother my head when my own books miss fire. And the point I am making to you is: why worry? Let the best effort of your heart and head miss fire. The best effort of my heart and head has missed fire with you, as it has missed fire with practically everybody else in the world who reads, and I do not worry about it. I go ahead content to be admired for my red-blood brutality and for a number of other nice little things like that which are not true of my work at all.

Heavens, have *you* read *my* "Christ" story?[3] I doubt that anybody has read this "Christ" story of mine, though it has been published in book form on both sides of the Atlantic. Said book has been praised for its red-bloodedness and no mention has been made of my handling of the Christ situation in Jerusalem at all.

I tell you this, not because I am squealing, which I am not; but to show you that you are not alone in this miss-firing. Just be content with being called the "greatest American stylist."[4]

Those who sit alone must sit alone. They must continue to sit alone. As I remember it, the prophets and seers of all times have been compelled to sit alone except at such times when they were stoned or burned at the stake. The world is mostly bone-head and nearly all boob, and you have no complaint if the world calls you the "great stylist" and fails to recognize that your style is merely the very heart and soul of your brain. The world has an idea that style is something apart from heart and brain. Neither you nor I can un-convince the world of that idea.

I do not know what more I can say, except, that, had I you here with me for half an hour I could make my point more strongly, namely, that you are very lucky, and that you should be content to receive what the world gives you. The world will never give you due recognition for your "Christ" book. I, who never read serials, read your serial of the Christ and turned always to it first when my *North American Review* came in. I am not the world, you are not the world. The world feeds you, the world feeds me, but the world knows damn little of either of us.

Affectionately yours,
Jack London

Notes

1. Mary Austin (1868–1934), essayist, novelist, and playwright who was a founder of the artists and writers colony in Carmel. At this time, she was in New York and had turned from her earlier, more regional writing to issues of socialism, feminism, and religion.

2. In her letter of October 26, 1915, Austin complained that the point of her book *The Man Jesus; Being a Brief Account of the Life and Teaching of the Man of Nazareth* (1915) had been missed: "nobody seems to have discovered that I have said that Christian banking should be administered on behalf of those who serve rather than those who own. I thought that was a fairly suggestive conclusion—that a man could borrow money on his capacity to serve society rather than on his wife's diamonds." Austin's book appeared in *The North American Review* from June to November 1915. (Jack London Collection, Henry E. Huntington Library.)

3. *The Star Rover,* chap 17.

4. In her letter of October 26 Austin wrote: "You don't know how tired I get of being called 'the greatest American stylist'—and there is H. G. Wells putting me on a lonely pedestal alongside Stephen Crane." (Jack London Collection, Henry E. Huntington Library.)

Part 3

THE CRITICS

Introduction

Earle Labor likes to recall how he was introduced by Sam Baskett, now professor emeritus of Michigan State University and first president of the Jack London Society, at a 1963 meeting of the Michigan College English Association: "I am proud to introduce the other Jack London scholar." Times have changed. Today, after the renaissance of critical interest in Jack London that has taken place in the last 20 years, in good measure due to the efforts of scholars like Baskett and Labor, the field is full of literary scholars examining London's canon from a wide variety of perspectives. The publication of *The Complete Stories of Jack London* by Stanford in 1993; dozens of dissertations, editions, critical books, and definitive articles in major academic journals; the founding of the Jack London Society and the *Jack London Journal;* regular panels on London at the American Literature Association and Popular Culture Association; and regular conferences devoted entirely to London have radically changed the face of London scholarship.

Although there is much excellent work from which to choose, beginning with critics who were contemporaries of London, I have made the selections presented here with the idea of representing as closely as possible the range of approaches to London's short works. Edgar Lucien Larkin's short piece from the 1917 issue of *The Overland Monthly* commemorating London's death gives us a view inside the author's study and writing practices and a sense of his life on the ranch. It also provides a feel for the worshipful attitude of many of London's admirers, which continues today. The excerpt from Carl Sandburg argues that London is great insofar as he remained true to his socialist beliefs. The remaining three essays address three distinct periods of London's short fiction career and touch upon key themes: Earle Labor and King Hendricks' seminal essay on the two versions of "To Build a Fire" offers an important formalist analysis of that well-known story and a clear sense of how London's revision reflected his matured thinking. Lawrence I. Berkove examines a tale from the middle part of London's career, "The Unparalleled Invasion," that addresses both the writer's complex attitude toward "the Yellow Peril" and his often-ignored irony and satire. "The

Unparalleled Invasion" is a story that has been seriously misread—like some others of London's—and Berkove offers a persuasive argument that more carefully reflects a sense of the writer's purpose. James Slagel's essay on "Koolau the Leper" also takes race as its topic, describing London's attitude toward the struggle of Koolau and his fellow Hawaiians against the white rulers of the islands, as well as London's own passion for Hawaii, which he considered a second home in his last years.

Edgar Lucien Larkin

On September 13, 1906, I spent a night at Jack London's home in Sonoma. The house was crowded with guests. Jack took me to the place he had chosen for me . . .

Jack opened the door of his den, bade me enter, and pointed to a huge arm chair. He lighted up, said a few pleasant words, opened a door looking into the other half of the building, showed me his bed, bade me goodnight. And when all alone I tore up things in an exploration exercise. I was in one of the greatest literary centers of the world. The working table was wide and long. It was heaped up with an incredible stock of writing paper of varying sizes, pens by the gross, pencils, not one well sharpened, quart bottles of ink, sheets of postage stamps and the like.

But see these things, stories almost finished, others half, a third or fourth written; tense, exceedingly dramatic humanity plots and plans of other writings; sketches for illustrations of books, highly ideal, letters in heaps from all parts of the world and from many publishers.

I was glad there was no room for me in the house.

There! I heard a sweetly sad and solemn bell, tuneful bell, then another, and soon another, no two sounding the same note. But they had been attuned by a master of harmonics. They were three sacred Korean temple service bells secured when Mr. London was Russian-Japanese war correspondent. They had been fastened to twigs. The well known "Valley of the Moon" breeze, just in from the ocean, swayed the branches and rang them with delicate, excessively harmonic notes. But I didn't know they were there.

Finally a gust caused one to strike the window pane. I explored and solved this apparently esoteric mystery. Esoteric, indeed, for the bells had been in use, maybe, for centuries, in archaic Asiatic mysteries greater than those of Eleusis in Greece.

From "Recollections of the Late Jack London," *The Overland Monthly* 68 (May 1917): 433–34.

On a shelf across a corner above the chairback I counted thirteen books. I arose and took them down, one by one, looked at their dates. They had all been written by Mr. London within five years. He was born in San Francisco on January 12, 1876. I was looking them over at 1 A.M., September 14, 1906. Go do this work, and you will begin to sense the true meaning of the word work.

There were Mr. London's Arctic and Klondike outfits, curios from Asia and many things belonging to his dogs for their comfort in cold. . . .

Here I was in a world of pure literature—story, drama—these that rock the soul like the rocking of a baby's cradle. I could not wait longer. I seized Jack's pen and a lot of paper at 1:40 and "wrote a piece" for the Examiner, which was published a few days later. Then to Jack's bed at 3:15 A.M.

Breakfast early, a few words for the ranch employees, and they were glad to be laborers on land owned by Jack London, an employer kind to the extreme to man and beast.

Then the guests to the porch, and Mr. London entertained us with the most fascinating conversation. And we talked some.

Then out came Charmian. She broke up the party in one minute, and without saying one word. Silently she looked into the eyes of her husband, then she looked at each of her guests. We knew, and we went. It was time, 8:30 A.M., for Mr. London to go to the den and write. Not a person in Sonoma County would ask Charmian's permission to interrupt Mr. London. None could see the little 16 feet square, 9 feet high, California redwood building, even if passing within twenty feet, so completely was it hidden by the luxuriant California undergrowth, chapparal, vines and trees.

We all held the forenoon to be sacred to Mr. London. That one look of Charmian was enough. He "skipped," went to the edge of the wildwood, lifted a great hanging, bent beneath and vanished. . . .

Charles A. Sandburg

Some writer not possessed of force enough to fasten his name in my memory has of late made an explanation of the socialism of Jack London. The explanation goes as follows: Jack London is of a super-combative nature and must in the order of things have something to fight. As socialism is too petty a thing to be fought against by a strong man, he girds himself with a big stick and goes after capitalism. In short, he fights the competitive system because the co-operative commonwealth has not yet evolved so that it may be hit over the head with a club.

The man who works out this lucid, cogent exegesis is himself not at all of the fierce and swarthy tribe to whom barriers are an insult. Our genial exegesist is of the acquiescent temperament. If the socialism at which he sneers were here today, he would assent to that. But as we have instead capitalism and the law of club and fang, he wraps the drapery of his couch about him and lies down before the juggernaut of competition. If this gentle-hearted conformist chances to walk through a slum district, he finds his solace in that hoary chant, "The poor ye have with ye even alway."

I have introduced this carping critic to show on what flimsy pretexts men will hang their reasons for the existing order, what absurd motives may be hunted out in the heart of one you don't understand. I am now to consider some of the life-phases of one of the more remarkable men produced on American soil.

The first and baffling thing in a study of the life of Jack London is the versatility, the many-sidedness of the fellow. As a boy he lived in the underworld of San Francisco. He sold newspapers on the streets. He was a stevedore, an oysterman, a scullion, a sailor before the mast. Look over this list of occupations and ask yourself if it isn't more likely to produce a strong, ruthless, crafty, insensate creature rather than one of high, clean, intelligent manhood. Note also that following these occupations he became a tramp, a hobo stealing rides on freight and passenger

Charles A. Sandburg, "Jack London: A Common Man," *Tomorrow Magazine* 2 (April 1906): 35–39.

trains, mingling with all the hopeless, degenerate life of discouraged workmen, beggars, and petty criminals. Note further that at Niagara Falls he was captured and sentenced to a workhouse so that behind the bars he might nurse his bitterness into that relentless hatred marking the habitual criminal, the hatred that outlaws itself and tells mankind to go to hell in a lump, that deep vindictive thing possessing Jean Valjean before he met a great beautiful soul that stabbed him with a kind deed.

Note further that this stripling not yet twenty was not shackled by his environment. He was master of himself—a spectator but not a partaker in the degradations that surrounded him. Climbing out of the underworld, writing books that sent his name around the world, he forced his way to the overworld where men think and control and to these men who think and control, he said, "The twentieth century, the common man says, is his day. The evidence is with him. The previous centuries, and more notably the nineteenth, have marked the rise of the common man. From chattel slavery to serfdom, and from serfdom to what he bitterly terms 'wage slavery,' he has risen. Never was he so strong as he is today, and never so menacing. He does the work of the world, and he is beginning to know it. The world cannot get along without him, and this also he is beginning to know. All the human knowledge of the past, all the scientific discovery, governmental experiment, and invention of machinery, have tended to his advancement. His standard of living is higher. His common school education would shame princes ten centuries past. His civil and religious liberty makes him a free man, and his ballot the peer of his betters. And all this has tended to make him conscious, conscious of himself, conscious of his class. He looks about him and questions that ancient law of development. It is cruel and wrong, he is beginning to declare. It is an anachronism. Let it be abolished. Why should there be one empty belly in all the world when the work of ten men can feed a hundred? What if my brother be not so strong as I? He has not sinned. Wherefore should he hunger—he and his sinless little ones. Away with the old law. There is food and shelter for all, therefore let all receive food and shelter."

It is the common man for whom Jack London pleads and as he pleads he wants it understood that he too is a common man. Nor is it merely a plea he makes. It is also a threat, "the threat of socialism." It is the threat Mark Hanna had in mind when he said, "We've got to change the conditions that are breeding Social Democrats or the Republican Party will be lost in the shuffle." The masses are pitiful and pathetic in some respects, but there resides in them a huge, crude power that pushed too far spells blood and destruction. It is this that London points out to the men who think and control.

London's fame as a writer has of recent days been hard pushed by his notoriety as an agitator. Howells, "the dean of American literature," Bliss Carman, Richard Le Galliene, Edwin Markham, and other literary men are socialists, but they have made no noise about it. London, however, has neglected no occasion to boom his theories. He has gone up and down the land talking to thousands urging the need of a new "System." For the upper and middle classes he has tried to picture the hellishness of the social pit that forever yawns for the man and woman out of work. His book, The War of the Classes is a vivid presentation of the facts of the class struggle.

But towering above these transitory events are his works in the way of fiction. At twenty-three years of age his first stories were published and immediately sprang into popularity. They dealt with the Klondike regions, experiences of the hardy gold-hunters, so many of whom left their bones in the shadow of the Arctic circle. It has been his part to interpret the fear of "the white silence," that vast and awesome loneliness of the far north.

Among his various studies in the north, none shows a higher appreciation of the present "System," none will set you thinking about how far the human race has progressed, the gulf between savagery and civilization, than the tale of Nam Bok the Unveracious. Nam Bok, after an absence of many years returns to an isolated fishing village on the shores of Alaska. They fear he has come from "the bourne whence no man returns," but he joins valiantly in a supper of fish and blubber and then asks triumphantly, "Can a shadow eat?" Late into the night they talk, and Nam Bok, who has been to California, tells them he has seen single houses in which lived more people than in all the village; he has been upon a boat larger than all the boats of the village in one; he describes the sails of the vessel and avers it made head against the wind as well as with it; he describes an iron monster that sped upon two streaks of iron faster than the wind, was fed upon black stones, coughed fire, and shrieked louder than the thunder. Early the next morning he is visited by his cousins and brothers, informed that his sense of truth is mournfully degenerate. Their message runs in this wise, "Thou art from the shadow-land, O Nam Bok. With us thou canst not stay. Thou must return whence thou camest, to the land of the shadows." So much for Nam Bok. I cannot name a piece of literature in which the contrasts of

Part 3

civilization and savagery are more livingly set forth. It should be a part of the reading-course of every school.

The Call of the Wild and The Sea-Wolf are his masterpieces. Of these not a great deal may be said that is not repetitive. The Call of the Wild is the greatest dog-story ever written and is at the same time a study of one of the most curious and profound motives that plays hide-and-seek in the human soul. The more civilized we become the deeper is the fear that back in barbarism is something of the beauty and joy of life we have not brought along with us. We all feel these artificialities that so easily cramp and fret our lives. But this sense of a too-extreme complexity of life, too many tailors, launderers and chefs, too many walls and ceilings that shut out the stars, too many carpets lacking the odor of green grass or the tang of crisp snow, it is this sense you can't educate or civilize out of man. It is in all of us. Not the rankest degenerate but vaguely feels this call back to "nature and his primal sanities," the call of the wild. That the race is soon ripe for new and saner modes of life is shown in the widespread reception of The Call of the Wild. The book appeals to people of red blood and clear eyes and the way I have seen boys and girls and old men and hacked-up literary connoisseurs take to this book, makes my heart beat high for the final destiny of the human mob.

The Sea-Wolf bore down on me for all my brain-traffic would bear. I read it first as it appeared in cereal form and found it wholesome and nutritious. Had I not held a policy in the Equitable and felt certain I was going to live, I would surely have written the publishers to tell me how it was all going to end. The reviews of The Sea-Wolf were fun. Almost every man-jack of the hired scribes missed the allegory of the book, the lesson. Wolf Larsen is one in whose character revolve the motives of ambition and domination in their most terrible form. He is a ship-captain and absolute master of the vessel's crew. What gets in his way goes overboard, be it scullion or first mate. Do you know of any Thing that relentlessly crushes whatever gets in its way, be it a frail child, a tender woman, or a strong man? Wolf Larsen is The System incarnate. London has him die of a slow, pathetic paralysis. No wonder the well-sleeked critics thought his end was not artistic!

It is the fashion nowadays in the cities when bridge, dancing, driving, or golf pall on the senses to go a-slumming. Tender-hearted, misguided people there are too, who want to "do good" and forthwith turn their steps to where poverty ferments. I have seen a woman carrying a basket of sandwiches into a ten-storey tenement and as she disappeared into the swirl of rags and dirt, it seemed to me the relief conveyed by the good woman into that abyss to want was about equal to that of a drop of water in the pits of hades.

When Jack London went a-slumming in London, England, he was original, as he always is. He dressed as a workingman. He looked for work. He applied for relief at the free-soup houses. He slept on the floors of police stations with the wretches that applied nightly. He knew what it was to be turned away, denied the balm of sleep on clammy stone floors. He "carried the banner"—walked the streets all night afraid to sit him down in fear that he would awake to the tattoo of a policeman's baton and be sentenced to the workhouse. Before you go a-slumming, read The People of the Abyss.

There, in "skeletesque" outline, you have Jack London. Not Gerald Thockmorton London, nor Francis Felix Quebec London. But just plain everyday Jack! I am not a prophet and I don't like to dabble in futurities, but I know London to be a tremendous worker and of simple habits, so I put him down as X, a dynamo of unguessable power.

If he were not a Common Man I would call him a Great Man.

Earle Labor and King Hendricks

. . . . Though London may have written the first "To Build a Fire" "for boys merely," he nevertheless worked his form to perfection. This form, one of the oldest types of short fiction, is the *exemplum*.[1] Because its primary function is moral edification, such structural elements as atmosphere and characterization are subordinated, in the *exemplum*, to theme; and what E. M. Forster has called the "mystery" of plot is sacrificed for the didactic explicitness of "story." London adheres closely to the conventions of his form by stating his moral at the outset ("a companion is absolutely essential") and reemphasizing it at the end (*"Never travel alone!"*). The narrative action is simple and direct; his "story" is an uncomplicated circle, moving from message through true-to-life illustration back to message. The tale's effectiveness depends upon two major factors: clarity of the statement and vividness of the illustration. Another important, if minor, factor is the attractiveness of his hero; Tom Vincent, notwithstanding his foolishness, is a sympathetic, clean-cut character—an admirable model for young men. The first "To Build a Fire" was, in short, one of the many fictional examples used by the editors of *The Youth's Companion* to vivify their weekly sermons to America's strenuous young manhood.

The second "To Build a Fire" is, as London himself indicated, an altogether different story. It is, for one thing, considerably longer than the earlier version (7,235 as compared to 2,700 words). Although expansion is of itself no criterion for artistic merit, in this case London obviously used his additional wordage for greater artistic effect, creating a narrative "mystery" and an "atmosphere" lacking in the first version. His awareness of the importance of such elements is revealed in one of his letters to a fellow writer: "Atmosphere stands always for the elimination of the artist, that is to say, the atmosphere is the artist; and when there is no atmosphere and the artist is yet there, it simply means that the

From "Jack London's Twice-Told Tale," *Studies in Short Fiction* 4 (1967): 334–47. Copyright 1967 by Newberry College.

machinery is creaking and the reader hears it."[2] Since Wayne Booth has
. . . explained in his *Rhetoric of Fiction* that there is really no such thing as
"eliminating" the author from the work, perhaps we should paraphrase
London's advice as follows: "The effect of certain kinds of fiction—particularly fiction informed by cosmic irony—depends heavily upon the
evoking of mood; and mood is most effectively evoked through a skillful
manipulation of setting and imagery, rather than through editorial comment by the author. In other words, rather than being 'told' the reader
must be made to hear, to see and—above all—*to feel.*"

Examination of the opening paragraph of the second "To Build a Fire"
reveals the devices through which London allows atmosphere to function as commentary:

> Day had broken cold and gray, exceedingly cold and gray, when the man
> turned aside from the main Yukon trail and climbed the high earth-
> bank, where a dim and little-traveled trail led eastward through the fat
> spruce timberland. It was a steep bank, and he paused for breath at the
> top, excusing the act to himself by looking at his watch. It was nine
> o'clock. There was no sun nor hint of sun, though there was not a cloud
> in the sky. It was a clear day, and yet there seemed an intangible pall
> over the face of things, a subtle gloom that made the day dark, and that
> was due to the absence of sun. This fact did not worry the man. He
> was used to the lack of sun. It had been days since he had seen the
> sun, and he knew that a few more days must pass before that cheerful
> orb, due south, would just peep above the sky line and dip immedi-
> ately from view.

By varied repetition of a textural motif, London achieves the same kind
of hypnotic impact that Hemingway is said to have learned from
Gertrude Stein: certain images recur and cluster to produce a mood that
is at once somber and sinister ("cold and gray, exceedingly cold and gray
. . . a dim and little-traveled trail . . . no sun nor hint of sun . . . intangible pall . . . a subtle gloom . . . day dark . . . absence of sun . . . lack of the
sun . . . days since he had seen the sun"). The story's dominant symbolism, the polarity of heat (sun-fire-life) and cold (darkness-depression-
death), is carefully adumbrated at the outset so that the reader *senses* the
protagonist's imminent doom. We are subtly oppressed by that "intense
awareness of human loneliness" that Frank O'Connor has identified
with the short story, and we are reminded of that haunting statement
from Pascal: *"Le silence eternal de ces espaces infinis m'effraie."*[3] It is undoubt-
edly such scenes as this that prompted Maxwell Geismar to remark that

"London's typical figure was a voiceless traveler journeying across the ghostly leagues of a dead world."[4]

Unlike Tom Vincent, the protagonist of this "To Build a Fire" is nameless. He is the naturalistic version of Everyman: a puny, insignificant mortal confronting the cold mockery of Nature as Antagonist. Yet, though nameless, he is distinguished by certain traits of character: the man is practical, complacent, insensitive, and vain—he must, for example, excuse to himself the impractical human act of pausing for breath; he is unawed by the mysterious other-worldness of his surroundings; caught in this weird *Urwelt*, he is foolish enough to put his faith in mere clock-time.

What has been hinted in the beginning becomes explicit in the third paragraph, the only place in the story where the author's voice may be detected. The man lacks the one asset that might equalize the odds against him—imagination: "He was quick and alert in the things of life, but only in the things, and not in the significances. . . . Fifty degrees below zero was to him just precisely fifty degrees below zero [actually it is seventy-five below]. That there should be anything more to it than that was a thought that never entered his head." The scope of his imagination is signified in his one stock comment: "It certainly was cold," a fatally inept response that recurs with increasing irony as the man's situation deteriorates. It is also in this paragraph that the theme of the story is subtly implanted in the reader's mind: "It [the extreme cold] did not lead him to meditate upon his frailty as a creature of temperature, and upon man's frailty in general . . . and from there on it did not lead him to the conjectural field of immortality and man's place in the universe." London drops the comment so deftly that it hardly ripples in the reader's consciousness, yet it is this idea precisely that gives the story its final impact: "unaccommodated man" is indeed a frail and pitiable figure when pitted against the awful majesty of cosmic force. . . .

But the nameless protagonist of "To Build a Fire" is unaware of these deeper implications, as we learn not only from his own behavior but also through the only other animated character in the story, the dog. The inclusion of this *ficelle* or "reflector" is the masterstroke of London's revised version. By employing the dog as foil, the author has obviated the necessity for further editorial comment. Instead of being *told* that one needs a companion in the Northland, we are made to *see* dramatically through his relationship with the animal that the man is a "loner." Because he lacks imagination, he fails to see, until too late, that a companion—even a dog—might possibly save him in a crisis;

more important, he is revealed as a man lacking in essential warmth. There is no place in his cold practical philosophy for affection or for what London called elsewhere "true comradeship." To this man the dog is only another of "the things" of life, an object to be spoken to with "the sound of whip lashes." From his relationship to the animal, we may infer a broader relationship—that to mankind. The protagonist is, in other words, a hollow man whose inner coldness correlates with the enveloping outer cold. And there is a grim but poetic justice in his fate.

The dog serves as a foil in the following manner also: his natural wisdom of conduct is juxtaposed against the foolish rationality of his master's behavior. By shifting point of view from man to dog, London provides a subtle counterpointing that enhances both theme and structural tension. For example,

> The animal [unlike the man] was depressed by the tremendous cold. It knew [without the convenience of a watch] that it was no time for traveling. . . . The dog did not know anything about thermometers [which are as useless as watches if one lacks the ability to interpret]. Possibly in its brain there was no sharp consciousness of a condition of very cold such as was in the man's brain [a consciousness vitiated in the latter by stock response]. But the brute had its instinct [a surer gauge than rationality]. It experienced a vague but menacing apprehension [absent in the man, because he is without imagination]. . . .

And, finally, by using the animal as objective correlative, London has managed to give an extra twist of irony to the conclusion of his story. After the man's last desperate attempt to save himself and after his dying vision of rescue, we shift once more to the dog's point of view:

> The brief day drew to a close in a long, slow twilight. There were no signs of a fire to be made, and, besides, never in the dog's experience had it known a man to sit like that in the snow and make no fire. As the twilight drew on, its eager yearning for the fire mastered it, and with a great lifting and shifting of forefeet, it whined softly, then flattened its ears down in anticipation of being chidden by the man. But the man remained silent. Later the dog whined loudly. And still later it crept close to the man and caught the scent of death. This made the animal bristle and back away. A little longer it delayed, howling under the stars that leaped and danced and shone brightly in the cold sky. Then it turned and trotted up the trail in the direction of the camp it knew, where were the other food providers and fire providers.

Through its natural responses the dog conveys the finality of the man's death more forcibly—and more artistically—than any overt statement by the author might do. And in this concluding paragraph all the key elements of London's story—the ironic polarity of life and death, the intransigence of Nature's laws, the cosmic mockery of the White Silence—coalesce to produce a memorable effect. As Frank O'Connor has written, a great story "must have the element of immediacy, the theme must plummet to the bottom of the mind. . . . It must have a coherent action. When the curtain falls everything must be changed. An iron bar must have been bent and been seen to be bent."[5] Surely, with the firm grasp of the master craftsman, London has "bent his bar" in this concluding scene; and we must applaud his strength. . . .

Notes

1. See Margaret Schlauch, "English Short Fiction in the 15th and 16th Centuries," *Studies in Short Fiction* 3 (Summer 1966): 399–402; and Henry Seidel Canby, *A Study of the Short Story* (New York: H. Holt and Company, 1913), 9–10, 22–26. Canby indicates that the *exemplum*, best known through Chaucer, was also a popular form for such later writers as Addison and Steele—and Dr. Johnson.

2. To Cloudesley Johns, June 16, 1900, *Letters from Jack London*, ed. King Hendricks and Irving Shepard (New York: Odyssey, 1965), 108.

3. "The eternal silence of those infinite spaces terrifies me." See Frank O'Connor, *The Lonely Voice* (Cleveland: World Publishing Co., 1965), 19.

4. Maxwell Geismar, *Rebels and Ancestors: The American Novel, 1890–1915* (Boston: Houghton Mifflin, 1953), 144.

5. O'Connor, 216.

Lawrence I. Berkove

For eighty years, since its publication in 1910,[1] Jack London's "The Unparalleled Invasion" has been regarded as an expression of his anti-Oriental racism. Calder-Marshall's estimate of it, that it "was a variation of the theme of 'the Yellow Peril,' a common nightmare of the first decade of this century,"[2] appears to be generally accepted. While this view may be justified by reference to London's previous racist attitudes, it does not take into sufficient account the deep and dramatic changes in his perspectives that occurred almost abruptly during the last decade of his life, when he wrote this story. Our view of him is still distorted by the popular stereotype we have of him as the he-man writer of the Yukon. Recent scholarship, however, now recognizes that London continued to grow both in literary skill and in philosophy until his death.[3] This new information makes possible a parallax correction of our view of "The Unparalleled Invasion" so that we may see it as a story more concerned with humanity than with fears of "the Yellow Peril" or with notions of white supremacy.

London's experience in 1904 as a war correspondent in Korea during the Russo-Japanese War re-introduced him to the Orient after his brief contact with it in 1893. He saw on this second visit how quickly and well the Japanese were absorbing Western technology. Crossing the Yalu River from Korea into China, London also had a glimpse of how industrious and entrepreneurial the Chinese were, though still far behind the Japanese in development. His dispatches back home noted the profound changes that were stirring the peoples of the western rim of the Pacific. There is no doubt that in 1904 London forecasted trouble for the West in the "awakening" of the East, but his predictions reflected his immediate perceptions and his preconceptions of "the Yellow Peril" rather than his deliberations on the meaning of what he saw. Unbeknownst even to himself, like the Orient, he, too, was being stirred and

"A Parallax Correction in London's 'The Unparalleled Invasion.' " From *American Literary Realism*, Vol 24:2 © 1992 by permission of McFarland & Company, Inc., Publishers, Jefferson, NC 28640.

awakened to new ideas as well as new experiences. He was on the verge of entering the intense final decade of his life when his powers of narrative would be stretched to new limits by the demands of his rapidly evolving philosophy.

Between April 1907 and July 1909, London and his second wife, Charmian, sailed on his boat, the *Snark*, to the island cultures of the South Pacific: Hawaii, Melanesia, and Polynesia. The twenty-six month voyage proved to be seminally important for London. Labor describes it as "a catalyst . . . for London's mythopoeic genius."[4] Certainly, in the seven years of life he had left from the time he returned until his untimely death in 1916 at the age of 40, London became more understanding and respectful of non-white cultures and he increasingly portrayed non-whites in a new way, as adherents of cultures in some respects more advanced than our own. Conversely, this voyage enabled him to see that what was underway all around the Pacific was an unparalleled invasion by whites of not only the lands but also the cultures of non-whites. But "The Unparalleled Invasion," written in 1907, precedes this experience and therefore is significant evidence of how much London's mind had changed since 1904 and how, even before his voyage, he was already prepared to regard white colonialism as an ominous phenomenon.[5]

The entire story, chillingly ironic from start to finish, is identified at the end as "certain extracts" from the works of a future historian named "Walt Mervin."[6] All that we know of Mervin is what we can infer from his account of the events leading to the destruction of China, but that is more than enough. It is impossible to believe that London would identify with a historian so obviously shallow and ethnocentric that his entire account reeks with racist prejudice. When Mervin, for example, describes the aftermath of the extermination of the Chinese people as "the great task, the sanitation of China" (120),[7] he displays a gift for grim euphemism prefigurative of Adolf Hitler's infamous phrase, "the Final Solution." Mervin shows his bias in the story's first paragraph when be blames China for causing the deferring of America's bicentennial celebration of liberty and for having "twisted" and "tangled" plans of other nations, when the facts in the story are that America and those other nations had put off their various plans in 1976 in order to collude to destroy the Chinese. Even the opening phase of his next sentence, "[W]hen the world awoke rather abruptly to its danger," is grimly ironic when it is considered that the statement excludes from "the world"

China, which by 1975 had grown to the point that "[t]here were two Chinese for every white-skinned human in the world" (115).

Mervin insidiously distinguishes the West from the Orient by biased metaphor. The former he describes in complimentary language: "the flower of France," "the nations of the world," and even "the world." When he mildly chides the Western nations in retrospect for their "race-egotism"—the only time in his entire account when he suggests criticism of the West—he neutralizes the comment by prefacing it with praise for the Western nations' "native optimism" (110).

The Orient, however, he often characterizes by sub-human imagery: Japan is "vulpine" and is likened to a "biological sport [freak] in the animal kingdom" (110); Japanese agents "swarmed" over China (111); a French army disappeared into China's "cavernous maw" (114); China's people consisted of "wretched creatures" (or, neutrally, merely "inhabitants") that constituted an "over-spilling monstrous flood of life" (116) variously described as "hordes," a "wave," "a fearful tide," or a "glacier." When attacked, China "withdrew like a turtle into her shell" (114). The West Mervin associates with masculine activity: intellectual drive and technological progress; its main achievements take place in the laboratory. The Orient, in contrast, is feminine and passive; its accomplishments derive from numbers and labor. China is discovered "asleep" (110); once she is "awakened" her power derives from the "fecundity of her loins" (113). Japan is only initially successful in imitating the West. In the long run she cannot maintain the imposture. When she is eventually expelled from the awakened China, Japan exits from the "world drama" and reverts to her natural feminine character: "Thereafter she devoted herself to art, and her task became to please the world greatly with her creations of wonder and beauty" (113).

In a story so saturated by irony, even the title suggests various ways of viewing its events. The basic meaning of the title is, of course, "the invasion of China" (119). The story ends with an unparalleled invasion of the now completely depopulated China by huge numbers of presumably white colonists from the nations of the West. The least part of the invasion is the military aspect of "old War," land incursions of armies. "China had laughed at war, and war she was getting, but it was ultra-modern war, twentieth-century war, the war of the scientist and the laboratory . . ." (119). What ultra-modern war turns out to be begins with aerial overflights—an "unparalleled" invasion that immediately steps up to bacteriological warfare, another unparalleled "invasion." The racially motivated invasion of China by microbes is ironic in the colors of the diseases associated with them: *scarlet* fever, *yellow* fever, the *Black* Death. More grimly ironic still is the fact that the microbes do not themselves care about color: the plague germs "hybridized" into a "new and frightfully virulent germ" (119).

The story's bacteriological warfare may also be regarded as a continuation of another, more subtle, unparalleled invasion: the invasion of the Orient by Western ideas. It was Western thought which "awakened" first Japan and then China. These ideas quickly materialized first as technological and then military power. Insofar as "ultra-modern war" is ultimately the intellectual product of "the scientist and the laboratory" (119), we can see London's association of Western "progress" with death. It is the same association that Mark Twain worked out between 1897 and 1900 in Chapter 8 of "The Chronicle of Young Satan":

> It is a remarkable progress. In five or six thousand years five or six high civilizations have risen, flourished, commanded the wonder of the world, then faded out and disappeared; and not one of them except the latest ever invented any sweeping and adequate way to kill people. They all did their best, to kill being the chiefest ambition of the human race and the earliest incident in history, but only the Christian Civilization has scored a triumph to be proud of. Two centuries from now [i.e. the twentieth century] it will be recognized that all the competent killers are Christian; then the pagan world will go to school to the Christian: not to acquire his religion, but his guns.[8]

London, however, envisioned two possibilities that did not occur to Twain. "The Unparalleled Invasion" clearly contemplates genocide, and in it even physicians are subordinated to the war effort. Instead of using their skills to treat the sick and wounded of all humanity, they, like the doctors of Nazi Germany, heal only their own troops and deny care to the victims, withdrawing from them like all the rest of the West's soldiers—"to escape contagion" (119).

Despite the story's bleak view of the West, London does not blame it for all of humanity's evils. When given a chance, China also exhibits a "natural" tendency to invade other countries. She has no "Napoleonic dream" of creating an instant empire beyond her needs; her method is simply to move her huge population surpluses made possible by Western machine-civilization into adjacent countries: French Indo-China, Siam, Burma, the Malay Peninsula, and Siberia (114). The narrative of this sequence quietly underplays the fact that of these countries only

Siam was independent: Indo-China had already been taken over by the French, Burma and the Malay Peninsula by England, and Siberia by Russia. The Western nations *were* Napoleonically imperial; China's empire was driven by the need for "*lebensraum.*"

Nevertheless, in its own way, China turns out to be as arrogant and self-centered as the West. "What does China care for the comity of nations?" asks one of its leaders, "We have our own destiny to accomplish" (115). Smugly depending upon the pressure of its amazing birth rate to displace its neighbors in an unparalleled invasion of its own, China—"rejuvenescent, fruitful, and militant!" (115)—fatally underestimates both the West's fear and its ability and resolve to fight back.

Mervin's rhetorical genius is at its best when he describes the final stages of the conflict. After he has painted the victim as an aggressor, he then depicts the West as being forced to defend itself. Next, he daringly permits himself a few moments of sympathy as he describes the ravages of the germs as "destroying angels that stalked through the empire of a billion souls" (120). This half-implies that the germs were agents of the Deity, but it is the only time in his account that Mervin credits the Chinese with having souls. Finally, he returns to his praise of the heroes of the West: small expeditions of scientists and troops that "bravely" ventured into the devastated interior of China once the diseases had run their course. These resolute men put to death any "desperate bandits"—i.e., survivors—they found, and began the great task of the sanitation of China.

London concludes his masterpiece of irony with two final touches. The first is the resettlement of China—i.e., its colonization—by the victors in the most progressive way imaginable. Instead of assigning each one of the allied nations its own zone, resettlement is accomplished "heterogenously, according to the democratic American program" (120). The victorious (white) nationalities intermingle and all live happily ever after. Again, however, we have the irony—in fact a double irony—that an American model is used. In the first place a racist state is established in which only all (white) nationalities are equal. In the second, the heterogeneity which makes America so vigorous is paralleled to the hybridized disease germs which were more virulent than any of the original elements. By extension, therefore, whatever democratic intermingling of white nationalities America has accomplished only serves to make it the deadliest country in the world, emulated by the colony planted on the "sanitized" homeland of the now extinguished Chinese race.

Part 3

Like the atom bomb, the development of Jacobus Laningdale's plan of bacteriological warfare destroys an Oriental enemy. Whether or not racism was one of the complex of motivations for deciding to drop the atom bomb on Japan, the use of the fictional weapon *is* overtly racist. China is not depicted as angelic or as intrinsically better than the Western nations, but it is impossible to believe that London created this "historical" essay from the twisted and tangled perspective of its narrator, Walt Mervin, unaware that its ironic reflections focused largely on the West and most particularly on America. Whatever his past inclinations toward racism were, therefore, London appears in "The Unparalleled Invasion" to have reconsidered his biases and found them not only unwholesome but potentially deadly.

This story is not a work in which Chinese, or any other Orientals, are to be pigeon-holed as the "Yellow Peril" and dismissed as inferior to the white race. On the contrary, London had at last opened his eyes to the double-standards of the West, to its gratuitous assumption that it was all right for Western nations only to adventure beyond their parallels into the lands of other peoples, to dispossess those peoples, and to regard their lands as appropriate territories for conquest and settlement. London did not believe that the West had the moral right to do this. He did not believe Japan and China had the right to invade other countries, either, but he understood that their modern inspiration to do so came not from their own inclination but from Western instruction and example.

Significantly, the story ends as a commentary on the fickleness of the West. Like the aftermath of the collaborative Western military campaign that put down the Boxer Rebellion in 1901, France and Germany, two of the nations in the story that allied in 1975 to form common cause against the "Yellow Peril," were again at each other's throats in 1987 as they renewed their "ancient quarrel" (120). All nations of the world (i.e., white nations) consequently "solemnly" pledged themselves not to do to each other what they all did to China. Inasmuch as Mervin has not reminded us that the nations of Europe have always invaded each other, and every reader of this story at all familiar with history is fully aware of how bogus and futile such non-aggression pledges have always been, what started out as Mervin's glorification of one of the West's finest hours ends, unintentionally, as an exposure of its duplicity and, beneath that, its racism.

London saw more clearly in 1907 than generations of readers since have realized. It was not the Yellow Peril that he attacked in "The

Unparalleled Invasion," or just the duplicity and racism of the West, but national and ethnic aggressiveness, never more inhuman than when it is augmented by intelligence but concealed by lofty rationalization. In a way, "The Unparalleled Invasion" returns to the theme of "survival of the fittest" more obviously addressed in London's earlier works. As he saw it, human beings or nations or races might be cunning, educated, and resourceful, but however advanced or superior they might appear, without a higher moral standard they were just animals pitted against each other in Nature's ring. Victory or death were the alternatives. From the beginning of his career London had always sought to discover and affirm moral and humanitarian values that the human race could use to progress beyond the brutal consequences of physical conflict. Obviously, in "The Unparalleled Invasion" London had not yet solved the enigma that so troubled him. But by the story's implied universal rejection of aggression in the service of national or racial goals he had at least made an advance.

Notes

1. Although the story was written before 1910 there is some difficulty in assigning an exact date to it. On the first page of the manuscript of the story in the Huntington Library, London wrote that it was completed on 11 March 1906. But it is likely that this date is incorrect. London's bound register of magazine sales of his stories might be a more accurate record. According to it (the register, labeled "Magazine articles: Book III. Feb. 11, 1903–Feb. 6, 1909," is also in the Huntington), the story was first mailed out to a magazine on 12 March 1907, when it was sent to *Collier's*. Taking into account London's habit of sending off stories as soon as he completed them, his occasional errors in dating, and the fact that the works he completed and sent off in March 1906 appear not to be thematically similar to "The Unparalleled Invasion," 11 March 1907 is probably the correct date of completion. At any rate, London sent the story to about a dozen publishers before *McClure's* bought it for $400 in February 1910, and published it in July 1910. I wish to thank Earle Labor for sharing information with me and for his advice and encouragement. I am solely responsible, however, for the content and factual accuracy of this article.

2. Arthur Calder-Marshall, "Introduction," *The Bodley Head Jack London*, Vol. 1 (London: Bodley Head, 1963), p. 15.

3. See, for example, Earle Labor, "The Pacific World of Jack London," *Critical Essays on Jack London*, ed. Jacqueline Tavernier-Courbin (Boston: G. K. Hall, 1983), pp. 205–222; Jeanne C. Reesman, "The Problem of Knowledge in Jack London's 'The Water Baby,' " *Western American Literature* 23, 3 (November

Part 3

1988), 201–214; and James I. McClintock, *White Logic* (Grand Rapids, MI: Wolf House Books, 1975).

4. "Pacific World," p. 208.

5. After his return from the South Pacific, London wrote and published a number of stories implicitly and explicitly sympathetic to non-whites who were dominated by cruel and even bloody whites. Among them are "The Chinago" (July 1909), "Koolau the Leper" (December 1909), "Mauki" (December 1909), and "The Inevitable White Man" (November 1910). But even earlier in his career, London had on occasion taken the point of view of non-whites, e.g., *Children of the Frost* (1902).

6. It is not possible to ascribe a definite influence of Ambrose Bierce upon London in this matter, but Bierce had long used the perspective of a future historian in some of his satires on American culture, and there is evidence that London might have encountered some of them. Two such satires were "The Jury in Ancient America," *Cosmopolitan* 39:4 (August 1905), 384–88; and "Insurance in Ancient America," *Cosmopolitan* 41 (September 1906), 555–57. London read the *Cosmopolitan* and wrote for it at this time. London's opinion of Bierce fluctuated, but he was taking notice of what Bierce wrote and did, for his letter of 24 June 1906 to George Sterling comments on a publicized debate between Bierce, on the one side, and the socialists Morris Hillquit and Robert Hunter, on the other. See *The Letters of Jack London*, 3 vols. ed., Earle Labor, Robert C. Leitz, III, and I. Milo Shepard (Stanford CA: Stanford Univ. Press, 1988). The debate was featured as an article entitled "The Social Unrest" in *Cosmopolitan* 41 (July 1906), 297–302.

7. This and all subsequent parenthetical page references to the text of "The Unparalleled Invasion" refer to *Curious Fragments: Jack London's Tales of Fantasy Fiction*, ed. Dale L. Walker (Port Washington, NY: Kennikat, 1957), pp. 109–120. The story is also available in *Short Stories of Jack London*, ed. Earle Labor, Robert C. Leitz, III, and I. Milo Shepard (New York: Macmillan, 1990), pp. 270–281.

8. Mark Twain, "The Chronicle of Young Satan," in *The Mysterious Stranger*, ed. William M. Gibson (Berkeley: Univ. of California Press, 1970), p. 137.

James Slagel

When we teach English as a subject, we teach literature and language, often politics, and occasionally the politics of language and literature. Sometimes politics forces its way into apparently innocuous discussions. Such a passage of playful banter turned powerful political statement is a brief exchange between Charmian and Jack London as they lounged side by side during their second day in Hawaii, a conversation she initiated and then recorded in *Jack London and Hawaii:*

> "You are a *malihini*—did you know that?"
> "No, and I don't know it now. What is it?"
> "It's a newcomer, a tenderfoot, a wayfarer on the shores of chance, a—."
> "I like it—it's a beautiful word," Jack curbed my literary output. "And I can't help it, anyway. But what shall I be if I stay here long enough?"
> Recourse to a scratch-pad in my pocket divulged the fascinating sobriquet that even an outlander, be he the right kind of outlander, might come in time—a long time—to deserve. It is kamaai-na, and its significance is that of old-timer, and more, much more. It means one who belongs, who has come to belong in the heart and life and soil of Hawaii. "I'd rather be (*'kamaaina'*) than any name in the world, I think. . . . I love the land and I love the people."[1]

Although it is fair to group London with Melville, Twain, Stoddard, Stevenson, and Michener as a visitor to the Islands, we must acknowledge London's desire to become a *kama'āina* as evidenced in his writing by lush descriptions of the land and generally sensitive portrayals of the people, and in his life by his remaining in Hawaii until failing health necessitated his return to the Valley of the Moon. Unlike those other

245

haole (white) writers, the man called sailor, farmer, adventurer, pirate, genius, and philosopher (as well as racist) desired above all to be a *kama'aina*, literally, a child of a land.

Some in the Hawaiian community would argue that any such attempt would be futile; only one born in Hawaii or of Hawaiian blood can be a *kama'aina*. Others believe it to be a function of time; one becomes a *kama'aina* after a certain period of time in the Islands, regardless of sympathies or values. Still others, including the Londons, believe that by coming to appreciate all that is Hawaiian, a *malihini*, or newcomer, can achieve the distinction of "adopted son," if you will, as opposed to *nā kanaka maoli*, the indigenous Hawaiians or true children of the land. To fall within this broader definition of *kama'aina*, London the "outlander" first had to develop a respect for the relationship between the people and the land, which, in turn, led to an acceptance by this union of flesh and soil that was Hawaii.

Acceptance came hard: the conflict between London's philosophical beliefs and his seemingly more emotional infatuation with Hawaii was evident in the incongruities between his personal dealings with the Islanders and his writing. Initially, London's view of Hawaii was blurred by Social Darwinist leanings and the resultant ethnocentric, white supremacist corollaries, which subordinate the Hawaiians to the more capable Anglo-Saxons. In the end, his path to acceptance was, as it should be, his fiction. One piece in particular, "Koolau the Leper," shows genuine empathy with *nā kanaka maoli*.[2] When London finally lays lonely yet defiant Koolau to rest in a ginger blossom thicket in the Kalalau Valley, he closes one of the most controversial stories and opens one of the most bitter debates in Hawaiian *haole* literary history, a debate that kept his work off local bookstore shelves and the writer all but shunned by the white population in Hawaii.

London's stated desire to be more than a passing observer and recorder of a foreign culture, then, cannot be dismissed as a whimsical comment uttered on a pleasant day. Still, however sincere London's attempt to become part of the Hawaiian culture, he was the product of a Western heritage, education, and life experience, and he thus possessed a Western perspective. In a discussion of this perspective, an application of the paradigm established in Edward Said's *Orientalism* proves useful.[3] Hawaii, of course, is not part of the Orient as discussed by Said, that is, the Middle or Near East; nor is it part of the Japan/China-centered Far East, which America obsesses over; nor is it any more Eastern than Western in its philosophical, institutional, or cultural heritage. Rich in its own history and cultural identity, Hawaii is nonetheless Oriental as opposed to Occidental in terms of providing an Other for the Western Reader.

Although the composition of this Other is less the issue than London's existence apart from it, an understanding of its construction allows useful comparisons to the characters in London's Hawaiian fiction. Stephen Sumida, in his discussion of Hawaiian literary traditions, outlines Western writers' fascination with and search for the "exotic," an erotic, languid extension of the European pastoral but set in the South Seas.[4] When we are dealing with the Pacific Island cultures, equating this Exotic with Orientalism as a means of coming to grips with our perceptions as Westerners, rather than developing a real understanding of the culture, requires some qualification. Said points out that the Occident's view of the Orient is imbued with a rich tradition of competition (actually, dominance and subservience); the relationship of the Occident to the Exotic is comparatively fresh, less than four centuries old, and, at least initially, based on a purely fanciful understanding. Where Europe sees the Orient through the nostalgic "what was" or "what was perceived to be," America has viewed the Exotic through "what could be." Both distortions show the Occident's desire to dominate; each creates a discourse based on "Western projections unto and will to govern" the culture (Said's phrase) and a virtual reality created by extrapolating from ill-informed texts.

In the case of the Exotic in general, and Hawaii in particular, those texts were grounded in the imaginative fiction created by the likes of Defoe and Swift, Rousseau's concept of the Noble Savage, the journals of the eighteenth-century South Pacific explorers—most notably, James Cook and Samuel Wallis—and later the provocative fiction of Stevenson, Melville, and others.[5] Melville's *Typee* (1846), set in the Marquesas Islands, initially perpetuated, then challenged the stereotype of an unblemished and dignified people living a carefree and quietly fulfilling existence in idyllic surroundings. Indeed, as the Western population in Hawaii steadily grew throughout the nineteenth century, and with it the recognition that sets of values differed between diverse peoples, especially between the missionaries and *nā kanaka maoli*, so did the number of pejorative tracts being shaped by and shaping Western perspectives. Given two opposing yet presumably accurate truths within the Exotic discourse, the Occident had to decide, as Sumida puts it, which view was "more true—that the natives were peaceful, domestic sorts, noble inhabitants of a paradise; or that the natives, although useful for replenishing the ships' stores, were depraved and were to be shot at the first threat of harm to the visitors."[6]

Shortly before London's first arrival in Hawaii, one writer in particular, Mark Twain, seemed to address this duality. In typical fashion, Twain's keen observations and wry comments satirize both visions.[7] Through his fictitious traveling partner, Mr. Brown, a parody of the boorish American abroad, Twain outlines many of the annoyances that, though superficial, tend to undermine the image of paradise. Brown's tirades against the scorpions, cockroaches, and "santipedes," as well as his diatribes mocking the language and customs, provide Twain the luxury of judging a culture under the guise of judging the judge.

However, Twain's historical narratives and comments on his own encounters with the native people reveal his ambivalence. He alternates jabs at such "barbaric" customs as human sacrifice with attacks on the selfish and intolerant *haole* intruders. One only has to read Twain's account of Captain Cook's death at Kealakekua Bay and his description of Britain's brief annexation of the kingdom in 1843 to be convinced of his sympathy for *nā kanaka maoli.* Yet he chides the missionaries for delivering the concept of Hell to a carefree, unburdened people, and at the same time he acknowledges, in a rare moment of sincerity, that "the wonderful benefit conferred upon the people by the missionaries is so prominent, so palpable, and so unquestionable, that the frankest compliment I can pay them, and the best, is simply to point to the conditions of the Sandwich Islanders of Captain Cook's time and their condition today. Their work speaks for itself."[8] The Occidental's placing himself in a position to make such a choice, and thus control the Exotic, is more germane to the discussion of perspective than which choice is made.

Such was the Exotic that London encountered; given a blank sheet of paper, what Hawaiian would he describe? The writer takes chances when he incorporates leprosy, a heinous serpent introduced into the garden by the West through the East. At one point in Hawaiian history, to utter the word in public was to commit a misdemeanor, and some 40 years before London's arrival, Twain had been admonished not to discuss the disease in his letters to the *Sacramento Union* for fear of losing readers in the business community.[9]

By transforming a bit of recent Hawaiian lore regarding a native leper's refusal to submit to the *haole* government, and thus raising the protagonist to near legendary status, London appears in "Koolau the Leper" to exploit the diseased few for the elevation of the healthy yet oppressed many. More important, he asks and answers political questions about the distribution of power, which *haole* society considered inappropriate. Was the writer the sensationalist, the betrayer of friends, and the "untruthful and ungrateful bounder," in the words of Lorrin Thurston, London's close associate who also spoke for the indignant white community?[10] Or was London simply writing as a *kama'aina*, the true child of the land Charmian claimed he longed to be? Or, given the relationship between the two perspectives, could he not be one without being the other?

A misplaced emphasis on the *fear* of leprosy that appears to be so pivotal invites the first conclusion. A closer look at the protagonist, especially in relation to the protagonists of London's two other "leper stories," Jack Kersdale in "Good-bye, Jack" and Lyte Gregory in "The Sheriff of Kona," reveals that the physical components of the disease, in particular the contagiousness, are minimized and that "Koolau the Leper" is the powerful and enduring political statement of a man struggling with and finally, in Hawaii's case, rejecting the imperialism spawned by Social Darwinism, ethnocentric doctrine, and Western perspectives on the Exotic. . . .

The degree to which Jack London achieved the status of *kama'aina* is uncertain. There is no litmus test for an outsider's acceptance into a foreign culture, and we are forced to use subjective standards. Obviously, London was not born in the Islands; nor did he reside in Hawaii long enough to qualify as a *kama'aina* merely as a function of time, although the creation of the Island-born protagonist John Lakana (London) in his last short story, "The Water Baby," might indicate the author's self-perception or desire. London's love of the land never wavers. The agrarian novels he penned and his work at his own Beauty Ranch in California attest to his reverence for the *'aina;* however, the Hawaiians cannot claim sole possession of this reverence, and London seems from early on to appreciate the land around him.

Ideally, the question of London's relationship with the Hawaiian people should be answered by the people themselves, and we must rely on anecdotal evidence. In an oft-quoted piece, Charmian relates the incident of a ukulele player in a Hawaiian orchestra in San Francisco, a young Hawaiian man who spoke through much emotion upon hearing of London's death, "Better than any one, he *knew* us Hawaiians—Jack London, the Story Maker. . . .The news came to Honolulu—and people, they could not understand. . . . They could not believe. I tell you this: Better than any one, he knew us Hawaiians."[11]

Equally touching is Charmian's story of the *mele*, the song Hawaiians composed for Jack and presented at his farewell *lū'au* in 1916, a series of long stanzas punctuated by a sweet refrain:

> Haianaia mai ana ka puana,
> No Keaka Lakana neia inoa.
>
> This song is then echoed,
> 'Tis in honour of Jack London.[12]

On a more personal level, I can speak to the enduring nature of London's relationship with the Islands. I teach at the Kamehameha Schools, a unique college-preparatory institution established more than a century ago by a descendant of the Hawaiian monarchy for the education of native Hawaiian children. Like many indigenous peoples compromised, betrayed, and eventually consumed by the Western world, Hawaiian students exhibit a certain skeptical resentment toward Western writers, especially when so much beautiful and important Hawaiian literature has been ignored in favor of these visitors. Yet Jack London, more than many other visiting *haole* writers, touches the lives of the students. In a story like "Koolau the Leper," my students see a sympathetic, somewhat indignant white writer speaking *to* a proud culture and *for* an otherwise unheard (to the ears of these students) segment of the population.

In the final analysis, London the writer will be judged on his writing, mostly the more popular fiction. As readers with late-twentieth-century sensibilities, we are tempted to view as clumsy and patronizing his early-twentieth-century attempts to redefine the traditional Exotic of Defoe, Rousseau, and Melville. London certainly misses much of the poetry that implicitly defines Hawaiian values in the writing of Pi'ilani and Ko'olau, and the overstated and vulgar presentation in some of his Hawaiian material might be as much a reflection of his lack of understanding as it is a necessary component of his literary style.

His loving respect for the Hawaiian people and his sympathy for their struggle against the ever-growing *haole* are evident in these early stories, though some readers regard these same stories as exploitive, and later stories, especially "The Bones of Kahekili," appear to present the Hawaiian groveling before the omnipotent white rancher, "a source of life, a source of food, a fount of wisdom, a giver of law, a smiling beneficence, a blackness of thunder and punishment."[13] "The Water Baby" can be viewed as London's last word on the matter, the Hawaiian is in the end elevated to a transcendental level: the wisdom and wholeness of the old Hawaiian compared to the more "civilized" whites are brought to surface in the relationship between Kokokumu and the *haole* Lakana. At best, London's portrayal of the Hawaiian people is a heavily qualified success; the writer seemed on more solid ground when he attempted to distinguish between *malihini* like Jack Kersdale and *kama'aina* like Lyte Gregory and, perhaps, John Lakana.

Of course, such judgment with no historical context is blatantly unfair and perhaps off the point. Even an effective writer like London must be judged as much on intent as product when we try to ascertain his feelings about a subject dear to him, and we must be allowed to consider London's attempt as much as his success in coming to appreciate Hawaii Nei. In truth, no writer, regardless of talent, could portray the fierce pride and simple dignity of Koolau the Leper without feeling some of that pride himself. Having recently commemorated the 100th anniversary of the overthrow of Queen Liliu'okalani, I believe using Jack London to help Hawaiian children gain an appreciation for the best the *haole* have to offer in terms of compassion and respect is a gratifying extension of his time spent in the Islands. It is an appropriate legacy for a man known for much, but wishing to be remembered as Keaka Lakana, *kama'aina*.

Notes

1. Charmian London, *Jack London and Hawaii* (London: Mills and Boon, 1918), 22–23.

2. The name of the historical figure that inspired London's story was Ko'olau, with the Hawaiian *'okina* (glottal stop) between the *o*'s. For the sake of clarity, I will use Koolau to refer to London's protagonist and Ko'olau to refer to the historical figure. In keeping with the Hawaiian language, no *s*'s are placed on plurals. Also, to avoid confusion, and in keeping with the language of London's time, I will use the term leprosy instead of the preferred designation, Hansen's Disease.

3. Edward Said, *Orientalism* (New York: Vintage Books, 1979).

4. Stephen Sumida, *And the View from the Shore: Literary Traditions of Hawai'i* (Seattle: University of Washington Press, 1991).

5. A. Grove Day, *Pacific Island Literature: One Hundred Basic Books* (Honolulu: University of Hawaii Press, 1971).

6. Sumida, 15–16.

7. A. Grove Day, ed., *Mark Twain's Letters from Hawaii* (Honolulu: University of Hawaii Press, 1975).

8. Ibid., 54–55.

9. Day, "Introduction," ibid., vii. See also Sumida, 47.

10. *The Letters of Jack London,* ed. Earle Labor, Robert C. Leitz, III, and I. Milo Shepard (Stanford: Stanford University Press, 1988), 861. Under the pseudonym "Bystander," Thurston wrote his editorial/letter in the *Honolulu Advertiser* following the publication of London's leper stories, initiating a series of public and private letters between the two friends.

11. Charmian London, *Jack London and Hawaii,* 238.

12. Ibid., 304.

13. London, "The Bones of Kahekili," *Stories of Hawaii* by Jack London, ed. A. Grove Day (Honolulu: Mutual Publishing Co., 1968), 135–36.

Chronology

1876   Jack London born John Griffith Chaney in San Francisco, California, on January 12, only child of Flora Wellman, who names as his father William Henry Chaney, an itinerant astrologer and lecturer with whom she had lived as common-law wife in 1874–1875. September: Flora marries John London, a widower with two daughters; baby is named John Griffith London.

1878   After Jack and his stepsister, Eliza, suffer near-fatal attacks of diphtheria, the family moves across San Francisco Bay to Oakland, where John London sells produce to local markets and runs a grocery store.

1881   Family moves to a farm in Alameda.

1886   Family purchases a house in Oakland after living on farms in San Mateo County and Livermore.

1891   London is graduated from Cole Grammar School (eighth grade) and takes a job in Hickmott's Cannery. A few months later, with money borrowed from family friend Virginia ("Aunt Jenny") Prentiss, he purchases the *Razzle-Dazzle*. London drinks with grown men and becomes an oyster pirate. Nearly drowns in San Francisco Bay while drunk.

1892   London works as a deputy patrolman for the California Fish Patrol in Benicia.

1893   January–August: London serves as an able-bodied seaman aboard the *Sophia Sutherland*, a sealing schooner on an eight-month voyage in the Northern Pacific. Late August: London takes a job in a jute mill at 10 cents an hour; the entire country is in the depths of an economic depression, the "Great Panic of 1893." November 11: "Story of a Typhoon Off the Coast of Japan," is published in a contest for young writers sponsored by the *San Francisco Morning Call.*

1894 London works as a coal heaver in the power plant of the Oakland, San Leandro, and Haywards Electric Railway. April: Leaves Oakland to join Kelly's Army, the western contingent of Coxey's Industrial Army of the Unemployed. May: Begins tramping on his own. Later arrested in Buffalo, New York; serves a 30-day sentence for vagrancy in the Erie County Penitentiary. Tours the East Coast and returns west by coal car across Canada, earning passage from Vancouver as a coal stoker aboard the *SS Umatilla.*

1895 London attends Oakland High School and publishes short stories and articles in *The High School Aegis.* He participates in the Henry Clay Debate Club and falls in love with Mabel Applegarth, later the model for Ruth Morse in *Martin Eden* (1909).

1896 April: London joins the Socialist Labor Party and leaves high school. He briefly attends the University Academy in Alameda to prepare for entrance examinations at the University of California, then studies independently for three months. He is admitted and attends one semester at the university.

1897 February: London leaves the university due to a lack of tuition money. After a brief period of writing and socialist work, he works in the laundry of the Belmont Academy. July: London sails with his brother-in-law, Capt. James H. Shepard, aboard the *SS Umatilla* for Port Townsend, Washington, then boards the *City of Topeka* for Juneau, Alaska, to join the Klondike Gold Rush. He spends the winter in an old cabin on Split-Up Island, between the Stewart River and Henderson Creek, 80 miles from Dawson City, Yukon Territory.

1898 Late July: Completing his journey of 2,500 miles from Dyea to St. Michaels on the Bering Sea, London returns to California penniless, suffering from scurvy. Starts an intensive regimen to become a professional writer. September: Completes first Klondike story, "The Devil's Dice Box."

1899   January: "To the Man on Trail" is published in the *Over-land Monthly*. July: "An Odyssey of the North" is accepted for publication in the January 1900 issue of *Atlantic Monthly*. December: London meets Anna Strunsky. During the year he publishes a total of 24 items, including essays, jokes, poems, and stories.

1900   April: London marries Bessie Mae Maddern. London's first book, *The Son of the Wolf* (Houghton Mifflin), is published.

1901   January 15: Birth of daughter Joan. Earning 245 votes, London is defeated as Socialist Democrats' candidate for Mayor of Oakland. *The God of His Fathers* (McClure, Phillips) is published.

1902   August–September: London lives in East End of London, collecting material for and writing *The People of the Abyss;* he travels in Europe for three weeks. October 20: Birth of daughter Bess (Becky). His first novel, *A Daughter of the Snows* (Lippincott), as well as a collection of Klondike stories focused upon the Indians of the Northland, *Children of the Frost* (Macmillan), and a children's book, *The Cruise of the Dazzler* (Century), are published.

1903   London falls in love with Charmian Kittredge and separates from Bessie London. He purchases the sloop *Spray* for sailing on San Francisco Bay. Has most successful publishing year yet, with *The Call of the Wild* (Macmillan) bringing him worldwide fame. *The Kempton-Wace Letters*, coauthored with Anna Strunsky (Macmillan) and *The People of the Abyss* (Macmillan) appear.

1904   January–June: London in Korea as a war correspondent for Hearst, covering the Russo-Japanese War. Returning on June 28, he is served with papers for divorce. *The Faith of Men* (Macmillan) and *The Sea-Wolf* (Macmillan) are published.

1905   March: London is once again defeated as Social Democrats' candidate for mayor of Oakland (981 votes). April–September: London spends summer at Wake-Robin Lodge in Glen Ellen, Sonoma County. Purchases the 129-acre Hill Ranch, the beginning of his "Beauty

Ranch." October: Begins lecture tour for the Intercollegiate Socialist Society of the East and Midwest. November: Marries Charmian Kittredge in Chicago the day after the divorce from Bessie London is final. December: Interrupts his lecture tour for a honeymoon in Jamaica and Cuba. Essay collection *War of the Classes* (Macmillan), the first prizefight novel, *The Game* (Macmillan), and *Tales of the Fish Patrol* (Macmillan) are published.

1906   January: London returns to United States from Jamaica to resume the lecture tour and ignites crowds with his socialist critique of American society at Carnegie Hall, Yale University, and the University of Chicago. He cancels end of tour because of illness and returns to Glen Ellen in mid-February. Spring: He begins building the *Snark* for projected seven-year around-the-world cruise, but the building is interrupted by the Great San Francisco Earthquake (April 18), which London reports for *Collier's*. *Moon-Face and Other Stories* (Macmillan), *White Fang* (Macmillan), and the play *Scorn of Women* (Macmillan) are published.

1907   April: After repeated delays, the *Snark* sails from Oakland for Hawaii. Its near-disastrous maiden voyage over, on May 20 the *Snark* drops anchor in Pearl Harbor and undergoes extensive repairs while the Londons visit the Hawaiian Islands. June: London finishes revision of "To Build a Fire." October: The *Snark* sails from Hilo for Marquesas, arriving at Nuka Hiva December 6. Sails from Marquesas to Tahiti December 18–27. *Before Adam* (Macmillan), *Love of Life and Other Stories* (Macmillan), and *The Road* (Macmillan) are published. London is publicly attacked by President Theodore Roosevelt for "nature-faking."

1908   January–February: London takes a round trip from Papeete to Oakland aboard the *Mariposa* to straighten out financial affairs. April–November: He resumes *Snark* voyage, sailing from Tahiti to Samoa. Sails to Fiji Islands, New Hebrides, Solomon Islands, Australia. He is hospitalized in Sydney, Australia, for double fistula operation; suffering from multiple tropical diseases. December: London announces that *Snark* voyage is being abandoned. Purchases the La Motte Ranch. *The Iron Heel* (Macmillan), London's most substantial socialist work, is published.

1909   July: London returns to Glen Ellen via Ecuador, Panama, New Orleans, and Grand Canyon. *Martin Eden* (Macmillan), his critically acclaimed novel about the life and suicide of a disillusioned sailor-turned-writer, is published.

1910   London hires his stepsister, Eliza Shepard, as business manager and superintendent of ranch. Purchases 700-acre Kohler-Frohling-Tokay Ranch. Devoting more and more of his time to building the ranch, London begins plans for Wolf House. June 19: Daughter Joy is born; she dies two days later. July: London reports Johnson-Jeffries world championship fight in Reno, Nevada. Four books appear: *Lost Face* (Macmillan), *Revolution and Other Essays* (Macmillan), *Burning Daylight* (Macmillan), and *Theft: A Play in Four Acts* (Macmillan).

1911   June–September: London drives his four-horse wagon, with Charmian and man-servant Nakata, on 1,340-mile trip to Oregon and back. The Londons move from Wake-Robin Lodge to new home on Kohler Ranch (Ranch House). December: They depart by rail for New York on Christmas Eve in order for London to meet with publishers. *When God Laughs and Other Stories* (Macmillan), *Adventure* (Macmillan), *The Cruise of the Snark* (Macmillan), and *South Sea Tales* (Macmillan) are published.

1912   January: London arrives in New York City and signs publishing contract with the Century Company, departing from his close association with Macmillan. March: The Londons sail from Baltimore for five-month voyage to Seattle around Cape Horn. August: London returns to Glen Ellen. He signs a five-year contract with *Cosmopolitan* for fiction. Charmian loses second child through miscarriage. *The House of Pride and Other Tales of*

Hawaii (Macmillan), *A Son of the Sun* (Doubleday, Page), and *Smoke Bellew* (Century) are published.

1913　London visits Los Angeles to discuss movie contracts with the Balboa Amusement Producing Company. He and Charmian enjoy the premiere of Bosworth's *The Sea-Wolf*, the first feature-length film produced in America. He undergoes operation for acute appendicitis. Wolf House is destroyed by fire probably caused by spontaneous combustion. *The Abysmal Brute* (Century), *John Barleycorn* (Century), and, in a return to publishing with Macmillan, *The Valley of the Moon* are published.

1914　London again travels to New York City to discuss business affairs; he pursues further business by entering into a contract with the Jack London Grape Juice Co., which fails in 1915. April: he departs with Charmian for Vera Cruz, Mexico, via Houston and Galveston, to report on the Mexican Revolution for *Collier's*. He is forced to return home by a severe case of dysentery, and also suffers attacks of rheumatism. *The Strength of the Strong* (Macmillan) and *The Mutiny of the Elsinore* (Macmillan) appear.

1915　February: The Londons depart for a five-month stay in Hawaii, hoping to improve his health. They return to Glen Ellen in July, then visit Hawaii again in December. *The Scarlet Plague* (Macmillan) and *The Star Rover* (Macmillan) are published.

1916　London's last California novel, *The Little Lady of the Big House* (Macmillan) is published, along with his California nature play *The Acorn-Planter* (Macmillan) and *The Turtles of Tasman* (Macmillan). He resigns from the Socialist Party. The Londons return from Hawaii in July, and, when attending the California State Fair in Sacramento in September, London is stricken with acute rheumatism once again; his doctors warn him to restrict his diet and drinking. He finds himself engaged in lawsuits with Charmian's relatives over water rights on the ranch, and his health continues to fail, with ptomaine poisoning and other gastric disorders. London is found unconscious in his bed by his servant Sekine on November 22; time of death is given as 7:45 P.M. after repeated attempts to revive him fail. Death is attributed to "[u]raemia following renal colic. Duration one plus days. Contributor chronic Intestinal Nephritis. Duration three years."

Selected Bibliography

Primary Sources

The Son of the Wolf. Boston: Houghton Mifflin, 1900.
The God of His Fathers. New York: Century, 1901.
Children of the Frost. New York: Century, 1902.
The Faith of Men. New York: Macmillan, 1904.
Tales of the Fish Patrol. New York: Macmillan, 1905.
Moon-Face and Other Stories. New York: Macmillan, 1906.
Love of Life and Other Stories. New York: Macmillan, 1907.
Lost Face. New York: Macmillan, 1910.
Revolution and Other Essays. New York: Macmillan, 1910.
When God Laughs and Other Stories. New York: Macmillan, 1911.
South Sea Tales. New York: Macmillan, 1911.
The House of Pride and Other Tales of Hawaii. New York: Macmillan, 1912.
A Son of the Sun. Garden City, NY: Doubleday, Page & Company, 1912.
Smoke Bellew. New York: Century, 1912.
The Night-Born. New York: Century, 1913.
The Strength of the Strong. New York: Macmillan, 1914.
The Turtles of Tasman. New York: Macmillan, 1916.
The Red One. New York: Macmillan, 1918.
On the Makaloa Mat. New York: Macmillan, 1919.
Dutch Courage and Other Stories. New York: Macmillan, 1922.
"No Mentor but Myself ": A Collection of Articles, Essays, Reviews, and Letters, by Jack London, on Writing and Writers. Edited by Dale L. Walker. Port Washington, N.Y.: Kennikat, 1979.
The Letters of Jack London. Edited by Earle Labor, Robert C. Leitz III, and I. Milo Shepard. 3 vols. Stanford, Calif.: Stanford University Press, 1988.
The Complete Short Stories of Jack London. Edited by Earle Labor, Robert C. Leitz III, and I. Milo Shepard. 3 vols. Stanford, Calif.: Stanford University Press, 1993.

Secondary Sources

Books

Hamilton, David Mike. *"The Tools of My Trade": Annotated Books in Jack London's Library.* Seattle: University of Washington Press, 1986.

Hedrick, Joan. *Solitary Comrade: Jack London and His Work.* Chapel Hill: University of North Carolina Press, 1982.

Hendricks, King, ed. *Jack London: Master Craftsman of the Short Story.* Logan: Utah State University Press, 1966.

Johnston, Carolyn. *Jack London—An American Radical?* Westport, Conn.: Greenwood, 1984.

Labor, Earle, and Jeanne Campbell Reesman. *Jack London: Revised Edition.* New York: Twayne, 1994.

McClintock, James I. *White Logic: Jack London's Short Stories.* Cedar Springs, Mich.: Wolf House Books, 1976. Reissued as *Jack London's Strong Truths.* Introduction by Sam Baskett. East Lansing: Michigan State University Press, 1997.

Walker, Franklin. *Jack London and the Klondike: The Genesis of an American Writer.* San Marino, Calif.: The Huntington Library, 1966. Reprint, with a foreword by Earle Labor, 1978.

Articles and Parts of Books

Auerbach, Jonathan. Introduction to *Northland Stories,* by Jack London, ed. Auerbach. Harmondsworth, U.K.: Penguin, 1997.

Berkove, Lawrence I. "A Parallax Connection in London's 'The Unparalleled Invasion.' " *American Literary Realism* 24 (Winter 1992): 33–39.

Campbell, Jeanne. "Falling Stars: Myth in 'The Red One.' " *Jack London Newsletter* 11 (May–December 1978): 87–101.

Chapman, Arnold. "Between Fire and Ice: A Theme in Jack London and Horacio Quiroga." *Symposium* 24 (Spring 1970): 20–24.

James G. Cooper. "The Summit and the Abyss: Jack London's Moral Philosophy." *Jack London Newsletter* 12 (January–April, 1979): 24–27.

Courbin, Jacqueline. "Jack London's Portrayal of the Natives in His First Four Collections of Arctic Tales." *Jack London Newsletter* 10 (September–December 1977): 127–37.

Day, A. Grove. Introduction to *Stories of Hawaii* by Jack London. New York: Appleton-Century, 1965.

Dhondt, Steven T. "Jack London's *When God Laughs:* Overman, Underdog, and Satire." *Jack London Newsletter* 2 (May–August 1969): 51–57.

Gair, Christopher. "Hegemony, Metaphor, and Structural Difference: The 'Strange Dualism' of 'South of the Slot.' " *Arizona Quarterly* 49 (Spring 1993): 73–97.

Graham, Don. "Jack London's Tale Told by a High-Grade Feeb." *Studies in Short Fiction* 15 (Fall 1978): 429–33.

Gurian, Jay. "The Romantic Necessity in Literary Naturalism: Jack London." *American Literature* 38 (March 1966): 112–30.

Hensley, Dennis. "Jack London's Use of the Linguistic Style of the King James Bible." *Jack London Echoes* 3 (July 1983): 4–11.

Kirsch, James. " 'The Red One.' " *Psychological Perspectives* 11, no. 2 (1980): 152–54. Reprinted in *The Critical Response to Jack London.* Ed. Susan M. Nuernberg. Westport, Conn.: Greenwood Press, 1995, 201–16.

Labor, Earle. "The Archetypal Woman as 'Martyr to Truth': Jack London's 'Samuel.' " *American Literary Realism* 24 (Winter 1992): 23–32.

———. "Jack London's Symbolic Wilderness: Four Versions." *Nineteenth-Century Fiction* 17 (September 1962): 149–61. Reprinted in *Jack London: Essays in Criticism.* Ed. Ray Wilson Ownby. Santa Barbara, Calif.: Peregrine Smith, 1978: 31–42.

———. "From 'All Gold Canyon' to The Acorn-Planter: Jack London's Agrarian Vision." *Western American Literature* 11 (Summer 1976): 83–102.

———. "Jack London's 'Planchette': The Road Not Taken." *Pacific Historian* 21 (Summer 1977): 138–46.

Labor, Earle, and King Hendricks. "London's Twice-Told Tale." *Studies in Short Fiction* 4 (1967): 335. Reprinted in *The Critical Response to Jack London.* Ed. Susan N. Nuernberg. Westport, Conn.: Greenwood Press, 1995, 9–16.

Littell, Katherine M. "The 'Nietzschean' and the Individualist in Jack London's Socialist Writings." *Jack London Newsletter* 15, no. 2 (1982): 76–91.

Malcolmson, Scott L. "The Inevitable White Man: Jack London's Endless Journey." *Voice Literary Supplement,* February 1, 1994, 10–12.

Moreland, David. "Violence in the South Sea Fiction of Jack London." *Jack London Newsletter* 16 (January–April 1983): 1–35.

———. "The Quest That Failed: Jack London's Last Tales of the South Seas." *Pacific Studies* 8 (Fall 1984): 48–70.

Pizer, Donald. "Jack London: The Problem of Form." *Studies in the Literary Imagination* 16 (Fall 1983): 107–15. Reprinted in Donald Pizer, *Realism and Naturalism in Nineteenth-Century American Literature.* Carbondale: Southern Illinois University Press, 1984, 166–79.

Reesman, Jeanne Campbell. "The Problem of Knowledge in 'The Water Baby.' " *Western American Literature* 23 (Fall 1988): 201–15.

———. " 'Never Travel Alone': Jack London, Naturalism, and the White Silence." *American Literary Realism* 29 (Winter 1996): 33–49.

Tavernier-Courbin, Jacqueline. "Jack London's Science Fiction." *Jack London Newsletter* 17 (September–December 1984): 71–78.

Tietze, Thomas R., and Gary Riedl. "Jack London and the South Seas." Jack London Collection, Sunsite Digital Library, University of California, Berkeley: Sunsite.Berkeley.EDU/London/Essays/southseas.html. (August 21, 1996).

———. " 'Saints in Slime': The Ironic Use of Racism in Jack London's South Seas Tales." *Thalia: Studies in Literary Humor* 12 (1992): 59–66.

Ward, Susan. "Jack London's Women: Civilization vs. The Frontier." *Jack London Newsletter* 9 (May–August 1976): 81–85.

————. "Jack London and the Blue Pencil: London's Correspondence with Popular Editors." *American Literary Realism* 14 (Spring 1981): 16–25.

Watson, Charles N. Jr. "Jack London: Up from Spiritualism." In *The Haunted Dusk: American Supernatural Fiction, 1820–1920*, edited by Howard Kerr, John W. Crowley, and Charles Crow. Athens: University of Georgia Press, 1983.

Wilcox, Earl. " 'The Kipling of the Klondike': Naturalism in London's Early Fiction." *Jack London Newsletter* 6 (January–April 1973): 1–12.

Anthologies of Criticism

Cassuto, Leonard, and Jeanne Campbell Reesman, eds. *Rereading Jack London.* Stanford, Calif.: Stanford University Press, 1996.

Nuernberg, Susan, ed. *The Critical Response to Jack London.* Westport, Conn.: Greenwood, 1995.

Ownby, Ray Wilson, ed. *Jack London: Essays in Criticism.* Santa Barbara, Calif.: Peregrine Smith, 1978.

Tavernier-Courbin, Jacqueline, ed. *Critical Essays on Jack London.* Boston: G. K. Hall, 1983.

Biographies

Kingman, Russ. *A Pictorial Life of Jack London.* New York: Crown, 1979.

————. *Jack London: A Definitive Chronology.* Middletown, Calif.: David Rejl, 1992.

Lasartemay, Eugene P., and Mary Rudge. *For Love of Jack London: His Life With Jennie Prentiss—A True Story.* New York: Vantage, 1991.

London, Becky Fleming. "Memories of My Father, Jack London." *The Pacific Historian* 18 (Fall 1974): 5–10.

London, Becky Fleming. *My Jack London: A Daughter Remembers.* American Literature on Video Series. Films for the Humanities. Princeton, N.J.: 1988.

London, Charmian. *The Log of the Snark.* New York: Macmillan, 1915.

————. *The Book of Jack London.* 2 vols. New York: Century, 1921.

————. *Our Hawaii.* Rev. ed. New York: Macmillan, 1922.

London, Jack. *John Barleycorn: Alcoholic Memoirs.* New York: Century, 1913.

London, Joan. *Jack London and His Times.* New York: Doubleday, 1939. Reprint, Seattle: University of Washington Press, 1968.

————. *Jack London and His Daughters.* Introd. Bart Abbott. Berkeley: Heyday Books, 1990.

Sinclair, Andrew: *Jack: A Biography of Jack London.* New York: Harper & Row, 1977.

Stasz, Clarice. *American Dreamers: Charmian and Jack London.* New York: St. Martin's Press, 1988.

Stone, Irving. *Sailor on Horseback: The Biography of Jack London.* Cambridge, Mass.: Houghton Mifflin, 1938.

Index

Aegis, The, (periodical), 7, 8, 18–19
"All Gold Canyon," 105–6, 115
"Aloha Oe," 146
"Apostate, The," xi, 78, 83, 87–89, 108, 125, 136
Applegarth, Mabel, 10, 18, 182n. 7
Arnold, Matthew, 16, 182n. 7, 188n. 54
Assassination Bureau, The, 95
Atlantic Monthly (periodical), xii, 11, 202
"At the Rainbow's End," 35
Auerbach, Jonathan, 53, 96, 185n. 25
Austin, Mary, 220nn. 1, 2, 4

Bamford, Frederick Irons, 74
Baskett, Sam, 223
"Batârd," 35–36, 186n. 36
Belmont Academy, 8
"Benefit of the Doubt, The," 87
Berkove, Lawrence I., 164, 194n. 89, 223
Bierce, Ambrose, 115, 207, 209, 244n. 6; "The Jury in Ancient America," 244n. 6; "Insurance in Ancient America," 244n. 6; "An Occurrence at Owl Creek Bridge," 115; *Soldiers and Civilians,* 207, 209–10
Black Cat (periodical), 10, 200
Blake, William, 29
Bocaccio, 22; *Decameron,* 22
"Bones of Kahekili, The," 172–73, 194n. 94, 250
Bookman (periodical), 94
Booth, Wayne, 233; *Rhetoric of Fiction,* 233
Brett, George, 11, 97, 104. *See also* Macmillan Company

Brooks, Van Wyck, 97
Browning, Robert, 7, 17, 116, 165
"Brown Wolf," 108–9
"Bunches of Knuckles," 80, 99–100, 176
Bunn, Charles, 33
Burning Daylight, xvi
Burroughs, Edgar Rice, 60
Bush, Glen P., 182n. 10
Butler, Samuel, 15
"By the Turtles of Tasman," 158–59, 187n. 40

Cain, William, 188n. 57
Calder-Marshall, Arthur, 237
Call of the Wild, The, xi, 35, 57, 73, 186n. 36, 230
"Captain of the *Susan Drew,* The," 158
Carlyle, Thomas, 188n. 54
Carman, Bliss, 229
Carroll, Lewis, 126; "The Hunting of the Snark," 126
Century Illustrated Monthly Magazine (periodical), 42
Chaney, William, 5, 10
Chapman, Arnold, 43
"Charley's Coup," 102
"Chased by the Trail," 32
"Cherry," 179
Children of the Frost, 53, 57–58, 60, 62–63, 244n. 5
"Chinago, The," 5, 136–38, 146–47, 244n. 5
Chrétien de Troyes, 81
"Chun Ah Chun," 71, 144–46
Cicero, 20; *On the Commonwealth,* 20
Collier's Weekly (periodical), 182n. 7, 243n. 1

Complete Short Stories, The, xii–xiii, xvi, 223
Conrad, Joseph, 16, 188n. 22, 198; *Heart of Darkness*, 192n. 77; "An Outpost of Progress," 184n. 22; *Victory*, 217
Cook, James, 247, 248
Coolbrith, Ina, 5
Cooper, James G., 40
Cosmopolitan (periodical), 99, 202, 212–14, 244n. 6
Cowper, William, 15
Coxey's Army, 7
Crane, Stephen, xii, 97, 220n. 4
Cruise of the Snark, The, 126–28
"Cry for Justice, The," Introduction, 74
"Curious Fragment, A," 85

Darwin, Charles, 32, 70, 129, 160, 182n. 7; *Origin of Species*, 70, 187n. 7
"Daughter of the Aurora, A," 37
Day, A. Grove, 177
"Day's Lodging, A," 34, 185n. 26
"Death of Ligoun, The," 62
Debs, Eugene V., 84
Defoe, Daniel, 247, 250
de Maupassant, Guy, 209; "Baa, Baa, Black Sheep," 209; "The Man Who Was," 209; "Necklace," 209; "Piece of String," 209
"Demetrios Contos," 101, 102
"Devil's Dice Box, The," 19, 20–22, 23, 27
"Devils of Fuatino, The," 155–56, 158
DeWindt, Harry, 13; *Through the Gold Fields of Alaska*, 13
Dickens, Charles: *Great Expectations*, 83; *Oliver Twist*, 83
"Dream of Debs, The," 83, 84–85
Dreiser, Theodore, xii, 97
Duyckinck, E. H., 206

Eames, Ninetta, 107, 190n. 70
Eames, Roscoe, 107
Editor (periodical), xi, 17, 97, 98
Emerson, Ralph Waldo, xii

"End of the Story, The," 34
"Enemy of All the World, The," 79, 83, 84
Engels, Friedrich, xiv
"Eternity of Forms, The," 114–15, 159
Eusebius, 20; *Life of Constantine*, 20
"Eyes of Asia," 179

Faith of Men, The, 61
Faulkner, William, xiii, 116, 186n. 36; *Absalom, Absalom!*, 186n. 36; *The Sound and The Fury*, 116
"Feathers of the Sun, The," 158
"Finis," 36
"Flutter in Eggs, A," 38
Forster, E. M., 232
"*Francis Spaight*, The," 129
Frazer, Sir James, 16; *The Golden Bough*, 16–17
Frazier, Francis, 149
Freud, Sigmund, 17, 161, 175
Furer, Andrew, 71
"'Fuzziness' of Hookla–Heen, The," 58

Gair, Christopher, 189n. 61
Game, The, 29
Garden Island (newspaper), 193n. 84
Geismar, Maxwell, 233
Gibbon, Percival, 218
Gilman, Charlotte Perkins, 114
"Goboto Night, A," 157–58
God of His Fathers, The, 53, 54
"God of His Fathers, The," 33, 130
"Goliah," 79, 80–83, 84, 108, 109, 143, 197
"Good-Bye, Jack," 146–48, 249
Graham, Don, 116
"Grit of Women," 54–56
Gurian, Jay, 185n. 31

Haeckel, Ernst, 40, 70; *History of Creation*, 70
Haggard, H. Rider, 209; *She*, 209
Hamilton, David Mike, 17, 184n. 24; *"Tools of My Trade": Annotated Books in Jack London's Library*, 17

Hanna, Mark, 228
Harte, Bret, 31
Hawthorne, Nathaniel, 83, 114,
    186n. 36
Haywood, William D. ("Big Bill"),
    84, 87
Hearst's (periodical), 175
"Heathen, The," 131, 136–37, 139
Hedrick, Joan, 85
Hegel, Georg Wilhelm Friedrich, 70
Hemingway, Ernest, 43, 128, 186n.
    36, 233; "The Snows of Kiliman-
    jaro," 186n. 36
Hendricks, King, 44, 223
Herrick, Robert, 17
Hewitt, James, 70; *The Ruling Races
    of Prehistoric Times*, 70
Hillquit, Morris, 244n. 6
Hinkle, Beatrice, 161, 163
Hitler, Adolf, 83, 238
"Hobo and the Fairy, The," 119,
    120–21
Homer, 12, 13, 19, 25–27, 29, 160,
    165, 182n. 7, 184n. 24; *Iliad*, 15,
    19; *Odyssey*, 15, 19, 25–26, 27,
    182n. 7
Honolulu Advertiser (newspaper),
    192n. 80, 252n. 10
Hopkins, Gerard Manley, 175
Houghton Mifflin, 11
"House of Mapuhi, The," 139–40, 147
House of Pride, The, 127, 140, 147,
    151, 187n. 36
"House of Pride, The," 5, 81, 142
Howard, June, 39
Howells, William Dean, xii, 229
"How I Became a Socialist," 74
Hunter, Robert, 244n. 6
"Hussy, The," 158
Huxley, T. H., 16, 70
"Hyperborean Brew, A," 79

"In a Far Country," 25, 31, 37, 43,
    81, 106, 182n. 22, 187n. 40
"Inevitable White Man, The," 5,
    133–35, 244n. 5
"In the Forests of the North," 60
Iron Heel, The, xi, 77

Jack London Journal (periodical), 223
Jack London Society, 223
James, George Wharton, 6, 67, 95
James, Henry, 114
Jerry of the Islands, 129
John Barleycorn, xii, xvi, 40, 197
Johnson, Jack, 71
"Jokers of New Gibbon, The,"
    156–57
Jones, Gail, 184n. 24
Jordan, David Starr, 70
Jung, C. G., 49, 69, 160–62, 164,
    169, 171, 176–77, 194nn. 89, 94;
    Psychology of the Unconscious, 160,
    164, 171
"Just Meat," 78, 89–90, 213

"Kanaka Surf, The," 80, 175–77
Kazin, Alfred, 77, 79
Keats, John, 17
"Keesh, the Son of Keesh," 59–60
Kesey, Ken, 116; *One Flew Over the
    Cuckoo's Nest*, 116
Kidd, Benjamin, 96, 133, 191n. 77
Kingman, Russ, 75, 76, 77, 131, 141,
    193n. 84
"King of Mazy May: A Story of the
    Klondike, The," 32
"King of the Greeks, The," 101
Kipling, Rudyard, 7, 12, 17, 31, 76,
    211, 219
Kirsch, James, 161–62, 165
"Klondike Christmas, A," 19
Klondike Gold Rush, 11
Ko'olau, 148–50, 250
"Koolau the Leper," 71, 146,
    148–51, 174, 224, 244n. 5, 246,
    248–50

Labor, Earle, 44, 162, 185n. 31,
    190n. 70, 193n. 88, 197, 223; *Jack
    London*, 162
Lanier, Sidney, 82
Larkin, Edgar Lucien, 223
Le Galliene, Richard, 229
"League of the Old Men, The,"
    62–64

Leitz III, Robert C., 197
Lenin, (Vladimir Ilyich Ulyanov), 33
Letters of Jack London, The, xii, 197
"Like Argus of the Ancient Times,"
    39, 48–50, 65, 155, 158, 163, 180
Littell, Katherine M., 77
Little Lady of the Big House, The, xvi,
    175, 176
"Little Man, The," 39
"Li-Wan the Fair," 58
London, Bess (Becky), 187n. 45
London, Bess (Bessie) Maddern, 68,
    108
London, Charmian Kittredge, 13,
    14, 16, 68, 69, 72, 99, 100,
    103–4, 107–8, 117, 126–28, 133,
    135, 161, 170, 175, 176, 180, 187
    n. 47, 190n. 70, 193 n. 84, 226,
    238, 245, 249
London, Eliza. *See* Shepard, Eliza
    London
London, Flora Wellman, 67–69, 107,
    187n. 45
London, Jack (John Griffith): advice
    to writers, xi, 17, 98–99, 211–12,
    214–16; alcoholism, views on,
    40–41, 92; American Scholar, as
    xii; critical response to, xii–xiii,
    39–40, 95–97, 218–19, 223–24,
    237; death of, 4, 180; early
    poverty of, 6–7, 18, 67, 199–201,
    228; early writing/ apprentice-
    ship, 3, 8, 14, 17–18, 98–99,
    200–202, 215; early years/influ-
    ences on, 4–7, 227–28; educa-
    tion of, 5, 7–8; family, attitude
    toward, 5–7, 10, 13–14, 67–69,
    95, 104, 160; father, 10, 68–69;
    fictional experimentation, xiv–xv,
    18, 30; first publications, 7,
    15–16; formula writing, 97,
    99–100, 103; habits as a writer,
    197, 225–26; in Hawaii, xv–xvi,
    104, 127, 141ff, 192n. 80, 193n.
    84, 245ff; health of, 153, 159–60;
    importance as short story writer,
    xi, 181; influence of other writers
    on, 7, 13, 14–15, 16–17, 206–10,
    217; in jail, 7, 76, 228; in
    Klondike, 11, 12, 13–14, 31–32;
    in Korea, 72–73, 237; language,
    xv, 26, 30, 63, 86, 91, 110–11,
    121, 137, 150; "Long Sickness,"
    109; mother, 5, 67–69; paternity
    concerns of, 5, 10, 69; point of
    view, xv, 56, 94, 120, 135, 142;
    psychology of, 161–64; and pub-
    lishing, 94, 212–13; and ranch
    life, 226–27; relationship to pub-
    lishers, 11, 97, 200, 212–16; in
    Sonoma, 104; sources, 13–20,
    31–32, 38, 48, 83–84; in South
    Pacific, xv–xvi, 127ff, 151ff, 238;
    theory of writing 211, 213, 215;
    war correspondence (Russo-
    Japanese War, 1904), 72–73, 237;
    as war correspondent, 72–73,
    225, 237–38

NARRATIVE TECHNIQUES
allusions: archetypal, 27, 122, 140,
    161, 163–65; Arthurian, 81–82,
    143, 174–75; biblical, 15, 30, 59,
    61, 66, 73, 74, 123, 138–39, 143,
    146, 150, 165, 192n. 78, 218–19;
    classical, 13, 19, 45, 48–50; Jun-
    gian, 30, 174, 177–78
bildungsroman, 36, 83
dialogic structures, xv, 30, 170
dramatic monologue, 116
essay-exemplum, 18, 57, 232
ficelle, 44, 234
flashback, 112
frame, vx, 9, 18, 26, 30, 57–58
horror, use of, 8, 114–15, 197, 206ff
irony and satire, 39, 47–48, 58–59,
    80–84, 89–93, 115, 117, 137,
    140, 148, 176, 178–79, 238–41
multiple narrators, xv, 120–21
mythic imagery: Apollo, See sun;
    Athena, 51, 122, 124; classical
    myth, 13, 18–19, 45, 48–50;
    Greek, xiii, 27, 73, 106, 108–9,
    146, 190n. 70; Helios, See sun;

Homeric, 12–16, 19; Mammon, 22, 46–47, 48, 184n. 21; Medea, 19, 49, 66; Medusa, 15, 29, 169–70; Norse, Old, 184n. 24; Odysseus, 14, 25–27, 48, 165; Sol, See sun; sun, 13, 19–21 23, 24, 25, 27, 28–29, 33, 79, 82, 89, 99, 106, 115, 151–52, 154, 163–64, 167, 177, 182n. 19, 184n. 22, 187n. 39; trickster, 29, 32, 34, 37–38, 45–46, 60, 63–64, 79, 103, 178
narrative ambiguity, xv
naturalist fable, 13
objective correlative, 235
science fiction, 9, 79–84, 182n. 6

PHILOSOPHY
class, xiv, 26–27, 50–51, 67–68, 78, 118–120, 170, 172
cultural relativity/ racial other, 52, 59–64, 66, 69, 71, 90–91, 103, 110–13, 128, 130, 137, 140, 146, 157, 179, 237ff, 246ff
Darwinism, 16–17
determinism, 111, 186n. 34
dualism, 29, 40, 77, 87, 114, 125, 135, 140, 147, 169,
materialism, 40, 73
miscegenation, 53, 61–62, 144
monism, 70, 73, 162, 185n. 31, 233, 248
naturalism, 4, 13, 39, 42–44, 125, 140, 146, 208–9
orientalism, 246–48
philosophy of life, xi; of work, 79–80, 87–88
race, 9,10, 31, 43, 50, 62, 67–69, 72, 77, 91, 101, 102, 130, 131–34, 139, 156–57, 170, 237ff
racialism, 57, 68–72, 101
racism, 68–72, 101, 158n. 57, 191n. 77
realism, 17
sincerity, xi, 98–99
social Darwinism, 8, 70, 129, 191n. 77, 246

socialism, xiv, 8, 68, 70, 73–78, 80, 188n. 58, 227
spirituality/spiritualism, 39, 41, 106–8, 125, 147
"whiteness," 43, 53–54, 71, 128, 131, 137, 156, 158, 186n. 36

THEMES/SUBJECTS
agrarian vision, 104–6
atavism, 10, 87, 96, 106, 108, 111, 113, 116
brotherhood, code of, 14, 20–22, 25–26, 73, 106, 114–15, 117, 131, 155, 159, 179
community, xiv, 4, 8, 24, 30, 33, 39, 41, 42, 48, 63, 67, 73, 84, 86, 102, 141, 155, 234–35
feminine, the, 64–65, 68–69, 92, 105, 118–21, 131, 167, 169, 172
gender, 9, 30, 50–52, 66, 68, 118–24, 131, 139, 169, 170, 179
hero, code of, 4–5, 14, 26–27, 30–50, 71, 113, 146, 151, 155
imagination, 4, 8, 37, 41, 44–45, 48, 63, 73, 84, 87, 101, 102, 107, 128, 136, 141
Indians/indigenous peoples, xi–xii, xv, 14, 24, 27, 30, 33, 43, 50, 52–66, 69–72, 77, 81–83, 118, 124, 127–44, 148–51, 155–58, 164–76, 178–79, 245ff
justice, xiv, 4, 8, 38 (Code of North), 41, 48, 52, 63, 67, 73, 84, 86, 101, 102, 106, 115, 117, 120, 130, 141, 151, 155, 190n. 70
knowledge, 41–44, 50, 59, 144, 177–79, 235
leprosy, 146–51, 191n. 73, 217, 248–49
love, 10, 22–23, 34, 54–56, 66, 87, 92–93, 113, 158–59
oathbreaking, 20, 21–23, 25–26, 27, 33–34
race/racialism/racism: *See* London, Jack: philosophy
sacrifice, 54–55, 62, 63, 69, 129, 131, 171

Index

WORKS: ESSAYS, LETTERS, AND COL-
  LECTIONS OF ESSAYS
Cruise of the Snark, The, 126–28
"Cry for Justice, The," Introduction,
  74
"How I Became a Socialist," 74
Letters of Jack London, The, xii, 197
*"No Mentor but Myself": A Collection of
  Essays, Reviews, and Letters on Writ-
  ing and Writers*, 197
People of the Abyss, The, xi, 29, 87, 197,
  231
"Revolution," 74
Revolution and Other Essays, 8, 12, 13,
  80
Road, The, 97, 197
"Shrinkage of the Planet, The,"
  182n. 7
"Terrible and Tragic in Fiction,
  The," xvi
"These Bones Shall Rise Again," 12
"War of the Classes," 74
War of the Classes, 75, 80, 188n. 54, 229
"What Life Means to Me," 8, 188n. 54

WORKS: NOVELS AND COLLECTIONS
  OF STORIES
Assassination Bureau, The, 95
Burning Daylight, xvi
Call of the Wild, The, xi, 35, 57, 73,
  186n. 36, 230
"Cherry" (ms.), 179
Children of the Frost, 53, 57–58, 60,
  62–63, 244n. 5
Complete Short Stories, The, xii–xiii,
  xvi, 223
"Eyes of Asia" (ms.), 179
Faith of Men, The, 61
Game, The, 29
God of His Fathers, The, 53, 54
House of Pride, The, 127, 140, 147,
  151, 187n. 36
Iron Heel, The, xi, 77
Jerry of the Islands, 129
John Barleycorn, xii, xvi, 40, 197
Little Lady of the Big House, The, xvi,
  175, 176
Lost Face, 42

Martin Eden, xi, xvi, 77, 197, 218
On the Makaloa Mat, 128, 140, 158,
  160, 163, 170, 172, 175
Sea-Wolf, The, 10, 77, 97, 218, 230,
  186n. 36
Smoke Bellew, xv, 30, 36–39, 65, 99
Son of the Sun, A, 99, 128, 151
*Son of the Wolf: Tales of the Far North,
  The*, 30, 36, 53, 54
South Sea Tales, 99, 127–30, 140, 146
Star Rover, The, xi, 34, 74, 192n. 78
Tales of the Fish Patrol, xv, 32, 99,
  100–101, 151
Turtles of Tasman, The, 128, 158
Valley of the Moon, The, xvi, 69, 102
When God Laughs, 128–29, 136
White Fang, 95, 186n. 36

WORKS: PLAYS
"Return of Ulysses—A Modern Ver-
  sion, The" (ms.), 182n. 7
Scorn of Women, The, 50–51

WORKS: SHORT FICTION
"All Gold Canyon," 105–6, 115
"Aloha Oe," 146
"Apostate, The," xi, 78, 83, 87–89,
  108, 125, 136
"At the Rainbow's End," 35
"Batârd," 35–36, 186n. 36
"Benefit of the Doubt, The," 87
"Bones of Kahekili, The," 172–73,
  194n. 94, 250
"Brown Wolf," 108–9
"Bunches of Knuckles," 80, 99–100,
  176
"By the Turtles of Tasman," 158–59,
  187n. 40
"Captain of the *Susan Drew*, The,"
  158
"Charley's Coup," 102
"Chased by the Trail," 32
"Chinago, The," 5, 136–38, 146–47,
  244n. 5
"Chun Ah Chun," 71, 144–46
"Curious Fragment, A," 85
"Daughter of the Aurora, A," 37
"Day's Lodging, A," 34, 185n. 26

"Death of Ligoun, The," 62
"Demetrios Contos," 101, 102
"Devil's Dice Box, The," 19, 20–22, 23, 27
"Devils of Fuatino, The," 155–56, 158
"Dream of Debs, The," 83, 84–85
"End of the Story, The," 34
"Enemy of All the World, The," 79, 83, 84
"Eternity of Forms, The," 114–15, 159
"Feathers of the Sun, The," 158
"Finis," 36
"Flutter in Eggs, A," 38
"Francis Spaight, The," 129
"'Fuzziness' of Hookla–Heen, The," 58
"Goboto Night, A," 157–58
"God of His Fathers, The," 33, 130
"Goliah," 79, 80–83, 84, 108, 109, 143, 197
"Good-Bye, Jack," 146–48, 249
"Grit of Women," 54–56
"Heathen, The," 131, 136–37, 139
"Hobo and the Fairy, The," 119, 120–21
"House of Mapuhi, The," 139–40, 147
"House of Pride, The," 5, 81, 142
"Hussy, The," 158
"Hyperborean Brew, A," 79
"In a Far Country," 25, 31, 37, 43, 81, 106, 182n. 22, 187n. 40
"In the Forests of the North," 60
"Inevitable White Man, The," 5, 133–35, 244n. 5
"Jokers of New Gibbon, The," 156–57
"Just Meat," 78, 89–90, 213
"Kanaka Surf, The," 80, 175–77
"Keesh, the Son of Keesh," 59–60
"King of Mazy May: A Story of the Klondike, The," 32
"King of the Greeks, The," 101
"Klondike Christmas, A," 19
"Koolau the Leper," 71, 146, 148–51, 174, 224, 244n. 5, 246, 248–50

"League of the Old Men, The," 62–64
"Like Argus of the Ancient Times," 39, 48–50, 65, 155, 158, 163, 180
"Little Man, The," 39
"Li-Wan the Fair," 58
"Lost Face," 32
"Love of Life," 33
"Madness of John Harned, The," 110–11, 137
"Make Westing," 129
"Man on the Other Bank, The," 37–38
"Marriage of Lit-Lit, The," 64
"Master of Mystery, The," 60
"Mauki," 5, 113, 133, 135–36, 244n. 5
"Men of Forty-Mile, The," 31
"Mexican, The," xiv, 111–13, 157
"Minions of Midas," 79, 80, 84
"Mission of John Starhust, The," *See* "The Whale Tooth"
"Mistake of Creation, The," 38
"Moon-Face," 100, 197
"Nam-Bok the Unveracious," 58–59, 64, 229–30
"Night-Born, The," xv, 29, 65, 121, 123–25, 163
"Night's Swim in Yeddo Bay, A," 8–9
"Odyssey of the North, An," xii, 4, 11, 19, 25–28
"O Haru," 8–9
"One More Unfortunate," 9
"One Thousand Dozen, The," 35
"On the Makaloa Mat," 144, 170–71
"Piece of Steak, A," xiv, 89
"Plague Ship, The," 9, 10
"Planchette," 80, 106–8, 190n. 70
"Priestly Prerogative, The," 19
"Princess, The," 91–93, 158, 180
"Proud Goat of Aloysius Pankburn, The," 155
"Race for Number Three, The," 37
"Raid on the Oyster Pirates, A," 101
"Red One, The," 15, 27, 29, 158, 161, 164–70, 176–78, 180, 194n. 94, 197

"Relic of the Pliocene, A ," 79
"Sakaicho, Hona Asi, and Hakadaki," 8
"Samuel," xv, 94, 121–23, 163
"Seed of McCoy, The," 71, 131,
    138–39, 147
"Sheriff of Kona, The," 146, 249
"Shin Bones," 85, 170, 173–75, 178
"Sickness of Lone Chief, The," 62
"Siege of the 'Lancashire Queen',
    The," 101, 102
"Siwash," 53, 54
"Son of the Sun, A," 152–53
"Son of the Wolf, The," 5, 19,
    23–24
"South of the Slot," 87
"Stampede to Squaw Creek, The,"
    37
"Story of a Typhoon Off the Coast of
    Japan," 3, 11, 18
"Story of Jees Uck, The," 53, 61, 62,
    139
"Story of Keesh, The," 60
"Strange Experience of a Misogy-
    nist, The," 9–10
"Strength of the Strong, The,"
    85–86, 219
"Sun-Dog Trail, The," 28–29, 64, 85
"Sunlanders," xi
"Taste of Meat, The," 36
"Tears of Ah Kim, The," 171–72
"Terrible Solomons, The," 118–19,
    132–33
"Test: A Clondyke Wooing, The,"
    19, 22–23
"Thousand Deaths, A," 9, 10, 34, 79
"To Build a Fire", xi, 29, 34, 36,
    39–48, 51, 129, 136, 151, 186n.
    36, 223, 232–36
"To Kill a Man," 115, 118, 119–20
"Told in the Drooling Ward," xv,
    116–18
"To the Man on Trail," 18, 19, 31,
    35
"Town Site of Tra-Lee, The," 38
"Two Gold Bricks," 8
"Under the Deck Awnings," 115,
    118–19
"Unexpected, The," 51–52

"Unparalleled Invasion, The,"
    90–91, 137–39, 223–24, 237–44
"War," 115
"Water Baby, The," xi, xv, 27, 128,
    140, 170, 176–80, 194n. 94,
    249–50
"Whale Tooth, The," 129–30
"When Alice Told Her Soul," 176
"When the World Was Young," 87,
    113–14, 115, 120, 159
"Where the Trail Forks, " 56–57
"White and Yellow," 101, 103
"White Man's Way, The," 64
"White Silence, The," 11, 19, 23
"Who Believes in Ghosts!," 9
"Whose Business It Is to Live," 158
"Wife of a King, The," 53
"Wit of Porportuk, The," 64–65
"Wonder of Women, The," 65, 155,
    158
"Yah! Yah! Yah!," 133, 135, 155
"Yeddo Bay, In," 9
"Yellow Handkerchief," 101, 103

London, Joan, 95, 96, 187n. 45
London, John, 5, 18, 68
López, Debbie, 189n. 59
Longfellow, Henry Wadsworth, 17
Lost Face, 42
"Lost Face," 32
"Love of Life," 33

Macmillan Company, 11, 101. *See
    also* George Brett
"Madness of John Harned, The,"
    110–11, 137
"Make Westing," 129
Malcolmson, Scott, 71
Malory, Sir Thomas, 82; *Morte
    d'Arthur*, 82
"Man on the Other Bank, The,"
    37–38
Markham, Edwin, 229
"Marriage of Lit-Lit, The," 64
Martin Eden, xi, xvi, 77, 197, 218
Marx, Karl xiv, 7, 17, 73, 78, 160,
    162, 163, 171, 173, 177, 194n. 94
"Master of Mystery, The," 60

"Mauki," 5, 113, 133, 135–36, 244n. 5
May, Charles E., 186n. 34
McClintock, James, xii, 40, 57, 59, 70–71, 116; *White Logic: Jack London's Short Stories*, xii
McClure's (periodical), 11, 33, 58, 202, 243n. 1
Melville, Herman, xv, 128, 131, 186n. 36, 245, 247, 250; *Typee*, 128, 247
"Men of Forty-Mile, The," 31
"Mexican, The," xiv, 111–13, 157
Michener, James, 245
Mill, John Stuart, 16
Milton, John, 22, 29, 160, 182n. 7, 184n. 21, 187n. 39; *Paradise Lost*, 22, 27, 32, 46–47, 182n. 7, 184n. 21, 187n. 39
"Minions of Midas, The" 79, 80, 84
"Mission of John Starhust, The," *See* "The Whale Tooth"
"Mistake of Creation, The," 38
Mitchell, Lee Clark, 186n. 34
"Moon-Face," 100, 197
Moreland, David, 128–29, 135, 166, 170, 174, 175
Morris, William, 7, 15, 16
Morrison, Toni, 186n. 36

"Nam-Bok the Unveracious," 58–59, 64, 229–30
Neumann, Erich, 169
Nietzsche, Friedrich, xiv, 43, 72, 77, 78, 96, 160–62, 218; *Thus Spoke Zarathustra*, 77
"Night-Born, The," xv, 29, 65, 121, 123–25, 163
"Night's Swim in Yeddo Bay, A," 8, 9
Noel, Joseph, 98
"No Mentor But Myself": A Collection of Essays, Reviews, and Letters on Writing and Writers, 197
Norris, Frank, xii, 8, 97
North American Review (periodical), 218–19

Oakland Public Library, 5, 14, 183n. 12
O'Connor, Frank, 233, 236
"Odyssey of the North, An," xii, 4, 11, 19, 25–28
"O Haru," 8–9
"One More Unfortunate," 9
"One Thousand Dozen, The," 35
"On the Makaloa Mat," 144, 170–71
On the Makaloa Mat, 128, 140, 158, 160, 163, 170, 172, 175
Orwell, George, 78–79
Outing Magazine (periodical), 14
Overland Monthly (periodical), 200
Ovid, 20; *Metamorphoses*, 20

Partington, Blanche, 99
Pattee, Fred Lewis, 53, 182n. 10
People of the Abyss, The, xi, 29, 87, 197, 231
Phillips, Roland, 99
"Piece of Steak, A," xiv, 89
Pi'ilani, 148–49, 250
Pizer, Donald, 13, 39
"Plague Ship, The," 9, 10
"Planchette," 80, 106–8, 190n. 70
Plato, 58–59; "Allegory of the Cave," 58–59
Poe, Edgar Allan, xi, 43, 83, 110, 114, 197, 206ff; "Berenice," 207; "Black Cat," 207; "Cask of Amontillado," 207; "Fall of the House of Usher," 207; "Masque of the Red Death," 207; *The Narrative of Arthur Gordon Pym of Nantucket*, 43; "Pit and the Pendulum," 207; *Tamerlane and Other Poems*, 206
Powers, Richard Gid, 95–96
Prentiss, Virginia, 5, 68, 187n. 45
"Priestly Prerogative, The," 19
"Princess, The," 91–93, 158, 180
"Proud Goat of Aloysius Pankburn, The," 155
Pyle, Howard, 82

"Race for Number Three, The," 37

"Raid on the Oyster Pirates, A," 101
Rand, Ayn, 83
"Red One, The," 15, 27, 29, 158, 161, 164–70, 176–78, 180, 194n. 89, 197
"Relic of the Pliocene, A ," 79
Renan, Ernest, 16
"Return of Ulysses—A Modern Version, The," 182n. 7
"Revolution," 74
Revolution and Other Essays, 8, 12, 13, 80
Riedl, Gary, 127, 130
Road, The, 97, 197
Roesler, Frank, 70; *The World's Greatest Migration: The Origin of the "White Man,"* 70
Rostand, Pierre, 17
Rousseau, Jean-Jacques, 247, 250
Ruskin, John, 7, 16

Sacramento Union (newspaper), 248
Said, Edward W., 246–47
"Sakaicho, Hona Asi, and Hakadaki," 8
"Samuel," xv, 94, 121–23, 163
Sandburg, Carl, 223
San Francisco Bulletin (newspaper), 15
San Francisco Morning Call (newspaper), 3
Schultz, Alfred, 70, *Race or Mongrel*, 70
"Scorn of Women, The," 50–51
Seattle Post-Intelligencer (newspaper), 12
Sea-Wolf, The, 10, 77, 97, 218, 187n. 36, 230
"Seed of McCoy, The," 71, 131, 138–39, 147
Seltzer, Mark, 96, 185n. 28
Shakespeare, William, 17, 180, 212
Shelley, Percy Bysshe, 78
Shepard, Eliza London, 5, 68, 70, 104, 187n. 45
Shepard, I. Milo, 104, 105, 197
Shepard, Irving, 104
Shepard, John, 48
"Sheriff of Kona, The," 146, 249
"Shin Bones," 85, 170, 173–75, 178

"Shrinkage of the Planet, The," 182n. 7
"Sickness of Lone Chief, The," 62
"Siege of the 'Lancashire Queen', The," 101, 102
Sinclair, Andrew, 96
"Siwash," 53, 54
Slagel, James, 224
Slocum, Joshua, 126; *Sailing Alone around the World*, 126
Sloper, Merritt, 31
Smoke Bellew, xv, 30, 36–39, 65, 99
Snark, cruise of, xv–xvi, 42, 72, 103, 104, 126–28, 165, 238
Son of the Sun, A, 99, 128, 151
"Son of the Sun, A," 152–53
"Son of the Wolf, The," 5, 19, 23–24
Son of the Wolf: Tales of the Far North, The, 30, 36, 53, 54
"South of the Slot," 87
South Sea Tales, 99, 127–30, 140, 146
Spencer, Herbert, 7, 32, 78, 96, 129, 160; *Philosophy of Style*, 7, 17
"Stampede to Squaw Creek, The," 37
Starr, Kevin, 96
Star Rover, The, xi, 34, 74, 192n. 78
Stasz, Clarice, 187n. 47
Stein, Gertrude, 233
Steinbeck, John, 116; *Of Mice and Men*, 116
Sterling, Carrie, 108
Sterling, George, 108, 164, 244n. 6
Stevenson, Robert Louis, 100, 103, 209, 245, 247; *Ebb Tide*, 211; *Strange Case of Dr. Jekyll and Mr. Hyde*, 209; *Treasure Island*, 103
Stoddard, Charles Warren, 245
Stoltz, Bert, 149
Stoltz, Louis, 148
Stone, Irving, 96; *Sailor on Horseback*, 96
"Story of a Typhoon Off the Coast of Japan," 3, 11, 18
"Story of Jees Uck, The," 53, 61, 62, 139
"Story of Keesh, The," 60

"Strange Experience of a Misogynist, The," 9–10
"Strength of the Strong, The," 85–86, 219
Strunsky, Anna, 42
Sumida, Stephen, 247
"Sun-Dog Trail, The," 28–29, 64, 85
"Sunlanders," xi
Swift, Jonathan, 247
Swinburne, Charles Algernon, 16
Symons, Julian, 95

Tales of the Fish Patrol, xv, 32, 99, 100–101, 151
"Taste of Meat, The," 36
Tavernier-Courbin, Jacqueline, 94, 182n. 6
"Tears of Ah Kim, The," 171–72
"Terrible and Tragic in Fiction, The," xvi
"Terrible Solomons, The," 118–19, 132–33
"Test: A Clondyke Wooing, The," 19, 22–23
"These Bones Shall Rise Again," 12
Thoreau, Henry David, 125; "Cry of the Human," 125
"Thousand Deaths, A," 9, 10, 34, 79
Thurston, Lorrin A., 192n. 80, 249, 252n. 10
Tietze, Thomas R., 127, 130
"To Build a Fire," xi, 29, 34, 36, 39–48, 51, 129, 136, 151, 186n. 36, 223, 232–36
"To Kill a Man," 115, 118, 119–20
"Told in the Drooling Ward," xv, 116–18
"To the Man on Trail," 18, 19, 31, 35
"Town Site of Tra-Lee, The," 38
Turtles of Tasman, The, 128, 158
Twain, Mark, xii, 4, 82, 92, 132, 147, 186n. 36, 240, 245, 248; "The Chronicle of Young Satan," 240
"Two Gold Bricks," 8

"Under the Deck Awnings," 115, 118–19

"Unexpected, The," 51–52
"Unparalleled Invasion, The," 90–91, 137–39, 223–24, 237–44

Valley of the Moon, The, xvi, 69, 102
Vance, Arthur T., 97
Vickery, John, 16

Walker, Franklin, 7, 11, 12, 31
Wallis, Samuel, 247
"War," 115
Ward, Susan, 50, 52, 97
War of the Classes, 75, 80, 188n. 54, 220
"War of the Classes," 74
"Water Baby, The," xi, xv, 27, 128, 140, 170, 176–80, 194n. 94, 249–50
Watson, Charles N. Jr., 185n. 31
Wells, H. G., 220n. 4
Welty, Eudora, 116; "Why I Live at the PO," 116
Whalen, Terry, 185n. 31
"Whale Tooth, The," 129–30
Wharton, Edith, xii, 97
"What Life Means to Me," 8, 188n. 54
"When Alice Told Her Soul," 176
When God Laughs, 128–29, 136
"When the Was Young," 87, 113–14, 115, 120, 159
"Where the Trail Forks, " 56–57
"White and Yellow," 101, 103
White Fang, 95, 187n. 36
"White Man's Way, The," 64
"White Silence, The," 11, 19, 23
"Who Believes in Ghosts!," 9
"Whose Business It Is to Live," 158
"Wife of a King, The," 53
Wilson, Christopher, 96
"Wit of Porportuk, The," 64–65
Woman's Home Companion (periodical), 97. *See also* Arthur T. Vance
"Wonder of Women, The," 65, 155, 158
Wood, Michael, 26–27

Woodruff, Charles, 153; *The Effects of Tropical Light on White Men*, 153

"Yah! Yah! Yah!," 133, 135, 155

"Yeddo Bay, In," 9
"Yellow Handkerchief," 101, 103
Youth's Companion (periodical), 32, 42, 101, 200, 232

The Author

Jeanne Campbell Reesman, professor of English and interim dean of Graduate Studies at the University of Texas at San Antonio, is the author of *American Designs: The Late Novels of James and Faulkner* (1991) and editor of *Speaking the Other Self: American Women Writers* (1997). She is the coauthor of *Jack London: Revised Edition* (with Earle Labor, 1994) and two editions of the widely known *A Handbook of Critical Approaches to Literature* (with Wilfred Guerin, et al., 1992, 1998). She is coeditor of *Rereading Jack London* (with Leonard Cassuto, 1996). She is presently at work on a volume on the trickster figure in American literature, a book on Jack London and Hawaii, and a study of the subject of race in Jack London's works. Founder and executive coordinator of the Jack London Society, Reesman is a member of the executive board of the American Literature Association.

The Editors

Gary Scharnhorst is professor of English at the University of New Mexico, coeditor of *American Literary Realism,* and editor in alternating years of *American Literary Scholarship: An Annual.* He is the author or editor of books about Horatio Alger Jr., Charlotte Perkins Gilman, Bret Harte, Nathaniel Hawthorne, Henry David Thoreau, and Mark Twain, and he has taught in Germany on Fulbright fellowships three times (1978–1979, 1985–1986, 1993). He is also the current president of the Western Literature Association and the Pacific Northwest American Studies Association.

Eric Haralson is assistant professor of English at the State University of New York at Stony Brook. He has published articles on American and English literature—in *American Literature, Nineteenth-Century Literature,* the *Arizona Quarterly, American Literary Realism,* and the *Henry James Review,* as well as in several essay collections. He is also the editor of *The Garland Encyclopedia of American Nineteenth-Century Poetry.*